THE CONTROL OF PEOPLE SMUGGLING
AND TRAFFICKING IN THE EU

Law and Migration

Series Editor
Satvinder S. Juss, King's College London, UK

Migration and its subsets of refugee and asylum policy are rising up the policy agenda at national and international level. Current controversies underline the need for rational and informed debate of this widely misrepresented and little understood area.

Law and Migration contributes to this debate by establishing a monograph series to encourage discussion and help to inform policy in this area. The series provides a forum for leading new research principally from the Law and Legal Studies area but also from related social sciences. The series is broad in scope, covering a wide range of subjects and perspectives.

The Control of People Smuggling and Trafficking in the EU

Experiences from the UK and Italy

MATILDE VENTRELLA
University of Liverpool Online Master Programmes, UK

ASHGATE

Published by
Ashgate Publishing Limited
Wey Court East
Union Road
Farnham
Surrey, GU9 7PT
England

Ashgate Publishing Company
Suite 420
101 Cherry Street
Burlington
VT 05401-4405
USA

www.ashgate.com

British Library Cataloguing in Publication Data
Ventrella, Matilde.
  The control of people smuggling and trafficking in the EU :
  experiences from the UK and Italy. -- (Law and migration)
  1. Human smuggling--European Union countries. 2. Human
  trafficking--European Union countries. 3. Human
  smuggling--European Union countries--Prevention. 4. Human
  trafficking--European Union countries--Prevention.
  5. Human smuggling--Law and legislation--Great Britain.
  6. Human smuggling--Law and legislation--Italy. 7. Human
  trafficking--Law and legislation--Great Britain. 8. Human
  trafficking--Law and legislation--Italy.
  I. Title II. Series
  345.2'40237-dc22

Library of Congress Cataloging-in-Publication Data
Ventrella, Matilde.
  The control of people smuggling and trafficking in the EU : experiences from the UK and Italy / by Matilde Ventrella.
     p. cm. -- (Law and migration)
  Includes bibliographical references and index.
  ISBN 978-0-7546-7466-5 (hardback) -- ISBN 978-1-4094-1221-2 (ebook)
  1. Human smuggling--European Union countries. 2. Human smuggling--Italy. 3. Human smuggling--Great Britain. I. Title.
  KJE8781.H86V46 2010
  345.24'0237--dc22

2010015529

ISBN 9780754674665 (hbk)
ISBN 9781409412212 (ebk)

Mixed Sources
Product group from well-managed
forests and other controlled sources
www.fsc.org Cert no. SA-COC-1565
© 1996 Forest Stewardship Council
FSC

Printed and bound in Great Britain by
MPG Books Group, UK

Contents

List of Abbreviations

AVID	Association of Visitors to Immigration Detainees
BID	Bail for Immigration Detainees
EC	European Community
ECHR	European Convention of Human Rights
ENP	European Neighbourhood Policy
EAW	European Arrest Warrant
EEW	European Evidence Warrant
EJN	European Judicial Network
ENP	European Neighbourhood Policy
EPP	European Public Prosecutor
EU	European Union
ILPA	Immigration Law Practitioners' Association
IOM	International Organization for Migration
JCWI	Joint Council for the Welfare of Immigrants
JHA	Justice and Home Affairs
LDSG	London Detainee Support Group
OLAF	Anti-fraud Office
PACE	Police and Criminal Evidence Act 1984
QMV	Qualified Majority Vote
RABITs	Rapid Border Intervention Teams
SAR	International Convention on Maritime Search and Rescue
SOLAS	International Convention for the Safety of Life at Sea
SOCA	Serious Organised Crime and Police Act 2005
TFEU	Treaty on the Functioning of the European Union
UKHTC	UK Human Trafficking Centre
UNTOC	United Nations Convention against Transnational Organized Crime
WTO	World Trade Organization

Preface

When I started my research on policing and judicial co-operation in the EU in 2001, I did not expect to concentrate on people smuggling by sea and on trafficking in human beings. I also did not expect that I would demonstrate that the smuggling of migrants by sea could be addressed by granting permanent visas to victims of this crime. I was aware that it would have been more straightforward to demonstrate this fact for victims of people trafficking because there is a lot of law at the international level that provides for their protection. There is no law that similarly protects victims of people smuggling by sea. There is also a widespread belief that people smuggling by sea is an uncontrollable phenomenon that can only be prevented by restrictive laws forbidding these people from entering the territory of EU Member States. These facts were problematic for my research, as I did not want to accept the position that favoured the victims of human trafficking over the victims of people smuggling by sea just because it is argued that they are not victims, having chosen to travel irregularly from their countries of origin. People smuggled by sea are not victims in the traditional sense because no one forces them to leave their country of origin, and so their decision can be considered freely taken.

The law does not support my views on this, and for this reason I decided to travel to Sicily to talk to experts who have been dealing with the smuggling of migrants by sea for years. I am deeply indebted to the individuals who spared their time to answer my questions in Lampedusa. I greatly benefited from the information they provided. They helped me to understand that smuggling of migrants by sea is controllable, and can be defeated by protecting the victims of these crimes. Having written this book, I am very pleased that the Lisbon Treaty has now entered into force. The Lisbon Treaty provides the possibility of enacting many of my findings by adopting effective laws against the criminal organisations who exploit poverty.

Acknowledgements

I am deeply indebted to the individuals who work for the Association Pope John XXIII who spared their time to answer my questions. I am also very grateful to the individuals of the Polizia di Stato (Italian police) in Rimini who helped me to understand how to deal with victims of people trafficking. In fact, I am most grateful to the Polizia di Stato in Italy for the very valuable information they provided to me on trafficking in human beings and smuggling of migrants by sea. I will never forget the professionalism of the individuals in Lampedusa and the fantastic members of Polizia di Stato I met in Siracusa. During my stay in Sicily, I greatly benefited from the help of the staff of Frontex and the Guardia di Finanza (Italian Frontier Police). It was the Guardia di Finanza who suggested that I contact the public prosecutors in Siracusa, and I will always be grateful for their advice. As a result of meeting the public prosecutors and learning about the important work they carry out, I came to understand more fully how smuggling of migrants by sea can be defeated.

I am also very grateful to the Italian Ministry of Internal Affairs, Department of Immigration which supplied me with the data on the number of people smuggled by sea from Africa to Lampedusa. They have been very patient, and have always sent me the updated figures.

I am very grateful to the International Organization for Migration (IOM) in Lampedusa and London, whose staff agreed to be interviewed by me. A particular thanks goes to the Italian Red Cross in Lampedusa, and in Sicily in general, who have given much of their time and who have provided me with very important documents on smuggling of migrants by sea.

I thank the Italian citizens I met in Milan who made themselves available to answer my questions. I also thank the individuals from the Poppy Project in London, one of the public prosecutors of the UK Human Trafficking Centre (UKHTC) in Sheffield who responded to my questions on trafficking in human beings, and the Smuggling Unit of Heathrow Airport in London.

I would like to thank my friend Darius who helped me to edit my manuscript.

I am very grateful to my father Antonio who helped me to write the Italian part of my book. My father was an estimated administrative lawyer whose suggestions were invaluable. It was his idea to go to Rimini to interview the police and the members of the humanitarian association I indicate in Chapter 5 of my book. My father also passed on to me all the law and case-law on Italian immigration. Thank you, dad, for having been my father!

To my beloved dad Antonio who passed away on 20th April 2010.

Chapter 1

Introduction

The Impact of the Lisbon Treaty

The ratification of the Lisbon Treaty provides the EU with an opportunity to show how it can be a force for good. In return, the Treaty allows EU citizens to form a decision as to the extent of EU power. One area where the Lisbon Treaty shows significant potential is in combating the crimes of trafficking in human beings and the smuggling of migrants by sea. As it currently operates, these areas of EU policing and judicial co-operation are governed by the use of framework decisions. Article 34 (2)(b) of the EU Treaty states that framework decisions do not entail direct effect, which means that individuals cannot rely on them before national courts. Another issue is the fact that the European Parliament has only a consultative role in these areas. That legal measures in this area were adopted unanimously by the Council of the EU (hereafter 'the Council') is also problematic. The Council is composed of the ministers of the Member States' governments who are there to represent the interests of national governments, not necessarily the interests of all the people of the EU. Conversely, the European Parliament is the only democratic body directly elected by the people of the EU whose representatives are supposed to aim specifically to improve the EU. Yet the European Parliament is limited to co-legislating with the Council in most of the areas covered by the EC Treaty, but not in the area of police and judicial co-operation (third pillar). This is significant because changes in the third pillar potentially threaten the fundamental human rights of EU citizens. Why should the European people passively accept what is decided behind closed doors? Why should the European people accept the decisions taken concerning their freedoms, their personal data and their rights as defendants and suspects in EU Member States? The whole purpose behind democracy is to give governments the legitimacy they need to act through gaining the support of their citizens. If the EU has the authority to make fundamental decisions affecting its citizens' rights, EU citizens should have a powerful say in what those decisions should be. If this is not the case, the EU will be seen as functioning as a dictatorship, and should therefore be abolished. There is a conviction that all bodies or new entities which threaten democracy do not have any legitimate reason to exist, and that it is the people's job to make sure that their fundamental rights are protected. Therefore, in this context, the ratification of the Lisbon Treaty is important as it will permit the European Parliament to co-legislate with the Council in the area of police and judicial co-operation. The Lisbon Treaty will also replace the unanimous voting procedure with majority votes in most of the areas covered by the EU. The Lisbon Treaty will also permit national parliaments to be consulted on draft legislation reinforcing the democratic process in the EU. Over the years, many conferences have taken place where academics have debated the role the national parliaments should play. Some academics have argued that consultation with national parliaments could potentially weaken the European Parliament. This view is contested here because it is felt that all legal measures concerning the rights of European citizens must be enacted with as much democratic involvement as possible. If this means involving national parliaments and encouraging a democratic dialogue with the European Parliament, such measures should be welcomed. Encouraging this dialogue would reassure the people of Europe that decisions will not be taken that disregard their interests. The power of the Council should be reduced in the decision-making procedure because the ministers sitting in this body are bearers of their particular national interests, which are not necessarily the interests of the people of Europe. For example, it seems that international terrorism is a threat within the EU, and for this reason the Council (and not the European Parliament, and thus not the people of Europe) is adopting tough legal measures that will limit the liberties of EU citizens. This endangers EU citizens' personal data, as there is a risk that their e-mails or telephone calls could be monitored without their knowledge. Some have noticed that their letters coming from foreign countries into Italy are often delivered opened. When the post office is asked why, it responds that they are being opened because they come from abroad, and must be checked for security reasons. This invasion of privacy is troubling, but what is more upsetting is that the staff of the post office can do this because an EU framework decision allows them to do so regardless of the wishes of Italian or other EU citizens. This would be of concern if members of the European Parliament, as the only direct representatives of EU citizens, had been involved in these decisions, but the fact that the Council made the decision on its own is absolutely unacceptable for anyone who believes in the democratic process. The Lisbon Treaty will make a difference by involving the European Parliament and national parliaments, giving EU citizens a direct say on most of the areas covered by the Treaty. The more EU citizens are involved in the decisions taken by the EU that directly affect their lives, the more they will invest in the effective functioning of the EU. At that point, they will be in a better position to make a judgement as to what direction they would like the EU to take. The Lisbon Treaty presents a chance for people to be brought closer to the EU, and thus to understand it better. In this way, the sovereign people of Europe will be fully entitled to say: 'We want or we do not want the EU as it stands.' The Treaty thus presents the citizens of Europe with an important opportunity.

Content of the Book

This book focuses attention on the two crimes of smuggling of migrants by sea and trafficking in human beings in the European Union. The subject is approached by analysing the United Nations Convention against Transnational Organized Crime

(UNTOC) Protocols against Smuggling of Migrants and Trafficking in Human Beings, and EU laws adopted relating to these crimes. The book explores EU police and judicial co-operation to counter smuggling and trafficking, and the amendments that the Lisbon Treaty will introduce.

A sizeable portion of the book is dedicated to examining the plight of victims of human trafficking and people smuggling, because their story can be a motivation for combating these two cross-border crimes. This research was undertaken as part of the search for a solution to these particular crimes. Initially, the difference between trafficking and smuggling was not clear, as it was believed that there was little to no difference between the victims of these two crimes. Indeed, there are similarities, as both groups are forced to go against their will. Victims of human trafficking are forced by criminal organisations to travel for the purpose of sexual or other forms of exploitation, such as forced labour. Victims of people smuggling are forced to travel, not by organised crime, but by the impoverished circumstances they are compelled to escape from in their countries of origin. However, the research early on revealed that according to international conventions and EU law, the difference between people who are smuggled and people who are trafficked is that the latter are considered victims, while the former are not. International conventions and EU law consider that when people who are smuggled leave their countries of origin, they are making a free choice which is absent in the case of victims of human trafficking. Nights and days were spent trying to understand this difference, and the conclusion was reached that this differentiation, although fully supported by the law, was not accurate. The research was carried out in Italy, where the crime of smuggling of migrants by sea is a major problem. Interviews were held with law enforcement authorities and members of humanitarian organisations who deal every day with smuggled migrants, in order to get their views, based on their experience, about the best way to tackle human trafficking and people smuggling. Discussions were initiated with many people in the north and south of Italy about victims of trafficking and people smuggling. The research made it clear that smuggled migrants are in fact victims, because their decision to leave their country of origin is not made freely, but as a result of extreme poverty. This book presents the results of these findings. It is clear that those smuggled are forced by circumstances to leave their countries of origin, and are aware that their trip will not be easy. They are aware that most people who attempt to leave countries in Sub-Saharan Africa do not even make it out of the desert. They are aware that even if they are lucky enough to reach the coast of Libya, many of them will be tortured in Libyan prisons before being able to take boats bound for Italy (see Chapter 5). Finally, they are aware that of those who actually get the chance to make the journey across the sea to Italy, many will drown as a result of travelling on sub-standard boats. Despite knowing that the odds are stacked against them, they still decide the risk is worth taking. Why would they make that choice? This is clearly not a decision to be taken lightly. They take this decision because they are forced, not by other people, but by the fact that they have no alternative if they want to survive and seek a better life for themselves. It is thus very difficult to see how trafficked people are classed as victims whilst smuggled migrants are not. It seems obvious that they are victims, and as such, they should be legally protected by their states of destination. Unfortunately, states of destination simply return them to their countries of origin, because it is much easier for them to ignore the larger problem of poverty that forces these people to take this decision. A different policy would not be presented in such a way as to make it a vote-winner, and thus would not be taken up by national governments. This book aims to demonstrate that a different policy concentrating on the integration of victims is both necessary and possible if these crimes are to be defeated. It is necessary because statistics show that in recent years, smuggling of migrants has increased, which means that the criminal organisations behind this crime are growing stronger. It is possible because the smuggling of migrants is not uncontrollable. Italy, for example, knows very well the number of people who are smuggled in every year.[1] In 2009, the number of migrants smuggled by sea arriving in Italy decreased because the government turned away boats carrying these people to its shores. However, by taking this decision, the Italian government has been in breach of different international conventions. Firstly, the Italian government has violated the United Nations Convention on the Law of the Sea, which states that States Parties of this convention have the legal obligation to rescue people found at sea who are lost or in danger.[2] Secondly, the Italian government has violated the Convention on the status of refugees and EU law on the protection of persons in need of subsidiary protection. This is because many of the people on the rejected boats are asylum seekers who are escaping from war or for other reasons covered by this convention, as well as EU law. Finally, the Italian government has violated the UNTOC Protocol on Trafficking in Human Beings and EU law on trafficking, because many people on the rejected boats are victims or potential victims of this crime. Nations do not have the right to ignore international conventions and EU law just because they go against their particular narrow interests.

If they decide to join the EU or to ratify international conventions, they must respect them to the same extent as they do their own domestic laws, and the EU should ensure that nations are respectful of the international and EU law they are a party to. The Lisbon Treaty will facilitate this, because national parliaments, along with the European Parliament, will be involved in the adoption of legal measures regarding most areas of the EU, including that of immigration. It is hoped that the European Parliament will be keener in pursuing the general interests of European people rather than the particular interests of one or of a few particular Member States. This is because the people of Europe will be vigilant in ensuring that their representatives pursue the general interests of the EU. Rejecting people smuggled by sea is not in the general interest of the European people because it does not resolve the problem of irregular entry.

---

1   See Chapter 5 of this book for the Italian statistical data on the smuggling of migrants by sea which I received from the Ministry of Home Affairs.

2   See Chapter 4.

Chapter 2 will show that most irregular migrants are over-stayers, and not the victims of people smuggling. Therefore, rejecting them does not address the problem of irregular migration at all, which clearly cannot be resolved by the mere adoption of repressive measures without regulating regular economic migration. The Lisbon Treaty, by promoting a common policy on immigration, will permit the adoption of legal measures on economic migration which will contribute to the reduction of irregular entry. It is unfortunate that the UK, Ireland and Denmark have decided to opt out of the measures regarding EU immigration policies.[3] They have missed an opportunity to improve the policy and law on immigration by co-operating with other EU Member States. Was opting out of these policies and laws what the citizens of these three countries really wanted? In the UK, there is much demagogy about the EU that might have misled the British people into being suspicious of it as an institution. Sectors of the British press in particular appear to take a very hostile approach towards the EU, which may influence public opinion and policy. A Labour politician once said that the UK should allow limitation of its sovereignty by the EU on economic issues only.[4] The problem is that the EU is already limiting national sovereignty in delicate areas such as data protection by framework decisions which result in people not having any say on the issues. The UK is party to the measures related to EU police and judicial co-operation, and this means that it, along with other Member States, has approved tough measures concerning the fundamental freedoms of EU citizens without allowing the European Parliament (representing the sovereign people of Europe, which includes the British people) to have its say. The Lisbon Treaty should allow these sovereign people the opportunity to understand the demagogic intent of their government through the European Parliament. Their right to decide on whether to stay or to leave the EU will be the result of their understanding of it, and should be given full respect. At the moment, the sovereign people of Denmark, Ireland, the UK and of all the EU Member States are not prepared to reject the EU, as a majority lack knowledge of what the EU is about. They do not have sufficient understanding of how the EU functions to be able to see the positive role the European Parliament can play as their representative in the EU.

Aims of the Book

The aims of this book are twofold. The first is to demonstrate that EU Member States alone cannot address these two crimes, because they have a cross-border

---

3   For the position of the UK, Ireland and Denmark on EU immigration law and policy, see Chapter 3, which explains their position under the EU Treaty, and their future position under the Lisbon Treaty.

4   Comments made by the Labour MP Gisela Stuart during a public lecture at the University of Buckingham, 2 June 2008.

dimension. This means that these crimes are committed across different EU Member States and in countries outside the EU. This explains the intervention of agencies such as Europol and Frontex. These international crime-fighting agencies must co-operate with the national police forces of EU Member States and facilitate communication with non-EU countries. However, allowing their presence on national territory means that EU Member States will have to limit their sovereignty concerning certain criminal investigations. This should only be done if the sovereign people of the EU are in agreement. EU citizens would have greater understanding of how important EU police and judicial co-operation are if there was improved dialogue between them and their representatives in the EU Parliament. In this way, the sovereign people could create a *cultural and moral movement* against the criminal organisations involved in the smuggling of migrants and trafficking, with the opportunity to vote in favour of legal measures on EU police and judicial co-operation. This cultural and moral movement should also aim to integrate victims of people smuggling and trafficking. In this way, they would escape from the intimidating power of criminal organisations and feel comfortable enough to co-operate with law enforcement authorities. Integration is possible by granting a permanent visa to these victims. The Lisbon Treaty could permit a more unified policy on migration and a more effective approach against these two cross-border crimes. This book will show that at the moment, there is a lack of mutual trust between the law enforcement authorities of EU Member States. New legal measures aimed at fostering mutual trust between the Member States have been adopted. However, they will not create mutual trust until the sovereign people of Europe understand how their personal rights and freedoms will be impacted, and how the reinforcement of mutual trust can be ensured without the sacrifice of fundamental human rights. Italy and the UK have been chosen as the focus of this research in order to demonstrate the difficulties that Member States with different legal systems and traditions may encounter when trying to co-operate with each other.

The other aim of this book is to demonstrate that the criminal organisations that commit these crimes can be defeated through the support of their victims. The research on which the book is based will show that criminal organisations are able to intimidate people by threatening them or their families, especially when these people are not integrated into the society where they live. In the case of smuggling of migrants and trafficking, their victims cannot be integrated if they do not have a long-term visa. A long-term visa would permit these people to work and to trust the law enforcement authorities, which would then assist and encourage them to testify against their smugglers and traffickers. In this way, criminal organisations would lose their power of intimidation, and could be defeated. One might ask how all this can be proven. This method has been successful in two Italian cities, and this would suggest that it could and should be applied elsewhere in Italy and in other Member States. The protection of victims of human trafficking has long been lacking. The two successful approaches are called the 'Rimini Method' (for victims of human trafficking) and the 'Siracusan Approach' (for victims of smuggling of migrants by sea). This book will share the findings of interviews carried out in the UK and in Italy, at the detention centre of Lampedusa (Italy), which further strengthen the argument that people smuggled by sea are in fact victims.

Chapter 2
The Limits of Law

Introduction

Preventive measures against the smuggling of migrants and trafficking in human beings should at minimum consist of supporting victims of these crimes, by facilitating their integration into the receiving country. This ensures that the victims feel safe to co-operate with the law enforcement authorities involved in fighting against these two crimes. In addition to offering support for victims of these crimes, EU police and judicial co-operation should also be enhanced. These two crime prevention measures are the focus of the next chapters of this book. This chapter specifically concentrates on the smuggling of migrants and trafficking in human beings at the international and EC/EU levels.

The first section of this chapter will define the crimes of the smuggling of migrants and trafficking in human beings. These definitions will be derived by analysing UNTOC[1] and the Council of Europe Convention on Action against Trafficking in Human Beings.[2] The second section of this chapter will examine the measures adopted at the international level intended to fight against the smuggling of migrants and trafficking in human beings. The third section will analyse EC/EU measures against smuggling of migrants and trafficking in human beings. Finally, this chapter will focus on reforming the EU Treaty in order to facilitate European integration in the criminal area, making the fight against smuggling of migrants and trafficking in human beings more effective. For this purpose, amendments that would be introduced by the Lisbon Treaty will be analysed.

One would think that the difference between international law and EC/EU law might be summarised by quoting an important UNTOC provision, which states:

> States Parties shall carry out their obligations under this Convention in a manner consistent with the principles of sovereign equality and territorial integrity of States...
>
> Nothing in this Convention entitles a State Party to undertake in the territory of another State the exercise of jurisdiction and performance of functions that

---

1   See *United Nations Convention against Transnational Organized Crime* (UNTOC), A/RES/55/25, Doc. A/55/383, 8 January 2001.

2   *Council of Europe Convention on Action against Trafficking in Human Beings*, CM (2005) 32 Addendum 1 final, 3 May 2005.

are reserved exclusively for the authorities of that other State by its domestic law.[3]

Instead, EU law should enable EU Member States the ability to fight against transnational crimes by co-operating with each other. The EU has developed, and continues to do so, important instruments that enable an effective fight against criminal organisations. These instruments are impeded at the international level because of a rigid respect for national sovereignty. The European Arrest Warrant (EAW), for example, is a very important EU measure that could really make a difference to international law in combating criminal organisations that smuggle migrants and traffic human beings. This chapter will suggest how to strengthen EU crime combating measures by reinforcing EU supremacy.

In order to achieve this objective, it is essential to define what smuggling of migrants and trafficking in human beings mean, by examining two international conventions, UNTOC and the Council of Europe Convention on Action against Trafficking in Human Beings.

Definition of Smuggling of Migrants and Trafficking in Human Beings

Definition of Smuggling of Migrants

Smuggling of migrants has been defined by the UNTOC Protocol on Smuggling of Migrants.[4] This Protocol was drafted with the purpose of punishing organised criminal groups that intentionally smuggle people for a financial gain.[5] Therefore, the Protocol does not address: the crime of assisting irregular entry without the purpose of a financial gain, the assisting of irregular migration that does not involve criminal organisations, or mere irregular entry itself. The reason for these exclusions is that the crime of assisting illegal entry by organised criminal groups (smuggling of migrants) has been recognised as transnational in nature. This demands that the Protocol is focused specifically on fighting this particular form of serious crime.[6]

The principal feature of the crime of smuggling migrants is a criminal group with the intention of committing the smuggling of migrants for financial gain.

---

3   See Art. 4 of UNTOC, op. cit. note 1.

4   See Arts 3 *et seq.* of *Protocol against the Smuggling of Migrants by Land, Sea and Air, Supplementing the United Nations Convention against Transnational Organized Crime, A/RES/55/25* (UNTOC Protocol), 8 January 2001.

5   See *Legislative Guide for the Implementation of the Protocol against the Smuggling of Migrants by Land, Sea and Air, Supplementing the United Nations Convention against Transnational Organized Crime*, p. 341.

6   See ibid., p. 340.

The importance of the 'financial gain' component of the crime is confirmed by the Protocol on Smuggling, which reads:

> 'Smuggling of Migrants' shall mean the procurement, in order to obtain, directly or indirectly, a financial or other material benefit, of the illegal entry of a person into a State Party of which the person is not a national or a permanent resident.[7]

The Protocol also makes reference to the 'financial gain' feature when it calls for States Parties to make the smuggling of migrants a criminal offence 'when committed intentionally and in order to obtain, directly or indirectly, a financial or other material benefit'.[8] The UNTOC Protocol states that this Protocol applies when the smuggling of migrants is committed by 'an organized criminal group',[9] demonstrating that the Protocol is in fact focused on criminal organisations' activity. The UNTOC Protocol calls for States Parties to adopt measures against persons who participate as accomplices, organisers or directors of other persons in order to commit smuggling of migrants.[10]

The UNTOC Protocol calls for serious measures to be taken against the smuggling of migrants; in addition, it allows Member States to be even more restrictive in their approach than the Convention demands. UNTOC states that: 'Each State Party may adopt more strict or severe measures than those provided for by this Convention for preventing and combating transnational organized crime.'[11] The elements of intentional illegal behaviour aiming to gain a profit must also be present in the criminal conduct of producing, procuring, providing or possessing fraudulent documents.[12] Another element, that must be added to those outlined above is the intention or purpose to use these documents to smuggle other people, and not for facilitating their own irregular entry.[13] Moreover, those persons who commit offences concerning documents must have the intention of procuring illegal entry, and not the intention of enabling illegal entry, although Member States can decide to punish this specific conduct.[14] In conclusion, the Smuggling Protocol is left open to wide interpretation, because it takes in consideration the different policies that States Parties can adopt against this crime and leaves them the choice of being more restrictive than the Protocol.

---

7   See Art. 3(a) of the UNTOC Protocol, op. cit. note 4.
8   Ibid.
9   See Art. 4 of the UNTOC Protocol, op. cit. note 4.
10   See ibid., Arts 6(2)(b) and (c).
11   See Art. 34(3) of UNTOC, op. cit. note 1. See also *Legislative Guide for the Implementation of the Protocol against the Smuggling of Migrants*, op. cit. note 5, p. 356.
12   See ibid., p. 344.
13   Ibid.
14   See Art. 34(3) of UNTOC, op. cit. note 1.

Definition of Trafficking in Human Beings

A clear definition of trafficking in human beings can be found in UNTOC[15] and in the Council of Europe Convention on Action against Trafficking in Human Beings.[16] Trafficking in human beings has been characterised by the combination of three elements: action, means and purpose.[17] The action required is 'the recruitment, transportation, transfer, harbouring or receipt of persons'.[18] The crime of trafficking in persons is committed:

> by means of the threat or use of force or other forms of coercion, of abduction, of fraud, of deception, of the abuse of power or of a position of vulnerability or of the giving or receiving of payments or benefits to achieve the consent of a person having control over another person ...[19]

These activities are perpetrated 'for the purpose of exploitation'.[20] The UNTOC Protocol requires States Parties to criminalise trafficking in human beings.[21] The UNTOC Protocol also states that conduct inclusive of all the elements described in this section shall be criminalised, and not individual actions.[22] States Parties may decide to criminalise the single acts, but the criminalisation of single acts is outside the scope of the Trafficking of Persons Protocol.[23] In both Conventions,[24] the exploitation element is not only required for human trafficking for the purpose of prostitution, but also other forms of exploitation, such as forced labour.[25] Indeed, the Council of Europe Convention on Action against Trafficking in Human Beings and the UNTOC Protocol on Trafficking of Persons state:

---

15   See Art. 3 (1)(a) of the *Protocol to Prevent, Suppress and Punish Trafficking in Persons, Especially Women and Children, Supplementing the United Nations Convention against Transnational Organized Crime, A/RES/55/25* (Trafficking in Persons Protocol), Doc. A/55/383, 8 January 2001.

16   See Art. 4(1)(a) of the Council of Europe Convention, op. cit. note 2.

17   See *Legislative Guide for the Implementation of the Protocol to Prevent, Suppress and Punish Trafficking in Persons, Especially Women and Children, Supplementing the United Nations Convention against Transnational Organized Crime*, p. 268.

18   See Art. 3(1)(a) of the Trafficking in Persons Protocol, op. cit. note 15. See also Art. 4(1)(a) of the Council of Europe Convention, op. cit. note 2.

19   Ibid.

20   Ibid.

21   See Art. 5 of the Trafficking in Persons Protocol, op. cit. note 15.

22   Ibid.

23   See the interpretative notes, A/55/383/Add. 1, para. 64.

24   See Art. 3(1)(a) of the Trafficking in Persons Protocol, op. cit. note 15. See also Art. 4(1)(a) of the Council of Europe Convention, op. cit. note 2.

25   Ibid.

Exploitation shall include, at a minimum, the exploitation of the prostitution of others or other forms of sexual exploitation, forced labour or services, slavery or practices similar to slavery, servitude or the removal of organs ...[26]

Therefore, trafficking in human beings not only consists of trafficking in prostitution, but includes other forms of trafficking in human beings as well. It has in fact been estimated that only one-quarter of the whole phenomenon of trafficking in human beings consists of trafficking in prostitution.[27] Although the data on human trafficking is not entirely reliable, it is safe to say that most victims are exploited for other purposes.[28]

UNTOC and protocols negotiators have also argued that the mere attempt to commit trafficking in persons should also be criminalised.[29] Nevertheless, not all States Parties punish the attempt to commit a crime.[30] This is the reason why the criminalisation of attempts to commit trafficking in persons is not mandatory,[31] as reflected in the UNTOC Trafficking Protocol, which states:

Each State Party shall also adopt such legislative and other measures as may be necessary to establish as criminal offences:
a.   Subjects to the basic concepts of its legal system, attempting to commit ...[32]

To summarise: the Council of Europe Convention on Action against Trafficking in Human Beings and the UNTOC Protocol require Member States to criminalise all forms of human trafficking. Therefore, States Parties should investigate who are the victims of human trafficking without excluding any groups of people, because anybody may be a potential victim.

People Smuggling, Human Trafficking and Economic Irregular Migration

A study by the International Organization for Migration (IOM) reveals that in 2004, trafficking in human beings was a phenomenon that remained mostly

---

26   Ibid.

27   See Obokata, T., 'Trafficking of Human Beings as a Crime against Humanity: Some Implications for the International Legal System', *International and Comparative Law Quarterly* 54:2 (2005), p. 447.

28   Ibid. Obokata quotes Hughes, D.M., 'The "Natasha" Trade: The Transnational Shadow Market of Trafficking in Women', *Journal of International Affairs*, pp. 625 and 628, which gives a statistic from the United Nations.

29   See Legislative Guide, op. cit. note 17, p. 271.

30   Ibid.

31   Ibid.

32   See Art. 5(2)(a) of the Trafficking in Persons Protocol, op. cit. note 15.

unreported. The statistics published by IOM are those of police, border guards and agencies that give assistance to traffickers' victims.[33] IOM data does not show the sex of victims, but in the health assistance programme carried out by the IOM, 392 victims of trafficking in human beings they received were all women aged 20–30.[34] Based on the data published by IOM on the top six nationalities of victims (Moldovian, Romanian, Ukrainian, Belarusian, Bulgarian and those from the Dominican Republic) revealing that trafficking in human beings is mostly committed for sexual exploitation, one might assume that the majority of victims are women.

However, such an assumption may be incorrect, as it has been reported that men, and especially boys, are also victims of sexual exploitation.[35] Certainly, the European Commission emphasised that 'trafficking in women and girls especially for commercial sexual exploitation is a wide reality'.[36] The data reported by IOM show that in 2004, approximately 78 percent of the victims were aged 18–24.[37] Nearly 13 percent of traffickers' victims from the top six nationalities were under 18 years old.[38] The IOM also reported that many of the victims are mothers or single mothers,[39] and UNICEF estimated that 1.2 million children are exploited in the sexual market, although there is very little knowledge on the true rate.[40] It is important to consider the possibility of other potential victims excluded from the data, since they are not reliable.

IOM research reveals that almost 25 percent of exploitation consists of forced labour and other illegal activities not specified.[41] IOM research also reveals that human trafficking is widespread throughout Africa.[42] It has been reported that many families literally 'sell' their children to criminal organisations that subsequently traffic them in Europe, not only for the purpose of sexual exploitation, but also to recruit them into forced labour. These IOM research findings demand that investigations into human trafficking be conducted at the EU, national and international level, so that all forms of trafficking in human beings can be combated effectively. Concentrating only on trafficking of women and children

---

33   See *World Migration: Cost and Benefits of International Migration* (Geneva: International Organization for Migration, 2005), p. 417.

34   Ibid.

35   See ibid., p. 421. See also *Fighting Trafficking in Human Beings: An Integrated Approach and Proposals for an Action Plan*, COM (2005) 514 final, 18 October 2005, p. 7.

36   See ibid.

37   See *World Migration: Costs and Benefits of International Migration*, op. cit. note 33, p. 418.

38   Ibid.

39   See ibid., p. 420.

40   See ibid., p. 335.

41   Ibid.

42   See Adepoju, A. (2005) 'Review on Research and Data on Human Trafficking in Sub-Saharan Africa', in Laczko, F., and Gozdziak, E., eds, *Data and Research on Human Trafficking: A Global Survey* (Geneva: International Organization for Migration, 2005).

may create the mistaken belief that only they can be victims of this crime, resulting in other irregular migrant groups being neglected. This assumption does not take into consideration that, as Europol has emphasised, although trafficking in human beings is characterised by sexual exploitation, child pornography, illicit trade in abandoned children and illicit trade in human organs and tissue, 'labour exploitation is becoming just as important for the Member States'.[43] Europol did not specify who the victims of trafficking in human beings are.

In addition, Europol has identified the push-factors for human trafficking: high unemployment, poverty, escaping persecution, violence or abuse, avoiding breaches of human rights, environmental conditions, labour markets forbidden to women, and sexual or ethnic discrimination.[44] Some push-factors are specific to women, others affect all people, including children. When analysing these push-factors, it seems clear that victims of human trafficking are predominantly people who leave their countries of origin for economic reasons, and they must not be ignored.

In conclusion, international law and EC/EU law mainly concentrate on women and children, because data show that they are the principal victims of this crime. However, other categories of victims and potential victims are possibly being excluded from the data, because there are no reliable data on trafficking which do not include sexual exploitation.[45] The unreliability of data on human trafficking makes it all the more important for there to be increased co-operation in investigating this crime. Such increased co-operation in investigating human trafficking and the smuggling of migrants is important not only for reasons of unreliable data, but also because these two crimes are transnational in nature.[46] Understanding the transnational element of trafficking and smuggling is essential in combating these two crimes.

The Transnational Elements of People Smuggling and Human Trafficking

Smuggling of Migrants as a Transnational Crime

The smuggling of migrants is not necessarily a transnational crime. If States punish any act directed to facilitate irregular entry disregarding whether or not the act has cross-border implications, smuggling of migrants will only remain conceptually a domestic offence. In British law, for example, any act that facilitates an irregular

---

43   See 'Trafficking in Human Beings for Sexual Exploitation in the EU: A Europol Perspective' (January 2004).

44   Ibid.

45   See Chapter 5 of this book.

46   See Chapter 5 for the connections between irregular migration, smuggling of migrants and trafficking in human beings.

entry is punishable, no matter whether this act has cross-border implications.[47] The reason is that British legislators believe that essentially, assisting irregular entry is a domestic offence. Indeed, the UK, although it does not foresee the crime of smuggling of migrants as a separate criminal offence from assisting irregular migration, states that a person commits the crime of assisting irregular migration to an EU Member State if she or he: 'does an act which facilitates the commission of a breach of immigration law by an individual who is not a citizen of the European Union'.[48] Furthermore, British law states that a person commits the offence of helping asylum seekers to enter the UK if she or he 'knowingly and for gain facilitates the arrival in the United Kingdom of an individual'.[49]

The transnational element of the smuggling of migrants is also ignored by Italian law. Italian law differs from British law by differentiating the smuggling of migrants done by criminal organisations from other forms,[50] it punishes the attempt to commit assisting irregular migration and the attempt to commit smuggling of migrants.[51] The attempt will not necessarily end up in an irregular entry involving the territory of another EU Member State. If smuggling of migrants is committed by the falsification of documents committed by criminal groups for financial gain and this act is only committed on Italian territory, the transnational element is not relevant.[52] UNTOC expressly specifies that States Parties can criminalise the offences which are within the scope of this Convention 'independently of the transnational nature or the involvement of an organized criminal group'.[53] Moreover, UNTOC establishes that: 'Each State Party may adopt more strict or severe measures than those provided for by this Convention for preventing and combating transnational organized crime.'[54] Nevertheless, the transnationality and the involvement of criminal organisations have to be common elements of smuggling of migrants to all States Parties in order for double criminality to apply.[55] Double criminality is essential to obtain international assistance and extradition

---

47   See ss. 25 *et seq.* of the Immigration Act 1971 as replaced by the Nationality, Immigration and Asylum Act 2002.

48   See s. 25(1(a)) inserted by the Nationality, Immigration and Asylum Act 2002.

49   See s. 25A(1(a)) inserted by the Nationality, Immigration and Asylum Act 2002.

50   See Art. 12(3) of Legislative Decree 286/1998, GU 191, 18 August 1998, Supplemento ordinario 139 as modified by Art. 11(1(b)) of Act 189/2002, GU 199, 26 August 2002.

51   See ibid., Art. 12(3).

52   Ibid.

53   See Art. 34(2) of UNTOC, op. cit. note 1. See also *Legislative Guide for the Implementation of the United Nations Convention against Transnational Organized Crime and the Protocol Thereto* (United Nations Office on Drugs and Crime, 2004), pp. 10 and 11.

54   See Art. 34(3) of UNTOC, op. cit. note 1.

55   See *Legislative Guide for the Implementation of the United Nations Convention against Transnational Organized Crime*, op. cit. note 53, p. 11.

between States Parties signing and implementing this Convention, as stated by Article 16(1) of UNTOC.[56]

The absence of the transnational element and of the involvement of criminal organisations does not mean that the act of assisting irregular migration which lacks these two elements should never be criminalised at domestic level, but it does mean that assisting irregular migration is not criminalised under UNTOC. Furthermore, it could be argued that transnational crimes are domestic offences which have, as further characteristic a cross-border dimension that makes international police and judicial co-operation necessary in order to fight against them. This is the reason why UNTOC focuses attention on the transnationality of smuggling of migrants.

UNTOC has outlined the characteristics that are the hallmark of transnational organised criminal offences, stating that transnational crime requires: either the commission of the offence in 'more than one State',[57] or that 'a substantial part of its preparation, planning, direction or control takes place in another State',[58] or 'an organized criminal group that engages in criminal activities in more than one State',[59] or that 'It is committed in one State but has substantial effects in another State.'[60]

In conclusion, the mere attempt to smuggle migrants, or other conduct such as producing falsified documents, are not considered transnational crimes. The smuggling of migrants becomes a transnational crime, punishable under UNTOC, when it is committed in more than one State and by organised crime.

The next section will focus on the transnational features of trafficking in human beings.

The Transnational Features of Human Trafficking

The Trafficking Protocol states that all the UNTOC provisions apply to the Protocol, and therefore must be read together.[61] In other words, the characteristics of transnational crimes listed by UNTOC are to be extended to trafficking in persons.[62] The crime of trafficking in human beings can take place in one country, while 'a substantial part of its preparation, planning, direction or control takes place in another State'.[63] Trafficking in persons might involve 'an organized criminal group that engages in criminal activities in more than one State',[64] and can have 'substantial effects in another State apart from the one in which it was

---

56   See ibid. See also Art. 16(1) of UNTOC, op. cit. note 1.
57   See ibid., Art. 3(2).
58   Ibid.
59   Ibid.
60   Ibid.
61   See Art. 1 of the Trafficking in Persons Protocol, op. cit. note 15.
62   See Art. 3(2) of UNTOC, op. cit. note 1.
63   Ibid.
64   Ibid.

committed'.[65] However, these transnational characteristics are not crucial to the crime of human trafficking, since it can be committed entirely in only one State. When it comes to human trafficking, these two Conventions are less focused on the transnational element of the crime, and on its exploitive features.[66] Trafficking in persons is a domestic offence when victims of this crime are transported within the borders of a given country.[67] These cases fall outside UNTOC's scope, as it is focused only on trafficking with a transnational dimension.[68] Even though trafficking in human beings that is committed within one country is not covered by UNTOC, it does fall within the scope of the Council of Europe Convention against Trafficking in Human Beings.[69]

International Co-operation against People Smuggling and Human Trafficking

Jurisdiction and Extradition

UNTOC does offer solutions for the establishment of jurisdictional control over crimes listed in the Convention and Protocols. Some solutions are based on objective criteria which do not require that the crime involves either a transnational element or organised crime.[70] One solution takes into consideration the territory where the offence has been committed. UNTOC states that each State Party shall establish jurisdiction over offences covered by this Convention and 'committed in the territory of that State Party'.[71] Another solution takes into account the vessel or aircraft on which the crime has been committed:[72]

> The offence is committed on board a vessel that is flying the flag of that State Party or an aircraft that is registered under the laws of that State Party at the time that the offence is committed.[73]

Other solutions are based on subjective criteria, because they take into account either the nationality of the person who is victimised by the offence or the nationality

---

65   Ibid.

66   See Art. 3(1)(a) of the Trafficking in Persons Protocol, op. cit. note 15. See also Art. 4(1)(a) of the Council of Europe Convention, op. cit. note 2.

67   See Obokata, 'Trafficking of Human Beings as a Crime against Humanity', op. cit. note 27, p. 448.

68   See Art. 3 of UNTOC, op. cit. note 1.

69   See Art. 2 of the Council of Europe Convention, op. cit. note 2.

70   See *Legislative Guide for the Implementation of the United Nations Convention against Transnational Organized Crime*, op. cit. note 53, p. 107.

71   See Art. 15 (a) of UNTOC, op. cit. note 1. All measures of the Convention shall be extended to the Protocols.

72   See ibid., Art. 15(1(b)).

73   Ibid.

or the residence of the offender.[74] Thus, UNTOC specifies that States Parties shall establish jurisdiction either if '[t]he offence is committed against a national of that State Party'[75] or if '[t]he offence is committed by a national of that State Party or a stateless person who has his or her habitual residence in its territory'.[76] Therefore, States Parties have the right to invoke extra-territorial jurisdiction when the crime has been committed against one national of their State or when the offender is their national or resident. This subjective criterion has the potential to create problems if the crime involves multiple States which may all decide to assert jurisdictional control against a person who has partly committed the transnational crime in their own territory. There could be problems if the offender is a national of a State where the offence has not been committed. If the State where the crime has been committed (requesting State) requests the extradition of an offender who is not one of their nationals, the requested State might refuse to extradite 'solely on the ground that he or she is one of its nationals'.[77] In this case, 'when the alleged offender is present in its territory and it does not extradite such person solely on the ground that he or she is one of its nationals'[78] the principle of *aut dedere aut iudicare* (extradite or prosecute) may not be sufficient to resolve potential conflicts of jurisdiction. The reason *aut dedere aut iudicare* may be ineffective is that the requested State may need to gather evidence in the requesting State in order to prosecute the offender. The requested State Party that has refused to extradite the offender may require the requesting State Party's legal assistance and other forms of legal co-operation to prosecute the offender.[79] UNTOC states that:

> A State Party in whose territory an alleged offender is found, if it does not extradite such person … shall, at the request of the State Party seeking extradition, be obliged to submit the case without undue delay to its competent authorities for the purpose of prosecution.[80]

Mutual legal assistance consists of assisting a foreign State in a trial by ensuring that the evidence is then submitted in the trial.[81] Mutual legal assistance might render the extradition superfluous, especially when the offender is a national of the

---

74   See *Legislative Guide for the Implementation of the United Nations Convention against Transnational Organized Crime*, op. cit. note 53, p. 105.
75   See Art. 15(2(a)) of UNTOC, op. cit. note 1.
76   See ibid., Art. 15(2(b)).
77   See ibid., Art. 16(10).
78   See ibid., Art. 15(3). See also *Legislative Guide for the Implementation of the United Nations Convention against Transnational Organized Crime*, op. cit. note 53, p. 105.
79   See ibid., p. 202.
80   See Art. 16(10) of UNTOC, op. cit. note 1.
81   See Joutsen, M. (2004) 'International Instruments on Cooperation in Responding to Transnational Crime', in Reichel, P., ed., *Handbook of Transnational Crime and Justice* (London: Sage Publications, 2004), p. 264.

State requesting extradition. However, mutual legal assistance may be refused if it is considered too invasive of a State Party's national sovereignty.

This type of assistance is requested when an offence is transnational in nature, and thus States Parties need to co-operate with each other to prosecute criminals.[82] Mutual legal assistance also means allowing authorities of the State which has jurisdiction over a transnational offence to enter the State where the cross-border crime has been committed and gather evidence, in accordance with methods approved by the requested State.[83] UNTOC recognises the importance of mutual legal assistance under Article 18, which states that mutual legal assistance might be requested when there is the suspicion that a transnational crime listed in the Convention and Protocols has been committed by organised crime.[84] Article 18 does not give a definition of judicial proceedings, thus States Parties have wide discretion in deciding 'the extent to which they will provide assistance for such proceedings'.[85] In the EU, for example, Member States have adopted other measures to reinforce mutual legal assistance in criminal matters. UNTOC States Parties may decide to refuse mutual legal assistance on other grounds,[86] one of which is: 'the requested State Party considers that the execution of the request is likely to prejudice its sovereignty, security, ordre [*sic*: order] public or other essential interests'.[87] This UNTOC provision lends itself to wide interpretation, possibly allowing UNTOC States Parties the ability to deny mutual legal assistance even when double criminality exists.

In other words, mutual legal assistance may be refused if the requested State thinks that it would be too invasive of its sovereignty – something expressly protected by UNTOC.[88]

Extradition and mutual legal assistance might even be refused by States Parties when there is no double criminality.[89] Under UNTOC, the State where the crime was committed may request the extradition of non-nationals in another territory with the involvement of a criminal group, 'provided that the offence for which extradition is sought is punishable under the domestic law of both the requesting State Party and the requested State Party'.[90] This provision applies to all crimes that are transnational for which double criminality is required.[91] Double criminality

---

82   *Legislative Guide for the Implementation of the United Nations Convention against Transnational Organized Crime*, op. cit. note 53, pp. 216 and 217.

83   Ibid., p. 217.

84   See Art. 18(1) of UNTOC, op. cit. note 1.

85   *Legislative Guide for the Implementation of the United Nations Convention against Transnational Organized Crime*, op. cit. note 53, p. 220.

86   See Art. 18(21) of UNTOC, op. cit. note 1.

87   See ibid., Art. 18(21)(b).

88   See ibid., Arts 4(1) and 18(21)(b).

89   See ibid., Arts 16(1) and 18(9).

90   See ibid., Art. 16(1).

91   See *Legislative Guide for the Implementation of the United Nations Convention against Transnational Organized Crime*, op. cit. note 53, p. 199.

may be difficult to achieve in many States Parties due to differing cultural and legal norms apart from those familiar to the EU. These barriers to extradition or mutual legal assistance may result in perpetrators of serious criminal offences such as smuggling of migrants and trafficking in human beings going unpunished.

Other limitations may lead to difficulties in mutual judicial co-operation in the form of extradition and mutual legal assistance against smuggling of migrants and trafficking in human beings. UNTOC requires States Parties to adopt other forms of international co-operation against crimes listed in the Convention, including joint investigation and law enforcement co-operation.[92] The conclusion of these agreements is not compulsory, although this provision will represent a sufficient legal basis for co-operation on a case-by-case basis for those States which do not permit the conclusion of agreements on joint investigations.[93] Although UNTOC calls for a transnational co-operative approach to law enforcement, this approach may have to yield to considerations of differences in national enforcement standards.[94]

In conclusion, being an instrument of international law, UNTOC cannot oblige States Parties to co-operate with each other, out of respect for the principles of sovereignty, nationality and double criminality.[95] Despite the barriers the principle of national sovereignty presents, the EU may be better able to fight against all forms of transnational crime by reinforcing EU integration in the area of crime.

Measures Established by UNTOC to Fight against the Smuggling of Migrants and Trafficking in Human Beings

The Protocols on Smuggling of Migrants and Trafficking in Human Beings and UNTOC must be read together. These two Protocols state: 'This Protocol supplements the United Nations Convention against Transnational Organized Crime. It shall be interpreted together with the Convention.'[96] Thus, the co-operation measures described in this chapter must be applied together with the provisions of the Smuggling and Trafficking Protocols.[97] The Smuggling Protocol

---

92 See Art. 19 of UNTOC, op. cit. note 1.

93 See *Legislative Guide for the Implementation of the United Nations Convention against Transnational Organized Crime*, op. cit. note 53, p. 236.

94 See Art. 27 of UNTOC, op. cit. note 1. See also *Legislative Guide for the Implementation of the United Nations Convention against Transnational Organized Crime*, op. cit. note 53, p. 235.

95 See Arts 4 and 11(6), 15(3), 16(1)(10) and 18(9) of UNTOC, op. cit. note 1.

96 See Art. 1(1) of the Smuggling of Migrants Protocol, op. cit. note 4. See also Art. 1(1) of the Trafficking in Persons Protocol, op. cit. note 15.

97 See Arts 7–18 of the Smuggling of Migrants Protocol, op. cit. note 4. See also Arts 9–13 of the Trafficking in Persons Protocol, op. cit. note 15.

includes measures to obtain general assistance when a State suspects that its vessel or a stateless vessel has been involved in the smuggling of migrants.[98]

Border measures include reinforcing border controls and co-operation between border control agencies.[99] The Smuggling of Migrants Protocol provides for: measures to ensure the authenticity of travel documents,[100] training measures to teach officials to prevent and fight against smuggling of migrants,[101] the return of smuggled migrants[102] and the formal exchange of information.[103] The Smuggling Protocol also specifies that 'States Parties shall consider the conclusion of bilateral or regional agreements or operational arrangements'[104] in order to prevent and combat effectively the crime of smuggling of migrants.[105] These measures in the Protocols may provide the foundation for the creation of a sophisticated structure to aid the EU in combating the smuggling of migrants, trafficking in human beings and other transnational crimes.

The UNTOC Protocol on human trafficking specifies that States Parties shall adopt policies and other measures in order to prevent trafficking in human beings and to protect victims.[106] The UNTOC Protocol calls for States Parties to take initiatives that are intended to reduce factors that facilitate human trafficking, such as 'poverty, underdevelopment and lack of equal opportunities'.[107] Law enforcement and immigration authorities are also called on to co-operate with each other in order to combat this criminal offence.[108] The UNTOC Trafficking Protocol states that border control and the control of passports or other identification documents must be reinforced if this is necessary to prevent and detect human trafficking.[109]

UNTOC and the Protocols impose obligations, while at the same time showing respect for national sovereignty. UNTOC imposes basic requirements that all States Parties should take into consideration when deciding how to combat the smuggling of migrants using greater police and judicial co-operation. UNTOC could not go further, because it has to respect the principle of sovereignty. The same limitations apply to the Council of Europe Convention on Action against Trafficking in Human Beings. This Convention establishes that States Parties must adopt measures to ensure the establishment of jurisdiction over human trafficking

---

98   See Art. 8(1) of the Smuggling of Migrants Protocol, op. cit. note 4.
99   See ibid., Art. 11(1–6).
100 See ibid., Art. 12.
101 See ibid., Art. 14(2).
102 See ibid., Art. 18(1–4).
103 See ibid., Art. 10.
104 See ibid., Art. 17.
105 Ibid.
106 See Arts 9(1)(a) and 9(1)(b) of the Trafficking in Persons Protocol, op. cit. note 15. For the protection of victims, see Chapters 4 and 5 of this book.
107 See Art. 9(4) of the Trafficking in Persons Protocol, op. cit. note 15.
108 See ibid., Art. 10.
109 See ibid., Arts 11(1) and 12.

when they refuse to extradite offenders.[110] The Council of Europe Convention also states that when more than one State Party claims jurisdiction over trafficking in human beings, they shall find an agreement 'on the most appropriate jurisdiction'.[111] Since this Convention is an international instrument, the principle of *aut dedere aut iudicare* can encounter the same limitations emphasised above. It can be difficult to resolve conflicts of jurisdiction between all States that signed the Council of Europe Convention against Trafficking in Human Beings, because the Convention itself does not impose a new, binding legal system on its signatories. The result is that the national sovereignty of these States Parties must be fully respected, which can create huge obstacles in the fight against human trafficking when committed across borders.

However, the EU has already agreed adequate instruments that can be effective against smuggling of migrants and trafficking in human beings.

This begs the question: should the EU limit national sovereignty more than UNTOC does? In other words, is the EC competent under criminal law?

The EC/EU and Migration

In order to answer the question of the EC's competence in the criminal area, and in particular in the fight against people smuggling and human trafficking, this chapter will firstly explore the EC's competence in immigration issues, as the immigration area and the crimes connected are linked with each other. EC competence means extending the co-decision procedure (the ordinary legislative procedure according to the terminology of the Lisbon Treaty) to EC immigration law and policy.

The EC has already made progress in this field since 2004. This progress has been achieved through the adoption of the Amsterdam Treaty, which amended Title IV of the EC Treaty and which states that for five years from the entry into force of the Treaty of Amsterdam, 'the Council shall act unanimously on a proposal from the Commission or on the initiative of a Member State and after consulting the European Parliament'[112] before adopting measures on asylum and immigration covered by Title IV of the EC Treaty. The result is that five years after the enactment of the Amsterdam Treaty, the European Council, in the Hague Programme,[113] requested the Council to enact a decision establishing that all

---

110   See Art. 31(3) of the Council of Europe Convention, op. cit. note 2.
111   See ibid., Art. 31(4).
112   See Art. 67(1) of 'Consolidated Version of the Treaty Establishing the European Community', OJ C 325/33, 24 December 2002.
113   See *Draft Multiannual Programme: The Hague Programme – Strengthening Freedom, Security and Justice in the European Union*, Doc. 13993/04 JAI 408, 27 October 2004, p. 8. Art. 67(2) of TEC, op. cit. note 112, states: 'After this period of five years: the Council shall act unanimously on a proposal from the Commission; the Commission shall examine any request made by a Member State that it submit a proposal to the Council; the

measures concerning Title IV EC Treaty should be adopted on the basis of Article 67(2) and 251 TEC.[114] For this purpose, it required the Council to adopt a decision based on Article 67(2) of the EC Treaty.[115] As a result, Decision 2004/927/EC was established.[116] This decision grants the European Parliament power to enact legislation in those areas covered by Article 62(1, 2(a) and 3), Article 63(2(b) and 3(b)) and Article 66.[117] Therefore, the European Parliament now has a say in laws concerning irregular migration, while legal migration issues and family law have been omitted by this decision. This means that all measures on irregular migration will be adopted by the Council acting by qualified majority voting (QMV) and by

---

Council, acting unanimously after consulting the European Parliament, shall take a decision with a view to providing for all or parts of the areas covered by this Title to be governed by the procedure referred to in Art. 251 and adapting the provisions relating to the powers of the Court of Justice.'

114   Ibid., Art. 251 is the co-decision procedure. Art. 67(2) states: '2. After this period of five years: the Council shall act on proposals from the Commission; the Commission shall examine any request made by a Member State that it submit a proposal to the Council; the Council, acting unanimously after consulting the European Parliament, shall take a decision with a view to providing for all or parts of the areas covered by this Title to be governed by the procedure referred to in Article 251 and adapting the provisions relating to the powers of the Court of Justice.'

115   *Council Decision Providing for Certain Areas Covered by Title IV of Part Three of the Treaty Establishing the European Community to be Governed by the Procedure Laid Down in Art. 251 of that Treaty*, Doc. 15226/04, 15 December 2004, p. 3.

116   See 'Council Decision 2004/927/EC of 22 December 2004 Providing for Certain Areas Covered by Title IV of Part Three of the Treaty Establishing the European Community to be Governed by the Procedure Laid Down in Art. 251 of that Treaty', OJ EU L 396/45, 31 December 2004.

117   See *Council Decision Providing for Certain Areas Covered by Title IV of Part Three of the Treaty Establishing the European Community to be Governed by the Procedure Laid Down in Art. 251 of that Treaty*, op. cit. note 115, p. 3. Arts 62(1 and 2(a) and 3) of TEC, op. cit. note 112, state: '(1) measures with a view to ensuring, in compliance with Article 14, the absence of any controls on persons, be they citizens of the Union or nationals of third countries, when crossing internal borders; (2) measures on the crossing of the external borders of the Member States which shall establish: standards and procedures to be followed by Member States in carrying out checks on persons at such borders; (3) measures setting out the conditions under which nationals of third countries shall have the freedom to travel within the territory of the Member States during the period of no more than three months.'

Art. 63(2(b) and 3(b)) state: '(2) measures on refuges and displaced persons within the following areas: promoting a balance of effort between Member States in receiving and bearing the consequences of receiving refugees and displaced persons; (3) measures on immigration policy within the following areas: illegal immigration and illegal residence, including repatriation of illegal residents.' Art. 66 of TEC states: 'The Council, acting in accordance with the procedure referred to in Article 67, shall take measures to ensure cooperation between the relevant departments of the administrations of the Member States in the area covered by this Title, as well as between those departments and the Commission.'

the European Parliament on the basis of the co-decision procedures.[118] Conversely, all measures on legal migration and family law will continue to be adopted by unanimous vote of the Council acting alone. The Court of Justice in a recent case stated that the European Parliament will decide jointly with the Council, under the co-decision procedure, which countries are deemed safe for returning irregular migrants.[119]

Denmark is not bound by this decision, whilst Ireland and the UK have expressed their wish to participate in it.[120] Denmark, the UK and Ireland have a different position towards EU asylum and immigration law and policy compared to other EU Member States, which is reflected in two protocols added to the Treaty of Amsterdam.[121] Article 1 of the Protocol on the UK and Ireland states that they do not have to take part in Title IV of the EC Treaty. In addition, Article 3 states that the UK and Ireland can notify the Council in writing whether they wish to participate in measures adopted under Title IV EC Treaty. If they decide to participate on a particular measure, the Council will decide by unanimous vote whether to allow these two Member States to participate in measures adopted under Title IV. Article 4 states that the UK and Ireland can notify the Council their wish to participate in a measure adopted under Title IV EC Treaty. Article 1 of the Protocol on Denmark establishes that this Member State will not take part in measures taken under Title IV. Article 5 states that Denmark shall decide within six months of the enactment of a measure adopted under Title IV whether to participate in that measure. If it decides to take part, the measure will create an obligation under international law between Denmark and the other Member States.

The UK and Ireland participate in Title VI of the EU Treaty and provisions of the Schengen Acquis related to police and judicial co-operation,[122] and have requested to participate in some repressive measures on irregular migration.[123] All policies on

---

118   See ibid., Arts 67 and 251.

119   See Case C-133/06 *Parliament* v. *Council*, not yet reported.

120   See Recitals 12 and 13 of Council Decision 2004/927/EC, op. cit. note 116.

121   See Protocol on the Position of the United Kingdom and Ireland. See also Protocol on the Position of Denmark. Protocols added by the Treaty of Amsterdam in TEC, op. cit. note 112.

122   For the participation of the UK in the Schengen Acquis, see 'Council Decision of 29 May 2000 Concerning the Request of the United Kingdom of Great Britain and Northern Ireland to Take Part in Some of the Provisions of the Schengen Acquis', OJ EC L 131/43. See also Annexes I and II of the Council Decision of 22 December 2004 on the 'Putting into Effect of Parts of the Schengen Acquis by the United Kingdom of Great Britain and Northern Ireland', OJ EC L 395/70.

123   The UK and Ireland participate in Directive 2002/90/EC. See para. 7 of 'Council Directive 2002/90/EC of 28 November 2002 Defining the Facilitation of Unauthorised Entry, Transit and Residence', OJ EU 2002 L 328/17, 5 December 2002. The UK and Ireland also participate in Council Decision 2004/573/EC. See para. 13 of 'Council Decision 2004/573/EC of 29 April 2004 on the Organisation of Joint Flights for Removals from the Territory of Two or More Member States of Third-country Nationals Who are Subjects of

family reunion, third-country national status and residence permits for victims of traffickers in human beings are not binding on the UK and Ireland. Denmark does not participate in all measures on legal migration and on irregular migration.[124]

It has been argued in relation to the UK that these opt-outs are essential to prevent the loss of the UK veto over EC immigration policies.[125] However, as Peers has pointed out, the UK veto cannot prevent other Member States adopting EC immigration and asylum law, as only a QMV is needed apart from legal migration and family law.[126] Therefore, the loss of the UK veto over immigration and asylum law does not justify its opting out.[127] Certainly, the British and Irish position over migration issues permits the Council to go ahead and apply a proposal even if they disagree, because now all measures on migration and asylum can be approved by QMV, apart from legal migration and family law.[128] If the UK and Ireland did not have the possibility of opting out of measures such as Directive 2004/81 on the protection of victims of people smuggling and human trafficking, they might have vetoed or forced the measure to be watered down. The UK and Ireland might have not agreed to extend the QMV in this area had they not had the option of opting out. Certainly, from a pragmatic point of view, this shows that it is much better for these Member States to have an opt-out rather than have them block progressive measures such as those intended to combat the smuggling of migrants and trafficking in human beings. The downside of the opt-out provisions is that they may contribute to the creation of two different European Unions – one more advanced than the other in fighting criminal organisations, including those engaged in human trafficking by sea. This would not be a beneficial state of affairs, resulting in some EU citizens suffering because of the reluctance of some Member States to accept European integration in as many areas as possible. It is argued by some that trafficking in human beings and smuggling of migrants by sea can only be defeated by considering legal migration, irregular migration, smuggling of migrants and trafficking in human beings as being interconnected, requiring common EU policies.

Individual Removal Orders', OJ EU L 261/28, 6 August 2004. Finally, the UK and Ireland participate in Directive 2003/110/EC. See para. 11 of 'Council Directive 2003/110/EC of 25 November 2003 on Assistance in Case of Transit for the Purposes of Removal by Air, OJ EU L 321/26, 6 December 2003.

124   See para. 8 of Directive 2002/90/EC, op. cit. note 123. See also para. 9 of Directive 2003/110/EC, op. cit. note 123, and para. 11 of Directive 2004/573/EC, op. cit. note 123.

125   See *Communication from the Commission to the Council and the European Parliament towards Integrated Management of the External Borders of the Member States of the European Union*, COM (2002) 233 final, 7 May 2002, p. 2. See also Peers, S., 'Statewatch Briefing: Vetoes, Opts-out and EU Immigration and Asylum Law', *Statewatch*, revised version, 23 December 2004.

126   Ibid.

127   Ibid.

128   See Peers, S., *EU Justice and Home Affairs Law* (Oxford: Oxford University Press, 2006), p. 56.

The Lisbon Treaty and New Horizons

The Treaty of Lisbon and Immigration

In 2007, Member States signed the Lisbon Treaty.[129] The Lisbon Treaty is divided into three parts. These parts are called the Consolidated Versions of the Treaty on European Union, the Treaty on the Functioning of the European Union (hereafter TFEU) and protocols and declarations. The first part is the EU Treaty, and includes common provisions, provisions on democratic principles, on the institutions, on enhanced co-operation, on EU external action, and specific provisions on Common Policy and Security Policy. The second part is the TFEU provisions on all the areas where the Union would have exclusive and shared competence with EU Member States. The TFEU includes the area of freedom, security and justice, which is inserted in Title V. The third and final part includes protocols and declarations, including the protocols concerning the UK, Ireland and Denmark in the area of freedom, security and justice.[130] The Lisbon Treaty amends the actual EU Treaty as most of Member States have signed and ratified it, including the Czech Republic and Poland. In Ireland, a referendum was held in 2008 and another in 2009. The result of the 2009 referendum was that the majority of Irish voted for ratification of this Treaty.[131]

The Lisbon Treaty abolishes the difference between the EC Treaty and the EU Treaty, referring to the EU as 'the Union' and stating that some measures in the criminal area can be adopted by the ordinary legislative co-decision procedure of Article 251 EC Treaty.

The TFEU which is part of the Treaty of Lisbon states that the Union has shared competence with the Member States in the area of freedom, security and justice.[132] In the EU Treaty, the area of freedom, security and justice were divided between Title IV of the EC Treaty and Title VI of the EU Treaty.[133] In contrast, Title V of the TFEU is called the Area of Freedom, Security and Justice, and it covers EU police and judicial co-operation and asylum and immigration law. The measures on EU police and judicial co-operation are dealt with in Chapter 3 of this volume. This section will analyse measures on asylum and immigration law. Article 77 of Title V requires the Union to develop a policy on border checks, asylum and immigration by:

---

129   See 'Consolidated Versions of the Treaty on European Union and the Treaty on the Functioning of the European Union' (the Lisbon Treaty), OJ EU 2010/C 83/01, 30 March 2010.

130   The positions of the UK, Ireland and Denmark in the area of freedom, security and justice are analysed fully in Chapter 4 of this book.

131   See <http://europa.eu/lisbon_treaty/countries/index_en.htm>.

132   See Article 4(j) of the Treaty on the Functioning of the European Union op. cit. note 129.

133   See, respectively, Arts 61 *et seq.* of Title IV TEC and Arts 29 *et seq.* TEC, op. cit. note 112.

ensuring the absence of any controls on persons ... when crossing internal borders; carrying out checks on persons and efficient monitoring of the crossing of external borders; the gradual introduction of an integrated management system for external borders.[134]

In order to achieve this object, Article 77 (2) states that the European Parliament and the Council shall enact legislation by the ordinary legislative procedure. Article 78 states that the Union shall adopt a common policy on asylum, subsidiary protection and temporary protection. Measures for a common European asylum system shall be adopted by the European Parliament and the Council in accordance with the ordinary legislative procedure. The Council and the European Parliament, according to Article 79, must enact legislation in accordance with the ordinary legislative procedure in order to establish:

a common immigration policy aimed at ensuring, at all stages, the efficient management of migration flows, fair treatment of third-country nationals residing legally in Member States, and the prevention of, and enhanced measures to combat, illegal immigration and trafficking in human beings.[135]

The TFEU of the Lisbon Treaty would also allow the European Parliament to adopt measures on legal immigration, including the protection of trafficking victims, now that it has entered into force.

Enhanced Co-operation and the Position of Ireland, the UK and Denmark on Measures on Migration Amended by the Lisbon Treaty

Another important amendment of the Lisbon Treaty concerns the law on enhanced co-operation. Article 20 of the amended EU Treaty incorporated in the Lisbon Treaty will launch enhanced co-operation, which means that the Council can allow Member States to increase co-operation if at least nine of them participate in it. Enhanced co-operation should be used by the Council as a last resort, and it should be promoted when it is established that the aims of this co-operation cannot be achieved adequately within a reasonable time scale. A provision on enhanced co-operation has been introduced in Title V of the Treaty on the functioning of the European Union. In particular, Article 83 states that if Member States do not find an agreement on the adoption of a draft directive, 'and if at least nine Member States wish to establish enhanced cooperation, they shall notify the European Parliament, the Council and the Commission accordingly'.[136] This provision is particularly important in the area of immigration, where the UK, Ireland and

---

134   See Art. 77(1) of the Treaty on the Functioning of the European Union op. cit. note 129.

135   See ibid., Art. 79(1).

136   See ibid., Art. 83(3).

Denmark are not willing participants. The position of these three Member States is regulated by two Protocols.[137] Article 2 of the Protocol on the UK and Ireland states that measures adopted under Title V of the Treaty on the Functioning of the European Union, including international agreements and judgments of the Court of Justice, shall be binding or applicable to the UK and Ireland. Article 3 of the same Protocol states that up to three months after a Title V proposal has been presented to the Council, the UK and Ireland may notify the Council President of their intention to participate in the measure. The Council has to decide unanimously whether or not to allow these two States to participate. In addition, Article 4 states that the UK and Ireland can decide to participate in measures based on Title V when they have been adopted, even if they have not expressed this intention before the measure being adopted. In this case, Article 331(1) of the Treaty on the functioning of the EU shall be applied. This Article requires Member States that wish to participate in enhanced co-operation to notify their intention to the Council and the Commission.

Article 2 of the Protocol on Denmark states that measures adopted under Title V of the Treaty on the functioning of the EU do not apply to Denmark. Article 4 states that Denmark has six months to decide whether it intends to take part in a measure based on a proposal built upon the Schengen Acquis. In any case, even if Denmark decides to participate, the measure will create an obligation under international law towards the other Member States.

The fact that the UK, Ireland and Denmark do not participate in measures adopted under Title V may create fragmentation in the fight against smuggling and trafficking. However, the positive aspect of the Lisbon Treaty is that it allows other Member States to go forward without them, adopting measures in the area of freedom, security and justice by the ordinary legislative procedure. The European Parliament and Council, through the ordinary legislative procedure, could recognise the status of victims of people smuggled by sea, making a difference in the fight against criminal organisations behind this crime and trafficking. One hopes that the Lisbon Treaty will allow these changes.

EC Criminal Competence

The EC and Criminal Law

The EC's competence in the area of criminal law is linked to its competence in immigration law. It has been shown that the EC's competence in immigration issues is very problematic. This situation should definitely change now that the Lisbon Treaty has been ratified by all Member States.

---

137   See Protocol 21 on the position of the United Kingdom and Ireland in respect of the Area of Freedom, Security and Justice. See also Protocol 22 on the position of Denmark, in the Lisbon Treaty, op. cit. note 129.

Before the entry into force of the Lisbon Treaty, the EC did not have competence in the area of criminal law. EC competence or jurisdiction in this section is intended as the power of the Parliament to co-legislate with the Council of EU (Council) in the third pillar of the EU Treaty: police and judicial co-operation.

This section will show on what basis in the past scholars and the Court of Justice have argued over the admissibility or inadmissibility of EC supremacy in criminal law. The issue will be considered by analysing the EU Treaty, secondary legislation and the opinion of Advocate General Colomer.[138]

The legal basis of EC competence in criminal law could have been found in Title VI of the EU Treaty, which aims to guarantee EU citizens 'an area of freedom, security and justice by developing common action among the Member States'.[139] The aims of Title VI EU Treaty, as pointed out by Advocate General Colomer, were to be achieved 'without prejudice to the powers of the European Community'.[140] Another important provision of EC competence in criminal law was Article 42 of the EU Treaty, which states that the powers of Title VI can be transferred to Title IV of the EC Treaty, which covers immigration and asylum policies.[141] Therefore, Article 42 EU Treaty could have established 'the communitisation of criminal law'.[142] This would have meant more involvement of European institutions, including the European Parliament, in all matters concerning criminal law.[143]

However, as Corstens argued, the introduction of Article 42 EU Treaty meant that the Member States did not believe that the approximation of criminal law can fall under EC competence.[144] This point of view was confirmed by the fact that Article 42 EU Treaty states that the Council, acting unanimously, shall take the decision on partly transferring areas concerning Article 29 of the EU Treaty into

---

138   Opinion delivered on 26 May 2005 in Case C-176/03 *Commission* v. *Council* [2005] ECR I-7879-Court of Justice.

139   See Art. 29(1) of 'Consolidated Version of the Treaty on European Union' (TEU), OJ C 325/1, 24 December 2002.

140   See ibid. See also Case C-176/03, Opinion of Colomer, op. cit. note 138, para. 13.

141   See Art. 42 of the Lisbon Treaty, op. cit. note 139. See also Case C-176/03, Opinion of Colomer, op. cit. note 138, para. 16.

142   See Corstens, G.J.M., 'Criminal law in the First Pillar?', *European Journal of Crime, Criminal Law and Criminal Justice* 11:1 (2003), p. 135. See also Art. 42 TEU, op. cit. note 139. Art. 42 states: 'The Council, acting unanimously on the initiative of the Commission or a Member State, and after consulting the European Parliament, may decide that action in areas referred to in Article 29 shall fall under Title IV of the Treaty establishing the European Community, and at the same time determine the relevant voting conditions relating to it. It shall recommend the Member States to adopt that decision in accordance with their respective constitutional requirements.'

143   Within five years of 1999, the European Parliament was to have a more important role in illegal migration. See Art. 67(1) TEC, op. cit. note 112.

144   See Corstens, 'Criminal law in the First Pillar?', op. cit. note 142, p. 136.

Title IV.[145] Thus, the communitisation of Title VI was considered an exception to be used only in special circumstances, the standard position being to consider criminal law as a matter to be dealt by Title VI of the EU Treaty.

The legal basis under which the EC could have had competence in criminal law might have been found in other legal instruments, even though this has not been expressly or clearly established. Advocate General Colomer stated that the Court of Justice has held in different cases[146] that for the attainment of EC objectives (Article 10(1) EC Treaty),[147] Member States can only impose appropriate civil or administrative penalties,[148] 'since the Community has no powers to impose criminal penalties'.[149] The Advocate General also pointed that the Court of Justice has held that Member States must impose effective, proportionate and dissuasive penalties of the same level as those applied by law enforcement authorities for breaches of national law.[150] It is therefore possible for Member States to choose to apply criminal penalties in order to comply with Article 10 EC Treaty.[151] Nevertheless, as pointed out above, the Court of Justice's case law does not explicitly recognise a power of the Community to require Member States to impose criminal penalties.[152] Moreover, the Court of Justice has affirmed that criminal law and criminal procedure do not fall within the EC's competence.[153] However, this statement does not prevent the EC adopting measures in the criminal area to protect the environment.[154]

EC competence, which requires Member States to impose criminal penalties, is also not expressly recognised in secondary legislation. There are measures that leave Member States to choose the type of penalties to apply for breaches of EC policy.[155]

---

145   See Art. 42 TEU, op. cit. note 139.
146   See: *Amsterdam Bulb* Case 50/76 [1977] ECR 137-Court of Justice; *Commission v. Greece* Case 68/88 [1989] ECR 2965-Court of Justice; *Zwartveld and Others* Case C-2/88 Imm [1990] ECR I-3365-Court of Justice; *Drexl* Case C-299/86 [1988] ECR 1213-Court of Justice; *Nunes and de Matos* Case C-186/98 [1999] ECR I-4883-Court of Justice.
147   Art. 10(1) TEC, op. cit. note 139, states: 'Member States shall take all appropriate measures, whether general or particular, to ensure fulfilment of the obligations arising out of this Treaty or resulting from action taken by the institutions of the Community. They shall facilitate the achievement of the Community's tasks.'
148   See Case C-176/03, Opinion of Colomer, op. cit. note 138, paras 30, 31, 32 and 33.
149   See ibid., para. 33.
150   See ibid., para. 34. See also *Amsterdam Bulb*, op. cit. note 146, para. 23.
151   See Case C-176/03, Opinion of Colomer, op. cit. note 138, paras 36 and 37.
152   See ibid., para. 38.
153   See ibid., para. 47. See also Case 203/80 *Casati* [1981] ECR 2595-Court of Justice, para. 27; Case C-226/97 *Lemmens* [1998] ECR I-3711-Court of Justice, para. 19.
154   See Case C-176/03, op. cit. note 138, para. 39.
155   See ibid., Opinion of Colomer, para. 40. Colomer mentions: Art. 1(2) Council Regulation (EEC) 2241/87 of 23 July 1987 establishing certain control measures for fishing activities, OJ EC 1987 L 207/1; Art. 31(1) of 'Council Regulation (EEC) 2847/93 of 12 October 1993 Establishing a Control System Applicable to the Common Fisheries Policy Council Regulation (EEC) No 2241/87 of 23 July 1987', OJ EU 1993 L 261/1.

Colomer has emphasised[156] that Directive 91/208/EEC[157] requires Member States to impose strict penalties to prevent money laundering, and these penalties may have a criminal nature.[158] There is then Directive 2002/90/EC,[159] which defines assisting irregular migration. However, this directive, as Colomer has pointed out, does not require Member States to impose criminal penalties. Directive 2002/90/EC only requires that Member States apply appropriate penalties against those who attempt, instigate or commit the infringement of assisting irregular migration procedures.[160] Colomer has pointed out that the criminal nature of these penalties is not qualified by the directive, but by Framework Decision 2002/946/JHA,[161] which is an EU Treaty measure adopted by the Council acting alone. Therefore, secondary legislation does not explicitly recognise the EC's competence in criminal law. However, in *Commission* v. *Council*,[162] Advocate General Mazàk stated that although there is the general rule that criminal law falls within the competence of Member States:[163]

> the Community legislature can, whenever criminal measures are necessary to ensure the full effectiveness of Community law and essential to combat serious offences in a particular area, require Member States to penalise certain conduct and to adopt in that regard effective, proportionate and dissuasive criminal sanctions.[164]

The EC could have required Member States to adopt criminal sanctions to penalise smuggling of migrants and trafficking in human beings because these crimes were considered serious offences. However, the intervention of the EC in the criminal area was considered exceptional.

To summarise, the EC's competence in criminal law was not expressly recognised by either the EU Treaty or the Court of Justice's case law or by secondary legislation. The Court of Justice has held that only in exceptional circumstances,

---

156   See Case C-176/03, Opinion of Colomer, op. cit. note 138, para. 41.

157   'Council Directive 91/308/EEC of 10 June 1991 on Prevention of the Use of the Financial System for the Purpose of Money Laundering', OJ EU 1991 L 166/77.

158   See Case C-176/03, Opinion of Colomer, op. cit. note 138, paras 41 and 50.

159   See 'Council Directive 2002/90/EC of 28 November 2002 Defining the Facilitation of Unauthorised Entry, Transit and Residence', OJ EU L 328/17, 5 December 2002.

160   See Case C-176/03, Opinion of Colomer, op. cit. note 138, para. 42. See also Arts 1, 2 and 3 of Directive 2002/90/EC, op. cit. note 159.

161   See Case C-176/03, Opinion of Colomer, op. cit. note 138, para. 42. See also Art. 1 of 'Council Framework Decision 2002/946/JHA on the Strengthening of the Penal Framework to Prevent the Facilitation of Unauthorised Entry, Transit and Residence of 28 November 2002', OJ EU L 328/1, 5 December 2002.

162   See Case C-440/05, *Commission* v. *Council*, Opinion of Advocate General Mazàk, ECR-19097-Court of Justice.

163   See ibid., para. 113.

164   See ibid., para. 112.

such as the protection of the environment, can the EC's competence encompass the criminal area. However, recent Court of Justice judgments have allowed for the possibility of the EC criminalising certain serious offences in order to achieve the objectives of Community law.

The EC has made progress in the criminal law area by focusing more closely on the recent Court of Justice judgment on the EC's competence in criminal law and the subsequent European Commission communication.

The Judgment of the Court of Justice on Environmental Protection and the Commission Opinion on the EC's Competence in Criminal Law

Before the entry into force of the Lisbon Treaty, the EC's competence in criminal law was been clarified by an important judgment.[165] The Court of Justice held that for the implementation of environmental policy, the EC can impose criminal penalties on those who do not respect EC environmental objectives.[166] On this occasion, the Court of Justice also re-emphasised that the EC does not have competence in criminal law or criminal procedure,[167] although this:

> does not prevent the Community legislature, when the application of effective, proportional and dissuasive criminal penalties by the competent national authorities is an essential measure for combating serious environmental offences, from taking measures which relate to the criminal law of the Member States ...[168]

The European Commission pointed out that the Court of Justice's judgment went further than the Advocate General's opinion.[169] Advocate General Colomer asserted that the EC's competence in criminal law consists only of determining the nature of an offence.[170] After the EC has given a uniform definition of an offence:

> the national legal systems must penalise that proscribed conduct, indicating the specific methods of punishment associated with the offence, to restore in that way the physical and legal positions which have been disturbed ...[171]

---

165 See Case C-176/03 *Commission* v. *Council*, op. cit. note 138, paras 47 *et seq.*
166 See ibid., paras 51 and 55.
167 See ibid., para. 47.
168 Ibid.
169 See *Communication from the Commission to the European Parliament and the Council on the Implications of the Court's Judgment of 13 September 2005 (Case C-176/03 Commission v. Council)*, COM (2005) 583 final/2, 24 November 2005, p. 3.
170 See Opinion of Advocate General Ruiz-Jarabo Colomer in Case C-176/03, op. cit. note 138, para. 84.
171 See ibid., para. 85.

Thus, as the Commission highlighted, Advocate General Colomer did not support the argument that the EC should have competence in imposing criminal penalties.[172] The EC's competence, according to Colomer, should be limited to defining a criminal activity. Moreover, Member States should only decide the type of penalty to impose, because:

> [i]n that enterprise, no party seems to be in a better position than the national legislature which, since it has first-hand knowledge of the legal and sociological particularities of its arrangements for coexistence, must opt, within the framework previously defined by the Community, for the response most apt to uphold Community law.[173]

The Court of Justice held an opposing view, stating that appropriate criminal measures could be adopted at EC level in specific areas, the better to achieve Community policy and objectives.[174] It is within the Commission's competence to evaluate, case by case, whether there is the need to adopt criminal measures at EC level.[175] The EC can intervene in the criminal area only when there are exigencies of necessity and consistency.[176] The Commission has argued that EC action in criminal law should only be exercised when it proves necessary and is carried out with respect for the principles of subsidiarity and proportionality.[177] In other words, the EC action has to be consistent, in the sense that the EC should only intervene in the criminal area when it is essential to achieve EC Treaty objectives.[178]

As a result of the Court of Justice's judgment on environmental protection, the European Commission has pointed out that many texts, including Directive 2002/90/EC and Framework Decision 2002/946/JHA, have been adopted on the wrong legal basis.[179] The framework decision should have been adopted on the basis of Articles 61(a) and 63(3)(b) of the EC Treaty.[180] Therefore, the Commission has to restore the order, as it is the 'guardian of the Treaties and the only body with the power to propose Community acts'.[181] These two instruments should be modified because 'the wrong legal basis of framework decisions could, in some cases, undermine the national implementing legislation'.[182] Could these same thoughts be extended to trafficking in human beings? Is it possible for EC's

---

172   Ibid.

173   Ibid.

174   *Communication from the Commission to the European Parliament and the Council on the Implications of the Court's Judgment of 13 September 2005*, op. cit. note 169.

175   Ibid.

176   See ibid., p. 4.

177   See ibid., p. 5.

178   Ibid.

179   See ibid., pp. 5, 7 and 8.

180   See ibid., pp. 7 and 8.

181   Ibid., p. 5.

182   Ibid.

criminal competence to be extended to measures on trafficking in human beings? The European Commission asserted that EC criminal measures can be adopted at sectoral level to ensure the attainment of the Community's objectives.[183] Therefore, one may think that the EC might have criminal competence on trafficking in human beings, although criminal measures on human trafficking have always been adopted on the basis of Title VI.

After the Court of Justice's judgment on environmental protection and the communication on the EC's competence in criminal law, it could be argued that the EC could have taken action in the criminal area on the basis of the principle of subsidiarity and proportionality if it was necessary and consistent. Even though the Court of Justice has not recognised a general EC competence in criminal law, it has asserted that EC competence can include the criminal area in specific cases.

The activities of assisting irregular migration and smuggling of migrants could be criminalised by the EC, a position that in the past was controversial. Nevertheless, after the Court of Justice's judgment on environmental protection, EC competence in criminal law has been recognised within the limits of consistency and necessity.

It is important now to analyse the reasons why it has been difficult to recognise general EC competence in any measures in the criminal area, and not only in terms of specific measures. It is also important to analyse the changes that should be introduced by the Lisbon Treaty.

Obstacles to the Recognition of the EC's Competence in Any Measure Adopted in the Criminal Area and Amendments of the Lisbon Treaty

The transfer of some areas of criminal law (the third pillar) should have been based on Article 42(1), TEU and the decision should have been agreed unanimously.[184] Certainly, the Council would still have been able to decide whether measures within the third pillar should have been approved by unanimity or qualified majority.[185] This would result in third pillar measures which would have been being approved by the co-decision procedure.[186] This fact does not necessarily mean that third pillar measures would be approved by qualified majority.[187] There are no provisions which state that the measures adopted when the co-decision procedure applies have to be agreed by qualified majority of votes.[188] However, the transfer of the third pillar into the first pillar could have meant that EU Member States had the intention of transferring their sovereignty in the criminal area. This transfer would

---

183   See ibid., p. 3.

184   See Peers, S., 'Statewatch Analysis: Transferring the Third Pillar', *Statewatch* (May 2006).

185   Ibid.

186   Ibid.

187   Ibid.

188   Ibid.

have been ideal, allowing for EC measures to combat the problem of trafficking in human beings and the smuggling of migrants. However, many EU Member States were firmly against this proposal, leading the British government at one point to state that according to Article 42 EU Treaty,[189] the idea of transferring some parts of the third pillar to the first pillar is 'over',[190] and that it is better 'to focus on practical cooperation rather than institutional change'.[191]

One might think that the fact that there are no reliable data on the extent of trafficking in human beings may cause problems, for example a possible imbalance to the internal market caused by public order. However, on this point the Court of Justice ruled in *Cullet*[192] that EU Member States have the competence to restrict free movement rights, although they can only be restricted on the basis that they represent a threat to the public order.[193] Indeed, EU Member States have to show that they are 'unable ... to deal with the consequences which an amendment of the rules in question ... would have upon public order and security'.[194] In *Commission* v. *France*,[195] the Court of Justice confirmed the rule delivered in *Cullet* by holding that 'the mere apprehension of internal difficulties cannot justify a failure to comply with Community law'.[196] Finally, in another case,[197] the Court of Justice stated that EU Member States have the competence 'to adopt all appropriate measures to guarantee the full scope and effect of Community law'[198] unless they can demonstrate 'that action on its part would have consequences for public order with which it could not cope by using the means at its disposal'.[199] Thus, EU Member States have to prove to the Court of Justice that they have done everything they could to avoid public disorder.[200] It is clear that EU Member States have exclusive competence to maintain public order, and protect internal security in their territories. This means that it is within EU Member States' competence to decide which methods to adopt that are most effective in countering threats to free movement rights.[201] It is logical, therefore, to conclude that EU Member States have specific competence to ensure that trafficking in human beings does

---

189   See Art. 42 EU Treaty, op. cit. note 139. See also *The Criminal Law Competence of the European Community*, Session 2005–2006, 42nd Report, HL 227, Minute of Evidence, p. 10.

190   See *The Criminal Law Competence of the EC: Follow-up Report*, Session 2006–2007, 11th Report, HL 63, Minutes of Evidence.

191   Ibid.

192   See Case 231/83 *Cullet* [1985] ECR 305-Court of Justice.

193   See ibid., paras 31, 32 and 33.

194   See ibid., para. 33.

195   See Case C-175/97 *Commission* v. *France* [1998] ECR I-963-Court of Justice.

196   See ibid., para. 13.

197   See Case C-265/95 *Commission v France* [1997] ECR I-6959-Court of Justice.

198   See ibid., para. 56.

199   Ibid.

200   See ibid., para. 65.

201   See Peers, *EU Justice and Home Affairs Law*, op. cit. note 128, p. 512.

not create an imbalance in the internal market, which can lead to problems of public disorder. Moreover, the Court of Justice can review whether Member States have adopted appropriate measures to ensure respect for Community law.[202] This is important, as these powers cannot be extended to violations of EU framework decisions, because Article 35 EU Treaty prevents the Court of Justice exercising them.

Now that the Lisbon Treaty has entered into force, the EC's supremacy will be extended to the criminal area. This Treaty will extend EC supremacy to the parts of the EU Treaty concerning the criminal area because the difference between the EC Treaty and the EU Treaty will be abolished. In addition, measures in the criminal area will no longer be adopted by framework decisions, but by directives. Article 288 of the TFEU, ex Article 249 of the EC Treaty, will be extended to the criminal area.[203] This is confirmed by Article 83 of the TFEU, which states:

> The European Parliament and the Council may, by means of directives adopted in accordance with the ordinary legislative procedure, establish minimum rules concerning the definition of criminal offences and sanctions in the areas of particularly serious crime with a cross-border dimension resulting from the nature or impact of such offences or from a special need to combat them on a common basis.[204]

The extension of the ordinary legislative procedure to the criminal area also means that all measures in this area will require the QMV in the Council to be adopted. As a result, the framework decision on trafficking in human beings that is examined below, and other framework decisions, should be replaced by directives, should be enacted by the ordinary legislative procedure, and adopted if there is a QMV in Council.[205] These modifications will make the fight against smuggling of migrants and human trafficking more democratic, and people will be involved in this fight with more success.

---

202   See ibid., p. 513.

203   See Art. 288 of the Treaty on the Functioning of the European Union op. cit. note 129. This Article replaces Art. 249 TEC, and states: 'To exercise the Union's competences, the institutions shall adopt regulations, directives, decisions, recommendations and opinions. A regulation shall have general application. It shall be binding in its entirely and directly applicable in all Member States. A directive shall be binding, as to the result to be achieved, upon each Member State to which it is addressed, but shall leave to the national authorities the choice of form and methods. A decision shall be binding in its entirely. A decision which specifies those to whom it is addressed shall be binding only on them. Recommendations and opinions shall have no binding force.'

204   See Art. 83(1) of the Treaty on the Functioning of the European Union op. cit. note 129.

205   See Peers, S., 'Statewatch Analysis: The EU's JHA Agenda for 2009', *Statewatch*, 2009.

The Cultural and Moral Case against Criminal Organisations

Trafficking and smuggling are committed by criminal organisations. Criminal organisations are mostly transnational in nature,[206] and they can be divided into indigenous criminal groups (criminal groups originating within the EU) and non-indigenous criminal groups (criminal groups originating outside the EU).[207] There are also intermediary situations, which include two main types of groups: second-generation groups and EU-based criminal organisations with a strong international dimension.[208] Second-generation groups can be further subdivided into non-EU-based and EU-based organised criminal groups.[209] These second-generation groups are very dangerous because they are prepared to use violence, corruption and/or influence in order to gain enhanced access to EU legal institutions. These groups gradually cut their ties with their countries of origin and blend into the EU through ethnic communities from which they obtain support, markets and recruitment. The EU-based groups with a strong international dimension include some traditionally indigenous groups which 'act with only "one foot" in the EU'.[210]

Criminal organised groups, especially indigenous groups and groups belonging to the intermediary category, are able to control the most important targets within the EU's public sector. These groups, being indigenous, tend to have strong criminal networks in the EU, making them more well connected within the EU Member States than those that are non-indigenous. The indigenous groups are more successful, through their connections, in influencing local and national politics, public tenders, land procurement processes and business deals.[211] Indigenous criminal groups and intermediary ones often use physical violence and the explicit or implicit threat of violence in order to gain influence in EU Member States.[212] Intermediary criminal groups may gain significant influence over non-integrated communities. It has been reported that criminal organisations influence communities that are not integrated with the surrounding society and concentrated in restricted geographical areas.[213] In the long term, this influence over non-integrated communities 'can spread to the rest of society and economy'.[214] If criminal groups in the EU gain an intimidating reputation through violence, threats or by influencing non-integrated communities, law enforcement authorities cannot

---

206   See Europol, *OCTA EU Organised Crime Threat Assessment 2007*, <http://www.europol.europa.eu/publications/European_Organised_Crime_Threat_Assessment_%28OCTA%29/OCTA2007.pdf>, p. 21.

207   See ibid., p. 8.

208   Ibid., pp. 14 and 15.

209   Ibid., p. 15.

210   Ibid.

211   Ibid., pp. 11 and 12.

212   Ibid., p. 13.

213   See Peers, 'Statewatch Analysis: The EU's JHA Agenda for 2009', op. cit. note 206, p. 14.

214   Ibid.

rely on the surrounding community because of its fear of retribution from those criminal organisations.[215] This makes the support of the surrounding community a very important factor in fighting against organised criminal groups in the EU. As Paolo Borsellino, an Italian anti-Mafia magistrate murdered by the Mafia, once emphasised about organised crime:

> Combating the Mafia ought to be the primary problem to resolve in our beautiful and unfortunate land and it must not simply be a detached act of repression. Indeed, the fight against the Mafia has to consist of creating a cultural and moral movement involving the entire population, especially the young. In fact, the young generation is more likely to experience the beauty of the fresh scent of liberty. This scent of liberty encourages people to refuse the price of the moral compromise, of the indifference, contiguity and therefore of complicity with the Mafia.
>
> I remember Falcone's happiness when, during a short period of enthusiasm, he said: 'People are supporting us.' By this thought, he not only referred to the comfort that the moral support of the population gives to the magistrates' work. He meant much more. He especially meant that our work was evoking public sentiments.[216]

Borsellino was making the point that it is important to involve all the surrounding population in the fight against organised crime. Facilitating the integration of the non-integrated communities, giving these communities a sense of belonging to society as a whole, means they might feel better able to resist organised crime. The victims of smuggling and trafficking can be made to feel less intimidated by criminal organisations by granting them legal protections such as the security of long-term visas. Feeling more secure as members of the society, they may be self-motivated to testify against the criminal organisations who smuggle and exploit them, leading to a reduction of these crimes throughout the EU.[217]

The creation of a unified cultural and moral movement against criminal organisations is important and necessary because criminal organisations do not limit themselves to the EU nation they originated in. They affect EU citizens and residents of other EU Member States, not only the citizens and residents living in

---

215   See ibid., pp. 13 and 14.

216   My translation of a speech that Paolo Borsellino gave during the ceremony in memory of Giovanni Falcone, his wife and escort, Palermo, 23 June 1992. Readers may object that institutions such as parliaments, not magistrates, should create a moral and cultural movement against criminal organisations. However, when States are absent in the fight against criminal organisations, as the Italian State was in those years, if courageous magistrates like Falcone and Borsellino do the State's work, they should only be admired for this. On this point, see Stille, A., *Excellent Cadavers: The Mafia and the Death of the First Italian Republic* (New York: Vintage, 1996).

217   See Chapters 4 and 5 on the protection of victims of smuggling and trafficking.

the EU Member States where the criminal groups are based. It has been reported, for example, that the majority of heroin destined for the UK is supplied by criminal organisations based in the Netherlands, and that these criminal organisations 'are the most active in the supply of hard drugs to the UK'.[218] What does 'cultural and moral movement' mean? We can answer this by means of a hypothetical situation. Let us assume that you know someone who is a British citizen who happens to be addicted to heroin. If you witnessed this person becoming completely destroyed by heroin, one question you might ask is what can be done to reduce the crime of drug trafficking. Upon being told that the heroin sold in the UK is largely provided by criminal organisations based in the Netherlands, you might try to prevent this criminal activity continuing. You might, for example, try to find ways to make UK citizens aware that heroin is being provided by criminal organisations based in the Netherlands. Through these efforts to bring the problem to public attention, citizens would start to understand that drug trafficking is a European problem that should be resolved at EU level. British citizens might be led to insist that their representatives in the EU Parliament adopt measures to prevent the trafficking of heroin from the Netherlands to the UK. People in the UK would have a vested interest in creating a cultural and moral movement against criminal organisations that commit drug trafficking in other EU Member States. This cultural and moral movement would reduce the power of criminal organisations. This is because people more exposed to criminal organisations might resist their threats and intimidations if they noticed that all EU citizens were pushing for reforms at EU level against criminal organisations, and that these measures were being concretely applied by all EU Member States. Moreover, this cultural and moral movement would promote more involvement of the European Parliament in the decision-making procedure regarding crime, as people of the EU would press their representatives in the Parliament for reforms. Giovanni Falcone, a highly successful Italian magistrate who was assassinated by the Mafia, highlighted that intimidation causes contiguity with the Mafia, for example.[219] However, Falcone also thought that surrendering to the Mafia meant recognising the Mafia's authority, so that people surrendering to the Mafia would be culpable.[220] The Italian Mafia's power is contingent upon the consent of the surrounding society. Falcone said that the consent of the Italian citizenry is obtained through intimidation. The same methods of coercion used by the Italian Mafia are employed by the Russian Mafia.[221] The smaller the enterprise, the more vulnerable it is, because

---

218   See Council of European Union Doc. 13788/1/05, *2005 EU Organised Crime Report*, 17 November 2005, p. 11.

219   See Falcone, G., *Cose di Cosa Nostra* (Milan: RCS Rizzoli Libri, 1991), pp. 91–3.

220   See ibid., p. 93.

221   See Varese, F., *The Russian Mafia: Private Protection in a New Market Economy* (Oxford: Oxford University Press, 2001), pp. 75–101, where Varese describes the findings of a case study conducted in Perm (Russia), although the whole volume should be read to understand how the Russian Mafia gains its power in civil society.

it is more isolated from the rest of the society, such as political and commercial networks.[222] Is it possible to ensure that society as a whole will oppose criminal organisations, even though people fear them? It is possible, if EU Member States take responsibility for reducing the intimidating power of criminal organisations by adopting effective EU measures against them. Member States should comply fully with EU measures in the criminal area, such as the EAW framework decision which is examined below. In this way, EU citizens, residents and victims of smuggling and trafficking would not be intimidated by criminal organisations. Their intimidating power is able to influence non-integrated communities such as the people smuggled and trafficked because they do not rely on law enforcement authorities. Firstly, victims of these crimes fear that the authorities may expel them, so they do not accuse their exploiters and smugglers. Secondly, victims of these two crimes fear that their families in their countries of origin may be killed by criminal organisations if accused by them. Consequently, these criminal organisations become stronger by intimidating these victims. Law enforcement authorities should impede this by protecting victims. In this way, they would gain trust and victims would feel encouraged to accuse their smugglers and traffickers. This goal could be reached by granting victims long-term visas. Such visas would permit victims to integrate in the hosting society, so they would escape the intimidating power of criminal organisations and would eventually report them to law enforcement authorities. However, a cultural and moral movement needs to be created so that EU citizens understand that restrictive measures against smuggling and trafficking do not contribute to reducing these crimes if law enforcement authorities do not gain the trust and support of victims.

How can a cultural and moral movement against criminal organisations based in the EU be created? – By extending EC supremacy into the criminal area; in other words, by allowing the European Parliament to enact legislation with the Council in the criminal area. The Lisbon Treaty, now that it has been ratified, will make an important contribution because it will allow the European Parliament to play an important role in the criminal area where vital measures will be adopted by the ordinary legislative procedure.

In the past, as earlier sections have highlighted, the EC did not have competence in the criminal area, and therefore in EU measures adopted by the Council regarding people smuggling and human trafficking. This is the main reason why there was a lack of mutual trust between law enforcement authorities of Member States and it was very difficult to achieve judicial co-operation.[223]

---

222   See ibid., p. 85.

223   The principles of mutual trust and mutual judicial recognition are analysed fully in Chapters 3 and 5 of this book.

A Role for the European Parliament

Before the entry into force of the Lisbon Treaty, the European Parliament was considered by EU citizens as an institution distant from them, because the topics of their jurisdiction only affected a limited number of citizens or residents – for example, EU citizens who moved from one EU Member State to another for reasons of work or study. Now that the Lisbon Treaty has entered into force, the European Parliament's jurisdiction is wider and covers delicate issues such as immigration and criminal law. Members of the European Parliament will have the important task of informing their voters about the draft legislation that will be discussed in the Parliament, and proposals that will affect EU citizens. The European Parliament will be a supra-national institution working for the interests of all EU citizens and residents. It is therefore the job of the parliamentarians to keep the citizens they represent informed about the measures being considered before the European Parliament. When topics related to transnational criminal organisations are discussed, members of the European Parliament should communicate what is being discussed to EU citizens and residents through blogs and other forms of communication. Members of the European Parliament can also communicate by distributing booklets with information about the measures they are taking and the impact they will have on EU citizens and residents. In this way, EU citizens and residents will understand why it is important to adopt a measure against criminal organisations with a cross-border dimension, and how this measure could benefit their everyday lives. By interacting with the EU citizens and residents they represent, European Parliamentarians can ensure that the measures they adopt are the most effective in serving their citizens in as reasonable and fair a manner as possible. If EU citizens understand this, they will organise anti-criminal organisation movements to support the adoption of draft legislation against these organisations.

Raising public concern over the crimes of people smuggling and human trafficking, and the criminal organisations behind them is not an easy thing accomplish. For comparison, take, for example, the crime of drug trafficking. It would be relatively easy to explain to EU citizens why a measure against criminal organisations that are involved in drug trafficking should be adopted. The negative impact of drug trafficking is felt throughout the entire EU Member States, as there are many people who are addicted to drugs. Drug trafficking affects a huge number of EU citizens and residents. Conversely, it is more difficult to persuade EU citizens and residents to be personally invested in seeing the crimes of human trafficking and people smuggling defeated. It may not be easy to understand why the smuggling of migrants and human trafficking requires that there be more liberal laws that are more focused on the protection of victims rather than on their criminalisation. Victims of these two crimes are usually not EU citizens, and people may not be interested in their protection. There is also too much demagogy on these issues, and people are not well informed about the two phenomena. There is a tendency to think that only creating barriers which keep illegal migrants out can resolve this problem.

This will place a much greater burden upon the European Parliament to demonstrate to EU citizens that a more restrictive approach will not ultimately succeed, because this approach does not address the root cause of the problem: organised crime. Liberal approaches have instead been more effective in resolving the problem of irregular migration and human trafficking, because the focus is on stopping the criminal organisations behind them, leading to a reduction in smuggling and trafficking.[224] Members of the European Parliament should inform their voters of the fact that security in their countries will not be improved simply by expelling all irregular migrants from the EU regardless of whether they are victims of smuggling or trafficking. Lasting security can be achieved by defeating the criminal organisations who victimise these people. This is why the law should offer support for victims who choose to testify against these criminals. However, if the law simply provides for the expulsion of irregular migrants without giving them the opportunity to accuse their smugglers and traffickers, irregular migration will only increase. No matter how tough the laws are and how big the barriers they build up, those who perpetrate these crimes will find a way round them if they continue to go largely unpunished. The European Parliament, bearing in mind the best interests of the EU, will have the task of informing its voters beyond demagogy. In this task, the European Parliament should be supported by national Parliaments, which can be consulted on draft legislation in accordance with the Lisbon Treaty. This consultation process is very important, because measures on immigration must be taken in the most democratic way possible to avoid inflaming anti-EU sentiment that could ultimately have a negative impact on the interests of EU citizens and residents. In the EU, possible abuses of governments can be reduced by enhancing the role of the European Parliament in the legislative process, and increasing its interaction with national parliaments which are the representatives of all people. The result of this interaction can be the creation of a cultural and moral movement in the EU, aimed at reducing irregular migration. The cultural and moral movement would achieve this goal by restoring a sense of humanity in approaching these issues, which governments of the EU Member States seem to have set aside.

A Role for EC/EU Law

The Crime of Assisting Irregular Migration

Council Directive 2002/90/EC[225] defines two criminal offences: the assisting of irregular migration and the smuggling of migrants. Assisting irregular migration

---

224   On this point, see Chapter 5 of this book.
225   See Art. 1(1(a)) of 'Council Directive 2002/90/EC of 28 November 2002 Defining the Facilitation of Unauthorised Entry, Transit and Residence of 28 November 2002', OJ

means assisting a person to enter irregularly into the territory of a State where they are not allowed.[226] The directive makes it possible for the criminalisation of any act aimed at assisting a person to enter the territory of one or more EU Member State, even those acts that are merely preparatory.[227] Those who assist in irregular migration are not necessarily members of organised crime. The perpetrators include migrants who regularly reside within the territory of a Member State, and who are attempting to reunite with family, prevent the persecution of relatives in war-torn countries, or aiding them in escaping unbearable economic conditions. Directive 2002/90/EC specifies that Member States shall impose sanctions on those anyone 'who intentionally assists a person who is not a national of a Member State to enter, or transit across, the territory of a Member State'.[228] Council Framework Decision 2002/946/JHA clearly states that assisting irregular entry in the way outlined above shall be punished by criminal penalties. Therefore, any assistance of irregular migration is punishable, whether organised crime is involved or not.[229]

Nevertheless, irregular migrants who are attempting to reunite with their families can invoke the protection granted them by the European Convention on Human Rights (ECHR).[230] In addition, migrants who regularly live in one Member State of the EU may rely on the ECHR[231] and the Convention on the Status of Refugees,[232] as the Framework Decision 2002/946/JHA indicates[233] they are entitled to in order to protect their relatives who are threatened by war or inhuman treatment. Furthermore, Directive 2002/90/EC specifies that EC Member States may decide: 'not to impose sanctions ... for cases where the aim of the behaviour is to provide humanitarian assistance to the person concerned'.[234] The EC might also provide policies in order to avoid returning irregular migrants who have been smuggled by sea and who have travelled in very poor conditions, because these people, as Chapters 4 and 5 will highlight, are victims of external circumstances, such as their state of poverty.

EU L 328/1, 5 December 2002.

226   Ibid.
227   Ibid.
228   Ibid.
229   See Art. 1(1) of 'Council Framework Decision 2002/946/JHA of 28 November 2002 on the Strengthening of the Penal Framework to Prevent the Facilitation of Unauthorised Entry, Transit and Residence', OJ EU L 328/1, 5 December 2002.
230   See Art. 8 of the *Convention for the Protection of Human Rights and Fundamental Freedoms* (ECHR), as amended by Protocol 11.
231   See ibid., Art. 3.
232   See the *Convention Relating to the Status of Refugees Adopted on 28 July 1951 by the United Nations Conference of Plenipotentiaries on the Status of Refugees and Stateless Persons*, convened under General Assembly Resolution 429 (V) of 14 December 1950, entered into force 22 April 1954, in accordance with Art. 43.
233   See Art. 6 of Council Framework Decision 2002/946/JHA, op. cit. note 231.
234   See Art. 1 (2) of Council Directive 2002/90/EC, op. cit. note 227.

Smuggling of Migrants in EC/EU Law

Directive 2002/90/EC states that:

> any person who, for financial gain, intentionally assists a person who is not a national of a Member State to reside within the territory of a Member State in breach of the laws of the State concerned on the residence of the aliens.[235]

The directive can include the assisting irregular migration committed by criminal organisations, although in comparison, UNTOC Directive 2002/90/EC, for reasons suggested above, is potentially much more repressive, stating that:

> 'Smuggling of migrants' shall mean the procurement, in order to obtain, directly or indirectly, a financial or other material benefit, of the illegal entry of a person into a State Party of which the person is not a national or a permanent resident.[236]

UNTOC also states that the procurement of irregular entry must be committed by criminal organisations[237] and in the form of a transnational crime in order to constitute smuggling of migrants.[238] In comparison, Directive 2002/90/EC does not limit the targets it is aimed at, potentially punishing those who are assisting irregular migration for honourable reasons as harshly as those who do so for financial gain, such as organised crime. The UK and Ireland take part in this repressive EC measure against assisting irregular migration and smuggling of migrants, whilst Denmark opted out from it.[239]

In conclusion, Directive/2002/90/EC punishes assisting irregular migration for financial gain no matter whether a criminal organisation is involved or not. The result is that the scope of this directive is wider than the scope of the UNTOC Smuggling Protocol.

People Trafficking at EU Level

Definition of Trafficking in Human Beings

Framework Decision 2002/629/JHA defines the crime of trafficking in human beings, requiring Member States to impose criminal penalties against persons

---

235   See ibid., Art. 1 (1(a)).
236   See Art. 3(a) of the UNTOC Protocol, op. cit. note 4.
237   See ibid., Art. 4.
238   Ibid.
239   See paras 7 and 8 of Council Directive 2002/90/EC, op. cit. note 227.

who commit this crime.[240] This framework decision requires Member States to criminalise 'the recruitment, transportation, transfer, harbouring, subsequent reception of a person',[241] which includes the use of force or threat, including abduction:[242]

> for the purpose of exploitation of that person's labour or services, including at least forced or compulsory labour or services, slavery or practices similar to slavery or servitude, or for the purpose of the exploitation of the prostitution of others or other forms of sexual exploitation, including in pornography.[243]

Framework Decision 2002/629/JHA creates uniformity in the definition of human trafficking in the EU, including not only trafficking in prostitution, but also other forms of exploitation. The Council requires uniformity in the definition of trafficking in human beings because:

> [i]t is necessary that serious criminal offence of trafficking in human beings be addressed not only through individual action by each Member State but by a comprehensive approach in which the definition of constituent elements of criminal law common to all Member States, including effective, proportionate and dissuasive sanctions, forms an integral part.[244]

The EU has also adopted legal measures against trafficking in children.

Trafficking in Children in EU Law

Measures against trafficking in children have been addressed by Council Decision 2000/375/JHA, which targets child pornography on the Internet,[245] and Council Framework Decision 2004/68/JHA, which targets sexual exploitation of children and child pornography.[246] Decision 2000/375/JHA calls for an array of measures to be adopted in order to fight against trafficking in human beings: these are Council

---

240   See Arts 1 and 3 of 2002/629/JHA of 'Council Framework Decision of 19 July 2002 on Combating Trafficking in Human Beings', OJ EU L 203/1, 1 August 2002.

241   See ibid., Art. 1(1).

242   Ibid.

243   Ibid.

244   See ibid., Recital 7.

245   Ibid.

246   See 'Council Framework Decision 2004/68/JHA of 22 December 2003 on Combating the Sexual Exploitation of Children and Child Pornography', OJ EU L 13/44, 20 January 2004.

Joint Action 96/700/JHA[247] and Joint Action 97/154/JHA.[248] Furthermore, Council Decision 2000/375/JHA emphasises that trafficking in human beings is a serious breach of fundamental rights. The decision also asserts that the sexual abuse of children, including the use, processing, possession and circulation of child pornography, can constitute a serious form of international organised crime that the EU must address adequately.[249]

Decision 2000/375/JHA requires Member States to establish: 'the widest and speediest possible cooperation to facilitate an effective investigation and prosecution of offences concerning child pornography on the Internet in accordance with existing arrangements and agreements'.[250] This co-operation is achieved by Member States informing Europol of suspected cases of pornography involving children.[251] Member States and Europol co-operate with each other in order to fight against child pornography on the Internet by organising meetings of authorities with expertise in the field, with the aim of enhancing the exchange of information and adopting criminal measures to combat this illicit activity.[252] Much in the same vein, Europol should be given greater authority in order to achieve the highest co-ordination in the fight against trafficking in children.

Framework Decision 2004/68/JHA[253] focuses on the sexual exploitation of children and child pornography. This framework decision uses the same instruments mentioned by Council Decision 2000/375/JHA,[254] intended to compliment other third pillar instrument measures. Framework Decision 2004/68/JHA also mentions other instruments that this measure should complement.[255] The instruments quoted by the framework decision refer to police and judicial co-operation that could contribute to combating this crime. Two important concepts introduced by this framework decision are the recruitment of children

---

247 See 'Council Joint Action of 29 November 1996 Establishing an Incentive and Exchange Programme for Persons Responsible for Combating Trade in Human Beings and the Sexual Exploitation of Children', OJ EU L322/7, 12 December 1996.

248 See 'Council Joint Action of 27 February 1997 Adopted by the Council Concerning Action to Combat Trafficking in Human Beings and Sexual Exploitation of Children', OJ EU L 63/2, 4 March 1997.

249 See the Preamble of Council Decision 2000/375/JHA, op. cit. note 247.

250 See ibid., Art. 2(1). For forms of police and judicial co-operation adopted in the EU, see Chapter 4 of this book.

251 See Art. 2(3) of Council Decision 2000/375/JHA, op. cit. note 247.

252 See ibid., Preamble.

253 See Council Decision 2000/375/JHA, op. cit. note 248.

254 See 'Council Joint Action of 29 November 1996 Establishing an Incentive and Exchange Programme for Persons Responsible for Combating Trade in Human Beings and the Sexual Exploitation of Children', op. cit. note 250.

255 See para. 13 of Council Decision 2004/68/JHA, op. cit. note 248.

'into prostitution or into participating in pornographic performances'[256] and the concepts of profiting from and exploiting children for sexual purposes.[257]

The framework decision requires Member States to prosecute offenders when:

a. the offence is committed in whole or in part within its territory;
b. the offender is one of its nationals; or
c. the offence is committed for the benefit of a legal person established in the territory of that Member State.[258]

Other measures have been adopted to fight against trafficking in human beings, in particular against trafficking involving women.

Other Legal Instruments against Trafficking in Women and Children

The EU has adopted a Council Resolution against trafficking in human beings, in particular women and children.[259] The main instrument this Resolution relies on is Article 5(3) of the Charter of Fundamental Rights, because it includes a prohibition on trafficking in human beings, the Hague Ministerial Declaration of 26 April 1997 on European Guidelines drafted in order to prevent and fight against Trafficking in Women for the purpose of sexual exploitation, the UN Convention on the Elimination of all Forms of Discrimination against Women, and the UN Convention on the Rights of Child and UNTOC.[260] This Resolution supports policies and practices and co-operation between EU Member States in order to combat trafficking in human beings, and in particular the sexual exploitation of children.[261]

The fact that trafficking in human beings is considered a serious crime by the EU is demonstrated by the passage of Resolution 2003/C 260/03 which states that the UN instruments: 'form a basis for enhanced global cooperation which is also reflected in developments regarding the European Union's relations with countries outside the Union'.[262] In other words, trafficking in human beings, especially women and children, can be adequately addressed by greater co-operation within the EU and by enhancing relations with countries that do not belong to the EU. Co-operation should not limited to increased police and judicial co-operation, but

---

256 See ibid., Arts 2(a) and (b).
257 See ibid., Art. 2(a).
258 See ibid., Art. 8(1).
259 See 'Council Resolution 2003/C 260/03 of 20 October 2003 on Initiatives to Combat Trafficking in Human Beings, in Particular Women', OJ EU C 260/4, 29 October 2003, paras 1, 2, 5 and 6.
260 See ibid., Recitals 1, 2, 5 and 6.
261 See ibid., Recital 13.
262 See ibid., Recital 15.

also co-operation on preventive measures against victimisation of more vulnerable people such as economic irregular migrants, and rehabilitation and reintegration of victims before it occurs.[263] The goal is to increase awareness that reintegration of the victims of human trafficking into the receiving State at EU level should more of a focus than is provided for in the Council of Europe Convention against Human Trafficking and the UNTOC Trafficking Protocol. This is also confirmed by the measures adopted at EC level against trafficking in human beings.

EC Initiatives on Human Trafficking

The European Parliament and the European Commission Initiatives on Trafficking in Human Beings

The European Parliament, in co-operation with the Council, adopted a decision in 2000[264] whereby the Parliament and the Council asserted that violence against children and other young people, including women, is:

> a breach of their right to life, safety, freedom, dignity and physical and emotional integrity and a serious threat to the physical and mental health of the victims of such violence.[265]

Parliament and the Council have argued that it is the EU that should take measures in the field of police and judicial co-operation to fight effectively against trafficking in human beings.[266] Instead, it should be the EC that provides supportive information on the issue of violence against children, young persons and women by adopting the necessary legal measures.[267] The EC can do this by creating a programme with the express purpose of facilitating the exchange of important information among Member States on their laws and the objectives to be achieved.[268] This undertaking, known as the Daphne Programme, was in line with the principle of subsidiarity, because it is at the EC level that such a programme is most effective, because the objectives can be better achieved by EC action.[269] The programme adopted in 2000 aimed to ensure greater protection for children, young persons and women from

---

263   See ibid., Recital 17.
264   See 'Decision 293/2000/EC of the European Parliament and the Council of 24 January 2000 Adopting a Programme of Community Action (the Daphne Programme) (2000 to 2003) on Preventive Measures to Fight Violence against Children, Young Persons and Women', OJ EU L 34/1, 9 February 2000.
265   See ibid., para. 1.
266   See ibid., para. 5.
267   See ibid., para. 8.
268   See ibid., para. 11.
269   See ibid., para. 12.

future exposure to violence.[270] Parliament and the Council stressed that trafficking in human beings should not only be addressed through EU police and judicial co-operation, but also through the establishment of initiatives such as the Daphne Programme that consider all aspects of trafficking in order to prevent it. The programme included setting up networks to exchange information, best practice and co-operation at EC level, with the purpose of strengthening co-operation between non-intergovernmental organisations and public authorities which take action in fighting against violence.[271] The programme also offered support for actions aimed at preventing human trafficking, including the sexual exploitation of children, commercial sexual exploitation and other sexual abuses.[272]

In 2004, the Parliament and the Council adopted another programme, called Daphne II,[273] a continuation of the programme adopted in 2000, to combat any form of violence against women, children and other vulnerable groups.[274] Daphne II's purpose was to fight against any form of violence, trafficking, sexual abuse and pornography against vulnerable groups with consequences that go beyond EU frontiers.[275] In this programme, the Parliament and the Council also pointed out that measures to prevent any form of violence against women and children should be taken by the EC in respect of the principle of subsidiarity.[276] Therefore, the EC intervened to better achieve a Community objective. In 2007, the European Parliament jointly with the Council launched the Daphne III.[277] The aims of this programme are to contribute to the protection of vulnerable groups such as women and children against all forms of violence and trafficking in human beings. For this purpose, Daphne III requires that the European Commission undertake research, seminars, conferences, interviews, polls and other studies, including publication of data and statistics aimed at detecting human trafficking. The Commission is also required to enlist the co-operation of non-governmental organisations to protect groups more vulnerable from becoming victims of this crime.

In conclusion, Parliament and the Council adopted programmes called Daphne I, II and III in order to prevent trafficking in human beings and to protect the

---

270 See ibid., Art. 1(2).

271 See ibid., Annex.

272 Ibid.

273 See 'Decision 803/2004/EC of the European Parliament and the Council of 21 April 2004 Adopting a Programme of Community Action (2004 to 2008) to Prevent and Combat Violence against Children, Young Persons and Women and to Protect Victims and Groups at Risk (the Daphne II Programme)', OJ EU L 143/1, 30 April 2004.

274 See ibid., Recital 1.

275 See ibid., Recital 8.

276 See ibid., Recital 13.

277 See 'Decision 779/2007/EC of the European Parliament and the Council of 20/6/2007 Establishing for the Period 2007–2013 a Specific Programme to Prevent and Combat Violence against Children, Young People and Women and to Protect Victims and Groups at Risk (Daphne III Programme) as Part of the General Programme "Fundamental Rights and Justice"', OJ EU L 173/19, 3 July 2007.

victims of this crime. These two European institutions together focused on sharing competence between the EC and the EU in order to achieve success in combating human trafficking. The European Commission has also adopted measures against trafficking in human beings.

The European Commission

In 2003, the European Commission adopted Decision 2003/209/EC,[278] in which it asserted that trafficking in human beings contravenes human rights and dignity, and that it should be approached by 'addressing the entire trafficking chain, comprising countries of origin, transit and destination alike'.[279] As a consequence, the Commission, set up a consultative group to establish measures for preventing trafficking in human beings and combating this crime.[280] However, the Commission stressed that these measures should be complementary to those adopted at the EU level in the criminal field for the attainment of an area of freedom, security and justice.[281]

The European Commission published a communication arguing that trafficking in human beings should be addressed by policies aimed at protecting potential victims of this crime.[282] Initiatives in this direction should be taken at international, EU and regional levels.[283] One of these initiatives should approach the crime of trafficking in human beings as a form of organised crime.[284] Therefore, the European Commission called for national law enforcement agencies to exchange information with Europol and maintain contact with Eurojust in order to facilitate the prosecution of traffickers in human beings.[285] The European Commission also stressed the importance of improving checks and surveillance of frontiers in order to fight against illegal immigration.[286] As suggested above, smuggling and trafficking in human beings are closely affiliated with each other. These two crimes are often linked together through international criminal networks.[287] However, law enforcement is not the only means by which trafficking in human beings should be

---

278   See 'Commission Decision of 25 March 2003 Setting Up a Consultative Group, to be Known as "The Expert Group on Trafficking in Human Beings"', OJ EU L 79/25, 26 March 2003.

279   See ibid., Recital 4.

280   See ibid., Recital 7.

281   See ibid., Recitals 1 and 2.

282   See Communication from the Commission to the European Parliament and the Council, *Fighting Trafficking in Human Beings: An Integrated Approach and Proposals for an Action Plan*, COM (2005) 514 final, 18 October 2005, p. 3.

283   Ibid.

284   See ibid., p. 4.

285   See ibid., p. 5.

286   See ibid., p. 6.

287   Ibid.

fought. Therefore, better investigations into what categories of persons are more exposed to human trafficking are necessary.

Moreover, the Commission emphasised that the need to reduce poverty should be adequately addressed, because it renders people vulnerable and easy targets for human traffickers.[288] The Commission concluded that EU institutions and EU Member States must continue to co-operate with international organisations such as the UN and the Council of Europe.[289] In order to do so, the Commission called for the UNTOC Protocol on Trafficking of Persons[290] and the Council of Europe Convention on Action against Trafficking in Human Beings to be ratified by Member States. It is these two Conventions that concentrate specifically on protecting the victims of human trafficking and of vulnerable persons,[291] although with limitations that will be indicated in Chapter 4.

In conclusion, the EC focuses attention on human trafficking victims. Moreover, it emphasises that it is not sufficient to address human trafficking through police and judicial co-operation. EU Member States and the EC should also concentrate on improving the economic conditions of countries that are more exposed to human trafficking, so that the smuggling of migrants and the human trafficking of economic irregular migrants can be prevented.

Conclusions

This chapter has focused on smuggling of migrants and trafficking in human beings at an international level. It explored the international measures adopted in order to fight against smuggling of migrants and trafficking in human beings. It also analysed the EC's competence in the criminal area, and it argued that in the past the EC did not have jurisdiction in this area because the European Parliament could not enact legislation with the Council.

The amendments introduced by the Lisbon Treaty will permit the European Parliament to play a more important role in the criminal area and in the fight against smuggling of migrants and trafficking in human beings. This is because the Union will be supreme, and all measures adopted in this area will require that the Council and the European Parliament enact legislation together.

Subsequently, this chapter analysed EC/EU measures on smuggling of migrants and trafficking in human beings. It argued that EC/EU law on smuggling of migrants has a wider scope compared to UNTOC, because it permits the punishment of assisting irregular migration that is not committed by criminal organisations and

---

288   See ibid., p. 11.

289   Ibid.

290   See Trafficking in Persons Protocol, op. cit. note 15. See also the Council of Europe Convention, op. cit. note 2.

291   See Arts 6 *et seq.* and 9 *et seq.* of Trafficking in Persons Protocol, op. cit. note 15. See also Arts 5 *et seq.* and 10 *et seq.* of the Council of Europe Convention, op. cit. note 2.

for a financial gain. This wider scope contributes to rendering EU law on assisting irregular migration tougher than UNTOC.

The next chapter concentrates on EU measures adopted regarding police and judicial co-operation. It will show that although the EU has made progress because it has adopted important measures in the third pillar that could make the fight against smuggling and trafficking more effective, it needs to become more democratic. The reason for this is because co-operation between EU Member States in the criminal area requires a high level of mutual trust that is currently weak in the EU. Mutual trust could be enhanced by creating a cultural and moral movement against criminal organisations committing cross-border crimes such as smuggling of migrants and trafficking in human beings. In other words, people should understand the importance of EU police and judicial co-operation in order to make it effective. This goal could be achieved by strengthening the role of the European Parliament in the criminal area. The European Parliament could explain to people what criminal organisations are and the measures that should be adopted, in a democratic way, to fight against them. All measures taken at EU level would protect people from the threat of criminal organisations. Moreover, these measures would take into consideration the fundamental freedom of people, and restrict them when it is necessary and when democracy is not in danger.

Chapter 3
EU Law Enforcement Measures

Introduction

The previous chapter analysed international and EC/EU measures on smuggling of migrants and trafficking in human beings.

This chapter's aim is to demonstrate that EU police and judicial co-operation has been enhanced by the adoption of important policy measures and by the introduction of the Lisbon Treaty. This chapter will stress that this new Treaty will replace framework decisions with directives, which means that all measures in the criminal area will be adopted by directives. Directives entail direct effect, and this means that individuals can rely on them in national courts. This chapter will explain the importance of the extension of direct effect in the criminal area. It will also explain that an effective fight against criminal organisations requires strengthening the European Parliament, and this result will be achieved because the Lisbon Treaty states that the European Parliament must enact legislation with the Council in the criminal area through the ordinary legislative procedure (co-legislative procedure).

The effectiveness of these measures will be dependent upon the judicial authorities in the Member States having mutual trust in each other. A lack of mutual trust can create obstacles in detecting persons who commit smuggling of migrants and trafficking in human beings. How does one establish mutual trust between EU Member States in the criminal area? This chapter will explore the progress the EU has made in enhancing mutual trust. Another goal of this chapter will be to determine whether measures adopted at EU level can overcome these obstacles alone, or whether it will be necessary to establish a supra-national criminal court to create mutual trust between EU Member States' judicial authorities. These issues will be examined in conjunction with the amendments in EU police and judicial co-operation now that the Lisbon Treaty has been ratified.

Europol

Management and Europol Control

Europol was set up in 1995 by the adoption of the Convention on Europol.[1] This Convention was replaced on 1 January 2010 by Council Decision 2009/371,

---

1   See 'Convention Based on Article K.3 of the Treaty on European Union, on the Establishment of a European Police Office' (Europol Convention), OJ EU C 316, 27

adopted in April 2009.[2] The Europol Convention established this police agency
with the intention of strengthening co-operation between Member States in
their fight against organised criminal groups.[3] Crimes falling within Europol's
mandate are those criminal offences listed by the Protocol amending the Europol
Convention.[4] The Europol Convention contains three protocols.[5] The first and
second entered into force on 29 March 2007, and the third one entered into force
on 18 April 2007.[6] Smuggling of migrants and trafficking in human beings were
included within Europol's mandate.[7] The legal basis of the Europol Convention
and its Protocols is Article 29 EU Treaty, which states that Member States shall
prevent and combat crime by strengthening police co-operation with Europol's
support.[8] Other legal bases of the Europol Convention are Article 30(1)[9] and
Article K3, now Article 31[10] TEU. The Europol Convention and Protocols should
be read together with Articles 39 *et seq.* of the Schengen Convention.[11] The reason
for this is because the Schengen Convention requires that Member States' police
authorities 'assist each other for the purposes of preventing and detecting criminal

---

November 1995.

2 See 'Council Decision 2009/371/JHA of 6 April 2009 Establishing the European
Police Office (Europol)', OJ EU L 121/37, 15 May 2009.

3 See Art. 2(1) of the Europol Convention, op. cit. note 1.

4 See Art. 2(1) of 'Council Act of 27 November 2003 Drawing Up, on the Basis of
Article 43(1) of the Convention on the Establishment of a European Police Office (Europol
Convention), a Protocol Amending that Convention', OJ EU C 2/1, 6 January 2004.

5 See Protocol drawn up on the basis of Art. 43(1) of the 'Convention on the
Establishment of a European Police Office (Europol Convention), a Protocol Amending
that Convention (the Money Laundering Protocol)', OJ EU C 358/2, 13 December 2000.
See 'Protocol Amending the Convention on the Establishment of a European Police Office
(Europol Convention) and the Protocol on the Privileges and Immunities of Europol,
the Members of its Organs, the Deputy Directors and the Employees of Europol' (the Jit
Protocol), OJ EU C 312/1, 16 December 2002; 'Council Act of 27 November 2003 Drawing
Up, on the Basis of Article 43(1) of the Convention on the Establishment of a European
Police Office (Europol Convention), a Protocol Amending that Convention', OJ EU C 2/1,
6 January 2004.

6 See 'German Council Presidency welcomes the entry into force of the extension
of Europol's operational powers', *Statewatch*, 20 April 2007, <http://www.statewatch.org/
news/2007/apr/europol-protocols-in-force.pdf>, p. 1.

7 See Art. 2(1) of 'Council Act of 27 November 2003 Drawing Up, on the Basis of
Article 43(1) of the Convention on the Establishment of a European Police Office (Europol
Convention), a Protocol Amending that Convention', op. cit. note 4.

8 See Art. 29 of 'Consolidated Version of the Treaty on European Union' (TEU), OJ
C 325/1-184, 24 December 2002.

9 See Recital (1) of Council Act 2004/C 2/01, op. cit. note 5.

10 See the Preamble of the Europol Convention, op. cit. note 1.

11 See Arts 39 *et seq.* of 'The Schengen Convention: Council Decision 1999/435/EC
of 20 May 1999', OJ EC L 239/1.

offences'.[12] Moreover, the Schengen Convention establishes other forms of police co-operation against criminals who have committed serious crimes such as trafficking in human beings.[13] The police co-operation indicated by the Schengen Convention may be facilitated by Europol.

Before the adoption of Council Decision 2009/371, Europol could not initiate investigation or arrest persons without previous authorisation from national authorities.[14] During the preparation of the Treaty of Maastricht, EU Member States made it clear that they considered Europol as 'an intergovernmental ... clearing house for information'.[15] In 2000, the European Council maintained that Europol's role should be enhanced by allowing this agency to initiate investigations.[16] This led to the adoption in 2000 of a Council recommendation[17] which established that Europol may request Member States to commence investigations, and they will decide independently on the basis of this request.[18] The approval of this recommendation did not mean that the Council recognised Europol as having inherent authority to require Member States to start investigations, because such recommendations are not binding.[19] In 2002, a protocol amending the Europol Convention was adopted,[20] with the result that Member States shall take into account Europol's requests to initiate investigations. If a request is rejected, Member States shall explain the reasons leading them to take this decision.[21] This protocol could have facilitated investigations in the Member States in three ways: by providing for the exchange of information between intelligence agencies, by enabling the collection and notification of data to the competent authorities of Member States in support of ongoing investigations,[22] and by granting Europol the authority to request that Member States initiate an investigation. In 2003, a

---

12   See Art. 39(1) of the Schengen Convention, op. cit. note 11.

13   See ibid., Arts 40(2 and 7). See also ibid., Arts 41–47.

14   From <http://www.europol.eu.int/indexasp?page=faq&language=>, accessed 3 October 2005.

15   See Fijnaut, C., 'Police Co-operation and the Area of freedom, Security and Justice', in Walker, N., *Europe's Area of Freedom, Security and Justice* (Oxford: Oxford University Press, 2004), p. 250.

16   See 'Presidency Conclusions of the Tampere European Council', S N 200/99, 15 and 16 October 1999, para. 45.

17   See 'Council Recommendation 2000/C 289/13 of 28 September 2000 to Member States in Respect of Requests Made by Europol to Initiate Criminal Investigations in Specific Cases', OJ EU C 289/8, 12 October 2000.

18   See ibid., Recital 2.

19   See Art. 249(5) TEU, op. cit. note 8.

20   See 'Protocol Amending the Convention on the Establishment of a European Police Office (Europol Convention) and the Protocol on the Privileges and Immunities of Europol, the Members of its Organs, the Deputy Directors and the Employees of Europol', op. cit. note 5.

21   See ibid., Art. 3(b).

22   See Art. 3 of the Europol Convention, op. cit. note 1.

new protocol was signed by Member States[23] introducing new amendments to the Europol Convention. One of these amendments allowed the Council, when acting unanimously, to extend Europol's jurisdiction to cover any form of serious international crime.[24] The protocol permitted further communication of data by an agreement with third States or third bodies 'which contains appropriate provisions on the exchange of information'.[25] However, these amendments were difficult to apply because of unwillingness on the part of Member States. This is the reason why the old Europol Convention has been replaced by a completely new Council Decision, as 'Decisions are more easily adaptable to changing circumstances and emerging political priorities.'[26] The Council Decision states that Europol has legal personality, and that the aim of this police agency is to strengthen police co-operation between 'the competent authorities of the Member States and their mutual cooperation in preventing and combating organised crime'.[27] The Council Decision grants Europol the authority to:

> collect, store, process, analyse and exchange information and intelligence; … notify the competent authorities … of information concerning them and of any connections identified between criminal offences; … aid investigations in the Member States, in particular by forwarding all relevant information to the national units; … ask the competent authorities of the Member States concerned to initiate, conduct or coordinate investigations and to suggest the setting up of joint investigation teams in specific cases; … provide intelligence and analytical support to Member States in connection with major international events; … prepare threat assessments, strategic analyses and general situation reports relating to its objective, including organised crime threat assessments.

Although this decision does not grant Europol the ability to initiate investigations, it can advise on them. In addition, Europol can assist with and encourage the use of relevant evidence for both national and EU investigations.[28] Europol can join with national police forces in a combined effort against organised crime.[29]

The Council Decision reaffirms the Europol Convention in allowing Europol the ability to request that Member States 'initiate, conduct or coordinate investigations in specific cases'.[30] This is an important provision, as there are crimes with a cross-

---

23   See Council Act 2004/C 2/01, op. cit. note 5, amending Arts 2 and 43(3) of the Europol Convention, op. cit. note 1.

24   See Arts 1(1) and 1(22)(b) of the Council Act 2004/C 2/01, op. cit. note 5. See also Peers, S., *EU Justice and Home Affairs Law* (Oxford: Oxford University Press, 2006), p. 537.

25   See Art. 1(9) of Council Act 2004/C 2/01, op. cit. note 5.

26   See para. 4 of Council Decision 2009/371/JHA, op. cit. note 2.

27   See ibid., Arts 2(1) and 3(1).

28   See ibid., Arts 5(1 and 2).

29   See ibid., Art. 6(1).

30   See ibid., Art. 7(1).

border dimension such as smuggling and trafficking where Europol can bring a broader perspective than that of national police forces. Europol's presence through the EU allows it to evaluate the impact of organised crime at multinational level.

Europol, People Smuggling and Human Trafficking

The Europol Convention focused on smuggling of migrants and human trafficking because those crimes were 'becoming increasingly professional'[31] under the direction of organised criminal groups.[32] The subsequent Council Decision also considers 'illegal immigrants smuggling' and 'trafficking in human beings' as 'serious crimes' which Europol must deal with.[33]

Europol itself has identified human trafficking and smuggling of migrants as two of the five priority crime areas,[34] in particular, the smuggling of Chinese migrants.[35] In 2004, Europol assisted in investigations into smuggling of migrants which led to multiple arrests in the Member States.[36] Europol reported that: 'The use of organised criminal groups to facilitate migration appears to be growing, as does the professionalism and organisation of the groups as they become more experienced.'[37] Smuggling of migrants from countries such as Iran, Iraq, Syria, Turkey and Afghanistan is very widespread. The areas most commonly used for transiting irregular migrants are the Balkans, Eastern Europe and North Africa. A study conducted by Europol shows that criminal organisations have a high capacity to adapt to new routes when old ones are discovered and closed by the competent authorities. The most frequent transit countries on the EU's external borders are Russia, Turkey, the Balkans and North Africa.

Based on the widespread multinational reach of organised crime, it is essential that Europol be reformed to widen its remit. Another important argument for expanding the remit of Europol is the indirect crimes that are associated with human trafficking that have no multinational dimension. Through human trafficking, organised crime may establish orphanages to facilitate organ trafficking – a crime currently outside the jurisdiction of Europol.

The crime of people smuggling by sea is also considered a priority by Europol. Often, those who are smuggled by sea participate willingly, but come to regret their choice once they discover the high cost associated with repayment. Many

---

31   See *Europol Annual Report 2004*, p. 7.
32   Ibid.
33   See Annex of Council Decision 2009/371/JHA, op. cit. note 2.
34   See *Europol Annual Report 2004*, op. cit. note 31, p. 6. The other four priority crime areas are: drug trafficking, counter-terrorism, forgery of documents, and financial and property crimes, including money laundering.
35   Ibid.
36   Ibid.
37   Ibid.

victims of people smuggling by sea do not get the chance to repay their victimisers because they die at sea while making the difficult journey across the Mediterranean. The death toll has been estimated at over 3,000 people in 2006 who drowned while travelling on boats from Africa to Europe.[38] Europol stated that although the crimes of trafficking and smuggling are different, they are often connected. For this reason, in 2007 Europol considered trafficking connected to smuggling as a priority crime to be fought against.[39] In conclusion, Europol in 2008 argued for increased investigation and co-ordination despite the improved efforts of national police agencies. Finally, in 2008 Europol affirmed that, although they were being addressed more effectively by national law enforcement authorities, people trafficking and smuggling were still increasing, as they needed further investigation and co-ordination.[40]

It is clear that the fight against these two crimes can be improved by strengthening the relationship between Europol and non-EU countries of transit for illegal migrants. Europol has signed agreements with third countries with the aim of combating cross-border crimes such as smuggling and trafficking.

Europol's External Relations

Europol emphasises that there are principally five routes that are used by smugglers of migrants: through the Baltic sea, Central Europe, the Balkans, the eastern Mediterranean and North Africa. This is why it is important for Europol to negotiate international agreements with third countries which are also confronting the crime of people smuggling. Two Council Acts approved in 1999 facilitated the two-way transmission of data between Europol and third.[41] Europol may also communicate personal data to third countries under the power conferred upon it by the Europol Convention.[42] In 2000, the Council passed Council Decision 2000/C 106/01, granting the Director of Europol the authority to negotiate and sign agreements with third States and non-EU bodies.[43] These agreements involve the exchange of personal data between Europol and non-EU States and non-

---

38   See *Europol Annual Report 2006*, p. 8

39   See ibid., pp. 9 and 10, and *Europol Annual Report 2007*, p. 9.

40   See *Europol Annual Report 2008*, pp. 18 and 19.

41   See 'Council Act 1999/C 26/03 of 3 November 1998 Laying Down Rules Concerning the Receipt of Information by Europol from Third Parties', OJ EU C 26/17, 30 January 1999. See also 'Council Act of 12 March 1999 Adopting the Rules Governing the Transmission of Personal Data by Europol to Third States and Third Bodies', OJ EU C 88/1, 30 March 1999.

42   See Art. 18 of the Europol Convention, op. cit. note 1.

43   See 'Council Decision 2000/C 106/01 of 27 March 2000 Authorising the Director of Europol to Enter into Negotiations on Agreements with Third States and Non-EU-related bodies', OJ EU C106/1, 13 April 2000.

governing bodies outlined in Decision 106/01.[44] These agreements are essential in supporting Europol's efforts to combat the smuggling of migrants and trafficking in human beings. Decision 106/01 has facilitated strategic agreements between Europol and Albania, Bosnia and Herzegovina, Colombia, the former Yugoslav Republic of Macedonia, Russia and Turkey. The agreement with Turkey is most significant because it is the country of transit for victims of people smuggling and human trafficking originating out of Africa. Another important agreement is the one Europol concluded with Interpol, the International Police Organisation which can provide critical intelligence about criminal organisations involved in people smuggling and human trafficking.[45]

As has been demonstrated, Europol plays an important role in investigating human trafficking and people smuggling, but other organisations also play a pivotal role.

Other Forms of Police and Border Co-operation

The European Border Guard Police

In 2001, the European Council emphasised the importance of concentrating on external borders in order to fight effectively against 'illegal immigration networks and the trafficking in human beings'.[46] In addition, according to the European Council, the fight against smuggling of migrants and trafficking in human beings ought to be addressed through strict management of the EU external borders. The management of entry via the EU external borders is regulated by Title IV EC Treaty and the Schengen Acquis.[47] The Commission has pointed out that the control of external borders requires mutual trust between Member States. One sign of mutual trust between Member States has been the abolishment of internal borders under the Schengen Acquis.[48] These challenges may only be achieved by reinforcing co-operation and co-ordination between border checkpoints which should agree to act jointly to secure external borders.[49] The Commission has recognised the lack of operational co-ordination within the EU and Member States in securing external borders.[50] The Schengen Convention states that 'Cross-border movement

---

44   See ibid., Art. 2.

45   See 'Agreement between Interpol and Europol', <http://www.europol.europa.eu/legal/agreements/Agreements/8890.pdf>.

46   See Laeken European Council of 14 and 15 December 2001, Conclusion 42.

47   See *Communication from the Commission to the Council and the European Parliament: Towards Integrated Management of the External Borders of the Member States of the European Union*, COM (2002) 233 final, 7 May 2002, p. 2.

48   See ibid., p. 3.

49   See ibid., p. 5.

50   See ibid., p. 6.

at external borders shall be subject to checks by the competent authorities'.[51] This means that these checks should be carried out on the basis of 'uniform principles, within the scope of national powers and national law and taking account of the interests of all Contracting Parties'.[52] Under the Schengen Acquis, Member States are responsible for checking external borders. However, this is not easy, as noted by the Commission, because Member States can find it difficult to decide who to grant access to their territories.[53] The Schengen Convention stipulates that persons can be refused entry to a Member State when they are considered to be 'a threat to public policy, national security or the international relations of any of the Contracting Parties'.[54] The interpretation of this may differ among Member States, making uniformity difficult.[55] The Commission highlighted that: 'Possible differences in national legislation and administrative practices can generate security differentials between sections of external borders controlled by different Member States.'[56] In the opinion of the Commission, the Schengen Convention places greater importance on entry checks than exit checks.[57] If this is the case, the Schengen Convention neglects the fact that smugglers of migrants and traffickers in human beings may repeatedly exit and re-enter the EU. For this reason, checks on those who enter the EU should be of equal importance to checks on those exiting the EU.

The European Commission asserted that there are two types of co-operation between Member States concerning checks and surveillance at external borders under the Schengen Acquis.[58] One type consists of exchange of liaison officers.[59] Another type of co-operation occurs through bilateral police co-operation agreements among Member States, on the basis of the Schengen Convention.[60] However, the Commission highlights that it is difficult to transfer these agreements from a bilateral dimension to the EU dimension.[61] It must be added that officials sent from one Member State to help another with external border checks cannot exercise functions of public authority.[62] This is why the Commission proposed to agree a common policy of management at external borders and to set up a European Corps of Border Guards.[63] The Commission national services of the Member States should be assisted by this body, which 'could exercise real *surveillance*

---

51   See Art. 6(1) of the Schengen Convention, op. cit. note 11.
52   Ibid. note 51.
53   See COM (2002) 233 final, op. cit. note 47, p. 9.
54   See Art. 5 (1)(e) of the Schengen Convention, op. cit. note 11.
55   Ibid.
56   See COM (2002) 233 final, op. cit. note 47, pp. 9 and 10.
57   See ibid., p. 10.
58   Ibid. See also Art. 7 of the Schengen Convention, op. cit. note 11.
59   See COM (2002) 233 final, op. cit. note 47, pp. 9 and 10.
60   Ibid. See also Art. 47 of the Schengen Convention, op. cit. note 11.
61   See COM (2002) 233 final, op. cit. note 47, pp. 9 and 10..
62   See ibid., p. 10.
63   See ibid., pp. 12 and 20.

functions at the external borders by joint multinational teams'.[64] The Commission also suggested that these Border Guards should be able to exercise public authority functions no matter what their nationality or where they are deployed.[65] This new body should contribute to surveillance and checks throughout the EU. Conflicts between national judicial authorities and the European Corps of Border Guards may lead to problems.

As a result of the Commission's communication, Regulation 377/2004 and Decision 2005/687/EC,[66] by which the UK and Ireland are bound, were passed.[67] Regulation 377/2004 creates Immigration Liaison Officers, who have the task of surveilling the EU's external borders. This regulation states that Immigration Liaison Officers are representatives of Member States with the task of 'contributing to the prevention and combating illegal immigration, the return of illegal immigrants and the management of legal migration'.[68] Liaison Officers can also be posted to a third country in order to facilitate the fight against smuggling of migrants.[69] The Council and Parliament have also established the Schengen Borders Code (Regulation 562/2006) in order to improve border checks.[70] According to Article 5 of the EC Treaty, Denmark had to decide within six months whether it wanted to take part in the Schengen Borders Code, and in 2008 it decided not to.[71] Ireland and the UK are not taking part in the Schengen Borders Code because it is a development of the Schengen Acquis.[72] Article 1 of Regulation 562/2006 introduces rules on crossing external borders. This regulation also mandates that border guards will be responsible for carrying out external border checks.[73] Article 12 provides for surveillance in order to prevent unauthorised entry, to monitor cross-border criminality and measures against persons who cross EU borders illegally. Article 5

---

64 See ibid., p. 20.

65 See ibid., p. 21.

66 See 'Council Regulation (EC) No. 377/2004 of 19 February 2004 on the Creation of an Immigration Liaison Officers Network', OJ EU L 64/1, 2 March 2004. See also 'Commission Decision 2005/687/EC of 29 September 2005 on the Format for the Report on the Activities of Immigration Liaison Officers Networks and on the Situation in the Host Country in Matters Relating to Illegal Immigration', OJ EU L 264/8, 8 October 2005.

67 See Recitals 11 and 12 of Regulation (EC) No. 377/2004, op. cit. note 66. See also Recitals 6 and 7 of Decision 2005/687/EC, op. cit. note 66. The position of these countries in EC immigration law and policy are examined in Chapter 2 of this book.

68 See Art. 1 of Regulation (EC) No. 377/2004, op. cit. note 66.

69 See ibid., Arts 2(3) and 3(1).

70 See 'Regulation (EC) No. 562/2006 of the European Parliament and of the Council of 15 March 2006 Establishing a Community Code on the Rules Governing the Movement of Persons across Borders (Schengen Borders Code)', OJ EU L 105/1, 13 April 2006.

71 See para. 7 of 'Regulation (EC) No. 296/2008 of the European Parliament and of the Council of 11 March 2008 Amending Regulation No. 562/2006', OJ EU L 97/60, 9 April 2008.

72 See paras 22, 27 and 28 of the Schengen Border Code, op. cit. note 70.

73 See ibid., Art. 7.

introduces entry conditions that third-country nationals must comply with in order to be allowed to enter EU territory. Article 13 states that if they do not meet these conditions, they will be forbidden entry.

In conclusion, Member States have adopted measures to police external borders in order to detect criminal organisations connected to irregular entry. Progress has been made in combating smuggling of migrants and trafficking in human beings. The creation of Liaison Officer networks and measures in the area of police and judicial co-operation may represent important efforts in preventing the entry of smugglers of migrants and traffickers in human beings.

There are further issues related to the victims of these criminal activities. There are clear differences between criminals and the irregular migrants who are victims of these criminals. However, the Schengen Borders Code does not make any distinction, and this is cause for concern. As has been demonstrated, the victims of smuggling may provide important evidence for law enforcement authorities investigating and prosecuting criminal organisations. As will be shown in Chapters 4 and 5, these victims must be made to feel secure in return for their testimony.

The EU's Border Agency: Frontex

Another EU border agency was established in 2004 by Regulation 2007/2004[74] to detect criminal activities connected to irregular migration, called the European Agency for the Management of Operational Cooperation at the External Border (Frontex). The UK, Ireland and Denmark are not parties to this regulation.[75] The UK challenged the legality of this regulation because it was excluded from the operations of the agency. The Court of Justice held that the regulation could not be annulled as it was a development of the Schengen Acquis.[76] According to Article 1 of this regulation, it is Frontex's purpose to improve 'the integrated management of the external borders of the Member States' by taking effective measures in order to manage external borders at Community level.[77] The main tasks of Frontex are to:

> coordinate operational cooperation between Member States in the field of management of external borders; assist Member States on training of national border guards, including the establishment of common training standards; carry out risk analysis; follow up on the development of research relevant for the control and surveillance of external borders; assist Member States in circumstances

---

74   See 'Council Regulation (EC) No. 2007/2004 of 26 October 2004 Establishing a European Agency for the Management of Operational Cooperation at the External Borders of the Member States of the European Union Amended by Regulation (EC) No. 863/2007 of the European Parliament and of the Council of 11 July 2007', OJ EU L 199/30, 31 July 2007.

75   See ibid., paras 24, 25 and 26.

76   See Case C-77/05 *UK v. Council* 2007 ECR I-11459-Court of Justice.

77   See Art. 1 of Council Regulation (EC) No. 2007/2004, op. cit. note 74.

requiring increased technical and operational assistance; provide Member States with the necessary support in organising joint return operations.[78]

To these tasks, others were added by amending Regulation 2007/2004. These new tasks include deploying Rapid Border Intervention Teams to EU Member States.[79] Regulation 2007/2004 also states that EU Member States can continue to agree bilateral co-operation between each other and with third countries which complement the work of the Frontex.[80] It also states that when Frontex fulfils executive acts, it will be subject to the national law of the Member State where the tasks are carried out.[81]

Frontex organises and co-ordinates joint operations and pilot projects conducted by Member States.[82] In these joint operations, guest officers may be sent to the hosting Member States in order to co-operate in surveillance of external borders.[83] Although the UK and Ireland are not parties to this regulation, they may well offer their expertise and facilities on a case-by-case basis, evaluated by the Management Board.[84]

Frontex may exchange information with the Commission and EU Member States and with Europol, international organisations and competent authorities of third countries.[85] In this way, an external relations policy may be established at EU level in order to manage external borders and fight against smuggling of migrants and human trafficking. Frontex has concluded a co-operation agreement with Europol.[86] The agreement's purpose is to enhance the role Frontex plays in fighting against trafficking in human beings and people smuggling. To these crimes can be added other related criminal activities committed in order to facilitate them.

In conclusion, the EU has created Frontex in order to strengthen its external borders. This agency should work in co-operation with EU Member States and competent third-country authorities, along with the Commission and Europol.

---

78   See ibid., Art. 2(1).
79   See ibid., Art. 2(1)(g).
80   See ibid., Art. 2(2).
81   See ibid., Art. 10.
82   See ibid., Art. 3(1).
83   See ibid., Art. 1(a).
84   See ibid., para. 27.
85   See ibid., Arts 11, 13 and 14. See also Peers, *EU Justice and Home Affairs Law*, op. cit. note 24, p. 143.
86   See 'Strategic Agreement between the European Agency for the Management of Operational Cooperation at the External Borders of the Member States of the European Union', <http://www.europol.europa.eu/legal/agreements/Agreements/Strategic%20coope ration%20agreement%20Frontex.pdf>.

Rapid Border Intervention Teams

Parliament and the Council presented a proposal in July 2006 on joint border teams.[87] Since Frontex became operational in 2005, it had become clear that this agency needed support and more technical and operational assistance in managing the EU's external borders.[88] This support might be needed to manage uncontrollable migration flows coming from the sea.[89] Therefore, on the basis of the proposal, the Regulation on the Rapid Border Intervention Teams (RABITs) was passed.[90] The preamble of the regulation states that trafficking in human beings and smuggling of migrants can be combated adequately through effective management of external borders. The efforts undertaken to secure the external borders must be supported 'by providing appropriate and sufficient resources, in particular personnel'.[91] Despite these efforts in securing the borders, the responsibility for doing so remains with the Member States. The regulation states that RABITs can be established in order to give assistance to the borders of one Member State that is facing the arrival of large numbers of irregular migrants.[92] The UK, Ireland and Denmark are not participating in the adoption of this regulation.[93] RABITs will follow the instructions of the hosting Member State. Members of RABITs are 'national border guards of their home Member States'.[94] Therefore, RABITs can co-operate with host Member States under their direction, but they are not dependent on them, as they are called to support the work of the national border police.

In conclusion, RABITs, Frontex and Europol should co-operate in order to fight more effectively against the smuggling of migrants and trafficking in human beings. These teams could support police co-operation between EU Member States and third countries.

It must be highlighted that measures establishing Europol and measures on external border controls have been adopted by different instruments and pillars. Measures on Europol have been adopted through decisions, and measures on RABITs have been adopted by a regulation with the intervention of the European Parliament. It is important to emphasise that all these measures against trafficking

---

87   See *Proposal for a Regulation of the European Parliament and of the Council Establishing a Mechanism for the Creation of Rapid Border Intervention Teams and Amending Council Regulation (EC) No 2007/2004 as Regards the Mechanism*, COM (2006) 401, 19 July 2006.

88   See ibid., p. 2.

89   Ibid.

90   See 'Regulation (EC) No. 863/2007 of the European Parliament and of the Council of 11 July 2007 Establishing a Mechanism for the Creation of Rapid Border Intervention Teams and Amending Council Regulation (EC) No. 2007/2004 as Regards that Mechanism and Regulating the Tasks and Powers of Guest Officers', OJ EU L 199/30, 31 July 2007.

91   See ibid., para. 4.

92   See ibid., Art. 1.

93   See ibid., paras 23, 24 and 25.

94   See, respectively, ibid., Arts 5 and 7.

and smuggling could be really effective if the people of EU felt EU co-operation was necessary in order to counter these cross-border crimes. In other words, it is important to create *a cultural and moral movement* against trafficking and smuggling. In this way, EU citizens can appreciate how essential is to strengthen Europol and co-operation on external borders. Without this cultural and moral movement in support of these efforts, the EU will always be considered by its citizens as an entity distinct from them, and not the expression of their common goals. It is unacceptable that the establishment of Europol and decisions that might affect national criminal justice are taken behind closed doors, as is now the case. It cannot be forgotten that Council Decisions are adopted without any co-operation from the most democratic European institution, the European Parliament. Democracy, as explained in Chapter 2, is essential in order to enable effective targeting of cross-border criminal organisations such as those involved in smuggling and trafficking.

Relevant changes in the criminal area will be introduced by the Lisbon Treaty. Various unsuccessful attempts have been made before the Lisbon Treaty to democratise the decisions reached in the EU criminal area. One of these was the establishment of the Constitutional Treaty and other brilliant proposals presented by very acute scholars.

The Constitutional Treaty, the Court of Justice, Policing and Judicial Co-operation

The Treaty establishing a Constitution for Europe (Constitutional Treaty), if ratified, would have created a European criminal judicial area. The modifications the Constitutional Treaty would have introduced could have ensured the application of the principle of supremacy in the criminal area. Indeed, the Constitutional Treaty abolished the difference between the EU and the EC. This is established by Article I-1, which states that: 'this Constitution establishes the European Union, on which the Member States confer competences to attain the objectives they have in common'.[95] The Constitutional Treaty also stated that the European Union and Member States have shared competence in the area of freedom, security and justice.[96] In addition, the Constitutional Treaty also stated that: 'European framework laws may establish minimum rules concerning the definition of criminal offences and sanctions in the areas of particularly serious crime with a cross-border dimension'.[97] The Constitutional Treaty introduced important modifications of the European Parliament's role in the area of police and judicial co-operation. Firstly, the co-decision procedure would

---

95   See Art. I-1 of 'Treaty Establishing the Constitution for Europe 2004' (Constitutional Treaty), OJ EU C 310/1, 16 December 2004.

96   See ibid. Art. I-14(2)(j).

97   See ibid., Art. III-271(1). European framework laws are directives. See Arnull, A., 'From Bit Part to Starring Role? The Court of Justice and Europe's Constitutional Treaty', *Yearbook of European Law* (2005), vol. 24, pp. 14 and 15.

have been required in the area of police and judicial co-operation.[98] Secondly, even if the co-decision procedure was not applied, the European Parliament would have been consulted and its consent would have been necessary in order to adopt a measure.[99]

The Constitutional Treaty included trafficking in human beings and sexual exploitation of women and children as two of the possible crimes that could have been the object of European framework laws.[100] Furthermore, as Weyembergh highlighted, the Constitutional Treaty would have reduced the democratic deficit, because national parliaments would also have been involved in the decision-making procedure.[101]

The Constitutional Treaty established the Court of Justice's jurisdiction in the criminal area. There was a provision which stated that the Court of Justice had competence in the area of freedom, security and justice, including police and judicial co-operation, apart from:

> operations carried out by the police or other law-enforcement services of a Member State or the exercise of the responsibilities incumbent upon Member States with regards to the maintenance of law and order and the safeguarding of internal security.[102]

Arnull pointed out that these restrictions had been established because, at national level, the criminal area causes much litigation.[103] Arnull emphasised that including the criminal area within the Court of Justice's jurisdiction would cause a dramatic increase in cases brought before it.[104] This is problematic as the Constitutional Treaty would require the Court of Justice to act with a minimum delay if the case referred involved a person in custody.[105] The potential for an overly burdened Court of Justice supports the idea that a new court should be created to alleviate this potential burden. However, this type of project is now considered an *ultima*

---

98   See Art. I-34 (1) of the Constitutional Treaty, op. cit. note 95. This Article refers to Art. III-396 of the Constitutional Treaty, which would replace Art. 251 EC Treaty (co-decision procedure). See also Weyembergh, A., 'Approximation of Criminal Laws, the Constitutional Treaty and the Hague Programme', *Common Market Law Review* 42:6 (2005), p. 1595.

99   Ibid. See Arts III-270 (2)(d) and III-271(1) of the Constitutional Treaty, op. cit. note 95.

100   See Arnull, 'From Bit Part to Starring Role?', op. cit. note 97.

101   Ibid. Weyembergh quotes Arts I-11, I-46 (2) and III-259 of the Constitutional Treaty, op. cit. note 95.

102   See Art. III-377 of the Constitutional Treaty, op. cit. note 95.

103   See Arnull, 'From Bit Part to Starring Role?', op. cit. note 97, p. 21.

104   Ibid.

105   Ibid. See also Art. III-369(4) of the Constitutional Treaty, op. cit. note 95.

ratio ('last resort').[106] The Lisbon Treaty also does not include any provision on the establishment of a new court.[107]

In conclusion, this section has analysed the modifications the Constitutional Treaty would have introduced in the criminal area. The Constitutional Treaty would have introduced relevant modifications to the Court of Justice's competence in the criminal field. However, these changes were not intended to interfere in EU Member States' different cultures. Despite the fact that the Constitutional Treaty has not been ratified, Member States may be keen to reform the Court of Justice or introduce other modifications to render more effective the fight against trans-national crimes such as smuggling of migrants and human trafficking. This should be done without jeopardising the cultural norms of each individual EU Member State, enhancing mutual trust between them. This is why it is thought that EU Member States should concentrate on enhancing mutual trust between their prosecuting and judicial authorities.

The European Public Prosecutor (EPP)

The Corpus Juris *2000*

The Constitutional Treaty introduced the office of European Public Prosecutor, 'In order to combat crimes affecting the financial interests of the Union'.[108] Moreover, the Constitutional Treaty stated that the European Council may extend the EPP's competence in order to include 'serious crime having a cross-border dimension'.[109] The Constitutional Treaty stated that the EPP could be established from Eurojust, and should be responsible for investigating, prosecuting and bringing to justice perpetrators and their accomplices against the European Union's financial interests.[110] The EPP would have been established by the Council by unanimity, after having obtained the European Parliament's consent.[111] Therefore, the procedure to follow in order to establish the EPP would have partly been inter-governmental, because the European Parliament could not have co-legislated with the Council in setting it up.

In the past, the EPP has been the subject of much research.[112] Different scholars have proposed the establishment of a *Corpus Juris* in order to fight against crimes

---

106 See below in this chapter.

107 See Art. 276 of the 'Consolidated Version of the Treaty on European Union and the Treaty on the Functioning of the European Union' (the Lisbon Treaty), OJ EU 2010/C 83/01, 30 March 2010.

108 See Art. III-274(1) of the Constitutional Treaty, op. cit. note 95.

109 See Art. III-274(4) of the Constitutional Treaty, op. cit. note 95.

110 See Art. III-274(1,2) of the Constitutional Treaty, op. cit. note 95.

111 Ibid.

112 See Delmas-Marty, M., and Vervaele, J.A.E., *The Implementation of the Corpus Juris in the Member States* (Mortsel: Intersentia, 2000), Arts 1–8 of the so-called *Corpus*

of fraud against the EC's financial interests, including market-rigging, money laundering, conspiracy, corruption, misappropriation of funds, abuse of office and disclosure of secrets pertaining to one's office.[113] Some scholars suggested that in order to act effectively against these criminal activities, an EPP should have been set up with competence to investigate, arrest and prosecute those who committed these offences.[114]

One first issue concerning this project, which was part of a code called *Corpus Juris* 2000,[115] is that important crimes such as smuggling of migrants and trafficking in human beings are not within the scope of the EPP's competence. This exclusion is not correct, because it is thought that these crimes are more serious than those listed in the *Corpus Juris* 2000. The *Corpus Juris* 2000 established that the EPP Office 'is an authority of the European Community'[116] and that it should be agreed by the co-decision procedure. The fact that a potential EPP would only have applied to EC instruments and not to EU instruments, demonstrates that the EC Treaty was only concerned with protecting the EC's economic interests. Smuggling of migrants and trafficking in human beings, although grave crimes with serious consequences for their victims, have been ignored, and the reason for this could be that they are not considered to a threat to the EC's financial interests. A second issue is that the EPP should have exercised its jurisdiction in EU Member States, which are considered 'a single legal area'[117] by the *Corpus Juris* 2000. How should the EPP have interacted with other national public prosecutors or the police? The *Corpus Juris* 2000 stated that police, public prosecutors and other national authorities should have informed the EPP of acts that might constitute one of the offences included in the EPP's jurisdiction.[118] National authorities should have transferred case files to the EPP if they discovered that one of the offences under the EPP's jurisdiction has been committed.[119] The EPP could only have decided whether to start an investigation[120] or to terminate it.[121] These obligations of the national authorities and the EPP's competence over certain crimes could have created problems related to national sovereignty. National authorities could have preferred to refer an act that can constitute a crime to their judicial authorities rather than the EPP. Why should they treat specific crimes in a different way to other crimes? It is possible that EU Member States did not support the EPP because it could have been considered too invasive, representing a threat to national

---

Juris 2000.
113 See ibid., Art. 18(2), pp. 189–92.
114 See ibid., Art. 18(2), p. 197.
115 Ibid.
116 Ibid.
117 Ibid. note 116.
118 See ibid., Art. 19(1), p. 199.
119 See ibid., Art. 19(2), p. 199.
120 See ibid., Art. 19(4), p. 199.
121 See ibid., Art. 21, p. 201.

sovereignty – an innovation far too radical at the time. At that moment, awareness of the possibility of creating an EU criminal area for EU citizens was low. The Lisbon Treaty offers new optimism that EU citizens will take the opportunity to fully understand what a potential EU criminal area would mean. With a better understanding of EU criminal area, they would be in a position to decided whether or not to give their consent through the European Parliament. Seeking the consent of the EU citizenry before creating an EU criminal area would confer legitimacy on such an endeavour.

In conclusion, it could be said that the EPP represents an important effort to find a solution in fighting crimes that have a cross-border dimension. The scholars who proposed the EPP recognised the need for a unified approach by EU Member States in fighting transnational crimes. Regrettably, the EPP project was too far ahead of its time, and was seen generally as a threat to national sovereignty.

The European Commission's Proposal on the European Public Prosecutor

In 2001, the European Commission proposed to establish an EPP in order to protect the European Community's financial interests.[122] The European Commission's proposal was based on the *Corpus Juris* 2000 proposal, which was the preparatory work which preceded the European Commission's study.[123] The Commission proposal contained all the limits which characterised *Corpus Juris* 2000. Indeed, as stated above, the EPP was only established to protect the EC's financial interests.[124] It is disappointing that the European Commission did not explain the reasons why the EC's financial interests were considered more important than the rights of people not to be smuggled, trafficked or reduced to slavery.

The EPP would have required uniformity in Member States, with the intention of creating a common investigation and prosecution area where the EPP would have enjoyed 'specialised jurisdiction, prevailing over the jurisdiction of the national enforcement authorities'.[125] This specific EPP competence could have been problematic, and could have provoked conflicts between Member States' national law enforcement authorities and the EPP, because national law enforcement authorities might have wanted to claim jurisdiction in investigating crimes committed in their territory, while the EPP might have invoked its special jurisdiction over the same crimes. Moreover, fragmentation in the interpretation of EU law could have been increased rather than reduced, because crimes against EC financial interests would have required a special approach, while for other crimes national legislation would have been enforced.

---

122   See *Green Paper on Criminal-law Protection of the Financial Interests of the Community and the Establishment of a European Prosecutor*, COM (2001) 715 final, 11 December 2001.

123   See ibid., pp. 5 and 6.

124   See ibid., p. 20.

125   See ibid., pp. 23 and 24.

Peers criticised the concept of the EPP, emphasising that the Commission did not consider other less ambitious measures that could have achieved the same objective.[126] Peers quotes important measures that have been taken in order to protect the financial interests of the EC.[127] There are also other 'third pillar measures strengthening the relationship between OLAF and national prosecutors and/or Eurojust'[128] that could have been adopted. [129] It is logical to argue that instead of concentrating on an ambitious project such as the EPP, other third-pillar measures should be taken into consideration that avoided the possibility of creating conflicts over national sovereignty. The efforts of the scholars who proposed the EPP are commendable, as they highlighted the need to reform the EU in the criminal area in order to fight serious crimes. The Lisbon Treaty establishes a European Public Prosecutor to fight against fraud against the financial interests of the EU, and future developments on the basis of the Treaty could be beneficial in the fight against this crime.[130] These efforts could form the basis for further developments in the future, provided that the Lisbon Treaty is brought into effect in a manner that increases democracy in the EU criminal area. The amendments that the Treaty of Lisbon will introduce in the criminal area, particularly in EU police and judicial co-operation, could contribute to establishing European criminal law.

The Lisbon Treaty and EU Police Co-operation

Following the rejection of the Constitutional Treaty by two referendums held in France and the Netherlands, the EU and its Member States moved to amend the existing EU Treaty rather than replace it. This section describes the amendments the Lisbon Treaty would introduce in the criminal area, particularly in EU police co-operation.

---

126   See Peers, *EU Justice and Home Affairs Law*, op. cit. note 24, p. 491.

127   See ibid., pp. 491 and 541. See also COM (2003) 154, 2 April 2003, not available in English, Italian, French or Spanish. The author also quotes: *Proposal for a Regulation of the European Parliament and the Council amending Regulation (EC) No 1073/1999 concerning Investigations conducted by the European Anti-Fraud Office (OLAF)*, COM (2004) 103, 10 February 2004; *Proposal for a Regulation of the European Parliament and of the Council on Mutual Administrative Assistance for the Protection of the Financial Interests of the Community against Fraud and Any Other Illegal Activities*, COM (2004) 509, 20 July 2004; *Proposal for a Regulation of the European Parliament and of the Council Amending Regulation (EC) No. 1073/1999 Concerning Investigations Conducted by the European Anti-Fraud Office (OLAF)*, COM (2006) 244, 24/5/2006. These measures are not analysed here because they are outside the scope of this book.

128   Ibid.

129   Ibid.

130   The EPP is not focused on here because crimes against EU financial interests are not analysed on this book.

Articles 87 *et seq.* of the TFEU are dedicated to EU police co-operation.[131] Article 87 states that the Parliament and the Council, by the ordinary procedure, can adopt measures on: 'the collection, storage, processing, analysis and exchange of relevant information … [and] common investigative techniques in relation to the detection of serious forms of organised crime'. Article 88 states that all measures on the structure, operations, fields of action and tasks of Europol, shall be enacted by the ordinary legislative procedure. These are important provisions because they allow Parliament to enact legislation in the criminal area along with the Council.[132] The EU Treaty does not allow Parliament to intervene in the criminal area, limiting it to a consultancy role on measures in the criminal area. Article 87 provides for enhanced co-operation between at least nine Member States in the event of the Council being unable to achieve unanimity in the adoption of measures on police co-operation. This means that the EU could take initiatives in the field of police co-operation even though not all Member States agree – a positive development when compared to the way things were done before. The requirement of unanimous agreement often blocked or delayed the adoption of effective measures which would have improved the criminal area. It is noteworthy that Member States took 14 years (from 1995 to 2009) to replace the Europol Convention with the Europol Council Decision. A negative aspect of Article 87 is that it mandates the Council to take unilateral actions when deciding on operational co-operation between Member States' law enforcement authorities. By giving the Council sole jurisdiction in some parts of the criminal area, the decision-making process dealing with police co-operation remains largely undemocratic. The European Parliament is the only EU institution that can claim to be directly representative of the citizenry of the EU. Therefore, it is not acceptable for decisions regarding measures on police co-operation which involve investigations and limitations of freedoms to be adopted without the European Parliament's consent. Moreover, in the interest of mutual trust between EU Member States and Europol, European and national Parliaments should be involved as much as possible. A recent report published by the House of Lords European Union Committee suggested that for Member States to trust Europol, there will need to be more democratic accountability.[133] On that occasion, an academic from the University of Leeds made a very commendable comment:

> I think the parliaments, the national parliaments in particular … need to become more proactive in stating what they want before technology is adopted … I think there is a role also for national parliaments in being very vigilant in defining the objectives and the competences of Europol … In addition to that, the national

---

131 See Arts 87 *et seq.* of the TFEU, op. cit. note 107.
132 See ibid., Arts 87(2)(a) and (c) and 88(2).
133 See House of Lords Select Committee on the European Union, *Europol: Coordinating the Fight against Serious and Organized Crime*, session 2008–2009, 29th Report, 12 November 2008.

parliaments might want to have some oversight over the output from joint investigation teams …[134]

More democratic accountability could pressure Europol to be more efficient, which is another argument for involving as many democratically elected institutions as possible. The House of Lords Select Committee agreed with this reasoning when it concluded that:

> It must be for the European Parliament to decide whether it wishes to adopt, in the spirit of the Treaty of Lisbon, a formal procedure for the scrutiny of Europol's activities, and whether, and if so how, to involve national parliaments of the Member States.

The functioning of Europol and its co-operation with Member States should be decided by using the ordinary legislative procedure along with the input of national parliaments, as established by the Lisbon Treaty and its Protocol on national parliaments. The ordinary legislative procedure should also be extended to cover decisions made on EU judicial co-operation. In fact, the Lisbon Treaty requires the use of the ordinary legislative procedure on these measures, and this will be examined later in this volume.

Third-pillar Measures

Eurojust

Eurojust was established by Council Decision 2002/187/JHA.[135] Eurojust is the European Judicial Co-operation Unit, which facilitates and co-ordinates national criminal investigations of serious transnational crimes and criminal judicial co-operation between the EU Member States.[136] Eurojust consists of 25 National Members chosen from EU Member States in accordance with their legal systems, with one member for each Member State.[137] National members are either judges, public prosecutors or police officers in their Member States.[138] Some Member States have appointed assistants to support their national members, as their

---

134   See ibid., p. 47.

135   See 'Council Decision 2002/187/JHA of 28 February 2002 Setting up Eurojust with a View to Reinforcing the Fight against Serious Crime', OJ EU L 63/1, 6 March 2002.

136   See Arts 29(2) and 31(2) TEU, op. cit. note 8.

137   See Art. 2 of Council Decision 2002/187/JHA, op. cit. note 135. See also *Eurojust Annual Report 2004*, p. 8. <http://www.eurojust.europa.eu/press_releases/annual_reports/2004/Annual_Report_2004_EN.pdf>.

138   Ibid.

workload increases every year.[139] Once the Council Decision has been ratified, Eurojust will be able to act as an electoral college. According to Sub-Committee F of the House of Lords, this will enable Eurojust to assert its authority to compel national authorities to commence investigations and prosecutions.[140]

Just like Europol, Eurojust is required to support criminal investigations against cross-border crimes, especially when these crimes are committed by criminal organisations.[141] Decision 2002/187/JHA adopting Eurojust is based on the third pillar, particularly Articles 31 and 34(2)(c) of the EU Treaty.[142] Article 31 EU Treaty states that judicial co-operation shall be encouraged by reinforcing co-operation among ministries in EU Member States and judicial authorities, 'including, where appropriate, cooperation through Eurojust, in relation to proceedings and enforcement of decisions'.[143] Moreover, it also states that judicial co-operation shall be supported by 'facilitating extradition between Member States'[144] and by 'preventing conflicts of jurisdiction between Member States'.[145] The EU Treaty also requires that the Council reinforce Eurojust's role in supporting co-ordination among the prosecuting authorities of EU Member States.[146] Eurojust is also required to intervene when serious and cross-border crimes have been committed, by facilitating closer co-operation between it and the European Judicial Network.[147] However, Article 34(2)(c) of the EU Treaty states that measures to promote co-ordination in the third pillar should be adopted by decisions that do not have direct effect,[148] and Decision 2002/187/JHA is based on this Article. Emphasis should be placed on the fact that on one hand the EU Treaty encourages enhancement of the Eurojust's jurisdiction in order to promote judicial co-operation, and on the other hand it requires the adoption of measures in this area by the Council acting alone. Wyngaert asserts that crimes which fall under Eurojust's jurisdiction are the same as those which fall under Europol's jurisdiction. This is because the Council Decision on Eurojust covers the same crimes listed by the Europol Convention.[149] Smuggling of migrants and trafficking in human beings are covered by Decision 2002/187/JHA.[150] The decision states that Eurojust's jurisdiction concerns all

---

139   Ibid.
140   See House of Lords Select Committee on the European Union, *Judicial Cooperation in the EU: The Role of Eurojust*, 23rd Report, HL 138, 21 July 2004.
141   See Art. 31(2) TEU, op. cit. note 8
142   See the Preamble of Council Decision 2002/187/JHA, op. cit. note 135.
143   See Art. 31(1)(a) TEU, op. cit. note 8.
144   See ibid., Art. 31(1)(b).
145   See ibid., Art. 31(1)(d).
146   See ibid., Art. 31(2)(a).
147   See ibid., Art. 31(1)(b and c).
148   See ibid., Art. 34(2)(c).
149   See Van Den Wyngaert, 'Eurojust and the European Public Prosecutor in the *Corpus Juris* Model', op. cit. note 15, p. 208. See also Art. 4(1(b)) of Council Decision 2002/187/JHA, op. cit. note 135.
150   See ibid., Art. 4(1(a)).

crimes over which Europol has jurisdiction, including smuggling of migrants and human trafficking.[151] Eurojust's jurisdiction also covers the crime of participation in a criminal organisation.[152] This means that Eurojust has a mandate to support judicial co-operation among Member States. Eurojust can therefore request a particular Member State to investigate and prosecute those who assist in the smuggling of migrants, as defined by Directive 2002/90/EC.[153]

Council Decision 2002/187/JHA on Eurojust[154] appears to widen the scope of Eurojust's jurisdiction, stating that Eurojust shall intervene when: 'It is necessary to improve judicial cooperation between the Member States … in particular in combating forms of serious crime often perpetrated by transnational organisations'.[155] The Council Decision requires Eurojust to support judicial co-operation in all transnational crimes, whether they involve criminal organisations or not.

Crimes connected to human trafficking and people smuggling should be included in Eurojust's competence on a case-by-case basis. The Council Decision also states that 'Eurojust may … assist in investigations and prosecutions on the basis of a competent authority of a Member State request'.[156]

Eurojust can request that a Member State not investigate or prosecute a particular crime because another Member State is in a better position to do so.[157] Eurojust can also establish a joint investigation team and provide all the information this body requires to fulfil its tasks.[158] Problems and difficulties in investigations may arise if one Member State refuses to start an investigation. Possible reasons for Member States' refusal include the protection of national security interest, and ensuring 'the success of investigations under way or the safety of individuals'.[159] Investigations may be stopped and criminals remain unpunished if Member States do not agree which domestic judicial authority is in a better position to deal with a crime with a cross-border dimension.

Council Decision 2002/187/JHA also established a Joint Supervisory Body (JSB).[160] This is an independent body that will monitor how Eurojust processes

---

151   See ibid., Art. 4(1(b)).

152   Ibid. For the definition of criminal organisation, see also 'Joint Action 98/733/JHA of 21 December 1998 Adopted by the Council on the Basis of Art. K.3 of the Treaty on European Union, on Making it a Criminal Offence to Participate in a Criminal Organisation in the Member States of the European Union', OJ EU L 351/1, 29 December 1998.

153   See Art. 2 of 'Council Directive 2002/90/EC of 28 November 2002 Defining the Facilitation of Unauthorised Entry, Transit and Residence', OJ EC L 328/17, 5 December 2002.

154   See Council Decision 2002/187/JHA, op. cit. note 135.

155   See ibid., Recital 1.

156   See ibid., Art. 4(2).

157   See ibid., Art. 7(1(a)(ii).

158   See ibid., Art. 7(1(a)(iii–v).

159   See ibid., Art. 8(I and ii).

160   See ibid., Art. 23.

personal data received by Member States and other partners.[161] Act 2004/C 86/01[162] established the tasks and powers of the JSB. The JSB was established to safeguard the personal data of those targeted by Eurojust investigations.[163] The JSB must intervene when, according to the Data Protection Officer, the data processing violates Council Decision 2002/187/JHA.[164] Furthermore, applicants whose request has been rejected by Eurojust can appeal the decision to the Joint Supervisory Body.[165]

Eurojust has co-ordinated important investigations with judicial authorities from Spain, Portugal and other European countries, and Portuguese and South America. These co-ordinated efforts have led to the successful arrest and prosecution of perpetrators guilty of money laundering and drug trafficking.[166] The House of Lords Select Committee (hereafter 'Select Committee') has recognised the important contribution Eurojust has made in co-ordinating investigations and judicial co-operation between police and judicial authorities of Member States.[167] The Select Committee stated that 'Eurojust received more requests for assistance by way of co-operation than for help to co-ordinate investigations and prosecutions'.[168] The Select Committee explained the discrepancy between requests for co-ordination and requests for investigation as resulting from national authorities' lack of confidence in Eurojust.[169] The Select Committee also highlighted that Eurojust must deal with the difficulties created by different national criminal justice systems among the 25 Member States.[170] The Select Committee pointed to the criminal procedural laws within the Member States as being the sources of the greatest differences, rather than the substantive criminal laws'.[171] In England, for example, criminal investigations are carried out by the police, while in France investigations are carried out by the police under the supervision of judicial authorities.[172] In 2006, Eurojust reported a 31 percent increase in the cases referred to it from the

---

161   See ibid., Arts 14, 22 and 23.

162   See 'Act of the Joint Supervisory Body of Eurojust of 2 March 2004 Laying Down its Rules of Procedure', OJ EU C 86/1, 6 April 2004.

163   See ibid., Art. 1. See also Arts 14, 22 and 23(1 and 7) of Decision 2002/187/JHA, op. cit. note 135.

164   See Art. 1 of Act 2004/C 86/01, op. cit. note 162. See also Art. 17(4(b)) of Decision 2002/187/JHA, op. cit. note 135.

165   See Art. 1 of Act 2004/C 86/01, op. cit. note 162. See also Art. 19(8) of Decision 2002/187/JHA, op. cit. note 135.

166   'Successful co-ordination', 9 September 2005, <http://www.eurojust.eu.int/press_releases/2005/09-09-2005.htm>, accessed 13 October 2005.

167   See *Judicial Cooperation in the EU: The Role of Eurojust*, op. cit. note 140, p. 6.

168   See ibid., p. 20.

169   Ibid.

170   See ibid., p. 16. See also Chapter 5 of this book, where differences in British and Italian law are analysed.

171   See *Judicial Cooperation in the EU: The Role of Eurojust*, op. cit. note 140.

172   Ibid.

EU Member States.[173] Eurojust has argued that this increase demonstrates 'that Member States are becoming more aware of the work and services provided by Eurojust'.[174]

In conclusion, Eurojust has improved judicial co-ordination among Member States, as proven by the fact that it has seen an increase in the numbers of cases referred to it over time. Lack of mutual trust might create obstacles in the functioning of Eurojust, but the Commission showed a willingness to address this problem when it issued a communication in 2007.[175] Eurojust also highlighted that this communication would represent a good opportunity 'to review progress and to consider refinements and improvements to the decision to make the Eurojust's internal working practices more effective'.[176] Eurojust is optimistic that the communication may improve the relationship of this agency with the competent authorities of EU Member States and with other organisations such the European Judicial Network (EJN). [177]

The European Judicial Network

The EJN was established by the Council in 1998,[178] and it is a contact point for Member States that need to set up judicial co-operation with other Member States in order to fight against serious crimes.[179] The EJN fulfils tasks to those performed by Eurojust, facilitating and accelerating judicial co-operation among Member States. A liaison magistrate can be appointed with the responsibility of completing these tasks.[180] Liaison magistrates 'may be linked to the European Judicial Network by the Member State appointing the liaison magistrate in each case'.[181] Contact points shall also provide Member States with practical information and legal assistance, when required.[182]

As pointed out by the Select Committee, the tasks of the EJN and those of Eurojust may overlap, creating duplication.[183] The Select Committee suggested that it would be better if there were a division of tasks between Eurojust and the EJN. The Select Committee specifically suggested that Eurojust should be 'a centralised EU agency

---

173   See *Eurojust Annual Report 2006*, p. 19.
174   Ibid.
175   See ibid., p. 74.
176   Ibid.
177   Ibid.
178   See 'Joint Action 98/428/JHA of 29 June 1998 Adopted by the Council on the Basis of Art. K.3 of the Treaty on European Union, on the Creation of a European Judicial Network', OJ EU L 191/4, 7 July 1998.
179   See ibid., Arts 1, 2 and 4.
180   See ibid., Art. 4(1).
181   See ibid., Art. 4(4).
182   See ibid., Art. 4(3).
183   See *Judicial Cooperation in the EU: The Role of Eurojust*, op. cit. note 140, p. 31.

and may be better placed to deal with complex requests or requests involving more than one Member State. The EJN … is about bilateral personal contacts'.[184]

The European Commission has also come up with a proposal to improve Eurojust and EJN co-operation in the fight against serious cross-border crimes.[185] In this communication, the Commission pointed out that the EJN has contributed to strengthening judicial co-operation between Member States. The Commission also suggested that Eurojust should co-operate with Europol. In order to achieve this, communication between these two agencies should be improved. According to the Commission, the protection of EU external borders can be achieved by fighting against the criminal organisations behind smuggling and trafficking. This is why the Commission encourages co-operation between Eurojust, Frontex and law enforcement authorities of non-EU countries. All these steps can be taken by amending Eurojust's decision so that this agency can reach its full potential.

The Council adopted Decision 2008/976/JHA in 2008[186] to improve judicial co-operation between Member States by allowing direct contact between the EJN and Eurojust through a system of secure telecommunication connections.[187] Articles 2 and 4 state that contact points of the EJN can be established in the Member States in order to reinforce international co-operation in the fight against serious crimes. Other modifications and supports to the EJN and Eurojust have been introduced by the Lisbon Treaty, which will change the way Eurojust operates. Article 85(1) states that Eurojust's task should be to enhance:

> coordination and cooperation between national investigating and prosecuting authorities in relation to serious crime affecting two or more Member States or requiring a prosecution on common bases, on the basis of operations conducted and information supplied by the Member States' authorities and by Europol.

Article 85(1) also states that measures dealing with how Eurojust operates shall be decided by the ordinary legislative procedure. Under this Article, Eurojust's tasks include: 'Initiation of investigations and prosecutions …; the strengthening of judicial cooperation, including by resolution of conflicts of jurisdiction and by close cooperation with the European Judicial Network'. Finally, Article 85(2) states that the European Parliament and national parliaments shall be involved in evaluating the activities of Eurojust. By requiring the involvement of those parliaments, this provision has the indirect benefit of improving democracy within the EU. As a result

---

184   Ibid.

185   See *Communication from the Commission to the Council and the European Parliament on the Role of Eurojust and the European Judicial Network in the Fight against Organized Crime and Terrorism in the European Union*, COM (2007) 644, 23 October 2007.

186   See 'Council Decision 2008/976/JHA of 16 December 2008 on the European Judicial Network', OJ EU L 348/130, 24 December 2008.

187   See ibid., para. 8.

of including the parliaments in this way, measures adopted concerning Eurojust will be more legitimate than those on EU police co-operation and Europol. In the case of EU police co-operation and Europol, it is more likely that particular interests of governments will prevail over the common good. This is problematic because as representatives of EU citizens who are directly affected by these measures, the European Parliament will not have the chance to give valuable input.

In conclusion, Eurojust and the EJN have been established to contribute to the fight against cross-border crimes such as smuggling of migrants and trafficking in human beings. Certainly, there is scope for improvements. Apart from all the initiatives in the criminal area that should be taken to reach decisions in a more democratic way, the importance of establishing mutual trust between EU Member States' judicial authorities should not be understated. In this way, Eurojust and the EJN's contribution to combating transnational crimes such as smuggling of migrants and trafficking in human beings will be improved. A step towards achieving this objective was taken in 2005 when Eurojust submitted a request to the Council that it be given the authority to issue and execute mutual legal assistance.[188]

Mutual legal assistance has the potential to strengthen judicial co-operation. Despite this fact, not all Member States have ratified the 2000 Convention on Mutual Legal Assistance, and the Protocol on Mutual Legal Assistance[189] that would replace the 1959 European Convention on Mutual Assistance.[190]

Gathering Evidence in the EU

Mutual Legal Assistance

The EU has adopted measures on mutual judicial assistance in order to facilitate the exchange between EU Member States of evidence in criminal cases.[191] These measures have built upon the existing international framework adopted by the

---

188   See *Eurojust Report on Judicial Powers of the national members of Eurojust*, Council Doc. 11943/05, 6 September 2005. See also Peers, *EU Justice and Home Affairs Law*, op. cit. note 24, p. 489.

189   See 'Convention Established by the Council in Accordance with Article 34 of the Treaty on European Union, on Mutual Assistance in Criminal Matters between the Member States of the European Union', OJ EU C 197/3, 12 July 2000. See also 'Protocol, Established by the Council in Accordance with Article 34 of the Treaty on European Union, to the Convention on Mutual Assistance in Criminal Matters between the Member States of the European Union', OJ EU C 326/1, 21 November 2001. See also <http://www.consilium.eu.int/accords>.

190   See *European Convention on Mutual Assistance in Criminal Matters*, Strasbourg 20. IV. 1959, Council of Europe ETS no. 30.

191   See Peers, *EU Justice and Home Affairs Law*, op. cit. note 24, pp. 474 and 475.

Council of Europe.[192] Subsequently, the EU has adopted its own measures on mutual recognition, supplementing the 1959 Convention on Mutual Legal Assistance.[193]

Mutual legal assistance was agreed by the 1959 Convention on Mutual Legal Assistance by the Council of Europe.[194] It consists of gathering evidence in different European States when cross-border crimes have been committed. In 2000, another convention was adopted by the EU between EU Member States.[195] The 2000 Convention on Mutual Legal Assistance supplements the 1959 European Convention on Mutual Legal Assistance, the 1978 Protocol to the 1959 Convention and the Schengen Acquis.[196] According to the 2000 Convention on Mutual Legal Assistance, mutual legal assistance is an exchange of information between the judicial authorities of Member States where a crime has been committed.[197] This convention regulates all the procedures that Member States should follow when they need such assistance.[198] The 2000 Convention states that legal assistance can be requested when a crime has been committed or when there is an administrative infringement related to an offence which requires mutual legal assistance.[199] This is different from UNTOC, which only permits mutual legal assistance for offences covered by the convention itself, and not for administrative infringements connected with that offence.[200]

The 2000 Convention expands well beyond the 1959 Convention by covering cases that had not been covered before.[201] The 2000 Convention states that the requested Member State (the State which is processing a request) 'shall comply with the formalities and procedures expressly indicated by the requesting Member State'.[202] The reason for this provision is to enable the facilitation of the use of information obtained for evidence in the proceedings of the requesting Member

---

192　Ibid.

193　Ibid.

194　See *European Convention on Mutual Assistance in Criminal Matters*, op. cit. note 190. See also *Judicial Cooperation in the EU: The Role of Eurojust*', op. cit. note 140, p. 15.

195　See 'Convention Established by the Council in Accordance with Article 34 of the Treaty on European Union, on Mutual Assistance in Criminal Matters between the Member States of the European Union', op. cit. note 189.

196　Ibid.

197　Ibid.

198　See ibid., Arts 6 *et seq.*

199　See ibid., Art. 3(1). See also the comment on Art. 3 of the 'Explanatory Report on the Convention of 29 May 2000 on Mutual Assistance in Criminal Matters between the Member States of the European Union', OJ EU C 379/7.

200　See Art. 18 of the *United Nations Convention against Transnational Organized Crime* (UNTOC), A/RES/55/25, Doc. A/55/383, 8 January 2001.

201　See also the comment on Art. 3 of the 'Explanatory Report on the Convention of 29 May 2000 on Mutual Assistance in Criminal Matters between the Member States of the European Union', op. cit. note 199.

202　See Art. 4(1) of the 'Convention on Mutual Legal Assistance', op. cit. note 195.

State.[203] The Explanatory Report also specifies that the expression 'formalities and procedures' should be widely interpreted in order to gather as much evidence as possible to be used in proceedings of the requesting Member State.[204] This liberal approach towards mutual legal assistance is also confirmed by a new provision in the 2000 Convention which states that judicial authorities can communicate directly with each other.[205] This provision makes direct communication among EU Member States' judicial authorities a general rule, replacing the 1959 method which required requests for mutual legal assistance to be forwarded between Ministers of Justice.[206] Nevertheless, direct communication between the different judicial authorities can be rather complicated, due to those judicial authorities not knowing each others' legal systems. There are also problems with mutual legal assistance that are caused by lack of trust that must be resolved. One problem concerns the double criminality that 'remains a potential ground for rejecting requests when the measure requested is coercive'.[207] Another problem is the differing criminal proceedings in EU Member States.[208] Double criminality is not an obstacle to mutual legal assistance, because serious crime are mostly punished in the same manner throughout the EU. There are exceptions that are allowed by EU legislation in cases of assisting irregular migration without financial purposes.[209] As mentioned above, difficulties with mutual legal assistance more often involve differences between the criminal procedures of Member States.[210] As a result, when requests for mutual legal assistance have been made, the judicial authorities of the requested State may act in a different way compared to previous times.[211] Indeed, sometimes they do not fulfil the formalities indicated by the requesting State.[212]

The 2000 Convention may resolve these problems by mandating that once mutual legal assistance has been agreed, the requested State shall fulfil 'the

---

203   See the comment on Art. 4 of the 'Explanatory Report on the Convention of 29 May 2000 on Mutual Assistance in Criminal Matters between the Member States of the European Union', op. cit. note 199.

204   Ibid.

205   See Art. 6(1) of the 'Convention on Mutual Legal Assistance', op. cit. note 195.

206   See the comment on Art. 4 of the 'Explanatory Report on the Convention of 29 May 2000 on Mutual Assistance in Criminal Matters between the Member States of the European Union', op. cit. note 199.

207   See 'Final Report on the First Evaluation Exercise: Mutual Legal Assistance in Criminal Matters', OJ EU C 216/14, 1 August 2001.

208   Ibid.

209   Ibid. See also Chapter 5 of this book, where Italian and British law on smuggling of migrants and trafficking in human beings are compared. See also Art. 1(2) of 'Council Directive 2002/90/EC of 28 November 2002 Defining the Facilitation of Unauthorised Entry, Transit and Residence', OJ EU L 328/17, 5 December 2002.

210   See *Judicial Cooperation in the EU: The Role of Eurojust*, op. cit. note 140, p. 16.

211   See 'Final Report on the First Evaluation Exercise', op. cit. note 207.

212   Ibid.

formalities and procedures expressly indicated by the requesting Member State'.[213] There are also issues that the 2000 Convention should resolve. These issues are related to the bureaucratic hierarchy 'which slows the dispatch of requests for mutual assistance considerably even when the Member State's laws authorise prosecutors to establish and dispatch them themselves'.[214] In some cases, judicial authorities in the requested State require formalities that are unnecessary and should be avoided in order to speed up the process. It is evident why the Council recommended that Member States ratify the 2000 Convention, because it overcomes obstacles concerning mutual legal assistance. The Council also recommended that to improve mutual legal assistance, Member States should contact the EJN in order to offer co-operation. However, the Council has noted that the EJN is not well known by practitioners, so it will be necessary for Member States and the EU to familiarise themselves with the EJN. The 2001 Protocol also suggests that Eurojust should intervene[215] when the requesting State request for mutual legal assistance is not successfully satisfied.[216] By means of this protocol, the Council aims to reinforce the role of Eurojust and the EJN in mutual legal assistance, even when, as the Council supports, there are only direct communications between judicial authorities.[217]

It is important that the first step of ratification be taken if mutual legal assistance is to improve. At the moment Italy, Greece, Ireland and Luxemburg have not ratified this convention.[218] In addition Estonia, Greece, Italy, Ireland and Luxembourg have not ratified the 2001 Protocol.[219] In other words, the lack of ratification of the Mutual Legal Assistance Convention and Protocol by all EU Member States represents a first obstacle to the full application of the principle of 'extradite or prosecute'. In the sense that if one EU Member State decides not to extradite a suspected smuggler of migrants, for example, according to the 2000 Mutual Legal Assistance Convention, mutual legal assistance should be agreed with the requesting State.[220] Nevertheless, mutual legal assistance may be refused either because that State has not ratified the 2000 Convention on Mutual Assistance yet, or because of lack of trust, which was the reason why, as will be shown below, extradition on the basis of the European Arrest Warrant (EAW) Framework Decision was refused by the House of Lords and the Italian Court of

213 See Art. 4(1) of the 'Convention on Mutual Legal Assistance', op. cit. note 195.
214 Ibid.
215 See 'Council Act of 16 October 2001 Establishing, in Accordance with Article 34 of the Treaty on European Union, the Protocol to the Convention on Mutual Assistance in Criminal Matters between the Member States of the European Union', op. cit. note 189.
216 See ibid., Art. 10.
217 See 'Final Report on the First Evaluation Exercise', op. cit. note 207. See also Art. 6(1) of the 'Convention on Mutual Legal Assistance', op. cit. note 195.
218 See <http://www.consilium.eu.int/accords>.
219 Ibid.
220 See Arts 1 *et seq.* of ' Convention on Mutual Legal Assistance', op. cit. note 195.

Last Resort (Corte di Cassazione) in different cases. EU Member States have not ratified the 2000 Convention and its Protocol because this ratification would mean enabling EU Member States' law enforcement authorities to gather evidence in other EU Member States. In other words, the application of mutual legal assistance would require a high level of mutual trust.

In conclusion, mutual legal assistance could improve investigation of the cross-border crimes of smuggling of migrants and trafficking in human beings. However, the effectiveness of mutual legal assistance depends on Member States' mutual trust. If there is no mutual trust between EU Member States, mutual legal assistance may be very difficult to achieve.

Another way to gather evidence in EU Member States in order to facilitate exchange of evidence is the European Evidence Warrant (EEW).

The European Evidence Warrant

In 2003, the Commission proposed a Framework Decision on the European Evidence Warrant.[221] Three years later, the Council reached an agreement on the text of the proposed framework decision, and in December 2008 a new Framework Decision on the EEW was agreed.[222] The EEW 'shall coexist with existing legal instruments'[223] agreed between Member States, such as mutual legal assistance and the other measures on mutual assistance.[224] The EEW is: 'a judicial decision issued by a competent authority of a Member State with a view to obtaining objects, documents and data from another Member State'.[225] The EEW may be issued in relation to criminal proceedings:

> brought by, or to be brought before, a judicial authority in respect of a criminal offence under the national law of the issuing State; in case of administrative proceedings concerning acts that are punishable in the issuing State and in case of violations considered infringement of the rule of law in the issuing State.[226]

---

221   See *Proposal for a Council Framework Decision on the European Evidence Warrant for Obtaining Objects, Documents and Data for Use in Proceedings in Criminal Matters*, COM (2003) 688, 14 November 2003. See also Peers, *EU Justice and Home Affairs Law*, op. cit. note 24, p. 476.

222   See *Proposal for a Council Framework Decision on the European Evidence Warrant (EEW) for Obtaining Objects, Documents and Data for Use in Proceedings in Criminal Matters*, Council Doc. 11235/06, 10 July 2006. See also 'Council Framework Decision 2008/978/JHA of 18 December 2008 on the European Evidence Warrant for the Purpose of Obtaining Objects, Documents and Data for Use in Proceedings in Criminal Matters', OJ EU L 350/72, 30 December 2008.

223   See ibid., Art. 21(1).

224   Ibid.

225   See ibid., Art. 1(1), p. 3.

226   See ibid., Art. 5(a).

The EEW can also be issued when proceedings are brought by judicial authorities for acts which are violations of the rule of law, even if these breaches are not considered criminal offences. The EEW can be addressed to proceedings carried out by administrative authorities and in relation to criminal offences, administrative violation or infringements of the rule of law for which a legal person may be considered liable in the issuing State.[227] Nevertheless, it is only the issuing State that can decide whether the EEW can be issued.[228]

Moreover, the EEW cannot be issued in order to:

a. conduct interviews, take statements or initiate other types of hearing involving suspects, witnesses, experts or any other party;
b. carry out bodily examinations or obtain bodily material or biometric data directly from the body of any person, including DNA samples or fingerprints;
c. obtain information in real time such as through the interception of communications, covert surveillance or monitoring of bank accounts;
d. conduct analysis of existing objects, documents or data; and
e. obtain communications data retained by providers of a publicly available electronic communications service or a public communications network.[229]

The issuing of the EEW shall not be subject to double criminality 'unless it is necessary to carry out a search or seizure'.[230] Finally, Member States shall adopt the necessary measures to transpose the EEW Framework Decision by 11 January 2011.[231] The EEW Framework Decision and the Mutual Legal Assistance Convention can coexist for a transitional period. Subsequently, the EEW will replace the previous convention.

In conclusion, the EEW is capable of facilitating the exchange of evidence between EU Member States. The EU Mutual Legal Assistance Convention establishes the exchange of evidence on the basis of the law of the *requesting* State, while the EEW provides for the exchange of evidence on the basis of the law of the *issuing* State. This might speed up the issuing of the EEW should the law of the requesting authority be respected. There are some concerns in relation to the fact that a measure such as the EEW is adopted by a framework decision without the involvement of the European Parliament, contributing to the democratic deficit. Another problem associated with the EEW is that judicial authorities may issue documents containing personal information of individuals, thus disclosing personal data. Such an intrusive measure, it can be argued, should have been

---

227 See ibid., Art. 5(b, c, d).
228 See Art. 6(1) of the agreed text in ibid.
229 See ibid., Art. 4(2).
230 See ibid., Art. 14(1).
231 See ibid., Art. 23(1).

agreed by the European Parliament, as it might jeopardise the fundamental rights of individuals. As has been shown, the EEW may contribute to increasing judicial co-operation, but there are other measures that have a role as well.

Extradition and Recent Improvements

Extradition in the EU

A first Extradition Convention was agreed in 1957.[232] This convention needed to be reformed because it allowed States Parties the right to refuse extradition of their nationals.[233] Another provision in the 1957 Convention that made extradition difficult required double criminality as an essential element for granting extradition.[234] The principle of double criminality requires that for extradition to be granted, the act with which the accused is charged in the requesting state must also be considered a crime in the requested state.[235] The problems of national exception and double criminality were not resolved by the Benelux Treaty on Extradition and Mutual Assistance in Criminal Matters.[236] This convention, as Deen-Racsmany and Blekxtoon have pointed out, is even more restrictive than the 1957 Convention on Extradition because 'it lays down an *obligation* not to extradite'[237] and 'it fails to provide for a corresponding obligation to prosecute domestically'.[238] The Benelux Convention also required double criminality as an essential requirement for extradition,[239] and the Schengen Convention did not expressly abolish the exception of nationality.[240]

In 1995, Member States adopted a convention aimed at simplifying, improving and accelerating the extradition procedure, goals which the 1957 Convention failed to achieve.[241] Member States were aware that extradition was essential

---

232   See *European Convention on Extradition 1957*, ETS No. 24.

233   See ibid., Art. 6(1(a)).

234   See ibid., Art. 2(1).

235   See Plachta, M., 'European Arrest Warrant: Revolution in Extradition?', *European Journal of Crime, Criminal Law and Criminal Justice* 11:2 (2003), p. 185.

236   See *Benelux Treaty on Extradition and Mutual Assistance in Criminal Matters* (Benelux Convention), 616 UNTS 120 1962.

237   See Deen-Racsmany, Z., and Blekxtoon, R. (2005) 'The Decline of the Nationality Exception in European Extradition?', *European Journal of Crime, Criminal Law and Criminal Justice* 13:3, p. 324.

238   Ibid.

239   Ibid. See also Art. 2(1) of the Benelux Convention, op. cit. note 236.

240   See Title III, Chapter IV of the Schengen Convention, op. cit. note 11. See also Deen-Racsmany and Blekxtoon, 'The Decline of the Nationality Exception in European Extradition?', op. cit. note 237, p. 325.

241   See Preamble of 'Convention Drawn up on the Basis of Article K.3 of the Treaty on European Union, on Simplified Extradition Procedure between the Member States of the

to improving mutual legal assistance and mutual judicial co-operation. In 1992, statistics had shown that the extradition procedure was needlessly long even when the person concerned had not been detained or prosecuted for other reasons in the requested State.[242]

Another step forward in improving the of extradition procedure was made by a new convention adopted in 1996.[243] This convention aimed to facilitate extradition among Member States by specifying that the nationality exception could be used in only exceptional circumstances,[244] stating that extradition 'may not be refused on the ground that the person claimed is a national of a requested Member State'.[245] The 1996 Convention on Extradition was only an amending convention; it did not replace any of the previous conventions on extradition, in particular the 1957 Convention and the Schengen Acquis.[246]

Despite the stated goal of the 1996 Convention being to limit the use of the nationality exception to only exceptional circumstances, Member States frequently continued to refuse extradition on the basis of nationality. This is because the 1996 Convention contained a contradicting statement that: 'any Member State may declare that it will not grant extradition of its nationals or will authorize it only under certain specified conditions'.[247] This meant that Member States continued to have a general right to refuse to extradite their nationals under the 1996 Convention on Extradition. The argument against the exercise of this general right is that Member States have shared values, including similarities in their judicial systems,[248] making the refusal to extradite on the basis of nationality nonsensical.

The 1996 Convention on Extradition is more advanced than UNTOC because UNTOC does not attempt to limit the ability of Member States to refuse extradition of their nationals in any way.[249] One limitation of the 1996 Convention was its affirmation of the double criminality principle. This meant, as stated above, that

---

European Union', OJ EU C 78/2, 10 March 1995.

242 See 'Convention on Simplified Extradition Procedure between the Member States of the European Union: Explanatory Report', OJ EU C 375/4, 12 December 1996.

243 See 'Convention Drawn up on the Basis of Article K.3 of the Treaty on European Union, Relating to Extradition between the Member States of the European Union' (Convention on Extradition 1996), OJ EU C 313/12, 23 October 1996.

244 See Deen-Racsmany and Blekxtoon, 'The Decline of the Nationality Exception in European Extradition?', op. cit. note 237, p. 325. See also Art. 7 of the Convention on Extradition 1996, op. cit. note 243.

245 See ibid., Art. 7(1). See also the Explanatory Report, op. cit. note 246.

246 See Art. 1 of the Convention on Extradition 1996, op. cit. note 243. See also 'Convention Relating to Extradition between the Member States of the European Union: Explanatory Report (Text Approved by the Council on 26 May 1997)', OJ EU C 191/13, 23 June 1997.

247 See Art. 7(2) of the Convention on Extradition 1996, op. cit. note 243.

248 See also 'Convention Relating to Extradition between the Member States of the European Union: Explanatory Report', op. cit. note 246.

249 See Art. 16(10) UNTOC, op. cit. note 200.

an offender could only be extradited if the specific conduct was considered a crime by both the requested and requesting State, save for the exception of conspiracy and association to commit offences.[250] As has been demonstrated, the principle of double criminality can be an obstacle to judicial co-operation, and therefore should be abolished by the EU. The European Arrest Warrant Framework Decision has attempted to overcome this limitation.

To summarise, the 1996 Convention attempted to restrict the use of exception of nationality as the basis for refusing to extradite. Despite the intended purpose of the 1996 Convention, real improvement in the efficiency of the extradition procedure was not achieved until the European Arrest Warrant Framework Decision of 2002.

The European Arrest Warrant

The EAW replaced all the conventions on extradition that came before it, including Title III, Chapter 4 of the Schengen Convention entitled 'Extradition'.[251] The EAW was established in 2002 by Framework Decision 2002/584/JHA,[252] which states that:

> The European arrest warrant is a judicial decision issued by a Member State with a view to the arrest and surrender by another Member State of a requested person, for the purposes of conducting a criminal prosecution or executing a custodial sentence or detention order.[253]

The EAW is more effective than the European Convention on Extradition 1996 because the exception of nationality is only an option under specific circumstances, containing no contradictory statement as found in the 1996 Convention.[254] The framework decision states that the executing judicial authority has the discretion, not the obligation, to refuse the execution of the EAW when 'the requested person is staying in, or is a national or a resident of the executing Member State'.[255] However, as Deen-Racsmany and Blekxtoon have pointed out, the importance

---

250   See Arts 2 and 3 of the Convention on Extradition 1996, op. cit. note 243.
251   See Arts 59 *et seq.* of the Schengen Convention, op. cit. note 11.
252   See 'Council Framework Decision 2002/584/JHA of 13 June 2002 on the European Arrest Warrant and the Surrender Procedures between Member States', OJ EU L 190/1, 18 July 2002.
253   See ibid., Art. 1(1).
254   Compare Art. 7 of the 1996 Convention on Extradition, op. cit. note 243, with Art. 4(6) of Framework Decision 2002/584/JHA, op. cit. note 252. See also Deen-Racsmany and Blekxtoon, 'The Decline of the Nationality Exception in European Extradition?', op. cit. note 237.
255   See Art. 4(6) of Framework Decision 2002/584/JHA, op. cit. note 252.

of nationality remains relevant in the EAW Framework Decision.[256] Article 5(3) of the EAW contains a provision that allows the relevant authorities of the executed State, once one of their nationals has been convicted in the executing State, to request that individual to be returned to them 'in order to serve there the custodial sentence or detention order'.[257] It appears that it was the intention of the Member States to reduce the importance of nationality as an exception when they implemented the framework decision.[258] The reason for the refusal to abandon the nationality exception altogether could be the lack of trust that exists between EU Member States.[259] This can be caused by the different traditions, cultures, points of view, laws and procedures among Member States. This lack of trust is the main reason why Member States are reluctant to establish a single judicial area that would remove the need for any extradition procedure. Douglass-Scott has claimed that 'Establishing such trust is surely part of the more general task of building a feeling of solidarity within the EU'.[260] This solidarity does not exist in the EU, and mutual recognition has only been successful for the completion of the internal market, and not in the criminal area.[261] In the criminal area, there is no mutual trust or judicial recognition, and as Douglass-Scott has pointed out, even if there was, in the case of EAW there are other barriers that must be taken into account.[262]

One of these barriers, as mentioned above, is the principle of double criminality. Framework Decision 2002/584/JHA abolishes the need for double criminality for certain forms of serious crimes.[263] Trafficking in human beings and smuggling of migrants are included in the list of these crimes.[264] Therefore, in these cases double criminality should not be a problem. However, the total abolition of double criminality is not conceivable due to differing cultural norms among the Member States. For example abortion and euthanasia[265] are crimes in some Member States but legal in others, and must be protected by the principle of double criminality.[266] It can be argued that criminalisation should not be applied because criminalisation of a conduct that is not a crime in the requested State would be in breach with the principle of double jeopardy (*nullum crimen, nulla poena sine lege*), explicitly

---

256   See Deen-Racsmany and Blekxtoon, 'The Decline of the Nationality Exception in European Extradition?', op. cit. note 254, pp. 343 and 344.

257   Ibid.

258   See ibid., p. 344.

259   See Chapter 5 of this book.

260   See Douglass-Scott, S., 'The Rule of Law in the European Union: Putting the Security into the Area of Freedom, Security and Justice', *European Law Review* 29:2 (2004), p. 227.

261   See ibid., p. 228.

262   Ibid.

263   See Art. 2(2) of Framework Decision 2002/584/JHA, op. cit. note 252.

264   Ibid.

265   See Douglas-Scott, 'The Rule of Law in the European Union', op. cit. note 260, p. 225.

266   Ibid.

recognised by Article 7 ECHR.[267] Harmonisation of Member States' criminal laws in delicate subjects such as euthanasia and abortion would be too invasive of Member States' national sovereignty.

Alegre and Leaf have highlighted that the issues arising from the abolition of double criminality could be manifold, because the amount and nature of offences that could be categorised as criminal in individual Member States are plentiful.[268] Therefore, many conflicts of jurisdiction can arise.

In conclusion, as Plachta emphasised, the EAW represents a very important measure in order to simplify and accelerate trials.[269] Indeed, the framework decision states that the EAW 'shall be dealt with and executed as a *matter of urgency*'.[270] Moreover, the framework decision states that the final decision on the EAW's execution should normally follow 'within a period of 60 days after the arrest of the requested person'.[271] Secondly, the framework decision establishes that the time limit for surrendering the suspected person should be not more than ten days.[272] Therefore, the EAW may contribute to accelerating trials, and it may be an effective instrument against smuggling of migrants and trafficking in human beings. However, the EAW can be controversial with regard to some delicate areas such as abortion and euthanasia.

Certainly, double criminality should not be applied by Member States to crimes such as human trafficking and people smuggling because they are serious, as they jeopardise the life[273] and the dignity of millions of people by reducing them to slavery. Euthanasia could also be considered a way to preserve the dignity of people. However, this statement is more controversial, and this is confirmed by the fact that the EAW Framework Decision abolished double criminality for trafficking in human beings and smuggling of migrants.[274] In contrast, euthanasia is not in the list of crimes that do not require the application of double criminality.

---

267   See Art. 7 of *Convention for the Protection of Human Rights and Fundamental Freedoms* (ECHR), Rome, 4 November 1950, as amended by Protocol 11. See also Douglas-Scott, 'The Rule of Law in the European Union', op. cit. note 260, p. 226. See also Alegre, S., and Leaf, M., 'Mutual Recognition in European Judicial Cooperation: A Step Too Far Too Soon? Case Study – the European Arrest Warrant', *European Law Journal* 10:2 (2004), p. 208.

268   See ibid., pp. 208 and 209.

269   See Plachta, 'European Arrest Warrant: Revolution in Extradition?', op. cit. note 235, p. 188.

270   See Art. 17(1) of Framework Decision 2002/584/JHA, op. cit. note 252; emphasis added. See also Plachta, 'European Arrest Warrant: Revolution in Extradition?', op. cit. note 235, p. 188.

271   See Art. 17(3) of Framework Decision 2002/584/JHA, op. cit. note 252. See also Plachta, 'European Arrest Warrant: Revolution in Extradition?', op. cit. note 235, p. 188.

272   See Art. 24(1) of Framework Decision 2002/584/JHA, op. cit. note 252. See also Plachta, 'European Arrest Warrant: Revolution in Extradition?', op. cit. note 235, p. 188.

273   See Chapter 4 of this book.

274   See Art. 2(2) of Framework Decision 2002/584/JHA, op. cit. note 252.

In other words, the allocation of double criminality should only be exceptional, and the EU should agree solutions to ensure that all EU Member States fully apply the EAW.

It is logical to argue that the EAW Framework Decision should be changed in order to enhance judicial co-operation between EU Member States and to ensure that the EU is supreme in the criminal area, an aim that could be achieved when the Lisbon Treaty enters into force. For this purpose, it is important to stress that the changes in the EAW should be enacted by the ordinary legislative procedure, and the framework decision should be replaced by a directive, because the Lisbon Treaty will abolish them. Article 288 (ex Article 249) states: 'To exercise the Union's competences, the institutions shall adopt regulations, directives, decisions, recommendations and opinions.' As the difference between the EC Treaty and EU Treaty will not exist any more, this provision applies to the criminal area, and this means that measures related to this area will not no longer be adopted by framework decisions which do not entail direct effect, but by directives and the ordinary legislative procedure.

The extension of direct effect to the criminal area is very important.

Extension of Direct Effect to the European Arrest Warrant and to All Framework Decisions

European integration in the criminal area must be facilitated, otherwise measures such as the EAW Framework Decision may be interfered with by EU Member States. One possible negative consequence of interference on the part of the Member States is ever-increasing involvement of criminal organisations in cross-border crimes, which may never be countered effectively. It is important to emphasise that this framework decision is a very advanced measure. The EAW Framework Decision allows for the surrender of a criminal or suspected criminal when a serious criminal offence such as smuggling of migrants and trafficking in human beings has been committed. The surrender is permitted even when the principles of double criminality and national exception have not been met. Specifically:

> The European arrest warrant is a judicial decision issued by a Member State with a view to the arrest and surrender by another Member State of a requested person, for the purposes of conducting a criminal prosecution or executing a custodial sentence or detention order.[275]

Paragraph 12 of the EAW Framework Decision states that: 'This Framework Decision does not prevent a Member State from applying its constitutional rules relating to due process.'[276] This means that if an executing Member State 'fears' that compliance with the EAW Framework Decision may create conflict with its own

---

275 See ibid., Art. 1(1).
276 See ibid., para. 12.

national constitution – in cases of double criminality, for example – it can refuse to surrender a suspected criminal to the executed Member State. Paragraph 12 of the EAW Framework Decision can be used by EU Member States as an excuse so that they may apply the national exception and the principle of double criminality even when serious transnational crimes have occurred. The European Commission has pointed out that while Member States have made improvements since 2005 to a satisfactory level, there remains work to be done on the transposition of the EAW Framework Decision. There are still problems that need to be overcome[277] which are capable, as Mackarel has argued, of again leading to national constitutions impeding full compliance of Member States with the EAW.[278] This raises the question: What is the point of agreeing to an advanced measure such as the EAW if EU Member States are able to use numerous excuses not to comply with it? In order to prevent Member States creating obstacles to compliance with the EAW Framework Decision, paragraph 12 should be amended to state that 'This framework decision requires that Member States adapt their constitutions to this instrument, in order to accelerate the extradition in the EU area.' If such an amendment was agreed to, it would mean that the EAW Framework Decision would now fully incorporate the principle of mutual recognition between Member States which is 'the 'cornerstone of judicial cooperation'.[279] Nevertheless, mutual recognition and mutual judicial co-operation presuppose that EU Member States trust each other's legal systems. If EU Member States were to agree to set aside their national constitutions, it would require that they trust each other. One way to enhance mutual trust between the Member States is for them to agree to common rules on fair trials.[280] The importance of this measure is that it would allow the EAW Framework Decision to become a vital tool in the fight against crimes such as smuggling of migrants and trafficking in human beings. In 1991, Falcone argued that co-operation between different States in criminal investigations was crucial in the fight against criminal organisations.[281] Falcone co-operated with Canada, the USA, France, Great Britain and Germany, and through his work, Italians were able to learn what the Mafia was and how it was structured.[282] Falcone argued that traditional extradition based on the principle of double criminality had often prevented the affiliates of the Mafia being extradited from abroad, from countries

---

277   See *Report from the Commission on the Implementation Since 2005 of the Council Framework Decision of 13 June 2002 on the European Arrest Warrant and the Surrender Procedures between Member States*, COM (2007) 407 final, 11 July 2007, p. 8.

278   See Mackarel, M., 'The European Arrest Warrant – the Early Years: Implementing and Using the Warrant', *European Journal of Crime, Criminal Law and Criminal Justice* 15:1 (2007), p. 49. See also this same article for a detailed description of obstacles that some Member States have created in the application of the EAW across the EU.

279   See para. 6 of Council Framework Decision 2002/584/JHA, op. cit. note 252.

280   Enhancing mutual trust between Member States legal systems is dealt with in greater detail later in this chapter.

281   See Falcone, G., *Cose di Cosa Nostra* (RCS Rizzoli Libri, 1991), p. 139.

282   See ibid., pp. 149–71.

like France. [283] Criminals would often decide to co-operate with Falcone.[284] This was the case in 1983, when a suspect named Francesco Gasparini was found in France with 6 kilograms of heroin.[285] The fact that Gasparini could not be extradited because the crime of associating with the Mafia was not recognised by French criminal law led to the loss of important evidence.[286] This case should be taken into consideration when deciding whether the third pillar should be more or less integrated than the EC Treaty. Preventing a similar scenario to that in the *Gasparini* case from taking place again would require that the principle of double criminality not be applied in rigid a way. An example might clarify the issue: when the crime assisting irregular migration without the purpose of financial gain has been committed, Member States should not surrender the person who has committed this offence to the requesting State. In such a circumstance, the principle of *favor rei* should be applied. *Favor rei* requires that the defendant remain in the territory where apprehended if the offence is of a minor grade.[287] Moreover, the entire circumstances of the case should be taken into consideration. If the offence is committed for justifiable reasons or they can contribute to the arrest of the criminals behind the smuggling of migrants or human trafficking, they should not be criminalised at all. The purpose of this approach is to enable the EU and its Member States to ensure that EU criminal measures are effective. This again would require the setting aside of national constitutions if necessary in order to defeat organised crime.

Despite the need for effectiveness, the EU Treaty expressly states that EU measures in the criminal area, such as the EAW Framework Decision, do not produce direct effects.[288] Understanding the connection between direct effect and supremacy is important in demonstrating how effective implementation of an EU measure is blocked. Should EU supremacy simply mean that EU law criminal provisions prevail over conflicting national provisions, even though direct effect does not apply?

Dougan defines the meaning of supremacy by explaining the two concepts of Primacy Model and Trigger Model.[289] The Primacy Model considers an EC provision supreme when it prevails over a national provision, resulting in the

---

283   See ibid., p. 141.

284   Ibid.

285   Ibid.

286   Ibid.

287   EU law also permits Member States to apply more favourable provisions in case of assisting irregular migration without a financial aim. See Art. 1(2) of 'Council Directive 2002/90/EC of 28 November Defining the Facilitation of Unauthorised Entry, Transit and Residence', OJ EC L 328/17, 5 December 2002.

288   See Art. 34(2)(b) TEU, op. cit. note 8.

289   See Dougan, M., 'When Worlds Collide! Competing Visions of the Relationship between Direct Effect and Supremacy', *Common Market Law Review* 44 (2007), p. 932.

incompatible national provision being set aside because it is hierarchically inferior to the said EC provision.[290] Dougan also points out that:

> For these purposes, the principle of direct effect is neither necessary nor even relevant: its threshold criteria have no particular function to perform, since the question is not whether the relevant Community norm is clear, precise and unconditional; but merely whether there exists an incompatibility between a rule of Community law and a rule of domestic law.[291]

In contrast, the Trigger Model means that a national provision is only set aside when an EC provision: 'has been rendered cognizable before the domestic courts, by satisfying the threshold criteria for enjoying direct effect'.[292] Lenaerts and Corthaut argue in favour of the Primacy Model, basing their assertion on the Court of Justice's decision in *Costa* v. *E.N.E.L.*, which shows that 'the real concern is consistency'.[293] What is important in EC law, and by extension in EU law, is that these laws produce a result that 'cannot be thwarted by incompatible national measures'.[294] The result could mean conferring rights upon individuals, but it could also entail 'an obligation on a government to create the conditions under which rights are granted to individuals',[295] as it is for directives where the criteria of precision, clarity and unconditionality have proved to be 'highly relative'.[296] Direct effect applicability is important, in that it confers rights that otherwise would not exist in the national legal order.[297] In addition, the principle of supremacy of EU law is necessary to avoid inconsistency between EU law and national law, and between EU law and international law.[298] An example of how this works is *Germany and Denmark* v. *Commission*,[299] where it was not the intention of the parties to show that the regulation in question granted rights to individuals. They only wanted to check whether the regulation was adopted in accordance with the correct procedures.[300] Indeed:

---

290   See ibid., p. 933.

291   Ibid.

292   See ibid., p. 934.

293   See Art. I-6 of the Constitutional Treaty, op. cit. note 95. See also Lenaerts, K., and Corthaut, T., 'Of Birds and Hedges: The Role of Primacy in Invoking Norms of EU Law', *European Law Review* 31:3 (2006), p. 290.

294   See ibid., p. 291.

295   Ibid.

296   Ibid.

297   Ibid.

298   See ibid., p. 297.

299   See Joined Cases C-465/02 and 466/02 *Germany and Denmark* v. *Commission* [2005] ECR I-0000-Court of Justice. See also Lenaerts and Corthaut, 'Of Birds and Hedges', op. cit. note 293, p. 297.

300   Ibid.

Nobody would claim that Germany and [D]enmark were precluded from relying on the basic regulation to obtain judicial review of the contested Commission act, until they convinced the Court that the provisions of the basic regulation ... they relied on were sufficiently clear, precise and unconditional.[301]

Furthermore, in *Wells*,[302] Mrs Wells was not interested in determining whether the directive concerned conferred rights upon individuals by seeing whether it was clear, precise and unconditional. Mrs Wells was only interested in checking whether the directive was binding on the government.[303] In any case, as Peers pointed out:

a detailed analysis of the case law to date indicates that, despite the best efforts of the high priests of European integration, the legal system established by the Third Pillar cannot sufficiently ensure an effective and uniform application of EU law or an adequate system of judicial control of the legality of EU measures. Such 'salvation' can only be found within the core Community legal order.[304]

The Court of Justice ruled on the third pillar, and made its best efforts to ensure judicial protection for individuals.[305] In *Spain* v. *Eurojust*, it stated that although the acts of Eurojust 'are not included in the list of acts the legality of which the Court may review'[306] under Article 230 EC Treaty, it reached the conclusion that in order to respect the rule of law, the acts of Eurojust are not exempt from judicial review.[307] The Advocate General also stated that: 'there is no obstacle preventing the Community system of law and the guarantees deriving from it from being extended to the European Union'.[308] The Advocate General stated that 'the rules and arrangements for reviewing legality'[309] in the EC and EU Treaties are not identical because the EC and the EU 'pursue, in part, distinct objectives and are subject to different conditions'.[310] However, the Advocate General further pointed out that:

---

301 Lenaerts and Corthaut, 'Of Birds and Hedges', op. cit. note 293, p. 290.

302 See Case C-201/02 *Wells* [2004] ECR I-723-Court of Justice.

303 See ibid., para. 33. See also Lenaerts and Corthaut, 'Of Birds and Hedges', op. cit. note 293, p. 300.

304 See Peers, S., 'Salvation Outside the Church: Judicial Protection in the Third Pillar after the *Pupino* and *Segi* Judgements', *Common Market Law Review* 44 (2007), p. 885.

305 See for example Case C-160/03 *Spain* v. *Eurojust* [2005] ECR I-2077-Court of Justice. For a better analysis of this case, see Peers, 'Salvation Outside the Church', op. cit. note 304, pp. 888–90.

306 See Case C-160/03, op. cit. note 305, para. 37.

307 See ibid., paras 41 and 42.

308 See ibid., para. 17 of the Opinion.

309 See ibid., para. 19 of the Opinion.

310 Ibid.

Article 35 EU must be interpreted as enabling certain applicants to seek the annulment of any measures adopted in the context of Title XVI which produce legal effects vis-à-vis third party.[311]

In any case, it must also be pointed out that at other times in the case law, EU courts have issued more restrictive judgments. For instance, in *Segi*,[312] the Court of First Instance stated that the Court of Justice's competence in the third pillar is exhaustively listed in Article 46 TEU:[313]

It follows from Article 46 EU that, in the context of Title VI of the EU Treaty, the only judicial remedies envisaged are contained in Article 35(1), (6) and (7) EU, and comprise the reference for a preliminary ruling, the action for annulment and the procedure for settling disputes between Member States.[314]

When interpreting the words of this judgment, it suggests that individuals cannot rely on third pillar measures because Article 35 TEU does not grant them this possibility. Therefore, if individuals cannot rely on framework decisions because they do not entail direct effect, the EU cannot be considered to have supremacy in the criminal area. The reason is that it is unclear what national provisions EU Member States should set aside if the EU norms in conflict with them are not recognisable. As Dougan pointed out in relation to the EC Treaty, which can also be applied to the EU Treaty, a judicial remedy in EC law 'presupposes the existence of an identifiable Community norm against which we can judge the validity of the relevant domestic rules'.[315] Dougan also emphasised that an EC provision is justiciable if it entails direct effect – meaning, as stated above, that it is clear, precise and unconditional.[316]

Therefore, the first objective to achieve in the EU criminal area should be to extend the direct effect to criminal measures such as framework decisions, or better, to replace them with directives, as the Lisbon Treaty now requires. The adoption of directives, and thus the extension of direct effect to the criminal area, would require that EU Member States set aside national provisions in conflict with recognisable and therefore justiciable EU law. The result would mean that the EU has supremacy in the criminal area.

---

311   See ibid., para. 21 of the Opinion.
312   See Case T-338/02 *Segi and Others* [2004] ECR II-1647-Court of Justice.
313   See ibid., para. 35. See also Art. 46 of the Constitutional Treaty, op. cit. note 293.
314   See Case T-338/02, op. cit. note 312, para. 36.
315   See Dougan, 'When Worlds Collide!', op. cit. note 289, p. 941.
316   Ibid.

Reforming the European Arrest Warrant Framework Decision by Setting Aside National Constitutions

The extension of direct effect in the criminal area does not change the fact that EU Member States can refuse to extradite a known or suspected criminal on the basis of paragraph 12 of the EAW Framework Decision. The EAW Framework Decision permits the executing Member State to refuse extradition if there is the possibility of violating the principle of due process in the executed Member State. By choosing to refuse the request, the executing Member State would not find itself in conflict with EU law. There is no conflict that would trigger the primacy of EU law over national law. This is based on the assumption that the EU criminal area was subject to the principles of supremacy which are intended to be an extension of direct effect to criminal measures such as framework decisions.

Is it correct to interpret the EAW Framework Decision as giving Member States wide latitude in deciding whether or not to execute a warrant if other Member States' rules would amount to a breach of due process as protected in the executing States' national law? Should the definition of EU supremacy also include the setting aside of national constitutions if they prevent the EAW's application? Should individuals rely on framework decisions even when there is a conflict between them and national constitutions? The answer is affirmative, because criminal organisations are transnational in nature, so the fight against them requires that EU measures in the criminal area be fully applied by all EU Member States in order to be effective. As a result, it would be desirable to amend paragraph 12 of the EAW Framework Decision in the way indicated above.

EU Member States may agree to set aside their national constitutions if they trust each other. One way to achieve this goal is by agreeing on common rules in the pursuit of fair trials. At the moment, concrete legislative measures on fair trials have not been adopted. There are only Commission proposals on the implementation of this principle,[317] although progress has been made by the Council, which adopted important framework decisions on mutual judicial recognition and trials *in absentia*.[318] The European Commission has also pointed out that there is no compliance with the ECHR, demonstrated by the fact that there are too many

---

317   See *Proposal for a Council Framework Decision on Certain Procedural Rights in Criminal Proceedings Throughout the European Union*, COM (2004) 328, 28 April 2004; *Green Paper on Mutual Recognition of Non-custodial Pre-trial Supervision Measures*, COM (2004) 562, 17 August 2004; *Communication from the Commission to the Council and the European Parliament: Communication on the Mutual Recognition of Judicial Decisions in Criminal Matters and the Strengthening of Mutual Trust between Member States*, COM (2005) 195. 19 May 2005. See also *Green Paper on the Presumption of Innocence*, COM (2006) 174, 26 April 2006; *Proposal for a Council Framework Decision on the European Supervision Order in Pre-trial Procedures between Member States of the European Union*, COM (2006) 468, 29 August 2006.

318   An analysis of these measures will be given later in this chapter.

applications before the European Court of Human Rights (Strasbourg Court). The amount of applications brought before the Strasbourg Court grew by over 500 percent between 1993 and 2000.[319] The EU should adopt legislative measures on fair trials that are intended to contribute to a full application of the ECHR in EU Member States. The minimum standards on fair trials that the EU adopts should not be lower than those established by the ECHR. If standards drop below the ones provided by the ECHR, as Peers emphasises,[320] it will result in Member States possibly making the assumption that they can 'get away with' the lower EU standards.[321] Moreover, common rules on fair trials should be based on the ECHR, because the EU Treaty states that: 'the Union shall respect fundamental rights, as guaranteed by the European Convention for the Protection of Human Rights and Fundamental Freedoms'.[322] It could be that by the time concrete legislative measures on fair trials are adopted, mutual trust between EU Member States have reached a point where they could foresee themselves setting aside their national constitutions in order to comply with EU measures in the criminal area. In this way, it would become possible for individuals to rely entirely on EU criminal measures such as framework decisions. Nevertheless, it is important that similar changes be adopted with the approval of the European Parliament. However, the EU could claim supremacy in the criminal area without its involvement, if EU supremacy is intended as extension of direct effect to third-pillar measures.

Enhancing the Role of the European Parliament to Strengthen EU Measures Such as the European Arrest Warrant in the Criminal Area

The European Parliament's role is a separate issue from EU supremacy concerning the legal effect of EU law, because the Court of Justice has never linked the issue with the level of involvement of the European Parliament. This is demonstrated by the Court of Justice's jurisprudence. Back when *Van Gend en Loos* and *Costa* were first decided, the European Parliament had very limited power and there was only a brief reference in these two cases to it. In their decision in *Van Gend en Loos*,[323] the court stressed that the objective of the customs union are relevant to individuals. Further, the court explained that individuals can claim their rights because the Preamble of the Treaty refers not only to governments, but also to people. The court then referred to 'the establishment of institutions',[324] and 'furthermore',[325]

---

319   See COM (2004) 328, op. cit. note 317, p. 3.

320   See Peers, S., 'Rights of Criminal Suspects and EU Law', *Statewatch*, <http://www.statewatch.org/news/2007/apr/Statewatch-analysis-crim-proced.pdf>.

321   Ibid.

322   See Art. 6(2) TEU, op. cit. note 8.

323   See Case 26/62 *Van Gend & Loos* v. *Netherlands Inland Revenue Administration* [1963] ECR 3-Court of Justice.

324   Ibid.

325   Ibid.

to the involvement of the nationals of Member States in the European Parliament and the Economic and Social Committee – this is in addition to the role of the court under Article 177 (now Article 234 of the EC Treaty). In *Costa*,[326] the court referred to the EC Treaty, which 'has created its own legal system'[327] 'of unlimited duration, having its own institutions, its own personality, its own legal capacity and capacity of representation on the international plane'.[328] This is a legal system where Member States have transferred their powers to the European Community in limited fields. However, there is no reference to the European Parliament's decision-making powers as such, and only an ancillary reference in *Van Gend en Loos*.

In key cases concerning the power of the European Parliament, such as *Les Verts*,[329] *Chernobyl*[330] and *Titanium Dioxide*,[331] the court does not make reference to the principles of supremacy and direct effect. In *Les Verts*, the court recognised the European Parliament's powers 'to determine its own internal organization given to it by the Treaty'.[332] Moreover, in *Chernobyl* the court recognised its own duty to ensure that the prerogatives of the European Parliament, described as 'one of the elements of the institutional balance created by the Treaties',[333] are respected.[334] In *Titanium Dioxide*, the court emphasised the importance of the co-operation procedure in the decision-making process.[335] What is common in all these cases is that the principle of direct effect is never mentioned. Can the effectiveness of EC/EU law be linked to how great a role the European Parliament plays in the process? If this were so, it would follow that EC measures in areas such as the common commercial policy would have less legal weight than EC Acts in other areas. This is not the case. In fact, the common commercial policy is one of the Community's activities in order to establish a common market.[336] Therefore, it can be concluded that the decision-making power of the European Parliament is a separate legal issue from the legal effect of EC/EU law. EC/EU supremacy may exist in areas such as the criminal area, where the European Parliament has only a marginal role. At the moment, the European Parliament has a mere consultative role in the criminal area, and a right to be informed by the presidency of the Commission

---

326   See Case 6/64 *Costa* v. *E.N.E.L.* [1964] ECR 1194-Court of Justice.
327   Ibid.
328   Ibid.
329   See Case 294/83 *Parti écologiste 'Les Verts'* v. *European Parliament* [1986] ECR 1339-Court of Justice.
330   Case C-70/88 *European Parliament* v. *Council of the European Communities (Chernobyl)* [1990] ECR I-2041-Court of Justice.
331   See Case C-300/89 *Commission of the European Communities v Council of the European Communities.* [1991] ECR I-2867-Court of Justice.
332   See Case 294/83, op. cit. note 329, para. 44.
333   See Case C-70/88, op. cit. note 330, para. 21.
334   See ibid., esp. paras 21–5.
335   See Case C-300/89, op. cit. note 331, para. 20.
336   See, respectively, Arts 2 and 3(1)(b) TEU, op. cit. note 8.

regarding discussions regarding the criminal area.[337] It can be argued that it might not be necessary to enhance the European Parliament's powers in the criminal area. Such an argument would be based on finding it sufficient to extend direct effect to EU measures in the criminal area as a means of integration. This extension might be inadequate in the fight against criminal organisations if a cultural and moral movement against them is not constructed. EU citizens and residents could create this movement in a response to learning that criminal organisations based in one Member State can affect citizens residing in other Member States, as shown above. Once EU citizens and residents have realised this, they may pressure the EU to adopt adequate measures in the criminal area by electing representatives to the European Parliament who desire to remove any barriers that may impede correct compliance with EU measures in the criminal area. EU citizens would be moved to push their European Parliament's representatives to adopt common measures such as fair trials, which would enhance mutual trust. The fight against criminal organisations would be more effective, making these criminal organisations appear less intimidating and more vulnerable before EU citizens and residents.

As stated above, the Lisbon Treaty will allow the Council and the European Parliament to adopt measures to fight against cross-border crimes by the ordinary legislative procedure. The national parliaments would also be involved in the activities of the EU, including the criminal area.[338] This is because the Lisbon Treaty states that Commission consultation documents must be forwarded directly by the Commission to national parliaments. The Commission must also send to national parliaments draft legislative Acts sent to the European Parliament and the Council.[339] Moreover, one of the Protocols of the Lisbon Treaty states that national parliaments can send their reasoned opinions on the draft legislative Acts.[340] The protocol also states that: 'The European Parliament and national Parliaments shall together determine the organisation and promotion of effective and regular interparliamentary cooperation within the Union.'[341] The Lisbon Treaty will also allow measures in the criminal area to be taken if at least nine Member States launch enhanced co-operation.[342] From a pragmatic point of view, this measure on enhanced co-operation will ensure that if nine Member States agree with a criminal measure, it will be adopted. However, this provision risks creating two different European Unions – one more advanced than the other. Those citizens and residents living in Member States that do not agree with one particular EU criminal measure would not enjoy the same benefits as those living in a Member State which launched enhanced co-operation. Reports have indicated

---

337   See ibid., Art. 39.

338   See 'Protocol (No. 1) on the Role of National Parliaments in the European Union', Lisbon Treaty, op. cit. note 107.

339   See, respectively, ibid., Arts 1 and 2.

340   See ibid., Art. 3.

341   See ibid., Art. 9.

342   See ibid., Art. 20(2).

that criminal organisations in the EU take advantage of the fact that there are: 'discrepancies between EU laws and national legislations in committing among others environmental crime and high technology crime'.[343] Allowing enhanced co-operation on criminal measures to be launched by only nine Member States, which can cause fragmentation by leaving all the others out, could create opportunities on which organised crime could capitalise. For this reason, it would be better to enhance the role of national parliaments in the criminal area by giving them the authority to monitor the actions of European institutions, including the European Parliament. This should be the approach, rather than adopting a measure to launch enhanced co-operation with only the approval of nine Member States. In any case, the ratification of the Lisbon Treaty is welcome (apart from the limitations presented by the provisions on launched co-operation), because it makes for greater integration in the EU criminal area due to the fact that amendments to the Lisbon Treaty are based on the EU Constitutional Treaty.[344] Framework decisions will disappear, while regulations, directives and decisions will be retained. There is hope that these reforms will support the introduction of direct effect and supremacy in the criminal area, amendments of the EAW Framework Decision, and a more influential role for the European Parliament in the criminal area. This would afford the European Parliament the ability to adopt measures establishing the conditions under which national constitutions could be set aside, and concrete legislative measures on fair trials.

To summarise, EU supremacy and EU integration in the criminal area might only consist of extending the direct effect to EU criminal measures such as framework decisions. However, this reform might not be enough in the fight against criminal organisations, which requires the creation of a popular cultural and moral movement against them. For this cultural and moral movement to be effective, EU citizens would have to advocate for greater involvement of the European Parliament in the criminal area through the use of the co-legislating procedure. Once this has been achieved, EU citizens, through their European Parliament representatives, should push for the adoption of measures on common rules such as fair trials that protect human rights. Conflicting national constitutions should be set aside if they conflict with the objectives of the EU in the criminal area. Now that the Lisbon Treaty has entered into force, criminal measures will be adopted by the Parliament and the Council acting together.

Reforms are necessary and can be achieved now that the Lisbon Treaty has been ratified. With the passage of the Lisbon Treaty, there is an opportunity for reinforcing mutual judicial recognition by strengthening mutual trust between EU Member States' judicial authorities.

---

343   See Council of European Union Doc. 13788/1/05 2005.

344   See Peers, S., 'Statewatch Analysis: EU Reform Treaty Analysis 1: JHA Provisions', *Statewatch*, 2 August 2007, <http://www.statewatch.org/news/2007/aug/eu-reform-treaty-jha-analysis-1.pdf>.

Mutual Judicial Recognition

Suggestions on How to Resolve Conflicts of Jurisdiction in Criminal Proceedings

Commission's proposal in the short term   Mutual judicial recognition is fundamental for the effective operation of the EAW. Framework Decision 2002/584/JHA states that: 'Member States shall execute any European arrest warrant on the basis of the principle of mutual judicial recognition'.[345] Mutual judicial recognition would require all other EU Member States to accept judicial decisions issued in another Member State.[346] The principle of mutual judicial recognition requires a high standard of mutual trust between Member States' judicial authorities. The Mutual Recognition Programme requires that Member States try to resolve issues related to conflicts of jurisdiction when one or more States seem to have jurisdiction over a single crime.[347] The solution proposed concerns Eurojust, which should facilitate co-ordination between Member States in order to resolve conflicts of jurisdiction.[348] It is possible for Eurojust to fulfil this task because the Council Decision that establishes it states that Eurojust can request the competent authorities of Member States to start investigations or prosecutions based on which Member State it feels is in the best position to do so.[349]

The Commission offered some guidance as to how to ensure that mutual recognition is constructed in EU Member States' criminal proceedings.[350] The Commission suggested that EU measures aimed at resolving conflicts of jurisdiction could be adopted in the form of framework decisions. These measures would be based on Article 31(1)(d) EU Treaty, which states that common action on judicial co-operation in criminal matters shall include 'preventing conflicts of jurisdiction between Member States'.[351] The Commission also made the suggestion that if necessary, Article 31(1)(c) EU Treaty could be taken into consideration as

---

345   See Art. 1(2) of Framework Decision 2002/584/JHA, op. cit. note 252.

346   See Jimeno-Bulnes, M., 'European Judicial Cooperation in Criminal Matters', *European Law Journal* 9:5 (2003), p. 623.

347   See the Introduction of 'Programme of Measures to Implement the Principle of Mutual Judicial Recognition of Decisions in Criminal Matters, 2001/C 12/02', OJ EU C12/10 2001, 15 January 2001, para. 2.3.

348   Ibid.

349   See *Commission Staff Working Document: Annex to the Green Paper on Conflicts of Jurisdiction and the Principle of Ne Bis in Idem in Criminal Proceedings*, SEC (2005) 1767, 23 December 2005, p. 23. See in particular Arts 6(a), 7(a) and 8 of Council Decision 2002/187/JHA, op. cit. note 135.

350   See *Green Paper on Conflicts of Jurisdiction and the Principle of* Ne Bis in Idem *in Criminal Proceedings*, COM (2005) 696, 23 December 2005.

351   See Art. 31(1)(d) of *Consolidated Version of the Treaty Establishing the European Community*, C 321 E/1, 29 December 2006. See also COM (2005) 696, op. cit. note 350, pp. 3 and 4.

a complementary basis to ensure 'compatibility in rules applicable in the Member States, as may be necessary to improve judicial cooperation'.[352]

On the basis of these provisions, the Commission proposed the creation of a mechanism for the choice of jurisdiction, 'aiming to allocate cases to an appropriate jurisdiction'.[353] For this purpose, two essential prerequisites must be met. One would be to ensure that the competent authorities are aware of criminal proceedings initiated in other Member States. In order to achieve this, the competent authorities would be permitted or obliged to exchange this information. The other prerequisite is to ensure that the competent authorities refrain from commencing prosecution or stopping an existing one when the same case is being prosecuted in another Member State. The result may be that Member States in this way would risk violating the principle of legality, which states that the competent authorities are obliged to prosecute any case that is within their competence. Nevertheless, the Commission pointed out that even if the principle of legality can be part of national constitutions, an exception to this principle could be agreed to in the future. This exception might provide that in the area of freedom, security and justice, the principle of legality is respected when the competent authorities of another EU Member State prosecute the case.

The Commission also explains that three procedural steps should follow when the prerequisites have been met. The first step would be ensuring that EU Member States interested in participating in the process of choosing the most appropriate jurisdiction for a case be informed of the process. The EU could adopt measures stating that either the prosecuting authorities, the judicial authorities, the law enforcement authorities or the investigating authorities (this depends on the particular features of the criminal judicial system of an individual EU Member State) of the initiating Member State shall inform the competent authorities of other interested Member States. Having been informed, the EU Member States would be required to communicate to the initiating state whether they have an interest in the case, otherwise the initiating Member State would be allowed to continue the prosecution of the case without further consultation, subject to the emergence of new facts that could change the scenario.[354]

If the competent authorities of two or more Member States show an interest in prosecuting the same case, they should consult with one another to decide which state is in a better position to prosecute that particular case. In this phase, the competent authorities might ask for Eurojust's assistance. When the best location to prosecute has been decided, the competent authorities of the designated EU Member State would initiate or continue the prosecution of the case in accordance with their national law. In addition, the competent authorities of the designated Member State could negotiate an agreement with the authorities of the interested

---

352   See Art. 31(1)(c) of C 321 E/1, op. cit. note 351. See also COM (2005) 696, op. cit. note 350, p. 4.

353   See also ibid., p. 4.

354   See ibid., p. 5.

EU Member States in order to ensure legal certainty by avoiding the possible reopening of the issue.

The third step is to be followed where an agreement between the interested Member States is not forthcoming and a settlement is needed. For this purpose, a body at EU level would act as a mediator, and the Commission proposed that Eurojust could take this role. The Commission also suggested that it might be beneficial to create a board or panel composed of senior national prosecutors and judges. A good suggestion would be to appoint criminal lawyers to this board or panel, but not the defence of the accused person. The reason for this is to achieve a more objective decision by supporting the involvement of three different perspectives (judges, prosecutors and lawyers). Including defence counsels of the accused would not be appropriate, because they may lack the necessary impartiality. In order to support transparency, the defence should, at the very least, be informed of the procedure in order to guarantee the fundamental rights of the accused. This step could be initiated on the request of any EU Member State which is interested in prosecuting the case. After this mediation, any dispute should be resolved.[355] In any case, Member States have to respect the principle of *ne bis in idem*.

Criteria for determining jurisdiction in the short term   The Commission has argued that there should be no single criterion in determining jurisdiction, because each case is unique.[356] The decision on who has jurisdiction when deciding in which Member State to try a case 'must be based on the particularities and the specific facts of the case at hand'.[357]

An important criterion in reaching such a decision is territoriality, because 'a prosecution should take place in the jurisdiction where the majority of the criminality occurred or where the majority of the loss was sustained'.[358] This criterion is important to consider, as the principle is widely recognised among EU Member States.[359]

Another criterion to determine jurisdiction should take into account the main residence of the defendant.[360] The nationality of the defendant might also be important if specific circumstances indicate that the defendant has a closer relation with the place of their nationality rather than with their place of residence.[361]

Another criterion takes into consideration the victims' interests when there is a concurrence between the criminal proceeding and civil or administrative actions for compensation.[362] The rights of victims should be balanced with those

---

355   See ibid., p. 6.
356   See SEC (2005) 1767, op. cit. note 349, p. 35.
357   Ibid.
358   See ibid., p. 36.
359   See ibid., pp. 36 and 37.
360   See ibid., p. 38.
361   Ibid.
362   Ibid.

of defendants.[363] In order to achieve this balance, the victims' interests should not be considered a primary criterion, but a second- or third-ranking criterion.[364]

The State's interests and criteria related to the efficiency and rapidity of the proceedings might also be taken into consideration when determining jurisdiction.[365] Eurojust has pointed out that 'time should not be the leading factor in deciding which jurisdiction should prosecute …'.[366] Efficiency and rapidity of the proceedings could be ensured by basing the decision on who has jurisdiction on where the most important items of evidence are, or where the presence of the suspect at the hearings is guaranteed, for instance.[367]

The competent authorities have to place greater priority on some criteria rather than others when determining jurisdiction.[368] This prioritisation has to take into account a wide array of interests.[369] The Commission pointed out that there are no rigid standards to follow, meaning that the competent authorities can decide which criteria to choose on a case-by-case basis when exercising their discretion.[370] The Commission suggested following the approach of the Framework Decision on Terrorism,[371] which considers territoriality as the first factor to be considered. The reason for this is due to the territoriality criterion being the most widely recognised one among EU Member States. The territoriality criterion is also the most objective, because it can take into consideration the interests of defendants, the interests of victims and the interest of the concerned State at the same time.[372]

The Commission further proposed the introduction of a new EU provision that would create national tribunals responsible for reviewing the decisions taken on the most appropriate competent authority of the Member State to deal with a specific case.[373] The judicial review should take into consideration if the principles of due process and reasonableness have been respected while making the decision on which Member State has jurisdiction.[374] Judicial review is indispensable when the interested Member States have concluded a binding agreement on the allocation of jurisdiction.[375] Moreover, the Court of Justice could deliver a preliminary ruling on

---

363   See ibid., p. 39.
364   Ibid.
365   Ibid.
366   See ibid., p. 40.
367   Ibid.
368   See ibid., p. 41.
369   Ibid.
370   See ibid., p. 42.
371   Ibid. See in particular Art. 9(2) of 'Council Framework Decision 2002/475/JHA of 13 June 2002 on Combating Terrorism', OJ EU L 164/3, 22 June 2002.
372   Ibid.
373   SEC (2005) 1767, op. cit. note 349, p. 35.
374   Ibid.
375   See COM (2005) 696, op. cit. note 350, pp. 6 and 7.

the mechanism chosen and on the criteria adopted for the allocation of jurisdiction, on the basis of Article 35 TEU.[376]

Relations with third countries   In addition, the Commission proposed that there should be 'a consultation mechanism in relation to certain third countries'.[377] The Commission mentioned the countries that are a party to the ECHR, and the Council of Europe, whose function is to protect fundamental rights to the same standard required by EU Member States with the same standards of data protection.[378] Eurojust could have the competence to conclude agreements with third-party countries.[379] This is due to the fact that by 2005, Eurojust had already concluded treaties with Norway, Iceland and Romania.[380] Eurojust was also negotiating treaties with the United States of America and Switzerland, while there was the possibility of concluding treaties with Ukraine and Russia.[381]

Suggestions for the long term   In the long term, the EU could set up an EU body that would be responsible for judicial review.[382] Nevertheless, this step is considered by the Commission a last resort, to be adopted when other forms of mediation described above fail to achieve an agreement.[383] If Eurojust were to carry out this task, its nature would change. This is because a mediator which takes binding decisions seems incompatible with the role a mediator should play.[384] Therefore, in the long term, it is better to establish a new body that would be able to issue binding decisions.[385] Such binding decisions should be subject to judicial control. At the moment, the Court of Justice does not have this competence under the treaties in force, and judicial control by national courts seems to be inappropriate and legally impossible. This is why some have made the suggestion that a European Preliminary Chamber be created, or an EU tribunal, subject to the Court of Justice control – either would be responsible for reviewing the decisions taken on the determination of jurisdiction from an EU perspective.[386] This suggestion would have the advantage of avoiding conflict over decisions taken by national courts, because the determination of jurisdiction would be taken at EU level. However,

---

376   Ibid. See also Art. 35 TEU, op. cit. note 8.

377   See SEC (2005) 1767, op. cit. note 349, p. 34.

378   Ibid.

379   Ibid.

380   See *Eurojust: Co-operation Agreement with the Kingdom of Norway*, Council Doc. 11641/04, 23 July 2004. The other agreements have not yet been published. On this point, see Peers, *EU Justice and Home Affairs Law*, op. cit. note 24, p. 489.

381   See *Eurojust Annual Report 2005*, <http://www.libertysecurity.org/article1509.html>, pp. 72 and 73.

382   See COM (2005) 696, op. cit. note 350, p. 7.

383   See SEC (2005) 1767, op. cit. note 349, p. 24.

384   Ibid.

385   See ibid., pp. 24 and 25.

386   See ibid., p. 28.

there are insufficient legal bases in the treaties for setting up a European Chamber under the Court of Justice's control. Certainly, Article 35 EU Treaty states that the Court of Justice can deliver preliminary rulings.[387] Beyond that, the Court of Justice cannot rule on individual cases, but only on disputes related to the validity and interpretation of the Treaty. It must be added that the competence to deliver preliminary rulings is subject to Member States' declaration. Furthermore, even if a national court can request a preliminary ruling, the Member State concerned is not obliged to do so. Finally, disputes on framework decisions cannot be started by concerned individuals. Therefore, at the moment, the creation of an EU body with the competence to allocate jurisdiction is impossible under the current EU Treaty.[388]

Now that the Lisbon Treaty has come into force, things may change. Article 267 of the Lisbon Treaty, which will replace Article 234 of the EC Treaty, will be applied to the criminal area because the pillar structure will disappear. As a result of the abolishment of the pillar structure, Article 35 EU (on the jurisdiction of the Court of Justice in the criminal area) and Article 68 EC (on the jurisdiction of the Court of Justice in asylum and immigration law) will be repealed. These two Articles required that each Member State issue a declaration recognising the jurisdiction of the Court of Justice and specifying the national courts that could have requested a preliminary ruling. This procedure will be eliminated and any national court will be able to request a preliminary ruling. In addition, as regards visas, asylum and immigration, any national court will be able to request a preliminary ruling to the Court of Justice and not only the courts of last instance.[389] Nevertheless, in the criminal area, Article 10 of Protocol 36 states that full jurisdiction will not apply until five years after the entry into force of the Lisbon Treaty. After these five years, the UK can declare that it does not accept the jurisdiction of the Court of Justice.[390]

---

387   See also Art. 35(1) TEU, op. cit. note 8.

388   See SEC (2005) 1767, op. cit. note 349, pp. 28 and 29.

389   See 'The Treaty of Lisbon and the Court of Justice of the European Union'. Court of Justice of the European Communities, Press Release No. 104/09, 30 November 2009, <http://europa.eu/rapid/pressReleasesAction.do?reference=CJE/09/104&format=HTML&aged=0&language=EN&guiLanguage=en>.

390   Art. 10 of Protocol 36 states: '1. As a transitional measure, and with respect to acts of the Union in the field of police cooperation and judicial cooperation in criminal matters which have been adopted before the entry into force of the Treaty of Lisbon, the powers of the institutions shall be the following at the date of entry into force of that Treaty: the powers of the Commission under Article 258 of the Treaty on the Functioning of the European Union shall not be applicable and the powers of the Court of Justice of the European Union under Title VI of the Treaty on European Union, in the version in force before the entry into force of the Treaty of Lisbon, shall remain the same, including where they have been accepted under Article 35(2) of the said Treaty on European Union. 2. The amendment of an act referred to in paragraph 1 shall entail the applicability of the powers of the institutions referred to in that paragraph as set out in the Treaties with respect to the amended act for those Member States to which that amended act shall apply. 3. In any case,

However, it must be stressed that national courts can only allocate jurisdiction at national level. In other words, the competence to allocate jurisdiction at EU level cannot be exercised by national courts. It must also be pointed out that national courts cannot review EU measures. As a result, at the moment, the creation of a mechanism of allocating jurisdiction consisting of creating a new EU body or consisting of giving the national courts this competence is impossible.

It was thought that modifications could have been adopted on the basis of the Constitutional Treaty. This is because the Constitutional Treaty contained a provision which stated that: 'European laws may establish specialised courts attached to the General Court to hear and determine at first instance certain classes of action or proceedings brought in specific areas.'[391] The Constitutional Treaty also stated that the decisions taken by specialised courts of first instance could be appealed before the Court of Justice.[392] The Commission proposed the possibility of amending the EU Treaty on the basis of this provision of the Constitutional Treaty.[393] However, this amendment has not been introduced by the Lisbon Treaty. It is clear

---

the transitional measure mentioned in paragraph 1 shall cease to have effect five years after the date of entry into force of the Treaty of Lisbon. 4. At the latest six months before the expiry of the transitional period referred to in paragraph 3, the United Kingdom may notify to the Council that it does not accept, with respect to the acts referred to in paragraph 1, the powers of the institutions referred to in paragraph 1 as set out in the Treaties. In case the United Kingdom has made that notification, all acts referred to in paragraph 1 shall cease to apply to it as from the date of expiry of the transitional period referred to in paragraph 3. This subparagraph shall not apply with respect to the amended acts which are applicable to the United Kingdom as referred to in paragraph 2. The Council, acting by a qualified majority on a proposal from the Commission, shall determine the necessary consequential and transitional arrangements. The United Kingdom shall not participate in the adoption of this decision. A qualified majority of the Council shall be defined in accordance with Article 238(3)(a) of the Treaty on the Functioning of the European Union. The Council, acting by a qualified majority on a proposal from the Commission, may also adopt a decision determining that the United Kingdom shall bear the direct financial consequences, if any, necessarily and unavoidably incurred as a result of the cessation of its participation in those acts. 5. The United Kingdom may, at any time afterwards, notify the Council of its wish to participate in acts which have ceased to apply to it pursuant to paragraph 4, first subparagraph. In that case, the relevant provisions of the Protocol on the Schengen acquis integrated into the framework of the European Union or of the Protocol on the position of the United Kingdom and Ireland in respect of the area of freedom, security and justice, as the case may be, shall apply. The powers of the institutions with regard to those acts shall be those set out in the Treaties. When acting under the relevant Protocols, the Union institutions and the United Kingdom shall seek to re-establish the widest possible measure of participation of the United Kingdom in the acquis of the Union in the area of freedom, security and justice without seriously affecting the practical operability of the various parts thereof, while respecting their coherence.'

391   See Art. III-359(1) of the Constitutional Treaty, op. cit. note 95.
392   See ibid., Art. III-359(3).
393   Ibid.

that this amendment might be desirable if it proved that binding agreements on the allocation of jurisdiction were only possible to achieve if Member States' mutual trust is high. This level of trust might require that EU Member States have a very in-depth knowledge of each other's legal systems. Certainly, the mechanism proposed by the Commission and analysed above could be adopted in the short term. A new EU provision could be established that obliges Member States to respect agreements reached with other interested Member States. This rule could be established by the ordinary legislative procedure that the Lisbon Treaty will introduce, which could oblige Member States to comply with it on the basis of the principle of direct effect. The infringement procedure could be extended to the criminal area, ensuring that EU Member States respect these laws. Nevertheless, creating an obligation on Member States in the pre-trial stage is not considered wise by the Commission.[394] This is because at this stage, the scenario might not be clear enough to allocate jurisdiction.[395] It must be added that according to the Commission, the most appropriate moment to allocate jurisdiction is when an accusation is sent to the national court, because all the information necessary to assess issues of jurisdiction, will have been collected.[396] From this moment, a binding agreement could be made, and an EU provision might oblige Member States to respect that agreement.

In any event, it is possible for binding agreements to provoke an increase in disputes between EU Member States and a mediator. In this scenario, the mediator might not be able to resolve some disputes, and there might be too many cases brought before the Court of Justice for infringement of procedure, causing a backlog of cases. For these reasons, the possibility of amending the new EU Treaty on the basis of the Constitutional Treaty should be taken into consideration. This possibility should only be considered if all EU Member States respect the rights of defendants and suspects in the same way. A new set of common rules on the rights of defendants in the EU should be introduced to achieve uniformity among the Member States. The establishment of a new court in order to resolve conflicts of jurisdiction should only be agreed after these common rules are introduced. This is because at the moment there are only common rules on the *ne bis in idem* principle, and not on other fundamental rights of defendants and suspects, such as the presumption of innocence.

In conclusion, the Commission proposed a three-step mechanism in order to resolve conflicts of jurisdiction between EU Member States' judicial authorities in order to enhance mutual recognition, which is essential for the effective application of the EAW. In the long term, the Commission suggested the possibility of amending the EU Treaty on the basis of the Constitutional Treaty. In the short term, even if EU Member States' judicial authorities do not find agreement, they at least have to respect the principle of *ne bis in idem*. EU Member States might insist on providing

---

394   Ibid.
395   Ibid.
396   Ibid.

exceptions to the application of the *ne bis in idem* principle.[397] The reason for this is that a Member State might find it difficult to accept that the judicial authorities of another Member State have already issued a final decision on a case, especially if the decision did not take into consideration the national interests that the Member State might have in the case.[398] All these problems would not exist if EU Member States trusted their legal systems and applied the principle of mutual recognition.

The *ne bis in idem* principle has been adopted by the Court of Justice, and on the basis of its interpretation, the Commission proposed some modifications.

The Principle of *Ne Bis in Idem*

Introduction

The aim of this section is to show that conflicts of jurisdiction can be resolved when there is a definitive decision through the application of the *ne bis in idem* principle and the accounting principle. However, as the Commission points out:[399]

> the ne bis in idem principle itself cannot provide adequate response to conflicts of jurisdiction: to avoid that it only bestows an exclusive effect to the 'fastest' prosecution, there needs to be a mechanism for determining the appropriate jurisdiction during proceedings.[400]

Therefore, it is important to introduce a consultation mechanism in EU Member States' criminal proceedings.

The *ne bis in idem* principle is expressly recognised by Protocol 7 of the ECHR.[401]

In the EU, the *ne bis in idem* principle is recognised by the Charter of Fundamental Rights.[402] The difference between the Charter and Protocol 7 of ECHR is that the Charter enlarges the territorial scope of the *ne bis in idem* principle, as it covers the whole EU, while Protocol 7 only provides that the principle should be applied in each Contracting Party's territory.[403]

---

397   See SEC (2005) 1767, op. cit. note 349, p. 7.
398   Ibid.
399   See ibid., p. 51.
400   Ibid.
401   See Art. 4 of Protocol No. 7 to the ECHR, op. cit. note 267, as amended by Protocol No. 11, ETS No. 117.
402   See Art. 50 of *Charter of Fundamental Rights of the European Union*, 2000/C 364/01, 18 December 2000.
403   See COM (2005) 195, op. cit. note 317, p. 12.

In the EU, the Schengen Convention also prohibits the violation of the *ne bis in idem* principle.[404] However, Article 55 of the Schengen Convention states that Member States can derogate from the respect of the *ne bis in idem* principle:

a. where the acts to which the foreign judgement relates took place in whole or in part in its own territory; in the latter case, however, this exception shall not apply if the acts took place in part in the territory of the contracting party where the judgement was delivered;

b. where the acts to which the foreign judgement relates constitute an offence against national security or other equally essential interests of that contracting party;

c. where the acts to which the foreign judgement relates were committed by officials of that contracting party in violation of the duties of their office.[405]

Seven Member States invoked option (a), four Member States have requested to apply option (b) and no Member States have invoked option (c).[406] Article 55(1)(b) of the Schengen Convention permits derogations to the *ne bis in idem* principle, while Protocol 7 of ECHR does not allow this derogation in cases of national emergency.[407] In the case of an exception to Article 55(1)(b), the Member State has to specify from which offences it intends to derogate.[408] A declaration of exception can be withdrawn at any time by a Member State that has issued one.[409] Moreover, the exception shall not be made if the Member State concerned has required another Member State, in relation to the same acts, to bring the prosecution or has authorised the extradition of the concerned person.[410]

The Court of Justice has ruled on the interpretation of rules on the *ne bis in idem* principle,[411] while two cases have been withdrawn.[412]

---

404   See Art. 54 of the Schengen Convention, op. cit. note 11.

405   See ibid., Arts 55(1)(a), (b) and (c).

406   See SEC (2005) 1767, op. cit. note 349, p. 47. See also Peers, *EU Justice and Home Affairs Law*, op. cit. note 24, p. 461.

407   See Art. 4(3) of Protocol No. 7, op. cit. note 401.

408   See Art. 55(2) of the Schengen Convention, op. cit. note 11.

409   See ibid., Art. 55(3).

410   See ibid., Art. 55(4).

411   See: Joined Cases C-187 and 385/01 *Gozutoc and Brugge* [2003] ECR I-1345-Court of Justice; Case C-469/03 *Miraglia* [2005] ECR I-2009-Court of Justice; Case C-436/04 *Van Esbroeck* [2006] ECR I-2333-Court of Justice; Case 467/04 *Gasparini* [2006] ECR I-0000-Court of Justice; Case C-150/05 *Van Straaten* [2006] ECR I-0000-Court of Justice; Case C-288/05 *Kretzinger* [2007] ECR I-6441-Court of Justice, Opinion of Advocate General of 5 December 2006; Case C-367/05 *Kraaijenbrink* [2007] ECR I-6619-Court of Justice, Opinion of Advocate General of 5 December 2006.

412   See Case C-491/03 *Hiebeler* [2005] ECR I-2025. See also Case C-272/05 *Bowens* [2006]-Court of Justice.

Application of the Ne Bis in Idem *Principle in Barred Prosecutions*

In the *Gozutoc and Brugge* joined cases,[413] the Court of Justice ruled on the interpretation of Article 54 of the Schengen Convention.[414] In particular, the national courts asked whether the *ne bis in idem* principle of Article 54 applies 'to procedures whereby further prosecution is barred'.[415] According to the Court of Justice, a procedure where further prosecution is barred is a procedure where the prosecuting authority decides to close a criminal proceeding against an accused. This will be the case if certain obligations have been fulfilled by the accused, or if the accused has paid a sum of money on the basis of a prosecuting authority's determination.[416] The Court of Justice ruled that in such a situation, 'the prosecution is discontinued by the decision of an authority required to play a part in the administration of criminal justice in the national legal system concerned'.[417] Again, it must be emphasised that the proceeding can only be discontinued if the accused fulfils specific obligations determined by the prosecuting authority.[418] In consequence, the unlawful conduct of the accused is penalised no matter whether a court has been involved and a similar decision did 'not take the form of a judicial decision ... since such matters of procedure and form do not impinge on the effects of the procedure'.[419] The Court of Justice ruled that the *ne bis in idem* principle applies where a proceeding is barred, even if a court is not involved and even if there is no harmonisation between the criminal systems and the criminal procedures of EU Member States.[420] This is because:

> there is the necessary implication that the Member States have mutual trust in their criminal justice systems and that each of them recognises the criminal law in force in the other Member States even when the outcome would be different if its national law were applied.[421]

The EU Treaty also states that its aims are to maintain and develop an area of freedom, security and justice where the free movement of persons is guaranteed.[422] The Protocol integrating the Schengen Acquis into the TEU also states that its purpose is to increase European integration in order to facilitate the EU's progress

---

413   Joined Cases C-187 and 385/01 [2003] ECR I-1345-Court of Justice.
414   See *Gozutoc and Brugge*, op. cit. note 411, para. 23.
415   See ibid., para. 25.
416   See ibid., para. 27.
417   See ibid., para. 28.
418   See ibid., para. 29.
419   See ibid., paras 29 and 31.
420   See ibid., paras 29, 31, 32, 33 and 34.
421   See ibid., para. 36. See also Art. 2 TEU, op. cit. note 8.
422   See *Gozutoc and Brugge*, op. cit. note 411, para. 36.

towards becoming an area of freedom, security and justice.[423] Article 54 aims to ensure that no one is prosecuted on the same facts in different Member States, and this objective is fully achieved when a decision is not taken multiple times, 'even where such decisions are adopted without the involvement of a court and do not take the form of a judicial decision'.[424]

The Court of Justice also added that a prosecution is only barred in EU Member States in relation to offences which 'are punishable only with relatively light penalties'.[425] If Article 54 was inapplicable in these circumstances, the free movement of persons that the *ne bis in idem* principle aims to protect would only be guaranteed for serious crimes. This is due to the fact that in these cases, the use of simplified methods not consisting of issuing a judicial decision is prohibited.[426] Nevertheless, in *Miraglia*,[427] the Court of Justice ruled that when a public prosecutor in a Member State has closed a proceeding without any determination on the merits of the case, this decision cannot be considered a final decision. This means that Article 54 of the Schengen Convention cannot be applied,[428] even though in *Van Straaten*[429] the Court of Justice ruled that an acquittal for lack of evidence is grounded on a determination of the merit.[430] In *Gasparini*,[431] the Court of Justice stated that the *ne bis in idem* principle can also be extended to decisions of acquittal 'because prosecution of the offence is time-barred'.[432] If in this case the *ne bis in idem* were not applied, the aim of Article 54 – ensuring the free movement of persons[433] – would not be achieved.[434] Therefore, even if there is no judicial decision, the case can be barred on the basis of a decision on the merit of the dispute, including acquittals for lack of evidence or as a result of the prosecution being time-barred, otherwise the *ne bis in idem* principle cannot be applied.

Application of the Ne Bis in Idem *Principle and the Meaning of 'Same Acts'*

In *Van Esbroeck*,[435] the Court of Justice confirmed the rules of *Gozutoc and Brugge*. As of a result, the Court of Justice confirmed the widest application

---

423   See ibid., para. 37. See also para. 1 of the Preamble of the Europol Convention, op. cit. note 1.

424   See *Gozutoc and Brugge*, op. cit. note 411, para. 38.

425   See ibid., para. 39.

426   See ibid., para. 40.

427   See Case C-469/03 *Miraglia*, op. cit. note 411.

428   See ibid., para. 30.

429   See Case C-150/05 *Van Straaten*, op. cit. note 411, paras 40–53.

430   See ibid., para. 60.

431   See Case 467/04 *Gasparini*, op. cit. note 411.

432   See ibid., para. 28.

433   *Gozutoc and Brugge*, op. cit. note 411, para. 38. See also *Van Straaten*, op. cit. note 411, para. 57.

434   See *Gasparini*, op. cit. note 411, para. 27.

435   See Case C-436/04 *Van Esbroeck*, op. cit. note 411.

of the *ne bis in idem* principle. Specifically in *Van Esbroeck*, the Belgian Hof van Cassatie asked whether the *ne bis in idem* principle applies to a criminal proceeding brought in a Member State for acts for which a person has already been convicted in another Member State even if the Schengen Convention was not yet binding in that Member State when that person was convicted.[436] The Court of Justice ruled that the *ne bis in idem* principle applies even if the judgment on a person was issued in a State where the Schengen Convention was not in force, in so far as the Schengen Convention was in force in the Member State in question at the time of the verification.[437] The Court of Justice also clarified the meaning of 'the same acts',[438] expressly indicated in Article 54 of the Schengen Convention. It ruled that the meaning of 'same acts' must not be based on a 'criterion based on the legal classification of the acts'[439] because there is no harmonisation of EU Member States' criminal systems.[440] As a result, the meaning of 'same acts' should be intended as 'material acts … which are inextricably linked together in time, in space and by their subject-matter'.[441] The Court of Justice also specified that it is within a national court's competence to establish this important criterion.[442] In *Kraaijenbrink*,[443] the Advocate General confirmed the necessity of having these criteria.[444] The Advocate General also added that the concept of 'same acts' can include acts that were not known 'at the material time to the prosecuting authorities or adjudicating courts of the first Member State'.[445] In any case, if these acts are inextricably linked to the main acts, they should be considered to be the same acts.[446] The meaning of 'same acts' based on the criterion of inextricability was also confirmed in *Van Straaten*[447] and in the pending case *Kretzinger*.[448]

The Accounting Principle and Detention Pending Trial

In *Kretzinger*, the Advocate General established more extensive interpretation of the application of the accounting principle. The Advocate General stated that if a custodial sentence has been issued and suspended in an EU Member State, this sentence must be regarded as an enforced penalty.[449] The accounting principle

---

436 See ibid., para. 18.
437 See ibid., para. 24.
438 See Art. 54(1) of the Schengen Convention, op. cit. note 11.
439 See *Van Esbroeck*, op. cit. note 411, para. 35.
440 Ibid.
441 See *Van Esbroeck*, op. cit. note 411, para. 38.
442 Ibid.
443 See Case C-367/05 *Kraaijenbrink*, op. cit. note 411.
444 See ibid., paras 27–33.
445 See ibid., para. 50.
446 See ibid., para. 52.
447 See Case C-150/05 *Van Straaten*, op. cit. note 411, paras 40–53.
448 See Case C-288/05, *Kretzinger*, op. cit. note 411, paras 35–40.
449 See ibid., para. 52.

must be applied to these sentences unless certain conditions established by the law of the State where the decision was given are not respected by the person concerned.[450]

The Advocate General also stated that detention pending trial cannot be regarded as 'enforcement of ... penalty for the purpose of Article 54'.[451] This is precisely due to the fact that a detention pending trial is applied pending a trial.[452] Instead, Article 54 requires a definitive penalty to be enforced.[453] As the Strasbourg Court has emphasised:[454]

> the aim of detention pending trial is to avert the risk that the accused will fail to appear for trial, or that, if released, he may take action to prejudice the administration of justice, commit further offences or cause public disorder.[455]

However, if the time spent in custody pending trial in one Member State is equal to or greater than the period of custody imposed by another Member State for the same acts, the accounting principle will apply, in the sense that further proceedings for the same acts will be prohibited by Article 54 of the Schengen Convention.[456] If the time spent in custody in one Member State is less than the final custodial sentence and the offender spends the rest of the term in prison, Article 54 is satisfied because the penalty is going to be enforced.[457] Instead, if the offender has spent some period of the detention pending trial in prison and is now at liberty, Article 54 cannot be applied because the penalty has not been enforced.[458]

The offender will be able to rely on the principle of setting-off in Article 56 of the Schengen Convention, which requires the deduction of any period spent in custody pending trial in a Member State, from the final penalty accorded in another Member State.[459] According to Advocate General Sharpston, the principle of setting-off should be distinguished from the *ne bis in idem* principle, 'even though both are manifestations of a general requirement of natural justice or fairness in criminal proceedings'.[460] The principle of setting-off is relevant when the *ne bis in idem* principle cannot be applied because the conditions of Article 54 are not met.[461]

---

450   Ibid.
451   See ibid., para. 58.
452   See ibid., para. 59.
453   See Art. 54(1) of the Schengen Convention, op. cit. note 11.
454   See *Smirnova* v. *Russia* (2003) 8, para. 59.
455   Ibid., quoted in Case C-288/05, *Kretzinger*, op. cit. note 411, para. 59.
456   See Case C-288/05, *Kretzinger*, op. cit. note 411, para. 65.
457   See ibid., paras 66 and 67.
458   See ibid., para. 68.
459   See ibid., paras 64 and 69.
460   See *Kraaijenbrink*, op. cit. note 411, para. 61.
461   See ibid., paras 55 and 61.

The Advocate General also stated that the same principles should be applied to periods of detention spent in police custody.[462] The *ne bis in idem* principle, conversely, should not be applied when an EAW has been issued for the purpose of enforcing a sentence issued after a trial and a conviction.[463] The reason for this is that Article 54 requires that a penalty is already being enforced or is in the process of being enforced.[464] In the case of an EAW being issued, the penalty has not been enforced and is not in the process of being enforced.[465]

Trials in Absentia, Ne Bis in Idem *and the Principle of Setting-off*

In the case of trials *in absentia*, the Advocate General stated that sentences issued in trials *in absentia* should be considered definitive sentences for the purposes of Article 54, even though the EAW Framework Decision does not make automatic the surrender of the person concerned and convicted *in absentia*.[466] However, trials *in absentia* have to respect the ECHR.[467] The national authorities also have to ensure that defendants have exercised their rights to attend trials or have deliberately absconded from the trial.[468] In any case, a judgment that does not respect the requirement of the ECHR cannot be considered a final sentence for the purpose of Article 54 of the Schengen Convention.[469]

The Commission asserted that there are cases where the *ne bis in idem* principle should be extended even when there is not an enforced penalty or a penalty in the process to be enforced.[470] The Commission also pointed out that the *ne bis in idem* principle has not been extended to penalties not enforced, to avoid cases of impunity when convictions are not enforced.[471] In any case, the Commission emphasised that the enforcement condition might no longer be necessary in an area of freedom, security and justice where transnational border enforcement is facilitated by the adoption of measures such as the EAW Framework Decision.[472] The Commission highlighted that the meaning of 'same acts' should be reconsidered and the exceptions of Article 55(1) of the Schengen Convention might not be necessary

---

462   See Case C-288/05, *Kretzinger*, op. cit. note 411, para. 75.

463   See ibid., paras 87 and 88.

464   See ibid., para. 88.

465   See ibid., paras 88 and 91.

466   See ibid., paras 95 and 104. See also Art. 5(1) of Framework Decision 2002/584/JHA, op. cit. note 252.

467   Se in Particular Art. 6 ECHR, op. cit. note 267. See also Case C-288/05 *Kretzinger*, op. cit. note 411, para. 95.

468   See *Sejdovic* v. *Italy* [GC], ECHR (2006), paras 81 *et seq.*, quoted in Case C-288/05, *Kretzinger*, op. cit. note 411, para. 95.

469   See Case C-288/05, *Kretzinger*, op. cit. note 411, para. 101.

470   See SEC (2005) 1767, op. cit. note 349, pp. 46 and 47.

471   See ibid., p. 47.

472   Ibid.

if a balanced mechanism of allocating jurisdiction is created.[473] The Council took into account the possibility of reconsidering the *ne bis in idem* principle, especially the exceptions to this principle.[474]

In conclusion, the Court of Justice has extensively applied the *ne bis in idem* principle and the principle of setting-off. The Advocate General has seemed to confirm the wide extension of these two principles. The *ne bis in idem* principle can also be applied in case of trials *in absentia*, unless the conditions of the ECHR have not been met. It should be added that Article 58 of the Schengen Convention permits EU Member States to apply more generous interpretations of the *ne bis in idem* principle and of the principle of setting-off.[475] Therefore, the Court of Justice and the Advocate General take fully into consideration the rights of accused persons. The Commission has also proposed improving the rules on *ne bis in idem* principle.

The Commission has also drafted proposals on how to guarantee the rights of defendants and suspects in EU Member States so that mutual trust can be enhanced. If mutual trust is reinforced, the EAW Framework Decision could be amended in order to ensure that national constitutions are adapted to this measure. Subsequently, other reforms could be considered in order to resolve conflicts of jurisdiction between EU Member States if the mechanism proposed by the Commission does not work.

Enhancing Mutual Trust and Mutual Judicial Recognition

The Rights of Defendants and Suspects

The rights of defendants and suspects should be protected to the same extent as the rights of victims of people smugglers and human traffickers which have been examined above. The Commission emphasised that it is important that 'mutually recognised judgements meet high standards in terms of securing personal rights',[476] in order to apply the principle of mutual recognition.[477] The European Council stated that 'the principle of mutual recognition should become the cornerstone of judicial cooperation in … criminal matters within the Union'.[478]

473　See COM (2005) 696, op. cit. note 350, pp. 8 and 9.

474　See ibid., p. 8. See in particular the Introduction of 'Programme of Measures to Implement the Principle of Mutual Judicial Recognition of Decisions in Criminal Matters, 2001/C 12/02', op. cit. note 347.

475　See Art. 58 of the Schengen Convention, op. cit. note 11. See also *Gozutoc and Brugge*, op. cit. note 411, para. 45; *Kraaijenbrink*, op. cit. note 411, para. 68.

476　See COM (2005) 195, op. cit. note 317, p. 6.

477　Ibid.

478　See Recital 1 of the Preamble of COM (2004) 328, op. cit. note 317, p. 21. This Proposal quotes the Conclusions of the Tampere European Council of 15 and 16 October

The EU Council stated that the principle of mutual recognition 'is designed to strengthen cooperation between Member States but also to enhance the protection of individual rights'.[479] The full implementation of mutual recognition requires that EU Member States trust each other's criminal justice systems[480] and that all actors involved in criminal trials have confidence in the 'decisions of the judicial authorities of other Member States ... and do not call in question their judicial capacity and respect for fair trial rights'.[481] Therefore, the Commission proposed a framework decision with:

> [t]he intention ... to ensure a greater balance in EU criminal law, which was (and still is) overwhelmingly focussed on ensuring more effective prosecutions and investigations, but made no significant contribution towards ensuring that the right to a fair trial was protected.[482]

This proposal was redrafted[483] in order to improve the focus on important rights, although some Member States (the UK, Ireland, Malta, Cyprus, the Czech Republic and Slovakia) did not want the redraft to be adopted through a binding measure, but through a draft resolution of Member States.[484] These dissenting States argued that the Council of Europe should have amended the draft, because they feared that the Proposed Framework Decision could have conflicted with Article 6 ECHR. On the basis of the Council of Europe's comments, the Proposed Framework Decision was redrafted by the German presidency. The new Proposed Framework Decision obligated Member States to ensure that any person arrested is promptly informed of the charges, the reason for these charges, the nature, causes and details of any accusation against them, and the relevant procedural rights they may exercise.[485] Article 3 provided for the right of every arrested person to have a defence, while Article 4 recognised gave arrested and charged persons the right to an interpreter if they did not understand the language of the court.[486] Finally, Article 7 stated that this framework decision could not limit or derogate rights and procedures safeguarded by the ECHR or by the laws of Member States which provided higher

---

1999, points 33–7. The most recent version of this Proposal was published in 2007.

479   See the Introduction of the 'Programme of Measures to Implement the Principle of Mutual Judicial Recognition of Decisions in Criminal Matters', op. cit. note 347. See also Recital 2 of the Preamble of COM (2004) 328, op. cit. note 317, p. 21.

480   See ibid., para. 3, p. 21.

481   See ibid., para. 4, p. 21.

482   See Peers, 'Rights of Criminal Suspects and EU Law', op. cit. note 320.

483   See *EU Council Document: Proposal for a Council Framework Decision on Certain Procedural Rights in Criminal Proceedings Throughout the European Union*, Doc 8182/07, 2 April 2007.

484   Ibid.

485   See ibid., Art. 2.

486   See ibid., Arts 3 and 4.

levels of protection.[487] The German text was criticised by the Council of Europe, and for this reason the German presidency will revise this text.[488] One hopes that the new text will be accepted, especially by EU Member States such as the UK that seem reluctant to accept that the EU should rule on domestic criminal proceedings, even if these rules are compatible with the ECHR. The new text should consider that fact that the redrafted framework decision, as Peers highlighted,[489] did not incorporate Article 5 and Articles 6(1) and 6(2) ECHR. A new draft has not been issued yet. The Commission issued a Green Paper on the presumption of innocence. However, there are no legislative proposals. Moreover, Article 7 ECHR, which rules on legality and non-retroactivity of criminal proceedings, right to appeal, compensation in case of wrongful conviction and prohibition of the *ne bis in idem* principle, has also been neglected by the new proposal, although the Schengen Convention allows the cross-border application of the *ne bis in idem* principle within the EU.[490]

The introduction of a framework decision on suspects' rights is very important in order to create a balance between EU criminal law and policy and the protection of human rights listed in the ECHR. However, one must agree with Peers when he states that if the minimum standards set out by the framework decision are lower than those of the ECHR, there is a risk that 'legislatures and national courts might … conclude that regardless of the ECHR, they can "get away with" the lower EU standards'.[491] For example, this could be the case in countries which are negotiating EU membership. Moreover, Peers makes another strong argument when he argues that:

> The dissenters' concern that the ECHR standards would be misinterpreted by the EU's Court of Justice relies on pre-2000 case law of the Court, not recognising that recent case law of the Court of Justice makes much greater reference to the case law of the European Court on Human rights … and has moreover overturned some of the earlier Court of Justice case law referred to.[492]

Further progress concerning mutual judicial recognition has been made by the Council, which in 2008 adopted Framework Decision 2008/909/JHA on mutual judicial recognition.[493] Article 1 of Framework Decision 2008/909/JHA states that

---

487 See ibid., Art. 7.
488 Ibid.
489 See Peers, 'Rights of Criminal Suspects and EU Law', op. cit. note 320.
490 Ibid.
491 Ibid.
492 Ibid.
493 See 'Council Framework Decision 2008/909/JHA of 27 November 2008 on the Application of the Principle of Mutual Recognition to Judgments in Criminal Matters Imposing Custodial Sentences or Measures Involving Deprivation of Liberty for the Purpose of their Enforcement in the European Union', OJ EU L 327/27, 5 December 2008.

this measure has the purpose of establishing when Member States shall recognise a sentence or judgment issued in another Member State in order to facilitate the rehabilitation of the sentenced person. It is interesting to note that Article 7 lists the crimes for which there is mutual judicial recognition without the need to verify the double criminality. Among these crimes are human trafficking and facilitation of unauthorised entry and residence.

In conclusion, the European institutions are aware that it is essential to enhance mutual trust in order to guarantee the full implementation of the principle of mutual recognition. This goal can be achieved by establishing at EU level common minimum standards on the protection of fundamental rights of suspects and defendants, including common measures on pre-trial detention. The Commission has also highlighted the importance of the presumption of innocence.

Presumption of Innocence

The presumption of innocence is another fundamental right that should be protected by EU Member States in order to enhance mutual trust and establish mutual recognition. The presumption of innocence is recognised by Article 6(2) ECHR, which states that: 'Everyone charged with a criminal offence shall be presumed innocent until proved guilt according to law.'[494] Furthermore, the Charter of Fundamental rights states that:

1. Everyone who has been charged shall be presumed innocent until proved guilty according to law.
2. Respect for the rights of the defence of anyone who has been charged shall be guaranteed.[495]

The presumption of innocence presupposes that persons are not considered guilty until they are recognised as such by a court.[496] The prosecutor must prove that the accused is guilty beyond reasonable doubts.[497] The Strasbourg Court also stated that the prosecutor needs to show sufficient evidence against the accused, and that any doubt should play in favour of the accused.[498]

The Commission emphasised that there are three situations where, according to the Strasbourg Court case law, the burden of proof should not only be placed on the prosecutor.[499] In cases of strict liability, the prosecutor need only prove that the accused committed the material act of the crime (*actus reus*), but does not

---

494   See Art. 6(2) ECHR, op. cit. note 267, as amended by Protocol 11.
495   See Art. 48 of *Charter of Fundamental Rights of the European Union*, op. cit. note 402.
496   See COM (2006) 174, op. cit. note 317, p. 5.
497   See ibid., p. 6.
498   See *Barberà, Messegué and Jabardo* v. *Spain,* (1989) 11 EHRR 360, para. 77.
499   Ibid.

have to adduce that the accused acted intentionally in a specific way in order to produce such a result.[500] In cases of strict liability, the accused is presupposed to be guilty.[501] In other situations, the prosecutor has to show that the accused acted in a specific way, while the accused must show that there is an innocent explanation that justifies the action.[502] The Strasbourg Court held that the heavier burden of proof for the accused can only be accepted for less serious crimes. A third situation where there can be a reversal of burden of proof is in the recovery of assets because they are considered proceeds of crime. In this case, the owner of the assets must be able to rebut the allegation that their assets are the proceeds of crime, and the court must take into consideration any claims of *bona fide*, especially where the right to property of third parties is endangered. In this case, Member States have to adopt mechanisms to protect property rights. Member States must also safeguard the accused's privilege against self-incrimination and the right of silence. The right of silence is recognised by the laws of EU Member States.[503] In most Member States, the law states that the accused must be advised of the right to remain silent, and the law of some Member States provides the inadmissibility of evidence gathered when the accused has not been advised of this right of silence. In other Member States, the law recognises the accused's right to appeal against a conviction when the obligation of advising the accused of the right to remain silent has not been fulfilled. Finally, in some Member States, the failure to advise the accused of their right might be considered an offence.

Nevertheless, the right of silence is not absolute. In *Murray* v. *UK*,[504] the Strasbourg Court stated that the right of silence:

> cannot and should not prevent that the accused's silence, in situations which clearly call for an explanation from him, be taken into account in assessing the persuasiveness of the evidence adduced by prosecution.[505]

Certainly, the court cannot base a conviction only on the fact that the accused decided to remain silent or refused to answer questions or give evidence.[506] However, if the evidence against the accused relies on explanations that the accused might be in the position to give, the accused's refusal to testify may lead the court to draw a conclusion of guilt.[507] In contrast, if the prosecutor shows little evidence, the accused's choice not to testify cannot lead the court to consider him

---

500   See *Salabiaku* v. *France* (1988) 13 EHRR 379, para. 28.
501   Ibid.
502   See COM (2006) 174, op. cit. note 317, pp. 7 and 8.
503   See ibid., p. 8.
504   See *Murray* v. *UK* (1996) 22 EHRR 29.
505   See ibid., para. 47.
506   See ibid., paras 47 and 51.
507   See ibid., para. 51.

or her guilty.[508] In any case, the Strasbourg Court asserted that the drawing of the conclusion that the accused is guilty when he or she decides not to testify when this would be very relevant does not transfer the burden of proof from the prosecutor to the defence 'so as to infringe the principle of the presumption of innocence'.[509]

In conclusion, it should be highlighted that the EU applies much importance to Article 6 ECHR on the presumption of innocence. The Commission considers this principle an important guarantee for the accused that all EU Member States have to take into consideration in order to improve mutual trust with the purpose of applying the principle of mutual recognition.

The same principles should be applied to pre-trial custody, for which the European Commission has presented various proposals.[510]

Proposals in Pre-trial Procedures

The Commission has also made proposals in an effort to enhance mutual recognition in cases of non-custodial pre-trial supervision measures.[511] These aim to explore alternatives to pre-trial detention between Member States.[512] The Commission noted that the excessive use and length of pre-trial detention leads to overcrowded prisons, with the risk that non-resident suspects are kept in custody while residents benefit from alternative measures.[513] Instead, pre-trial detention should be used only in exceptional circumstances under national law.[514] Subsequently, alternatives adopted in one Member State should permit suspects to be transferred to the Member State where they have residence.[515] At the moment, such transfers are not possible because EU Member States do not recognise foreign judicial decisions on pre-trial detention.[516] The Commission has encouraged the adoption of measures on pre-trial detention because the programme on implementing the principle of mutual recognition of decisions in criminal matters states that it should do so.[517]

The Commission also proposed a framework decision on a European supervision order in the pre-trial stage to implement the principle of mutual recognition highlighted by the programme of 2000.[518] The Commission emphasised that the mutual recognition programme revealed that specific aspects of mutual

508   Ibid.
509   See ibid., para. 54.
510   See COM (2004) 562, op. cit. note 317. See also COM (2006) 468, op. cit. note 317.
511   See COM (2004) 562, op. cit. note 317.
512   See ibid., p. 5.
513   See ibid., p. 3.
514   Ibid.
515   See ibid., p. 4.
516   Ibid.
517   See 'Programme of Measures to Implement the Principle of Mutual Judicial Recognition of Decisions in Criminal Matters', op. cit. note 347, measures 9 and 10.
518   See COM (2006) 468, op. cit. note 317, p. 2.

recognition regarding pre-trial orders have not been addressed at international level.[519] Indeed, the EU network of independent experts in fundamental rights revealed that the statistics of the Council of Europe show that there are many pre-trial detainees in many Member States.[520] Therefore, the Commission proposed a framework decision in order to strengthen the right to liberty and the presumption of innocence, and to 'promote equal treatment of all citizens in the *common* area of freedom, security and justice'.[521] The proposal establishes a European Supervision Order, which is:

> a judicial decision issued by a competent authority of a Member State in respect of a non-resident suspect for the purpose of the return of that person to his Member State of residence under the conditions that he complies with supervision measures, in order to ensure that due course of justice and in particular, to ensure that the person will be available to stand trial in the issuing Member State.[522]

This proposal is based on Articles 31(1)(a) and 31(1)(c) and Article 34(2)(b) TEU, and on the principles of subsidiarity and proportionality.[523] The European Supervision Order could be refused by the requested State 'if it is clear that criminal proceedings for the offence in respect of which that order has been issued would infringe the *ne bis in idem* principle'.[524] The suspect would also have 'the right to request the issuing authority to review the European supervision order no later than 60 days after it has been issued or last reviewed'.[525] The issuing authority could also revoke a European Supervision Order either because the suspect had fulfilled all the obligation contained in the order or because the suspect had breached it.[526] Finally, the proposal states that:

> A Member State which has experienced repeated problems on the part of another Member State in the execution of European supervision orders shall inform the Council with a view to evaluating the implementation of this Framework decision at member state level.
>
> The Council shall conduct a review, in particular of the practical application of the provisions of this Framework Decision by the Member States.[527]

---

519   See ibid., p. 3.
520   Ibid.
521   See ibid., p. 4.
522   See ibid., Art. 1(2), p. 11.
523   See ibid., Preamble and Recital 7, pp. 10 and 11.
524   See ibid., Art. 10(1), p. 14.
525   See ibid., Art. 13(1), p. 16.
526   See ibid., Arts 14 and 17, pp. 16 and 17.
527   See ibid., Art. 23, p. 20.

What if Member States do not implement this framework decision when adopted by the Council, and individuals are affected by the lack of implementation of this measure? If the direct effect was extended to framework decisions, Member States should be obliged to set aside national provisions in conflict with this framework decision. It is important that measures in the criminal area have direct effect, and this would be facilitated if measures taken in the criminal area were adopted by the ordinary legislative procedure. This is due to the fact that the European Parliament would participate in the decision-making procedure concerning the criminal area. People of the EU may feel led to pressure their representatives to adopt measures having direct effect if they realised that they are important to fighting against criminal organisations involved in people smuggling and human trafficking. The impact that the direct effect of a framework decision would have on the criminal area is analysed later in this chapter.

In conclusion, the European Commission has presented a variety of proposals on pre-trial measures, especially a Framework Decision on the European Supervision Order to reduce the use of pre-trial detention. There is another aspect of criminal proceedings that should also be improved. This aspect concerns the admissibility of trials *in absentia* in EU Member States.

Trials in Absentia

The European Commission has pointed out that definitions of trials *in absentia* differ in EU Member States.[528] The laws of some Member States allow trials *in absentia*, while other EU Member States' laws state that the accused is obliged to attend the process, and any violation of this obligation can be punished.[529] This section seeks to explain when trials *in absentia* should be allowed, with the conviction that they should not be abolished, although they have to respect the fundamental rights of the accused as expressly protected by the ECHR.[530] Subsequently, this section will focus attention on Council Decision 2009/299/JHA,[531] which amended other framework decisions, including the EAW Framework Decision, with the intent of allowing trials *in absentia* in certain circumstances.

The Strasbourg Court stated that trials *in absentia* do not violate Article 6 ECHR.[532] However, it also held that a denial of justice occurs when the accused

---

528   See COM (2006) 174, op. cit. note 317, p. 9.

529   Ibid.

530   See in particular Art. 6 ECHR, op. cit. note 267.

531   See 'Council Framework Decision 2009/299/JHA of 26 February 2009 Amending Framework Decisions 2002/584/JHA, 2005/214/JHA, 2006/783/JHA, 2008/909/JHA and 2008/947/JHA, Thereby Enhancing the Procedural Rights of Persons and Fostering the Application of the Principle of Mutual Recognition to Decisions Rendered in the Absence of the Person Concerned at the Trial', OJ EU L 81/24, 27 March 2009.

532   See *Sejdovic* v. *Italy* [GC], ECHR (2006), para. 82.

does not have the opportunity to hear a fresh determination of the merit of the charge in relation to matters of law and fact, when the accused does not have the opportunity to be present during the trial in order to defend themselves.[533] The court also asserted that although States Parties have wide discretion in choosing the means of ensuring that their legal systems respect Article 6 ECHR,[534] guaranteeing the right of an accused to be present during the trial is one of the fundamental requirements of Article 6.[535] The court also highlighted that persons accused of a criminal offence do not have to prove that they were absent for *force majeure*.[536] This is because the burden of proof lies with the national authorities.[537]

The use of trials *in absentia* should not be abolished. In Italy, for example, since some dangerous criminals such as those belonging to Mafia have deliberately absconded for 30 or 40 years. These Mafiosi have committed serious crimes such as ordering the car bomb killings of the two anti-Mafia judges Giovanni Falcone (along with his wife) and Paolo Borsellino and eight policemen of their escorts in two different attempts in 1992.[538] If trials *in absentia* were abolished, it would be difficult for investigative teams to keep evidence against these criminals. The Strasbourg Court also held that prohibiting all trials *in absentia*:

> may paralyse the conduct of criminal proceedings, in that it may lead, for example, to dispersal of the evidence, expiry of the time-limit for prosecution or a miscarriage of justice.[539]

It must be added that it would be incorrect to think that trials *in absentia* should only be retained in exceptional circumstances such as in case of crimes committed by Mafia affiliates. This is because in Italy, for example, there have been people who have raped, tortured, killed and who afterwards have absconded. This was the case with convicted murderer Andrea Ghira, who has been a fugitive from 1975 after having tortured and raped two girls of 17, murdering one of them.[540] If Ghira

---

533   See *Colozzza* v. *Italy* (1985) 13 EHRR 516, para. 29. See also *Einhorn* v. *France*, Application no. 71555/01, 16 October 2001 (unreported), para. 33; *Krombach* v. *France* (2001) ECHR 88, para. 85; *Somogyi* v. *Italy* (2004) ECHR 203, para. 66.

534   See *Sejdovic* v. *Italy*, op. cit. note 532, para. 83.

535   See *Stoichkov* v. *Bulgaria* (2005) ECHR 186, para. 56.

536   See *Colozzza* v. *Italy* (1985) 13 EHRR 516, para. 30.

537   See *Medenica* v. *Switzerland* (2001) ECHR 395, para. 57.

538   See, for example, the case of Bernardo Provenzano, missing for 40 years. 'Profile: Bernardo Provenzano', 11 April 2006, <http://news.bbc.co.uk/1/hi/world/europe/4899512.stm>. See also the case of Salvatore Riina, known as 'Totò': 'Mafia suspects held in 'Godfathertown', 5 June 2002, <http://news.bbc.co.uk/1/hi/world/europe/2027306.stm>.

539   See *Colozzza* v. *Italy*, op. cit. note 533, para. 29.

540   'The Circeo Murder (Andrea Ghira)', <http://www.chilhavisto.rai.it/CLV/english/misteri/2004-2005/CirceoDelittoGhira.htm>, accessed 12 April 2007. See also

returned to Italy, unless it was proved that he was dead,[541] he would be arrested and detained for the rest of his life. Trials *in absentia* permit that criminals are arrested if found. However, if trials *in absentia* were abolished, criminals might be encouraged to abscond and to circulate freely in the territory where they have committed crimes. The result would be the risk that they are never convicted if evidence against them is lost while they are at large. Trials *in absentia* are crucial to convict criminals, as long they respect the ECHR, and in particular Article 6 of this convention. This is demonstrated by the fact that Framework Decision 2009/299 states that:

> The right of an accused person to appear in person at the trial is included in the right to a fair trial provided for in Article 6 of the Convention for the Protection of Human Rights and Fundamental Freedoms, as interpreted by the European Court of Human Rights. The Court has also declared that the right of the accused person to appear in person at the trial is not absolute and that under certain conditions the accused person may, of his or her own free will, expressly or tacitly but unequivocally, waive the right.[542]

Therefore, the framework decision allows trial *in absentia* with respect to the ECHR.

In conclusion, the Strasbourg Court does not consider trials *in absentia* a breach of Article 6 ECHR. However, the Strasbourg Court indicates that States Parties must ensure that their legal systems provide that trials *in absentia* respect the requirements of Article 6 ECHR. The Council adopted a framework decision in order to guarantee common standards in trials *in absentia* with respect to Article 6 of the ECHR.

The next section analyses the changes that the Lisbon Treaty would introduce, and one recommendation made by the European Parliament with the intent of constructing an EU criminal justice area.

Limitations to the Development of an EU Criminal Justice System

The Lisbon Treaty states that judicial co-operation shall be based on mutual judicial recognition, and measures in this area should be enacted by the ordinary legislative procedure. Article 82 of the Lisbon Treaty lists measures that should be adopted. These measures ensure the recognition of all judgments and judicial

---

'Circeo, Ghira è morto 11 anni fa scoperta la tomba a Melilla', 29 October 2005, <http://www.repubblica.it/2005/j/sezioni/cronaca/ghiracirceo/andreaghira/andreaghira.html>.

541   See 'Circeo, Ghira è morto 11 anni fa scoperta la tomba a Melilla', 29 October 2005, <http://www.repubblica.it/2005/j/sezioni/cronaca/ghiracirceo/andreaghira/andreaghira.html>.

542   See Para. 1 of Framework Decision 2009/299/JHA, op. cit. note 531.

decisions in EU Member States, measures aimed at preventing and settling conflicts of jurisdiction among Member States, measures supporting the training of the judiciary and judicial staff, and measures having the purpose of facilitating co-operation between judicial authorities of all Member States. For this purpose, the European Parliament and the Council can establish minimum rules in order to reinforce mutual judicial recognition and police and judicial co-operation, especially in the face of cross-border crimes. These rules must 'take into account the legal traditions and systems of the Member States'.[543] The EU's supremacy in the criminal area is fully supported by the author of this book, and is partially recognised by the Lisbon Treaty. The Lisbon Treaty increases the legislative powers of the European Parliament in the criminal area, but must respect specific limitations. This is because it must take into account that supporting EU supremacy in the criminal area risks creating a negative reaction to EU integration in this area.[544] Such a negative reaction would certainly damage its effectiveness and further development in future, especially if its limitations are not indicated. One of these limitations is related to the imposition of criminal sanctions on individuals, which has to remain under Member States' competence. These thoughts are supported by the recent EC case law. In *X*,[545] the Court of Justice held that unimplemented directives have to respect the principles of legal certainty and non-retroactivity, and thus they cannot determine or aggravate the criminal liability of a person who is in breach of those directives.[546] In *Berlusconi*,[547] the court had to evaluate whether the Italian civil code's provisions which entered into force long after the implementation of the First Companies Directive should prevail. These codes were seen as being more favourable to Berlusconi and his friends. According to the Italian Penal Code, more lenient criminal sanctions always prevail regarding stricter criminal penalties, and the former shall be applied retroactively in pending cases.[548] Unsuprisingly, the Court of Justice held that according to well-established case law,[549] if the national courts find that the new national provisions are not appropriate, they should set aside these provisions.[550] However, the court also highlighted 'that a directive cannot of itself impose obligations on an individual

543 See Art. 82 (2) of the Lisbon Treaty, op. cit. note 107.

544 On this point, see Peers, 'Salvation Outside the Church', op. cit. note 304, p. 923.

545 See Case C-60/02 *X* [2004] ECR I-0000-Court of Justice.

546 See also Case C-80/86 *Kolpinghuis Nijmegen* [1987] ECR 3969-Court of Justice, paras 12 and 13.

547 See Case C-387/02 *Berlusconi* [2005] ECR I-3565-Court of Justice.

548 See Art. 2 of 'Codice Penale. R.D.N. 1398, 19/10/1930', GU 251, 26 October 1930.

549 See Case C 106/77 *Simmenthal* [1978] ECR 629-Court of Justice, paras 21 and 4. See also Joined Cases C-13/91 and C-113/91 *Debus* [1992] ECR I-3617-Court of Justice, para. 32; Joined Cases C-10/97 to C-22/97 *IN. CO. GE'90 and Others* [1998] ECR I-6307-Court of Justice, para. 20.

550 See *Berlusconi*, op. cit. note 547, para. 72.

and cannot therefore be relied on as such against that individual'.[551] Moreover, as pointed out above, a directive cannot aggravate or determine the criminal liability of an individual.[552] For these reasons, the court concluded that the directive could not have been relied upon.[553]

EU case law has also confirmed that EC/EU provisions cannot impose criminal sanctions on individuals. In *Pupino*,[554] the Court of Justice asserted that the principles of the EC Treaty should be applied to the EU Treaty. Specifically, the Court of Justice held that national legislation should be interpreted on the basis of framework decisions, typical third-pillar instruments.[555] The Court of Justice highlighted that Article 34(2)(b) EU Treaty defines framework decisions with the same words as Article 249 EC Treaty uses to define directives.[556] According to the Court of Justice, the similarity between Articles 249(3) EC Treaty and 34(2)(b) TEU indicates that framework decisions are binding at the same level as directives, and that national courts have the obligation to interpret national law in conformity with EU law.[557] Directives are EC measures, and thus, like all EC measures, have to be interpreted on the basis of the principle of conformity with Article 10 EC Treaty, which is the principle of loyal co-operation.[558] The Italian and the UK governments noted that the obligation of conformity that national courts should respect is established by Article 10 EC Treaty, which does not encompass the EU Treaty.[559] The Court of Justice rejected these observations by arguing that the fact that the EU Treaty aims to create 'an ever closer union among the peoples of Europe, in which decisions are taken as openly as possible and as closely as possible to the citizens'[560] means that the authors of the EU Treaty had intention to approve 'legal instruments with effects similar to those provided for by the EC Treaty, in order to contribute effectively to the pursuit of the Union's objectives'.[561] Furthermore, the Court of Justice has pointed out that jurisdiction would be deprived of having the most useful effects if individuals could not rely on framework decisions to obtain conformity of interpretation of national laws.[562] In other words, even in the area of EU police and judicial co-operation, Member States shall interpret their national laws in the light of framework decisions on the

---

551   See ibid., para. 73.
552   See ibid., para. 74.
553   See ibid., para. 78.
554   See Case C-105/03 *Criminal Proceedings against Maria Pupino* [2005] 2 ECR I-5285-Court of Justice.
555   Compare Art. 34(2)(b) TEU with Art. 249(3) TEC.
556   See Case C-105/03, op. cit. note 554, para. 33. Compare Art. 34(2)(b) TEU with Art. 249(3) TEC.
557   See Case C-105/03, op. cit. note 554, para. 34.
558   See Art. 10 TEC.
559   See Case C-105/03, op. cit. note 554, para. 39.
560   See Art. 1(2) TEU.
561   See Case C-105/03, op. cit. note 554, para. 36.
562   See ibid., para. 38.

basis of the principle of loyalty,[563] a typical principle of the EC Treaty.[564] From the wording of the observation by the Court of Justice, it can be implied that this principle can be extended to all Member States' national courts, including those of EU Member States that have not accepted the Court of Justice jurisdiction. As the Court of Justice has stated, the uniform interpretation of national law in the light of framework decisions is a general principle that all Member States national courts shall follow.[565] Nevertheless, the Court of Justice imposed limitations to the principle of conforming interpretation which are 'the general principles of law, particularly those of legal certainty and non-retroactivity'.[566] An unimplemented framework decision cannot impose criminal liability or aggravate such liability upon individuals, as the principle of the legality of criminal law would be violated.[567] These limitations cannot be extended to the criminal procedure and to the means by which the evidence is collected.[568] Indeed, in these cases, national laws have to be interpreted in the light of framework decisions, unless this interpretation would cause a violation of the right to a fair trial expressly recognised by Article 6 ECHR.[569]

What impact could this limitation of the EU supremacy in the criminal area have if EU supremacy only meant extension of the principle of direct effect to this area? In this case, the fact that individuals will not be subject to EU criminal penalties unless national laws provide for this to happen would guarantee the protection of the fundamental rights of individuals. The fact that framework decisions have direct effect (assuming that EU supremacy consists of extension of direct effect to the criminal area) would not encroach on national sovereignty as far as substantive criminal law (imposition of criminal sanctions) is concerned. There is EC/EU case law that prohibits this intrusion. Could the same thoughts be applied if EU supremacy in the criminal area meant setting aside national constitutions? At the moment, there cannot be a certain answer because the EU is still making progress in adopting common rules on fair trials. As a side note, it could be asserted, for example, that if the EAW Framework Decision was amended as indicated above, there is a necessity for all EU Member States to have the obligation to set aside their constitutions if required. This should be the case even if an EU measure provided criminal sanctions to be imposed on individuals, if this was necessary in order to comply fully with the EAW Framework Decision. Certainly, the Court of Justice's case law would impede this. However, there would definitely be a negative reaction to EU integration in the criminal area, as many Member States might think that the EU aims to

---

563 Ibid.
564 See Art. 10 TEC.
565 See Case C-105/03, op. cit. note 554, para. 43.
566 See ibid., para. 44.
567 See ibid., para. 45.
568 See ibid., para. 46.
569 See ibid., paras 46, 47, 48, 58 and 59.

create an EU dictatorship where national constitutions would no longer be able to protect individuals' rights.

The issue is rather problematic because, as stated above, setting aside national constitutions in order to comply with EU measures in the criminal area might be necessary in order to combat transnational criminal organisations. This is why EU supremacy in the criminal area would require reforming the European Parliament's role in this area. Therefore, ratification of the Lisbon Treaty was a pivotal moment, as it sought to introduce the ordinary legislative procedure when adopting certain measures in the criminal area. After this reform, the European Parliament should push the EU to introduce more criminal measures and enhance mutual trust between EU Member States, and therefore mutual judicial recognition, by the introduction of common rules on fair trials, which is currently in progress. If the European Parliament, as a body representing the citizenry of the EU, co-legislated with the Council and adopted common rules on fair trials, mutual trust could be established. EU citizens might be more willing to set aside their national constitutions if they realised that this was necessary in order to defeat trans-national criminal organisations. Setting aside national constitutions would not appear as EU dictatorship, but the will of EU citizens who have achieved this by creating a cultural and moral movement against criminal organisations. Finally, EU citizens could agree what limitations should be imposed on the EU in the criminal area, the relationship between EU criminal law and national constitutions, and whether the EU should have the power to impose criminal sanctions. However, in order to achieve this objective, it is crucial for Member States to have common rules with respect to human rights. Indeed, measures such as mutual judicial co-operation require a high degree of trust between EU Member States' criminal justice systems. Certainly, there is the ECHR. However, the fact that this convention is not part of Member States' constitutions creates fragmentation with regard to the ECHR's principles, as there are Member States that respect it less than others. Furthermore, as stated above, the European Commission revealed that there are instances of non-compliance with the ECHR, and this is evidenced by the fact that there are too many applications pending before the Strasbourg Court, which grew by over 500 percent in the period 1993–2000.[570] At the moment, the EU is trying to introduce common rules regarding respect of human rights. The Council adopted Regulation 168/2007 establishing a European Union Agency for Fundamental Rights.[571] The aims of the agency are:

> To provide the relevant institutions, bodies, offices and agencies of the Community and its Member States when implementing Community law with assistance and expertise relating to fundamental rights in order to support them

---

570   See COM (2004) 328, op. cit. note 317, p. 3.

571   See 'Council Regulation (EC) No. 168/2007 of 15 February 2007 Establishing a European Union Agency for Fundamental Rights', OJ EU L53/1, 22 February 2007.

when they take measures or formulate courses of action within their respective spheres of competence to fully respect fundamental rights.[572]

For this purpose, the regulation states that the Agency will work in co-operation with inter-governmental organisations, the European Council, civil society and Member States in respect of the Charter of Fundamental Rights and the ECHR.[573] The project might create uniformity in the respect of human rights in Member States. However, there are some concerns related to the relationship between the agency and the EU police and judicial co-operation in criminal matters. Indeed, the regulation addresses monitoring the respect of fundamental rights when Community policies must be implemented by Member States. The agency would not interfere in the criminal area, and this could lead to fragmentation in the respect of human rights when EU criminal measures are implemented by Member States. This shortcoming might be overcome if the Lisbon Treaty entered into force, because it abolishes the difference between the EC and EU Treaties. Respect for fundamental human rights is very important, especially now that the European Parliament is proposing a recommendation to the Council in order to establish an EU criminal justice system.[574] In this proposal, the European Parliament principally recommends the Council to review the state of judicial co-operation in the EU criminal area, to implement mutual judicial co-operation and the EAW in the criminal area, and to prepare a study on the similarities and differences between Member States' criminal law systems. The European Parliament specifies that all these initiatives should be taken with respect to the Charter of Fundamental Rights. This means that the European Parliament is aware of the importance of preserving fundamental rights in the development of an EU criminal justice system.

Conclusions

This chapter has focused on Europol and on how this agency could contribute to combating cross-border crimes such as smuggling of migrants and trafficking in human beings. The chapter also concentrated on Eurojust and on other measures in order to improve judicial co-operation in the EU. We then analysed the modifications that the Constitutional Treaty would have introduced in the criminal area, and the more democratic approach by which measures on the criminal area would be adopted according to the Lisbon Treaty. Subsequently, we moved on to analyse mutual legal assistance and the EAW which reformed the rules on extradition.

---

572   See ibid., Art. 2.
573   See, respectively, ibid., para. 2, Arts 8, 9 and 10.
574   *See European Parliament Report with a Proposal for a European Parliament Recommendation to the Council on development of an EU Criminal Justice Area (2009/2012 (INI))*, A6-0262/-2009, 8 April 2009.

This measure has been adopted at EU level by framework decisions (Council acting alone), and at the EC level, where the Council, European Parliament and the Commission co-operate in order to defeat trafficking in human beings and people smuggling. The approach at the EC level is preferable, as measures are adopted through a more democratic approach by including the European Parliament in the decision-making process. The EU governments have reached the point where they must decide whether or not EU integration should involve the criminal area, and in what way. Should citizens of the EU, people resident in the EU, and victims of smuggling and trafficking be involved in this process of integration? If EU supremacy in the criminal area only means extending direct effect to EU criminal measures, would this be an insufficient step in showing EU citizens that the EU can play a vital role in combating organised crime? The status quo suggests that governments of EU Member States would prefer that the EU remain a issue that only a few lucky or unlucky (depending on the different views) academics are capable of analysing and understanding. However, if EU Member States decided to make a concerted effort to bring the EU closer to EU citizens and residents, victims of smuggling and trafficking, and their needs, then they would have to implement measures that go beyond extending direct effects to the third pillar. In fact, the extension of direct effect to the criminal area does not require that EU Member States set aside national constitutions, even potentially in instances where a criminal measure would be important, leading to the arrest of criminals belonging to dangerous criminal organisations. The intervention of the European Parliament in the decision-making process in the criminal area is important in order to adopt measures that could potentially require Member States to set aside their national constitutions. The European Parliament could be instrumental in informing the EU citizenry so that they may understand that reinforcing the EU criminal area would mean living in a more secure environment. With this awareness, citizens would have the incentive to create a cultural and moral movement that would make the EU territory less accessible to criminal organisations. The adoption of repressive measures such as the EAW without the involvement of the European Parliament would not contribute to this increased understanding among the EU population of the reasons why it is necessary to combat organised crime in a unified manner that goes beyond national borders. Under the current framework, these decisions would be made in secret without the justification for making them being made public. This is the reason why the European Parliament, in co-operation with national parliaments, as established by Article 9 of the Lisbon Treaty Protocol on National Parliaments, would see the involvement of the citizens of the EU in the development of the criminal area. On 19 July 1992, the Italian anti-Mafia magistrate Borsellino, just a few hours before he died with his escorts, wrote these words:

> I became magistrate because I had a great passion for civil law and ... up until 1980 I worked mostly on civil cases. ... On May 4, Captain Emanuele Basile was murdered and chief prosecutor Chinnici asked me to handle the case. Meanwhile

my childhood friend Giovanni Falcone had joined my same office and from that time forward I understood that my work had changed. I had decided to remain in Sicily and I needed to give that choice a meaning. Our problems were the very one I had begun to deal with, almost by accident, and if I loved this land I had to work on them exclusively. From that day forward I have never left that job. ... And I am optimistic because I see that young people, Sicilian or otherwise, have a much greater awareness than the culpable indifference in which I lived until I was forty. When these young people are adults they will react with much greater force than I and my generation have.[575]

Again, it must be stated that the choice of extending EU supremacy into EU criminal measures only through direct effect will leave EU citizens and residents indifferent to the threats from criminal organisations. Without Member States' governments leading the way in creating a cultural moral movement by involving EU citizens through their European Parliament representatives, EU citizens will remain indifferent towards the activities of organised crime taking place around them. If this is the case, EU Member States' governments have to accept the fact that people, including victims of smuggling and trafficking, may understandably refuse to co-operate with law enforcement authorities in testifying against criminal organisations, for example, because they fear them. EU Member States' governments will also have to accept that as things stand now, measures in the criminal area may prove inadequate against criminal organisations because they are conducted in isolation and do not supersede national constitutions, as these measures do not involve the entire population of the EU.

Following the alternative route of reforming the EU Parliament's role and the role of national parliaments in the criminal area could make the fight against criminal organisations more effective. However, it must be emphasised that initiatives such as setting aside national constitutions should not be taken until the European Parliament is reformed and common rules on fair trials are adopted. Indeed, it is important for a civil society like the EU to protect the fundamental rights of defendants and suspects.

This chapter also highlighted how important it is to find ways to resolve conflicts of jurisdiction in order to ensure the full application of these measures. Furthermore, this chapter focused attention on the Framework Decision on Mutual Judicial Assistance and on ways to resolve conflicts of jurisdiction.

Member States must ensure a fair trial where the presumption of innocence and rules on trials *in absentia* are respected equally in all EU Member States. Unfortunately, at the moment there are no common rules on the respect of human rights in the criminal area. The Council has established an agency to monitor the respect of human rights in Member States. Nevertheless, this agency can only have competence to intervene in the implementation of Community policies,

575 Stille, A., *Excellent Cadavers: The Mafia and the Death of the First Italian Republic* (New York: Vintage, 2006).

and the criminal area is not part of the EC Treaty, but of the EU Treaty. Happily, the Lisbon Treaty has now been ratified by Ireland, so that common rules on the respect of human rights in the criminal area may be constructed. This is as a result of the Lisbon Treaty abolishing the difference between the EC and the EU. All measures adopted by the European Community will also apply to the European Union, especially in the criminal area, where the ordinary legislative procedure will be adopted to enact legislation.

The next chapter focuses in particular on victims of smuggling and trafficking, because it is thought that the fight against these two cross-border crimes could be improved by their contribution. Victims are intimidated by the criminal organisations involved in the commission of these crimes. This is the reason why victims of smuggling and trafficking should be encouraged to testify against criminal organisations and contribute to arresting the criminals responsible for these crimes. Law enforcement authorities must encourage to testify by gaining their trust. The EU could contribute to achieving this result by adopting and implementing measures to support victims. The next chapter examines these issues in depth.

Chapter 4
EU Migration Policies

Introduction

The last two chapters focused on defining people smuggling and human trafficking, and enhancing EU police and judicial cooperation in order to fight these two crimes. This chapter will focus on the victims of trafficking in human beings and on victims who are smuggled by sea. This chapter will propose that people smuggling by sea be treated the same as people trafficking. In order to achieve this objective, it will be argued that the EU directive on persons in need of subsidiary protection should be reformed. It is important that people smuggling by sea be considered wholly separate from people smuggling in general because of the unique nature of the former. People smuggling by sea involves victims who are forced to leave their countries of origin due to extreme poverty, making up 4–12 percent of people smuggled as whole, as this section will show. The High Commissioner for Human Rights, Louise Arbour, has argued that people who escape from poverty, famine and epidemics should be protected to the same extent as asylum seekers. This should be done, the Commissioner argues, by recognising a general right to escape poverty.[1] This would result in those being smuggled by sea, intending to escape poverty, being recognised as having a right to do so.

Bade emphasised that there are four forms of irregular migration.[2] The first form of irregular migration begins with regular entry by a person who enters as a tourist or a seasonal worker, for example.[3] The regular entry becomes irregular once that person remains for more than the time allowed.[4] This phenomenon is quite widespread in Euro-Mediterranean countries such as France which call these

---

1   See_*Request of Declaration of Inconstitutionality Requested by the Tribunale di Pesaro – Sezione Penale, RNR 2823/09*, RG TRIB 829/09, 31 August 2009, para. XV, which quotes the opinions of the High Commissioner for Human Rights Louise Arbour.

2   See Bade, K.J., *Legal and Illegal Immigration into Europe: Experiences and Challenges* (Ortelius-lezing, 2003), p. 15. See also paras 7, 8 and 9 of 'Proposal for a Comprehensive Plan to Combat Illegal Immigration and Trafficking in Human Beings in the European Union', OJ EC C142/23, 14 June 2002. This Proposal distinguishes three types of illegal migration. Two of these can be called irregular migration (over-stayers and illegal entrants who do not commit crimes); see *Communication from the Commission to the Council and the European Parliament on a Common Policy on Illegal Immigration*, COM (2001) 672 final, 15 November 2001, p. 7.

3   See Bade, *Legal and Illegal Immigration into Europe*, op. cit. note 2, p. 15.

4   See ibid., p. 16.

people *sans-papiers* ('without papers' – over-stayers).[5] According to Bade, the second form of irregular migration is entry gained by using false documents. Once they have gained entry to the country, these migrants continue to stay without being registered, and do undeclared work.[6] The third form, Bade pointed out, is the smuggling of human beings carried out by international organisations.[7] Finally, Bade distinguishes a fourth and final form of irregular migration which takes place with the purpose of avoiding criminal prosecution.[8]

The category of over-stayers is very widespread, even though there are no reliable data on the phenomenon. The European Commission has stated on various occasions that it is impossible to estimate how many irregular migrants live in the EU Member States.[9] However, in Italy, a nation of transit for many irregular migrants smuggled by sea, the government has gathered data showing that in 2002–2003, 75 percent of irregular migrants were over-stayers, 15 percent entered Italy using fraudulent documents, and 10 percent were smuggled in by sea.[10] In 2004, only 4 percent of all irregular migrants entered Italy by sea with the aid of criminal organisations, 29 percent used fraudulent documents, and 67 percent were over-stayers.[11] In 2005, the proportion of irregular migrants who entered Italian territory by sea with the support of criminal organisations increased from 4 percent to 12 percent of all irregular migrants.[12] The number of over-stayers decreased by 6 percent, from 67 percent to 61 percent, and those using fraudulent documents decreased from 29 percent to 27 percent.[13] These data cannot be completely relied upon as they do not account for those living in hiding across the EU. The point these data are intended to make is that irregular migrants who are smuggled in by sea are a small sub-category of the total irregular migrant population. Why should people smuggled by sea be distinguished from the other irregular migrants? The answer is that people smuggled by sea tend to suffer uniquely poor conditions as they make their journey. The United Nations Convention on the Law of the Sea (UNCLOS) argues that these people should be rescued. It states that:

> 1. Every State shall require the master of a ship flying its flag, in so far as he can do so without serious danger to the ship, the crew or the passengers;

---

5   See note 2 above.

6   Ibid.

7   Ibid.

8   Ibid.

9   See, for example, *Communication from the Commission to the Council, the European Parliament, the European Economic and Social Committee and the Committee of the Regions: First Annual Report on Migration and Integration*, COM (2004) 508, 16 July 2004, p. 13. See also COM (2001) 672 final, op. cit. note 2, p. 7.

10   *Rapporto Annuale 2005 sullo 'stato della sicurezza in Italia'*, 14 August 2005, <http://www.interno.it//assets/files/&/20058141464>, accessed 23 March 2007, pp. 41 and 42.

11   Ibid.

12   Ibid.

13   Ibid.

(a) to render assistance to any person found at sea in danger of being lost;
(b) to proceed with all possible speed to the rescue of persons in distress, if informed of their need of assistance, in so far as such action may reasonably be expected of him;
(c) after a collision, to render assistance to the other ship, its crew and its passengers and, where possible, to inform the other ship of the name of his own ship, its port of registry and the nearest port at which it will call.

2. Every coastal State shall promote the establishment, operation and maintenance of an adequate and effective search and rescue service regarding safety on and over the sea and, where circumstances so require, by way of mutual regional arrangements co-operate with neighbouring States for this purpose.[14]

This convention Article cannot be derogated by agreements between States Parties because, as Vassalli Paleologo has emphasised, it is intended to protect the fundamental right of solidarity.[15] The prohibition on derogating from UNCLOS can be found in the Article 311 of UNCLOS, which states that such a derogation would be 'incompatible with the effective execution of the object and purpose of this convention, and provided further that such agreements shall not affect the application of the basic principles embodied herein'.[16] Other conventions that require the rescue of people who are shipwrecked are the 1974 International Convention for the Safety of Life at Sea (SOLAS) and the 1979 International Convention on Maritime Search and Rescue (SAR).[17] People smuggled by sea should not be abandoned to face an uncertain future. However, what should States do after having rescued them? One answer is to offer visas to those smuggled by sea (4–12 percent of all irregular migrants). Having been provided with the security of a visa, the victims would be more likely to share valuable information on the criminal organisations running the operations. For this reason, it is advantageous for Member States to grant visas to those smuggled into the EU by sea, since victims would be more inclined to trust the law enforcement authorities' ability to protect them from retaliation. In order to increase protection for people smuggled by sea, EU legislation would need to be amended.

Other ways to fight against the smuggling of migrants by sea should involve the EU common policy on immigration, strengthening the European Neighbourhood

---

14   See Art. 98 of the *United Nations Convention on the Law of the Sea* (UNCLOS), Montego Bay, 10 December 1982. See also Vassallo Paleologo, F., 'Obblighi di protezione e controlli delle frontiere marittime', *Diritto Immigrazione e Cittadinanza* 9:3 (2007), p. 24.

15   See note 14 above.

16   See Art. 311(3) UNCLOS, op. cit. note 14.

17   These Conventions are not examined in this book because it has a different aim. For a detailed analysis of these two Conventions and their impact on people smuggled by sea, see Vassalli Paleologo, 'Obblighi di protezione e controlli delle frontiere marittime', op. cit. note 14.

Policy (ENP) and adopting legal measures on economic legal migration. Finally, another factor which can have an effect on combating the smuggling of migrants by sea are the changes which will come into force with the ratification of the Lisbon Treaty.

This chapter will refer to illegal entrants as 'irregular migrants', avoiding word 'illegal' in favour of 'irregular' because it is not accurate to label these migrants as criminals, since many leave their country of origin due to circumstances beyond their control. As Cholewinski has pointed out, the term 'illegal' 'constitutes contributory factors in the construction of the migrant from outside the EU as someone to be suspected and not to be trusted'.[18] Cholewinski also points to terminology used by Title IV EC Treaty and Title VI EU Treaty as reinforcing the idea that illegal migration (in the sense of irregular migration) is a phenomenon to fight, prevent and combat.[19] The use of the term 'illegal' is also inaccurate because not all countries hold irregular migration to be a crime. If States that consider irregular migration a crime do call them 'illegal', they should apply criminal law in the correct way. This means that States which want to treat irregular migrants as criminals should be made to detain them with charge. Charging would give economic irregular migrants, for example, the possibility of raising defences such as duress by threat (victims of trafficking in human beings) or duress by circumstances (victims of people smuggling). It is important that EU Member States avoid inaccurate labels associated with irregular migrants in their legislation.

International Conventions

UNTOC[20] and the Council of Europe Convention on Trafficking in Humans[21] provide certain protections for victims of human trafficking.[22] Unfortunately, these two international conventions do not establish an adequate form of protection for smuggled people. UNTOC in particular states that trafficking in human beings is committed:

---

18   See Cholewinski, R., 'The Criminalisation of Migration', draft paper presented to the ILPA, British Institute for International and Comparative Law and JUSTICE Conference on 'How Much Freedom, Security and Justice? Developments in EU Asylum and Immigration Law', 13–14 May 2005, p. 2. The author of this book has obtained the speaker's permission to quote this paper.

19   Ibid.

20   See Art. 3 of the *Protocol to Prevent, Suppress and Punish Trafficking in Persons, Especially Women and Children, Supplementing the United Nations Convention against Transnational Organized Crime* (UNTOC Trafficking Protocol), A/RES/55/25, Doc. A/55/383, 8 January 2001.

21   See Art. 4 of *Council of Europe Convention on Action against Trafficking in Human Beings* (Council of Europe Convention on Trafficking), CM (2005) 32 Addendum 1 final, 3 May 2005.

22   See ibid., s. 5.1.

by means of the threat or use of force or other forms of coercion, of abduction, of fraud, of deception, of the abuse of power or of a position of vulnerability or of the giving or receiving of payments or benefits to achieve the consent of a person having control over another person ...[23]

As mentioned earlier, the Smuggling Protocol states:

'Smuggling of Migrants' shall mean the procurement, in order to obtain, directly or indirectly, a financial or other material benefit, of the illegal entry of a person into a State Party of which the person is not a national or a permanent resident.[24]

Scholars highlight differences between people smuggling and human trafficking, based on the difference between consent and coercion.[25] Victims of human trafficking are 'coerced' to leave their countries of origin, and for this reason they are considered innocent and deserving protection from States where they arrive.[26] In contrast, smuggled migrants choose to leave their countries of origin irregularly, and therefore do not deserve any form of protection.[27] In reality, the difference is not so clear, as Bhabha and Zard have pointed out:

There are certainly 'pure' cases of trafficking and smuggling – of children kidnapped without their parents consent, of migrant workers defrauded from the outset or, at the other end of the spectrum, of completely transparent cross-border transportation agreements where a fee is mutually agreed and the relationship between transporter and transported ends.[28]

There are also cases where smuggled migrants are forced to leave their country of origin because otherwise they would die due to starvation:[29]

There is no question that smugglers are taking advantage of the smuggled persons' desperation or vulnerability. But not all exploitative offers are coercive ... a parent forcing a child to travel abroad to practice a foreign language before an exam is coercive but not exploitative. So just because the smuggler's offer is

23   See Art. 3(1)(a) of the Trafficking Protocol, op. cit. note 20. See also Art. 4(1(a)) Council of Europe Convention, op. cit. note 21.

24   See Art. 3(a) of the *Protocol against the Smuggling of Migrants by Land, Sea and Air, Supplementing the United Nations Convention against Transnational Organized Crime* A/RES/55/25 (Smuggling Protocol), Doc. A/55/383, 8 January 2001.

25   See Bhabha, J., and Zard, M., 'Smuggled or Trafficked', *Forced Migration Review* 25 (May 2006), p. 6.

26   Ibid.

27   Ibid.

28   See ibid., p. 7.

29   Bhabha, J., and Zard, M., 'Human Smuggling and Trafficking: The Good, the bad and the Ugly', <http://www.fmreview.org/pdf/bhabha&zard.pdf>, accessed 6 May 2007.

exploitative does not necessarily mean that the smuggled migrant is coerced …
If the smuggled migrant has no other acceptable options, then the exploitative
offer becomes coercive: if he or she would starve, or be unable to get medicine
for a child unless he or she took up the offer, then we could say that the offer is
coercive.[30]

An indirect form of coercion can be caused by natural disasters such as
hurricanes.[31] Natural disasters can cause food insecurity in the regions
affected,[32] and force people who have lost all their belongings to leave their
country by boat. Criminal organisations can exploit these people, convincing
them to embark on boats in poor condition that leave their countries of origin
irregularly. This is a form of mental rather than physical coercion, as these
people seemingly have no alternative. These victims of natural disasters fit
the definition of 'vulnerable' provided by the Trafficking Protocol.[33] People
smugglers prey on the vulnerability of their victims, and once they have them
under their control, are in a position to abuse them.[34] As Obokata emphasises,
irregular migrants:[35]

> by placing themselves in the hands of smugglers, individuals have already
> ceded control of their fate, and are therefore in a position of vulnerability. It
> could also be argued that charging a large amount of money for smuggling
> may itself be seen as subsequent exploitation, as many of those smuggled
> are compelled to pay back the cost to the smugglers after they reach their
> destinations. All of this means that there is a danger that those in need of
> adequate attention and care might not receive enough protection from
> States.[36]

The possibility of the States and courts broadening their definition of what it
means to be vulnerable under the Trafficking Protocol will depend on their
willingness to do so.[37] The States and national courts would have to include in

---

30   Ibid.
31   On this point. see *The State of Food Insecurity in the World 2006*, UNFAO, 2006,
p. 19, <http://download.repubblica.it/pdf/FAOSOFI2006.pdf>.
32   Ibid.
33   See Bhabha and Zard, 'Smuggled or Trafficked', op. cit. note 25, pp. 7 and 8. See
also Art. 3(1)(a) of the Trafficking Protocol, op. cit. note 23.
34   Ibid., p. 7.
35   See '"Trafficking" and "Smuggling" of Human beings in Europe: Protection of
Individuals Rights or States' Interests', [2001] 5 *Web JCLI*.
36   Ibid.
37   Bhabha and Zard, 'Smuggled or Trafficked', op. cit. note 25, pp. 7 and 8. See also
Art. 3(1)(a) of the Trafficking Protocol, op. cit. note 23.

the interpretation of the Trafficking Protocol[38] coercive methods that go beyond the use of physical force, fraud or deceit.[39]

Unfortunately, at present there are no provisions in the UNTOC Protocols that offer strong legal protection for victims of people smuggling to the same extent as victims of human trafficking. The UNTOC Trafficking Protocol requires States Parties to provide victims with:

(a) Appropriate housing;
(b) Counselling and information, in particular as regards their legal rights, in a language that the victims of trafficking in persons can understand;
(c) Medical, psychological and material assistance; and
(d) Employment, educational and training opportunities.[40]

In addition, the UNTOC Trafficking Protocol calls for States Parties to adopt legislative measures that enable victims to remain in the receiving State's territory temporarily or permanently.[41]

The UNTOC Trafficking Protocol specifies that States Parties shall take the necessary initiatives:

including through bilateral and multilateral cooperation, to alleviate the factors that make persons, especially women and children, vulnerable to trafficking, such as poverty, underdevelopment and lack of equal opportunities.[42]

Here the UNTOC Trafficking Protocol is recognising that developing the poorer economies of victims' countries of origin is an important step in preventing human trafficking.

The Council of Europe Convention on Trafficking in Human Beings also provides for specific programmes to be established in order to prevent human trafficking.[43] The Council of Europe Convention specifies that victims of human trafficking shall receive adequate assistance,[44] stating that:

Each State Party shall adopt such legislative or other measures as may be necessary to ensure that assistance to a victim is not made conditional on his or her willingness to act as a witness.[45]

---

38 See also Art. 3(1)(a) of the Trafficking Protocol op. cit. note 23.
39 See Bhabha, and Zard, 'Smuggled or Trafficked' op. cit. note 25, p. 8.
40 See Arts 6(3)(a)(b)(c) and (d) of the UNTOC Trafficking Protocol, op. cit. note 20.
41 See ibid., Art. 7(1).
42 See ibid., Art. 9(4).
43 See Art. 5(2) of the Council of Europe Convention on Trafficking, op. cit. note 21.
44 See ibid., Art. 12(1).
45 See ibid., Art. 12(6).

The Council of Europe Convention also states that a residence permit shall be issued to victims not only when they decide to co-operate in investigations and criminal proceedings,[46] but also when 'the competent authority considers that their stay is necessary owing to their personal situation'.[47] Smuggled persons do not enjoy the same protection as human trafficking victims at international level.[48] The UNTOC Convention establishes as a general rule that:

> Each State Party shall take appropriate measures within its means to provide assistance and protection to victims of offences covered by this Convention, in particular in cases of threat of retaliation or intimidation.[49]

In addition, Article 25 states that victims of crimes covered by this convention shall receive compensation. These rules are applicable both to the human trafficking and the smuggling of migrants protocols.[50] However, the issue of granting a residence permit to victims of people smugglers remains unaddressed, and the protective provisions found in the UNTOC Protocol on Trafficking in Human Beings have yet to be enacted. Certainly, the victims of smuggling of migrants should be protected from 'torture or other cruel, inhuman or degrading treatment or punishment'.[51] Moreover, victims of smugglers should be protected from violence.[52] In any case, the UNTOC Smuggling Protocol also states that the victims shall be returned to their countries of origin, and it does not establish the possibility of obtaining a residence permit. One hopes that the concept of 'abuse of vulnerable protection' indicated by Article 3(1)(a) of the Trafficking Protocol will be extended to victims of people smuggling who have no alternatives except to leave their countries of origin to escape natural disasters and starvation.

The European Convention on Human Rights and Smuggling of Migrants by Sea

The ECHR[53] does not include any provision that draws a distinction between victims of people smuggling and other irregular migrants. The ECHR does have a provision that prohibits slavery and forced labour,[54] but this provision, as

---

46   See ibid., Art. 13(1)(a).

47   See ibid., Art. 13(1)(b).

48   See Obokata, T., 'Smuggling of Human Beings from a Human Rights Perspective: Obligations of Non-State and State Actors under International Human Rights Law', *International Journal of Refugee Law* 7:2 (2005), pp. 397 and 398.

49   See Art. 25 (1) of the UNTOC Trafficking Protocol, op. cit. note 20.

50   See, respectively, ibid., Art. 1. See also Art. 1 of the Smuggling Protocol, op. cit. note 24.

51   See ibid., Art. 16(1).

52   See ibid., Art. 16(2).

53   See ibid., s. 3.1.

54   See Art. 4 of *Convention for the Protection of Human Rights and Fundamental Freedoms* (ECHR), Rome, 4 November 1950.

Cholewinski has pointed out, does not grant any form of protection to irregular migrants apart from prohibiting collective expulsion,[55] the deportation of persons who are at risk of inhuman and degrading treatment within the meaning of Article 3 ECHR when they are returned to their countries of origin,[56] and the deportation of persons who would be in breach with Article 8 ECHR (irregular migrants for family reasons).[57] Certainly, it is clear that victims of human trafficking may find protection under Article 4 ECHR. The ECHR guarantees the right to liberty, and it considers detention of irregular migrants an exception that must be interpreted strictly.[58] In any case, the ECHR allows the expulsion and detention prior to deportation of irregular migrants without drawing any distinction between victims of criminal organisations and other categories of irregular migrants.[59] Article 5(1)(f) states:

> Everyone has the right to liberty and security of person. No one shall be deprived of his liberty save in the following cases and in accordance with a procedure prescribed by law:
> (f) the lawful arrest or detention of a person to prevent his effecting an unauthorised entry into the country or of a person against whom action is being taken with a view to deportation …[60]

Article 5 ECHR states that the detainee but be informed of 'the reasons of his arrest and the charges against him',[61] and has the right 'to take proceedings by which the lawfulness of his detention shall be decided speedily by a court and his release ordered if the detention is not lawful'.[62] The ECHR also states that the detainee has the right to compensation if he or she has been unlawfully detained.[63] These are minimum guarantees against unlawful detention of irregular migrants in order to ensure: 'that any deprivation of liberty should be in keeping with the purpose of Article 5, namely to protect the individual from arbitrariness'.[64] Despite

---

55   See Cholewinski, R., 'The Need for Effective Individual Legal Protection in Immigration Matters'. In *European Journal of Migration and Law* 7:3 (2005), p. 241. The author quotes Art. 4 of Protocol. 4 to the ECHR.

56   See Cholewinski, 'The Need for Effective Individual Legal Protection in Immigration Matters', op. cit. note 55, p. 238.

57   Ibid.

58   See House of Lords and House of Commons Joint Committee on Human Rights, *The Treatment of Asylum Seekers*, Session 2006–2007, 10th Report, HL 81-1 and HC 60-I, *Volume I: Report and Report and Formal Minutes*, p. 70.

59   See Art. 5(1)(f) ECHR, op. cit. note 54.

60   Ibid.

61   See ibid., Art. 5(2).

62   See ibid., Art. 5(4).

63   See ibid., Art. 5(5).

64   See *Kemmache v. France*, judgment of 24 November 1994, Series A no. 296-C, para. 42.

its importance, demonstrated above, there are no provisions that draw a distinction between people smuggled by sea and other irregular migrants. The European Court of Human Rights (Strasbourg Court) interpretation of Article 5(1)(f) ECHR[65] may actually make matters worse by facilitating the expulsion of irregular migrants who are victims of criminal organisations. This is because , as Rogers pointed out,[66] the Strasbourg Court has recognised that immigration matters are within the competence of national laws, therefore giving Member States a wide margin of discretion in the way they deal with matters of immigration. The Strasbourg Court has emphasised that States have the right to decide who can or cannot enter and reside in their territories. The Strasbourg Court has no problem with the detention of illegal aliens for an extremely lengthy period,[67] 'as long as deportation proceedings are in progress'.[68] The Strasbourg Court has also recognised that the right of States to expel aliens must be balanced with the right to respect for private and family life.[69] This right has always been a high priority in the Strasbourg Court's jurisprudence, even where crimes have been committed.[70] The Strasbourg Court has stated that there is a breach of Article 5(1)(f) ECHR when authorities use their right to expel over-stayers 'by misleading them about the purpose of a notice so as to make it easier to deprive them of their liberty'.[71] The Strasbourg Court has also pointed out that it is not sufficient 'that the deprivation of liberty is executed in conformity with national law but it must also be necessary in the circumstances'.[72] However, the Strasbourg Court has also stated that detention of a potential asylum seeker or immigrant when there is no risk of absconding is in fact lawful, and it will not be considered excessive if it extends for up to seven days.[73] As suggested above, the interpretation of the Strasbourg Court does not draw the important distinction between irregular migrants who are victims of criminal organisations, and all other irregular migrants.

One might certainly be inclined to agree that States Parties to the ECHR should be able to decide who should be allowed to stay in their territories, a right recognised under international law.[74] However, it is logical to allow States to treat certain categories of irregular migrants differently, such as those smuggled by sea,

---

65   See *Moustaquim* v. *Belgium* (1991) 13 EHRR 802. See also *Chahal* v. *United Kingdom* (1996) 23 EHRR 413.

66   See Rogers, N., 'Immigration and the European Convention on Human Rights: Are New Principles Emerging?', *European Human Rights Law Review* 8:1 (2003), p. 53.

67   See *Chahal* v. *United Kingdom* (1996) EHRR 413, paras 119 and 123.

68   See ibid., para. 113.

69   See *Berrehab* v. *The Netherlands,* (1998) EHRR 138. See also *Slivenko* v. *Latvia* (2003) ECHR 2002-II, para. 113; *Moustaquim* v. *Belgium*, op. cit. note 65, paras 13 *et seq.*

70   See ibid., paras 13 *et seq.* See also *Radovanovic* v. *Austria* (2005) 41 EHRR 6.

71   See *Conka* v. *Belgium* 51564/99 [2002] ECHR 14, para. 42.

72   See *Witold Litwa* v. *Poland*, no. 26629/95, ECHR 2000-III, para. 78.

73   See *Saadi* v. *United Kingdom*, Application no. 13229/03, paras 42 and 45.

74   See *Report of the United Nations International Law Commission*, 57th Session, A/60/10, 2005, p. 123.

if they want to be serious in the fight against criminal organisations who are the root cause of this crime. The right of States to expel aliens must be balanced with the right of irregular migrants to be protected against human traffickers, and also against the people smugglers. Humanitarian organisations can also play a role by providing shelter for both victims of smuggling committed by sea as well as victims of human trafficking so they may feel encouraged to report their smugglers and traffickers. The Council of Europe Convention specifies that victims of trafficking in human beings must be identified and a residence permit should be issued.[75] This is made difficult by restrictive national immigration laws that mandate the automatic arrest, imprisonment and deportation of all irregular migrants with no form of legal protection. These tough national laws do not take into consideration that these irregular migrants are highly susceptible to re-victimisation by the same traffickers and smugglers who exploited them in the first place. These people are vulnerable if left to their fate when they are in detention camps or when they are outside EU territory. UNTOC expressly requires States Parties to prevent re-victimisation, which is contradicted by the automatic detention and expulsion of these groups. A distinction between the different categories of irregular migrants should be drawn.

Can the EU provide new protection for people smuggled by sea? This will be a reality now that the Lisbon Treaty has been ratified. Before the entry into force of this Treaty, at EU level there was legislation to protect irregular migrants who had been victims of criminal organisations, which is examined below. This legislation should be reformed in order to guarantee protection to victims smuggled by sea. Before the entry into force of the Lisbon Treaty, the opting out of Ireland, the UK and Denmark, along with ability of the Council to act on its own on matters related to legal migration, in particular Article 63(3)(a) and (4),[76] which was subject to the Council's unanimous votes and European Parliament's mere consultation,[77] made it difficult to establish a common EU policy to combat organised crime responsible for victimising irregular migrants. This was because granting temporary visas to victims of people smuggling by sea was an aspect of legal migration which was outside the competence of the EC. Moreover, there was fragmentation in the criminal measures adopted to counter people trafficking and smuggling and

---

75 See Art. 10 of the Council of Europe Convention on Trafficking, op. cit. note 21.

76 See Recital 7 of 'Council Decision 2004/927/EC of 22 December 2004 Providing for Certain Areas Covered by Title IV of Part Three of the Treaty Establishing the European Community to be Governed by the Procedure Laid Down in Article 251 of that Treaty', OJ EU L 396/45, 31 December 2004. See also Arts 63(3(a)) and 4 *Consolidated Version of the Treaty Establishing the European Community*, C325/1-184, 2002, which states: 'measures on immigration policy within the following areas: conditions of entry and residence, and standards on procedures for the issue by Member States of long term visas and residence permits, including those for the purpose of family reunion, ... (4) measures defining the rights and conditions under which nationals of third countries who are legally resident in a Member State may reside in other Member States.'

77 See Arts 67 and 251 of TEC op. cit. note 76.

measures related to migration or irregular migration. According to the EU Treaty, all measures related to the criminal area were taken by unanimous vote of the EU Council and the other institutions, though Parliament and the Commission played a marginal consultative role.[78] Measures adopted in the EU criminal area were therefore anti-democratic, which conflicts with the creation of a cultural and moral movement needed to fight against the criminal organisations behind smuggling and trafficking of human beings.

The Lisbon Treaty will permit the European Parliament to co-legislate with the Council, and decisions on immigration and the criminal area could be enacted by QMV. These reforms could make a difference in the protection of irregular migrants who have been the victims of organised crime. The European Parliament will be able to push for ad hoc measures for them by reinterpreting the law previously adopted on the protection of human trafficking victims. People smuggled by sea already fall within the scope of the directive on the protection of victims of trafficking, which will be covered later in this chapter. These people are victims, and they should be considered victims by Member States. This is because when these people leave their countries of origin by boat to reach the EU, they travel in very inhuman conditions, risking death. It has been reported that since 1988, 7,180 persons have died while trying to reach the EU by boat.[79] The highest death rate was reported in 2006, when 1,582 persons died – almost twice the number who died in 2005, and almost three times the number in 2004. Indeed, in 2005, 822 persons died and in 2004, 564.[80] These people would not travel in these conditions if they had other options in their countries of origin, which is why the directive on the protection of trafficking victims is important. Irregular migrants smuggled by sea may be reluctant to give information on the criminal organisations which have exploited them, for fear of retaliation.[81] In many cases when smuggled migrants are asked to identify the port they travelled from and the people who helped them, they give conflicting versions, and it is not possible to establish with certainty where they travelled from and who was in control of the operation.[82] Some sources suggest that the trips by boat to the EU are organised from Al Zwara in Libya, where the majority of criminal organisations that commit smuggling of migrants are based.[83] Other sources report that the main ports where

---

78   See Art. 39 of 'Consolidated Version of the Treaty Establishing the European Union', OJ C 325/1-184, 24 December 2002.

79   See 'Fortress Europe – L'osservatorio sulle vittime dell'immigrazione clandestina', *Melting Pot Europa*, 6 February 2007, <http://www.meltingpot.org/articolo9778.html>.

80   Ibid.

81   See Obokata, 'Smuggling of Human Beings from a Human Rights Perspective', op. cit. note 48, p. 410.

82   See 'Migrants land in Mauritania', News24, 12 February 2007, <http://www.news24.com/News24/Africa/News/0,2-11-1447_2068220,00.html>.

83   See Pecoraro, A., 'Lampedusa, la strage dimenticata dei migranti', *Il Manifesto*, 24 February 2007.

these trips are organised are in Turkey, and some suggest Senegal.[84] These people who are victims of smugglers should be distinguished from the other irregular migrants such as over-stayers or irregular migrants who travel to the EU in less precarious conditions. Indeed, not all smuggled migrants should be considered victims, but only those who travel in very poor conditions, avoiding certain death because of starvation or natural disasters, and who would not be protected by the Refugee Convention as they do not leave their countries of origin to escape war or persecution. Whether or not an irregular migrant can be said to be a victim should not be assumed, but investigated. All smuggled migrants should be looked after by humanitarian organisations, which could assist law enforcement authorities in distinguishing victims from other irregular migrants. The fact that people travel on old boats that sink, killing many migrants, for example, should lead to their being automatically considered as victims. Irregular migrants from countries that have recently suffered natural disasters or famine should also automatically be considered victims. Police in the countries of arrival, under Europol, should investigate irregular migrants to make sure they are not falsifying their claims in an attempt to avoid being returned to their countries of origin. Humanitarian organisations could support the investigations by reassuring the victims of smuggling. Chapter 5 will show the value of reassuring victims and encouraging them to report their smugglers and traffickers. The directive on the protection of trafficking victims might support this different approach.

How Should the Directive on the Protection of Victims of Smuggling of Migrants and Trafficking in Human Beings be Modified?

In 2004 the Council adopted Directive 2004/81/EC[85] on the protection of trafficking victims and optional protection of smuggling victims. The EU should make the protection of people smuggled by sea mandatory, not optional. The UK, Ireland and Denmark are not bound by this directive,[86] which may lead to inconsistencies in how human trafficking and people smuggling are combated throughout the EU. As stated above, criminal organisations are transnational in nature, which requires a transnational approach to counter them. The directive refers to victims of trafficking and 'third-country nationals who have been the

---

84 'Three missing after migrant boat sinks off Turkey', *Turkish Daily News*, 5 December 2006, <http://www.turkishdailynews.com.tr/article.php?enewsid=60887>, accessed 29 March 2007. See also 'Mueren 28 immigrantes frentes a las costas de Mauritania cuando se dirigìan en caiucos a Canarias', *El Mundo*, 13 August 2006, <http://www.elmundo.es/elmundo/2006/08/12/espana/1155400365.html>.

85 See 'Council Directive 2004/81/EC of 29 April 2004 on the Residence Permit Issued to Third-country Nationals Who are Victims of Trafficking in Human Beings or Who Have Been the Subject of an Action to Facilitate Illegal Immigration, Who Cooperate with the Competent Authorities', OJ EU L 261/19, 6 August 2004.

86 See ibid., Recital 21.

subject of an action to facilitate illegal immigration'.[87] This means that victims of trafficking and victims of smuggling, including victims of single acts committed to facilitate illegal entry, fall under the scope of the directive. However, the issue of issuing residence permits to persons who are not victims of trafficking is left to Member States' discretion. Member States can decide whether to extend the scope of this directive to victims of people smugglers.[88] Residence permits could be issued after a reflection period, during which victims of human trafficking, and eventually victims of smuggling of persons, could have an opportunity 'to recover and escape the influence of the perpetrators'.[89] Residence permits could be issued to those who decide to co-operate with the national prosecuting and judicial authorities in order to arrest and detain perpetrators of these crimes.[90] Furthermore, residence permits could be issued to victims 'for the investigation or the judicial proceedings, and ... whether he/she has shown a clear intention to cooperate and ... whether he/she has severed all relations'[91] with the human traffickers and the people smugglers. Directive 2004/81/EC also states that a residence permit may be withdrawn if the victim to whom it has been issued does not co-operate with the competent authorities, if the co-operation is fraudulent, if the victim actively and voluntary renews contact with her or his traffickers, and for other reasons related to public order.[92] Moreover, those who hold residence permits might only have access to vocational training and education for the duration of the permit.[93] There is also one provision that supports the integration of victims in the hosting Member State.[94] This provision states that Member States can introduce specific schemes for victims, and for this purpose their residence permits can be renewed.[95] As Chapter 5 shows, renewal of permits is relevant when investigations are complex and require a longer stay by the victim in the hosting Member State.

This directive might guarantee a form of legal protection to victims of human trafficking. However, it must be pointed out that granting legal protection to victims of people smuggling is only optional. For this reason, Directive 2004/81/EC should be amended so that it obliges EU Member States to grant legal protection to victims who have been smuggled by boat who decide to co-operate with law enforcement authorities. In this way, the criminal organisations behind these crimes may be defeated.

---

87   See ibid., Recital 9.
88   Ibid.
89   See ibid., Art. 6(1).
90   See ibid., Art. 8.
91   See ibid., Art. 8(1).
92   See ibid., Art. 14.
93   See ibid., Art. 11(2).
94   See ibid., Art. 12.
95   Ibid.

As emphasised above,[96] criminal organisations gain power by intimidating the surrounding society. If criminal groups in the EU successfully gain a reputation for violence, it makes it difficult law enforcement authorities to win the support of a surrounding community terrified of criminal organisations. In the case of smuggling of migrants and trafficking in human beings, this might mean forfeiting the support of victims in combating these two crimes and risk losing valuable evidence. For this reason, it is essential for law enforcement authorities to gain the trust of the victims of human trafficking and people smuggling. For example, there have been reports that show that victims are more likely to testify against their exploiters if they obtain residence permits. Permits offer protection for victims, making them more confident that they can trust law enforcement bodies in their efforts to combat organised crime.[97] There is no similar evidence for people smuggled by sea. Police officers at the Smuggling Unit of Heathrow Airport in the UK[98] have been told by smuggled migrants that they do not want to make accusations against their smugglers because they fear them. These findings, along with the data on the effects of offering residence permits, support reforming Directive 2004/81/EC, requiring all EU Member States to grant residence permits to all victims of human trafficking and those smuggled by sea without making any distinction between the two categories of irregular migrants.

This reform is certain to encounter resistance from EU Member States which fear that such an amendment might encourage irregular migrants to make false claims. A way to avoid this at EU/EC level is by adopting legal measures that discourage smuggled migrants from making false claims. Once it has been proven that irregular migrants have been victims of criminal organisations, they should be legally protected by granting them temporary visas. This issue will be examined more thoroughly in Chapter 5, where we present the findings of interviews held in the detention centre at Lampedusa in Italy and the investigative office of Siracusa in Italy.

Protection of Irregular Migrants Who are Victims of Criminal Organisations Even if They Decide Not to Co-operate with Law Enforcement Authorities

Victims of trafficking and smuggling should also be protected even if they decide not to co-operate with law enforcement authorities. Law enforcement authorities in Italy and the UK have found that in order to defeat the crime of trafficking, it was necessary to grant visas to victims whether they decided to co-operate with them or not. The findings of interviews and reasons for these thoughts will be explored in greater detail in Chapter 5. This section will focus on how and why the law should be reinterpreted in order to protect victims

---

96   See Chapter 2 of this book.
97   Interview with Polizia di Stato in Rimini held on 12 June 2006.
98   Interviews held on 16 June 2006 at Heathrow Airport.

of smuggling and trafficking even when these victims do not co-operate with law enforcement authorities. This section will also argue that granting legal protection to victims of smuggling and trafficking is crucial to investigations of the criminal organisations behind these two crimes.

Specifically, it is Directive 2004/83/EC which recalls the Convention on Refugees that must be reinterpreted.[99] This directive states that persons entitled to subsidiary protection are those who cannot apply for the status of refugees as defined by the Geneva Convention, but who may suffer serious harm if returned to their countries of origin or their habitual residence.[100] Directive 2004/83/EC explains what is meant by the term 'serious harm'. Serious harm consists of the death penalty, torture or other inhuman treatment, threat and violence against civilian populations in times of internal or international conflicts.[101] Article 6 states that the actors that may persecute or commit serious harm are States, and organisations controlling States. Non-State actors are also mentioned as perpetrators of serious harm in the directive where it can be demonstrated that States or other organisations controlling the State 'are unable or unwilling to provide protection against serious harm'.[102] Directive 2004/83/EC may protect victims of smuggling by sea if these victims can demonstrate that they have suffered serious harm at the hands of smugglers (non-State actors), and therefore should obtain visas because States or organisations representing States have failed to protect them.

States might be unable to protect victims because criminal organisations are strong and able to organise themselves despite the restrictions imposed by State actors. As Europol has noted, the criminal networks of organised crime 'are becoming increasingly professional'[103] in assisting irregular migration.[104] These organised criminal groups make a huge profits by doing so.[105] In particular, criminal networks benefit from the smuggling of Chinese migrants.[106] Europol has also identified fighting human trafficking and the smuggling of migrants as one of its five highest priorities.[107] In 2004, Europol fought against smuggling of migrants through the investigations of organised groups and through joint

---

99   See Recital 2 of 'Council Directive 2004/83/EC of 28 April 2004 on Minimum Standards for the Qualification and Status of Third-country Nationals or Stateless Persons as Refugees or as Persons Who Otherwise Need International Protection and the Content of the Protection Granted', OJ EU L 304/12, 30 September 2004.

100   See ibid., Art. 2(1)(e).

101   See ibid., Art. 15.

102   See ibid., Arts 6(a), (b) and (c).

103   See *Europol Annual Report 2004*, p. 7.

104   Ibid.

105   See ibid., p. 11.

106   Ibid.

107   See ibid., p. 6. The other four priority crime areas are: drug trafficking, counter-terrorism, forgery of documents, and financial and property crimes, including money laundering.

actions that facilitated multiple arrests in Member States.[108] Europol reported that: 'The use of organised criminal groups to facilitate migration appears to be growing, as does the professionalism and organisation of the groups as they become more experienced.'[109] Smuggling of migrants from Iran, Iraq, Syria, Turkey (of Kurdish origin) and Afghanistan is also very widespread.[110] The areas used to transit irregular migrants include the Balkans, Eastern Europe and North Africa.[111] A study conducted by Europol shows that criminal organisations have a high capacity to adapt to new routes when those previously chosen have been discovered and closed by the competent authorities.[112]

For these reasons, Directive 2004/83/EC should be reinterpreted to include trafficking and people smuggled by sea who can demonstrate that State actors are unable to protect them. As stated above, these people should obtain visas in order to encourage them to report their smugglers. This method has been employed by Italian public prosecutors in the Italian city of Siracusa, and the results of their investigations are reported in Chapter 5.

To summarise, victims of smuggling and trafficking should be protected whether they decide to co-operate with law enforcement authorities or not. The purpose is to encourage victims to testify against criminal organisations, eventually leading to the defeat of criminal organisations that commit people smuggling by boat and trafficking in human beings. Humanitarian organisations should provide them with assistance in presenting their case that they are in fact victims of organised crime. Unfortunately, the present governments of EU Member States are not focused on rooting out the causes of people smuggling and human trafficking, but are more concerned with the quickest ways to return irregular migrants to their countries of origin. Certainly, it is understandable that people who live irregularly in the EU should be returned to their countries of origin if they do not have any right to live there. However, this principle should not be applied indiscriminately, as there are victims of smuggling and trafficking who must be protected. These victims die every day in the Mediterranean, as will be shown in Chapter 5. These people should not be dismissed, but supported and encouraged to report the criminals behind these crimes.

---

108   *Europol Annual Report 2004*, p. 11.

109   See   <http://www.europol.eu.int/index.asp?page=news&news=pr050921.htm>, The Hague, 21 September 2005, accessed 6 October 2005. See also the Europol press releases for other Europol achievements, <http://www.europol.eu.int/index.asp?page=news&language=>, accessed 6 October 2005.

110   Ibid.

111   Ibid.

112   Ibid.

EU Return Policies

In 2005, the EU proposed a Return Directive.[113] The proposed directive established common rules that EU Member States should follow in order to return irregular migrants. This proposed directive allowed the removal of irregular migrants when they do not opt for voluntary departure.[114]

The proposed directive also introduced a ban on re-entry into the EU for a maximum of five years for those irregular migrants who have been expelled and returned to their countries of origin.[115]

The proposed directive has been criticised and changed a number of times. The main problems lie with the provisions on voluntary return, monitoring forced return, entry bans, and legal aid. The latest version has modified these provisions. The new modification requires consideration of the specific circumstances of the person being returned when determining the period allowed for voluntary departure.[116] The amendment to the proposed directive also stated that those irregular migrants who lack sufficient resources should be provided with legal aid.[117] Moreover, another amendment to the previous proposal stated that Member States should have many opportunities to monitor forced return.[118] However, the length of the entry ban was not reduced.[119] It must be added that the new proposal stated that the detention of irregular migrants could last 18 months.[120] The proposed directive was adopted by the European Parliament under the co-decision procedure on 18 June 2008,[121] and it was published in the EU *Official Journal* in December 2008.[122] It has been agreed to that detention cannot last more than six months, with a possible extension of 12 months.[123] The

---

113   See *Proposal for a Directive of the European Parliament and of the Council on Common Standards and Procedures in Member States for Returning Illegally Staying Third-country Nationals*, COM (391) 2005, 1 September 2005.

114   See ibid., Arts 6(2) and 7(1), pp. 15 and 16.

115   See ibid., Art. 9, p. 16.

116   See para. 6 of *Proposal for a Directive of the European Parliament and of the Council on Common Standards and Procedures in Member States for Returning Illegally Staying Third-country Nationals*, Council Doc. 8812/08, 16 May 2008.

117   See ibid., para. 7.

118   See ibid., para. 9.

119   See ibid., para. 10.

120   See ibid., Art. 14, paras 4 and 5.

121   See 'Parliament adopts directive on return of illegal immigrants', <http://www.europarl.europa.eu/news/expert/infopress_page/018-31787-168-06-25-902-20080616IPR31785-16-06-2008-2008-true/default_en.htm>.

122   See 'Directive 2008/115/EC of the European Parliament and of the Council of 16 December 2008 on Common Standards and Procedures in Member States for Returning Illegally Staying Third-country Nationals', OJ EU L 348/98, 24 December 2008.

123   See ibid., Arts 15(5) and (6).

Court of Justice stressed in a recent case[124] that detention can never exceed 18 months. The Court of Justice also held that the maximum period of detention: 'must include a period of detention completed in connection with a removal procedure commenced before the rules in that directive become applicable'.[125] The court held that the duration of detention must not include the time a person has been detained while awaiting a decision on their request for asylum.[126] Furthermore, the time the decree of deportation has been suspended because of a judicial review procedure initiated on request of the person concerned must be taken into consideration when calculating the detention period of the person to be deported.[127] If it appears unlikely that the person expelled will be admitted to a third country, they must be released immediately.[128] The facts that a person is aggressive, not in possession of valid documents and not in a condition to support him or herself cannot be considered good reasons to continue to detain the person if 18 months have passed and it is unlikely that the person concerned will be admitted to a third country.[129]

The entry ban has not been abolished, but it is left to the discretion of Member States to waive, cancel or suspend it.[130] It has also been agreed that particular attention should be given to children and families, who can be placed in detention only as a last resort.[131] Unaccompanied minors shall be provided accommodation in institutions with personnel who take into consideration the specific needs of people of their age.[132]

Member States may decide not to apply this directive to irregular migrants who have been intercepted or apprehended by the competent authorities while crossing borders by land, air and sea.[133] This might mean that Member States could consider more favourable provisions such as legal protection for irregular migrants who, for example, are victims of people smuggling by sea. It must be added that Member States can apply more favourable provisions in any case.[134] Nevertheless, there is the risk, as Peers pointed out regarding the proposed directive, that Member States whose laws provide the lowest standards permitted by the directive are very unlikely to improve them. Conversely, there is a real risk that those Member States which have higher standards than the directive

---

124   See Case C-357/09 PPU *Kadzoev*, judgment of 30 November 2009, not yet reported.
125   See ibid., para. 39.
126   See ibid., para. 48.
127   See ibid., para. 57.
128   See ibid., paras 60 and 67.
129   See ibid., para. 71.
130   See Art. 11 (3) of Directive 2008/115/EC, op. cit. note 122.
131   See ibid., Art. 17(1).
132   See ibid., Art. 17(4).
133   See ibid., Art. 2(2)(a).
134   See ibid., Art. 4.

will reduce them to the minimum permitted by the directive.[135] The risk of fragmentation increases even more when we consider that the UK, Ireland and Denmark are not participating in this directive.[136] The UK has justified its lack of participation by emphasising that this directive makes the return of irregular migrants more difficult. The difficulty is created, the UK points out, by the directive introducing restrictions on detention, and an obligation to provide legal aid, and it increases the chances of challenges to the Return Directive even though EU asylum and refugee law provides strong protections.[137] The last argument is the weakest, as there are categories of irregular migrants such as those smuggled by sea who cannot claim the protection provided by EU asylum and refugee law, even though they may be in a position of vulnerability and danger if returned to their countries of origin. Article 14 of the directive only states that during the period pending the voluntary return of irregular migrants, Member States shall take into consideration the needs of vulnerable persons. People smuggled by sea could be considered vulnerable persons, though this provision does not change the fact that these categories of irregular migrants will be returned to their countries of origin, unless Member States decide to adopt more favourable provisions.

More favourable provisions can be adopted if victims of smuggling of migrants by sea decide to co-operate with law enforcement authorities to contribute to the arrest of their smugglers. In support of this provision, Article 11(3) of the directive states that victims of human trafficking and people snuggling who co-operate with law enforcement authorities shall not be subject to the entry ban. These provisions may facilitate co-operation of these victims, and this may contribute to defeating the criminal organisations which are behind the smuggling of migrants by sea, as Chapter 5 will show.

This book does not focus on all aspects of irregular migration, but concentrates on smuggling and trafficking, proposing ways to defeat these crimes. However, the next sections will briefly examine economic irregular migration, and the EU policies intended to prevent it by co-operating with countries of origin. Specifically, the next sections will focus attention on the decline of the working population in the EU, economic migration and the European Neighbourhood Policy. The aim is to demonstrate that irregular migration can be defeated not only by addressing the crimes which facilitate it, but also by promoting economic initiatives in the countries of origin of irregular migrants that could discourage them from leaving and becoming victims of smuggling and trafficking.

---

135   See Peers, S., 'The Returns Directive', *Statewatch*, 9 June 2008, <http://www.statewatch.org/news/2008/jun/eu-analysis-returns-directive-june-2008-final.pdf>.

136   See paras 25, 26 and 27 of Directive 2008/115/EC, op. cit. note 122.

137   See Peers, 'The Returns Directive', op. cit. note 135.

Irregular Migration and the Ageing Population in the EU

The EU needs immigrants because, as the European Commission revealed in 2003, the EU-25 by 2020 the population of working age will decrease from its current total of 303 million to 297 million, and by 2030 it will fall to 280 million.[138] The Commission pointed out that by 2030, the decline in birth rate that began in the 1970s will by increase the proportion of people aged over 65 in the EU to 40 percent, an increase from 23 percent when the trend first started.[139] The number of people aged 80 and over in the EU will increase from 16 million in 2000 to 30 million in 2030.[140] The European Commission also highlighted that these figures cannot be changed by an unexpected growth in the birth rate in the EU, as it would take more than 20 years before the babies reached working age.[141] Therefore, the Commission has asserted that the EU must retain its existing human resources and migrant workers resident in the EU.[142] This is why Member States and the EU should adopt measures on legal migration. In this way, people who want to emigrate from their countries of origin to EU Member States could do so by following legal alternatives. If instead the EU and its Member States do not approve any legislation on legal migration, irregular migration and all the crimes connected with it will always increase, no matter how tough national law are, as people will remain motivated to escape their country of origin. As Europol has pointed out, no matter how tough Member States try to act towards irregular migration, criminal organisations are always able to rearrange their routes.

Many EU Member States are generally keen to support legal migration to facilitate integration and employment, and to decrease the risk of irregular migration.[143] The Commission has emphasised that temporary migration should not be encouraged, because only permanent migration can alleviate the demographic instability in the EU.[144] Therefore, the European Commission supports the entry of migrants to the EU to make the labour market more stable.[145] In 2004, the European Commission noted that without migration, many Member States would face a decline in their population.[146] Migrants account for 3.6 percent of the total employed population of the EU, and they contributed 22 percent of the growth in employment in 1997–

---

138 See *Communication from the Commission to the Council, the European Parliament, the European Economic and Social Committee and the Committee of the Regions on Immigration, Integration and Employment*, COM (2003) 336, 3 June 2003, p. 12.

139 Ibid.
140 Ibid.
141 Ibid.
142 See ibid., p. 15.
143 Ibid.
144 See ibid., p. 16.
145 Ibid.
146 See *Communication from the Commission to the Council, the European Parliament, the European Economic and Social Committee and the Committee of the*

2002.[147] Further support for migrant workers is offered by the fact that in 2007 the European Commission reported that there were some Member States which were suffering shortages of highly skilled workers.[148] The European Commission has stated that Member States require not only highly skilled workers, but also low skilled workers, especially in Southern European countries.[149] Low-skilled workers are needed in households, for hotels and restaurants, in construction, and in seasonal work such as agriculture.[150]

Amnesty could be granted to some irregular migrants who already live in EU Member States, such as those who are victims of smuggling by sea and trafficking. In the UK, for example, the Institute for Public Policy and Research reported that:

> regularising the nearly half million people who currently live and work in the
> UK could net the Treasury around £1 billion a year compared to the 4.7 billion
> it would cost to deport them forcibly.[151]

If these data are found to be similar in other Member States, an amnesty could be offered for this category of migrants. It is unacceptable to adopt tough laws on irregular migration at EU level without approving legislation on legal migration. It is indisputable that people who live in EU Member States without having the right to do so should be returned to their countries of origin if they are not asylum seekers or victims of serious crimes such as human trafficking and people smuggling. However, it is also important to adopt legal measures on economic legal migration to prevent irregular entry of many people who contact criminal organisations because they cannot otherwise emigrate.

Legal Migration and the Protection of Specific Categories of Economic Irregular Migrants

The introduction of laws on economic legal migration has been considered since 2001 by a Commission proposal of a directive and a subsequent communication

---

Regions: First Annual Report on Migration and Integration, COM (2004) final 508, 16 July 2004, p. 3.

    147   Ibid. note 146.

    148   See *Communication from the Commission to the European Parliament, the Council, the European Economic and Social Committee and the Committee of Regions: Towards a Common Immigration Policy*, COM (2007) 780, 5 December 2007, p. 8.

    149   See COM (2004) final 508, op. cit. note 146, p. 4.

    150   See COM (2007) 780, op. ct note 148, p. 8.

    151   See 'Jacqui Smith should back amnesty for illegal workers', IPPR, 15 July 2007, <http://www.ippr.org.uk/pressreleases/archive.asp?id=2794>.

on migration for employment and self-employed economic activities.[152] The Commission's proposal set out the common rules that EU Member States should establish to allow third-country nationals to enter and stay in the EU as employers or self-employed workers.[153] The Commission's proposal was intended to establish common criteria such as '"economic needs tests" and "beneficial effects tests"'[154] to permit third-country nationals to enter and stay in EU Member States as employers or self-employed workers.[155] The aim of the proposal was also to provide 'procedural and transparency safeguards, in order to assure a high level of legal certainty and information for all interested actors'.[156] These safeguards focus on the rules and administrative practices applied by EU Member States on the entry and stay of third-country nationals who want to work as employers or self-employed workers.[157] The Commission's proposal was also intended 'to simplify and harmonise the diverging rules currently applicable in Member States'[158] regarding residence and work permits. The proposal also aimed to provide rights for third-country nationals 'whilst respecting Member States discretion to limit economic migration'.[159] Moreover, the proposal intended to provide a flexible framework that could allow all Member States and other interested parties to adapt 'quickly to changing economic and demographic circumstances'.[160] The proposal sought to give Member States the opportunity to exchange views on ways to apply the proposed directive 'within an open coordination mechanism on Community immigration policy'.[161] Finally, the proposed directive's intentions included 'adding real meaning to the commitments that the EC and its Member states have undertaken in the context of the WTO GATS Agreement'[162] and allowing Member States to impose quotas or ceilings to limit the admission of third-country nationals to their territories.[163]

This proposed directive could have facilitated a common policy between Member States on legal migration because it established the possibility for a third-country national to apply for 'a residence permit worker' when a valid

---

152   See *Proposal for a Council Directive on the Conditions of Entry and Residence of Third-country Nationals for the Purpose of Paid Employment and Self-employed Economic Activities*, COM (2001) 386, 11 July 2001. See also *Communication from the Commission to the Council and the European Parliament on an Open Method of Coordination for the Community Immigration Policy*, COM (2001) 387, 11 July 2001.

153   See COM (2001) 386, op. cit. note 152, pp. 2 and 3.

154   See ibid., p. 3.

155   Ibid.

156   See ibid., p. 4

157   Ibid.

158   Ibid.

159   Ibid.

160   Ibid.

161   Ibid.

162   Ibid.

163   Ibid.

work contract had been offered.[164] Some economic irregular migrants could have been legalised if it had been demonstrated that certain posts could not be filled by categories of workers such as EU citizens and others indicated by the proposed directive.[165] In these circumstances, economic irregular migrants coming from very poor countries could have been assessed with 'a test, intended to verify shortages within the EU labour market'.[166] Member States could have had an incentive to legalise economic irregular migrants if it had been proven they would not become 'a financial burden for the host Member State'.[167] The proposed directive also provided the possibility for Member States, in exceptional circumstances, 'to grant work permits without granting a right of residence'.[168] Member States could have addressed this possibility in order not to return some economic irregular migrants from very poor countries.

The subsequent communication also focused attention on economic migration policy.[169] In this communication, the Commission confirmed that economic migrants should be recruited, in agreement with their countries of origin, 'to meet labour market needs'.[170] Regrettably, the Council did not show much interest in these initiatives.[171] Subsequently, the Commission prepared a Green Paper on economic migration.[172] In the Green Paper, the Commission asserted that EU legislation should establish common rules and criteria on the admission of economic migrants, while Member States should remain responsible for setting out the quota of migrants to admit on the basis of the needs of their labour markets.[173] The Commission also highlighted that the principal issue to resolve was whether preference in recruitment should be given to third-country nationals already present in EU Member States, or to new migrants.[174] The solution to this problem could address the question of whether or not to return certain economic irregular migrants on the basis of the needs of the Member States labour market. A directive on economic migration could allow some economic irregular migrants from very poor countries smuggled by sea or by human trafficking to remain in EU Member States if their presence was necessary to supply the needs of the States' labour markets. The price for remaining could be co-operation with law enforcement authorities in order to combat the criminal organisations behind

---

164   See ibid., Arts 5(1) and (3), p. 9.
165   See ibid., Art. 6(1), p. 10.
166   See ibid., Art. 8, p. 13.
167   See ibid., Art. 10(3), p. 13.
168   See ibid., Art. 13, p. 15.
169   See COM (2001) 387, op. cit. note 152.
170   See ibid., pp. 8 and 9.
171   See Peers, S., *EU Justice and Home Affairs Law* (Oxford: Oxford University Press, 2006), p. 223.
172   See *Green Paper on an EU Approach to Managing Economic Migration*, COM (2004) 811, 11 January 2005.
173   See ibid., p. 5.
174   See ibid., p. 6.

these crimes. Having secured their stay, these people might trust law enforcement authorities more. However, the Commission Green Paper was withdrawn and replaced by another proposal.[175] This new proposal emphasised the importance of checking demographic trends. Demographic trends will not affect all Member States in the same way: some are already experiencing a decline in their population of working, while others will experience this problem in the future.[176] In the short term, immigration may solve the problem of the decline of working population, although precedence should be given to EU citizens and migrants already residing legally in the EU.[177] Therefore, this proposal suggested that four directives should be adopted for specific fields of the economy and for broad categories of migrants:[178] a directive on the conditions of entry and residence of highly skilled workers, and a general framework directive on the conditions of all persons admitted for employment to be adopted in 2007;[179] a directive on the conditions of entry and residence of seasonal workers, to be adopted in 2008,[180] and two directives on intra-corporate transferees and on the conditions of entry for remunerated trainees, to be adopted in 2009.[181] The directive on seasonal workers should be addressed specifically to the many irregular migrants who work in precarious conditions in EU Member States.[182] The sectors interested in recruiting seasonal workers are tourism, agriculture and building.[183] Economic irregular migrants who are victims of smuggling and trafficking could be included in this directive. This would permit legalising many irregular migrants in the EU, benefiting the economic interests of many EU Member States where many local workers do not want to do certain jobs. Directives on economic legal migration have not been adopted yet, and the European Commission emphasised again in 2007 that:

> A common immigration policy represents a fundamental priority for the EU if we want to be successful together in harnessing the benefits and addressing the challenges at stake. This common policy should aim at a coordinated and integrated approach to immigration both at European, national and regional level. This implies looking at the different dimensions of the phenomenon and

---

175   See 'Withdrawal of Commission Proposals Following Screening for their General Relevance, their Impact on Competitiveness and Other Aspects', OJ EU C 64/3, 17 March 2006. See also *Communication from the Commission: Policy Plan on Legal Migration*, COM (2005) 669, 21 December 2005. This Communication replaced COM (2004) 811, op. cit. note 172.
176   See COM (2005) 669, op. cit. note 175, pp. 4 and 5.
177   See ibid., p. 5.
178   See ibid., p. 6.
179   See ibid., pp. 6 and 7.
180   See ibid., p. 7.
181   See ibid., p. 8.
182   See ibid., p. 7.
183   Ibid.

factoring immigration into the main strands of EU policy – *prosperity, solidarity and security.*

In conclusion, the Commission has proposed different directives on economic legal migration. This legislation could facilitate legal migration, permitting the legalisation of many economic irregular migrants, including those who are victims of smuggling and trafficking. As a result, these irregular migrants would be encouraged to trust law enforcement authorities and report the criminal organisations involved. Nevertheless, specific legislation on economic migration has not been adopted yet. As Peers emphasises:

> as long as there are jobs available that the local labour force cannot or is unwilling to do, the absence of legislation in this area leaves open the attraction of irregular entry and stay, which could be reduced by enlarging the avenue of legal entry.[184]

And Bade points out:

> Where no legal 'main gates' or 'front doors' are open, and even legal 'side doors' seem hardly accessible, despite migrants' willingness to adapt, apparently legal or illegal 'back doors' are being used more and more.[185]

The limited access to EC territory for third-country nationals was confirmed by Advocate General Geelhoed. He highlighted the fact that national laws on immigration are becoming very restrictive, as Member States try control immigration flows, meaning 'for nationals of non-Member States there are only limited opportunities for entering the territory of the European Union'.[186]

It is necessary for the EU to concentrate its efforts on economic legal migration in order to prevent irregular migration. It is hoped that the law on economic migration will be adopted, because at the moment the legislation on legal migration, including economic legal migration, is lacking. Directive 2003/109/EC[187] covers the status of third-country nationals, and Directive 2003/86/EC[188] covers the right

---

184   See Peers, *EU Justice and Home Affairs Law*, op. cit. note 171, p. 224.

185   Bade, K.J., *Legal and Illegal Immigration into Europe: Experiences and Challenges* (Ortelius-lezing, 2003), p. 15.

186   See Case C-109/01 *Secretary of State for Home Department* v. *Hacene Akrich*, Opinion of Advocate General Geelhoed, ECR I-09607, 27 February 2003, para. 47.

187   See 'Council Directive 2003/109/EC of 25 November 2003 Concerning the Status of Third-country Nationals Who are Long-term Resident', OJ EC 2004 L 16/44, 23 January 2004.

188   See 'Council Directive 2003/86/EC of 22 September 2003 on the Right to Family Reunification', OJ EC L 251/12, 3 October 2003.

of third-country nationals to be reunited to their families, but the UK, Ireland and Denmark have opted out of both.[189]

Another way to prevent irregular migration is by enhancing relationships with third-party countries. Indeed, it is in the EU's interests to try to reduce poverty in less-developed countries through the European Neighbourhood Policy and other initiatives.

Policies

The European Neighbourhood Policy

Amnesty International reported that in 2005, the governments of the world have not met many of their goals in reducing poverty.[190] The objective agreed to by 180 nations in 1996 to reduce hunger by 2015 will not be achieved.[191] The Food and Agriculture Organization (FAO) of the UN reported that: 'Ten years later, we are confronted with the sad reality that virtually no progress has been made towards that objective.'[192] Poverty forces many people to emigrate irregularly, and if efforts are not made to reduce it, economic migration will continue to increase. Economic irregular migration could also increase if States impose restrictions on legal migration.

The EU could contribute to reducing poverty and the connected phenomenon of economic irregular migration through the European Neighbourhood Policy (ENP). The ENP was established to prevent a dividing line between the enlarged EU and its neighbours.[193] Initially, the ENP included agreements with Euro-Mediterranean countries and with Ukraine and Moldova.[194]

The ENP includes Algeria, Armenia, Azerbaijan, Belarus, Egypt, Georgia, Israel, Jordan, Lebanon, Libya, Moldova, Morocco, the Palestinian Authority of the West Bank and Gaza Strip, the Russian Federation, Syria, Tunisia and Ukraine.[195]

---

189   See paras 25 and 26 of the Preamble to Council Directive 2003/109/EC, op. cit. note 187. See also paras 17 and 18 of the Preamble to Council Directive 2003/86/EC, op. cit. note 188.

190   See *Amnesty International Report 2006: The State of the World's Human Rights*, <http://www.amnesty.org/en/library/asset/POL10/004/2006/en/ec4588bf-d443-11dd-8743-d305bea2b2c7/pol100042006en.pdf>, p. 22.

191   See *The State of Food Insecurity in the World*, op. cit. note 31, p. 4.

192   Ibid.

193   See *The Policy: What is the European Neighbourhood Policy?*, <http://ec.europa.eu/comm/world/enp/policy_en.htm>.

194   Ibid.

195   See Annex of 'Regulation (EC) No. 1638/2006 of the European Parliament and of the Council of 24 October 2006 Laying Down General Provisions Establishing a European Neighbourhood and Partnership Instruments', OJ EU L 310/1, 9 November 2006.

The EU's aim is to promote regional and sub-regional co-operation and integration to achieve political and economic stability, and to reduce poverty and social division.[196] It has been shown that the EU's eastern neighbours have many economic problems, and the Mediterranean region has also faced conditions of absolute poverty for a long time.[197] In response, the European Commission has stated that trade investments should be implemented to improve economic conditions in these countries.[198] In addition, the European Commission has encouraged the free movement of persons between the EU and its neighbours and the adoption of a long-stay visa policy.[199]

However, trafficking in human beings and the smuggling of migrants, especially when carried out by sea, should be fought. Some of the priority areas focused on by the ENP include co-operation on justice, security and migration.[200] One important objective of the ENP is to increase co-operation with countries of origin, transit and destination in order to control migration flows, with the larger goal of combating irregular migration and human trafficking.[201] The EU needs to co-operate with all the countries bordering the Mediterranean and the countries of transit and origin in order to achieve this objective.[202] An important way to reinforce international co-operation against trafficking and smuggling is through policy and judiciary reform, and through training and technical assistance for police officers.[203] The EU has announced that from 2010, co-operation in order to counter smuggling of migrants and human trafficking will be extended to cover irregular migration from sub-Saharan African countries.[204] For this reason, victims could provide useful support for law enforcement authorities, therefore logic dictates they should not be automatically returned.

The EU has also held the view that long-term objectives intended to address smuggling of migrants and trafficking in human beings should consist of creating and improving 'integrated border management systems'[205] and improving 'the management of migration, including asylum'[206] with neighbouring countries.[207]

---

196   See *Communication from the Commission to the Council and the European Parliament. Wider Europe-Neighbourhood: A New Framework for Relations with our Eastern and Southern Neighbours*, COM (2003) 104 11 March 2003, p. 3.

197   See ibid., p. 7.

198   Ibid.

199   See ibid., p. 11.

200   See *European Neighbourhood and Partnership Instrument (ENPI). Regional Strategy Paper (2007–2013) and Regional Indicative Programme (2007–2010) for the Euro-Mediterranean Partnership*, EUROMED, p. 14.

201   See ibid., p. 15.

202   Ibid.

203   Ibid.

204   Ibid.

205   See ibid., p. 13.

206   Ibid.

207   See ibid., p. 12.

These objectives should achieve '[m]ore efficient, safe and effective border management, leading to improved stability and security in the region'.[208] Other goals should include enhanced co-operation between law enforcement authorities, an increase in technical capacity, and strengthening co-operation with border guards and judicial authorities in the area of asylum and immigration.[209] Through the ENP, the European Commission has instigated 'an €8 million border assistance mission providing on the job training and advice to Moldovan and Ukrainian officials'[210] on the Moldova–Ukraine border.[211]

In any case, the Commission is aware that the phenomenon of human trafficking can be significantly reduced by fighting poverty.[212] A European Commission communication[213] has proposed a regulation that 'establishes a Neighbourhood and Partnership to provide assistance ... for the development of an area of prosperity'[214] encompassing the EU and its neighbours. Regulation 1638/2006 was adopted in October 2006.[215] This regulation could contribute to reducing poverty in the EU's neighbouring countries, although other measures should also be implemented to address poverty in those countries and in other less-developed countries to reduce the threat of irregular migration and the related phenomena of smuggling of migrants and trafficking in human beings.

In conclusion, two of the priorities of the ENP are to tackle trafficking in human beings and smuggling of migrants. The ENP aims to achieve these objectives by enhancing international co-operation with the EU's neighbours. In addition, the EU is seeking the involvement of sub-Saharan Africa in the ENP.

Other Policies in Order to Prevent Economic Irregular Migration

The European Commission has highlighted that the push factors for migration in general are poverty, armed conflicts, ethnic cleansing, human rights abuses, poor governance, environmental catastrophes, high population growth, unemployment, unequal distribution of resources and lack of domestic development policies.[216]

---

208   See ibid., p. 13.

209   Ibid.

210   See 'Speech delivered by Dr Benita Ferrero-Waldner, European Commissioner for External Relations and European Neighbourhood Policy on "Combating Trafficking in Human Beings": The EU's Response, 17 March 2006, <http://www.osce.org/item/18396.html>, p. 3.

211   Ibid.

212   Ibid.

213   See *Proposal for a Regulation of the European Parliament and of the Council Laying Down General Provisions Establishing a European Neighbourhood and Partnership Instrument*, COM (2004) 628 final, 29 September 2004.

214   See ibid., p. 14.

215   See Regulation (EC) No. 1638/2006, op. cit. note 195.

216   See *Communication from the Commission to the Council and the European Parliament: Integrating Immigration Issues in the European Union's Relations with Third*

The main pull factors for migration are 'safety and socio-economic improvements stemming from labour demand in host countries'.[217] The Commission has pointed out that both EU and non-EU countries should address these causes of irregular migration, and adopt prevention policies.[218] The Commission has suggested that the push factors be addressed through development policies in poorer countries.[219] The European Council in Seville confirmed the importance of tackling the causes of irregular migration through 'closer economic cooperation, trade expansion, development assistance and conflict prevention'.[220] The Council confirmed that in the long term, the EU objective should remain to fight against smuggling of migrants and trafficking in human beings, coupled with eradicating poverty.[221]

To further this end, the EU has developed good relationships with some countries of origin of irregular migrants.[222] The countries that are co-operating with the EU are Albania, China, Russia, Morocco, Serbia Montenegro, Tunisia and Ukraine.[223] The EU has made recommendations to expand co-operation with other third countries,[224] including Sri Lanka, Algeria, Hong Kong, Macao and Pakistan.[225]

The EU has also granted financial assistance to some non-EU countries.[226] Regulation 491/2004 states that:

> The Community ... establishes a cooperation programme ... which aims to give specific and complementary financial and technical aid to third countries in order to support their efforts to improve the management of migration flows in all their dimensions.[227]

The co-operation programme is mainly directed at countries that have concluded admission agreements with the EU, although other countries may also be

---

Countries, COM (2002) 703, 3 December 2002, p. 10.

217   See ibid., p. 11.

218   See ibid., p. 20.

219   See ibid., p. 21.

220   Ibid. See also Conclusions of the European Council, Seville, 21 and 22 June 2002; See Peers, *EU Justice and Home Affairs Law*, op. cit. note 171, pp. 292 and 293.

221   See EU Council Doc. 8927/03, 5 May 2003, p. 5.

222   See *Communication from the Commission to the Council on the Monitoring and Evaluation Mechanism of the Third Countries in the Field of the Fight against Illegal Immigration*, COM (2005) 352, 28 July 2005. See also Peers, *EU Justice and Home Affairs Law*, op. cit. note 171, p. 294.

223   See COM (2005) 352, op. cit. note 222, p. 2.

224   See ibid., p. 10.

225   Ibid.

226   See 'Regulation (EC) No. 491/2004 of the European Parliament and of the Council of 10 March 2004 Establishing a Programme for Financial and Technical Assistance to Third Countries in the Areas of Migration and Asylum (AENEAS)', OJ EU L 80/1, 13 March 2004. See also Peers, *EU Justice and Home Affairs Law*, op. cit. note 171, p. 295.

227   See Art. 1(1) of Regulation (EC) No. 491/2004, op. cit. note 226.

involved.[228] The programme states that financial support should be given to non-EU countries in order to develop laws on legal migration, irregular migration and readmission agreements, and in order to support the capacity building of third countries 'in the field of reception conditions and protection capacity for asylum seekers'.[229] The regulation is intended to support programmes of socio-economic reintegration of irregular migrants returned to their countries of origin.[230]

To summarise, the EU is building up co-operation programmes and development initiatives in order to reduce irregular migration and human trafficking. The EU is supporting integration policies that may improve the economic situation in some countries of origin. In the long term, these policies may reduce the phenomenon of irregular migration.

Conclusions

This chapter dealt with victims of trafficking and smuggling of people by sea. It was emphasised that people smuggled by sea should be considered victims, just like trafficked people, because they do not always make a free choice to leave their countries of origin. It was also argued that victims of human trafficking and people smuggling should obtain visas (working visas, as will be emphasised in the next chapter) in the EU. This is to encourage victims of these crimes to testify against the organisations which smuggled and trafficked them. However, in order to achieve this objective, it is also important that law enforcement authorities gain the trust of smuggled and trafficked people. While there is a specific law on people trafficking that supports this approach, none relates to people smuggling, and a similar law needs to be developed. The chapter also discussed EC laws that facilitate the return of irregular migrants. There is much focus by Member States on the best ways to return irregular migrants, while neglecting the protection of victims of trafficking and those smuggled by sea.

Economic legal migration was also demonstrated to be a way to prevent irregular migration. Laws on economic legal migration should be adopted so that many people can be encouraged to come to the EU legally, as opposed to irregularly. The EU should devote more attention to legal migration, and fully address the smuggling of migrants by sea and human trafficking. In some cases, trafficking in human beings may be linked to smuggling of migrants, since victims of people smuggling can become victims of human trafficking in order to repay the price of their journey.[231] Finally, this chapter analysed the ENP as a way to reduce poverty in the countries of origin of many irregular migrants. It is thought that if poverty is reduced, irregular migration will also be reduced, as third-country

---

228   See ibid., Art. 1(2).
229   See ibid., Arts 2(a)–(k).
230   See ibid., Art. 2(1).
231   See COM (2001) 672 final, op. cit. note 2, p. 7.

nationals will look for opportunities in their countries of origin rather than in EU Member States.

The next chapter focuses on legal measures regarding smuggling of migrants and trafficking in human beings adopted in the UK and Italy. These two countries are analysed because they approach these phenomena in different ways. The UK does not participate in EC Directive 2004/81/EC on the legal protection of human trafficking victims; in contrast, Italy is bound by this directive, and has very advanced laws covering the protection of the victims of people smugglers and human traffickers. The next chapter will also examine the results of interviews held in Italy and in the UK on trafficking in human beings and on the smuggling of people by sea.

Finally, the next chapter will focus on the impact of legal measures concerning EU police and judicial co-operation on the UK and Italy.

Chapter 5
Comparative Analysis of British and Italian Law

Introduction

The previous chapter emphasised that victims of smuggling of migrants by sea and of trafficking should be granted legal protection in order to encourage them to report the criminal organisations behind these two crimes. This chapter presents a comparative analysis of Italian and British law on smuggling of migrants, trafficking in human beings and irregular migration. The aim of this chapter is to demonstrate that granting permanent visas to victims of smuggling of migrants by sea and trafficking could support investigations against these two crimes. For this purpose, this chapter will present findings based on interviews conducted in Italy and with UK police officers, members of humanitarian organisations and public prosecutors. This research has established two successful approaches to stopping human trafficking and people smuggling by sea, which will be referred to as the Rimini Method and the Siracusan Approach. These approaches have demonstrated that trafficking and smuggling of migrants by sea can be defeated by focusing on the victims. Indeed, when victims of trafficking and smuggling of migrants by sea have obtained long-term visas, they have been more willing to co-operate with law enforcement authorities and their evidence has contributed to the arrest and detention of those who perpetrate these crimes. Law enforcement authorities have stated that granting permanent visas to victims is crucial in gaining their trust and convincing them to implicate their victimisers.

Before we analyse the research findings, it must be emphasised that there is a difference between victims of human trafficking and victims of people smuggling by sea. Indeed, while it is clear that trafficked people are victims of their exploiters, UNTOC states that the same cannot be said about victims of smuggling by sea. As was shown in Chapter 4, the UNTOC Smuggling Protocol does not consider people who are smuggled to be victims of their smugglers. This is mainly because those who are smuggled make a free choice based on circumstances. Surely, those who can afford the costs associated with some forms of people smuggling can make the decision to migrate through legal means? This cannot be said of those who are smuggled by sea, as they are very likely escaping from object poverty and have little or no alternative if they wish to find a better life for themselves and their families. These people are often unaware of the dangers they face when crossing the sea, which has the potential to cost them their lives. This is the reason why these people should be considered universally as victims. This chapter will strengthen this point of view by presenting the findings of a visit and interviews conducted in the detention centre at Lampedusa in Italy.

Another purpose of this chapter is to highlight possible conflicts of jurisdiction between the UK and Italy that the measures adopted by the Council, proposals of the Commission and the Lisbon Treaty should help to resolve. This issue is explored by comparing the British and Italian legal systems.

British and Italian Laws on Smuggling of Migrants

Sections 25, 25A and 25B of the Immigration Act 1971, which have been modified by the Nationality, Immigration and Asylum Act 2002, are respectively entitled: 'Assisting unlawful immigration to member State',[1] 'Helping asylum-seekers to enter United Kingdom',[2] and 'Assisting entry to United Kingdom in breach of deportation or exclusion order'.[3] However, British law does not distinguish between the crime of assisting irregular migration and the crime of smuggling of migrants. English law does make a distinction between assisting irregular migration for financial gain and assisting without this motive.[4] Despite this, British law does not make the more important distinction between irregular migration which is facilitated by organised crime, and irregular migration without such assistance. Irregular migration assisted by criminal organisations can be considered a crime under the section entitled 'Helping asylum-seekers to enter United Kingdom'[5] of the Immigration Act 1971. This is important because the 1971 Immigration Act states that when criminal organisations have perpetrated this crime, the maximum penalty can be applied.[6]

The Italian law on immigration has recently been modified by Act 94/2009, and it is examined in detail below.[7] Legislative Decree 286/1998 incorporates the crimes of assisting irregular migration and smuggling of migrants, which requires the involvement of criminal organisations.[8]

Italian and British laws on immigration both meet the requirements of the Schengen Acquis (although the UK is not party to it), which states that 'The Contracting Parties undertake to impose appropriate penalties on any person who,

---

1   See s. 25 of Immigration Act 1971 as replaced by s. 143 of Nationality Immigration and Asylum Act 2002.
2   See s. 25A. of Immigration Act 1971, op. cit. note 1.
3   See ibid., s. 25B.
4   Ibid.
5   Ibid.
6   See ibid., s. 25(6(a)).
7   See Legge 15 July 2009 no. 94, 'Disposizioni in material di sicurezza pubblica', GU 170, 25 July 2009, Supplemento ordinario no. 128.
8   See Art. 12(1, 3 and 3*bis*) of Legislative Decree 286/1998, GU 191, 18 August 1998 as modified by Art. 11(1(a,b,c)) of Act 189/2002, GU 199, 26 August 2002.

for financial gain, assists or tries to assist an alien' to enter or stay in one of the Schengen Acquis States Parties.[9] Moreover, Italian and British laws on immigration reflect the requirements of Directive 2002/90/EC,[10] which repealed Article 27 of the Schengen Convention,[11] and added the assisting of irregular migration with the purpose of a financial gain and the mere assisting irregular migration without gaining an economic advantage.[12]

Through Directive 2002/90/EC, the EU has made the law on assisting irregular migration more restrictive, although Member States may decide to apply less severe penalties to those who assist irregular migration without financial gain. Indeed, in the case of assisting irregular migration without the purpose of financial gain, British judicial authorities may decide to apply a penalty not exceeding six months' imprisonment. The reason for this is that British law establishes two types of penalties:

> imprisonment for a term not exceeding 14 years, to a fine or both, or ... imprisonment for a term not exceeding six months, to a fine not exceeding the statutory maximum or both.[13]

Before Act 94/2009 entered into force, Legislative Decree 286/1998 established that people who committed the crime of assisting irregular migration could be punished with imprisonment up to three years and a fine up to €15,000 if they did not have the purpose of a financial gain.[14] Act 94/2009 increased the penalties for the crime of assisting irregular migration by making it punishable by imprisonment for up to five years and a fine up to €15,000 for each person who enters Italy irregularly.[15] Act 94/2009 established the same penalty if the crime was committed by a criminal organisation. Therefore, the new law has abolished the difference between assisting irregular migration and smuggling of migrants, as they are punished in the same way.

The Italian and British laws are similar to the UNTOC Smuggling Protocol provisions,[16] although the Smuggling Protocol is narrower in scope. This is due

---

9   See Art. 27(1) of the Schengen Convention, in 'The Schengen Acquis: Council Decision 1999/435/EC of 20 May 1999', OJ EU C 176, 10 July 1999.

10   See Art. 1(1) of 'Directive 2002/90/EC of 28 November 2002 Defining the Facilitation of Unauthorised Entry, Transit and Residence', OJ EU 2002 L 328/17, 5 December 2002.

11   See ibid., Art. 5.

12   See ibid., Art. 1(1(a)).

13   See s. 25(6(a)) of Immigration Act 1971, op. cit. note 1.

14   See Art. 12(1) of Legislative Decree 286/1998, op. cit. note 8 as modified by Art. 11(1(a)) of Act 189/2002, op. cit. note 8.

15   See Art. 1(26) of Act 94/2009, op. cit. note 7.

16   See Arts 3 and 4 of *Protocol against the Smuggling of Migrants by Land, Sea and Air, Supplementing the United Nations Convention against Transnational Organized Crime* (Smuggling Protocol), A/RES/55/25, 8 January 2001.

to the fact that the Smuggling Protocol only covers assisting irregular migration 'where the offences are transnational in nature and involve an organized criminal group'.[17] However, it is indisputable that British, Italian laws and the Smuggling Protocol punish the crime of smuggling of migrants, although British law does not punish people smuggling expressly, but only implicitly.

In conclusion, both British and Italian laws have responded to the requirements of the Schengen Acquis and the UNTOC Smuggling Protocol. However, British and Italian laws are more restrictive than the UNTOC Smuggling Protocol because they not only punish smuggling of migrants, but also the assisting of irregular migration not involving a criminal organisation and not having the purpose of a financial gain. It must be stressed that British law is less restrictive than Italian law in punishing the mere assisting of irregular migration because Italian law applies the same punishment to assisting irregular migration and people smuggling.

British and Italian Laws on Trafficking in Human Beings

British Law

British law on trafficking in human beings has been inadequate for many years. It had only one provision on trafficking in prostitution, and did not take into consideration other forms of human trafficking expressly indicated by the UNTOC Trafficking Protocol[18] and by the Council of Europe Convention on Action against Trafficking in Human Beings.[19] The British Sexual Offences Act 1956 stated that it was an offence 'to procure a woman to become, in any part of the world, a common prostitute'.[20] British law also stated that it was a criminal offence to detain a woman against her will and to constrain her to have intercourse with one particular man or with other men or to detain a woman against her will in a brothel.[21] British law punished abduction and the exercise of control over prostitutes.[22]

The Sexual Offences Act 1956 was amended in 2003, when new provisions on trafficking in prostitution were introduced. Sections 47–51 of the Sexual Offences Act 2003 are entitled 'Abuse of children through prostitution and pornography'.[23]

---

17   See ibid., Art. 4.

18   See Art. 3 of *Protocol to Prevent, Suppress and Punish Trafficking in Persons, Especially Women and Children, Supplementing the United Nations Convention against Transnational Organized Crime* (UNTOC Trafficking Protocol), A/RES/55/25, Doc. A/55/383, 8 January 2001.

19   See Art. 4(a) of *Council of Europe Convention on Action against Trafficking in Human Beings* (Council of Europe Convention on Trafficking), CM (2005) 32 Addendum 1 final, 3 May 2005.

20   See s. 22(1)(a) of the original Sexual Offences Act 1956.

21   See ibid., s. 24(1).

22   See ibid., ss. 30 and 31.

23   See ss. 47–51 of Sexual Offences Act 2003.

Section 47 punishes a person who 'intentionally obtains for himself the sexual services of another person (B)',[24] if 'before obtaining those services, he has made or promised payment for those services to B or to a third person'[25] and 'either B is under 18, and A does not reasonably believe that B is 18 or over, or … B is under 13'.[26] In all these cases, British law envisages imprisonment of up to 14 years unless B is under 13 years old, in which case the penalty is life imprisonment.[27] Therefore, British law punishes the sexual exploitation of children no matter whether there is an element of trafficking involved. The following sections of the Sexual Offences Act 2003 punish persons who cause or incite child prostitution or pornography,[28] who control a child prostitute or a child involved in pornography,[29] and who arrange or facilitate child prostitution or child pornography.[30] Sections 52–55 punish exploitation of prostitution, which consists of causing, inciting or controlling prostitution for financial gain.[31] The Sexual Offences Act 2003 punishes trafficking for sexual exploitation both within and outside the UK.[32] Section 57 states that 'A person commits an offence if he intentionally arranges or facilitates the arrival in the United Kingdom of another person (B)'[33] and either intends to commit a criminal offence involving B or knows that another person intends to commit a criminal offence involving B in the UK only.[34] In all these cases, the offenders will be imprisoned for a term not exceeding 14 years.[35] Section 58 punishes anyone who facilitates the arrival in the UK of a person to facilitate trafficking for sexual exploitation in the UK or in any other parts of the world.[36] Moreover, Section 59 punishes trafficking for sexual exploitation committed outside the UK.[37] The Nationality, Immigration and Asylum Act 2002 introduced other provisions which covered trafficking of persons for sexual exploitation.[38] One of these provisions states that it is an offence to arrange and facilitate the arrival of a person in the UK for the purpose of prostitution.[39]

However, the most important modification to British law on human trafficking came in 2004, when more provisions on human trafficking were adopted to meet

---

24 See ibid., s. 47(1)(a).
25 See ibid., s. 47(1)(b).
26 See ibid., s. 47(1)(c)(i) and (ii).
27 See ibid., s. 47(2)(3)(4).
28 See ibid., s. 48.
29 See ibid., s. 49.
30 See ibid., s. 50.
31 See ibid., ss. 52 and 53.
32 See ibid., ss. 57 and 58.
33 See ibid., s. 57(1).
34 See ibid., s. 57(1)(a and b).
35 See ibid., s. 57(2)(b).
36 See ibid., s. 58(1)(a and b).
37 See ibid., s. 59(1)(a and b).
38 See ss. 145 and 146 of the Nationality, Immigration and Asylum Act 2002 (C. 41).
39 See ibid., s. 145(1).

the requirements of Framework Decision 2002/629/JHA, which came into force on 1 August 2004.[40] The UK communicated the measures taken to implement this framework decision to the Commission in February 2005.[41]

Trafficking in human beings for the general purpose of exploitation is now considered a criminal offence.[42] British legislation states that exploitation includes any behaviour which contravenes Article 4, entitled 'Prohibition of slavery and forced labour', of the Human Rights Convention.[43] British legislation provides that human trafficking also encompasses traffic in human organs[44] and any form of force, threat or deception to induce a person '(i) to provide services of any kind',[45] '(ii) to provide another person with benefits of any kind',[46] and '(iii) to enable another person to acquire benefits of any kind'.[47] Moreover, British legislation states that trafficking in human beings is a criminal offence if committed against a vulnerable person who:

> is mentally or physically ill or disabled, he is young or he has a family relationship with a person, and … a person without the illness, disability, youth or family relationship would be likely to refuse the request or resist the inducement.[48]

British legislation imposes penalties not exceeding 14 years' imprisonment on persons who plead guilty to human trafficking.[49] It also provides a summary penalty not exceeding 12 months' imprisonment.[50] Other provisions on human trafficking have recently been introduced by the Borders, Citizenship and Immigration Act 2009. The new Act states that trafficking is also committed when:

---

40   See Art. 10(1) of 'Council Framework Decision of 19 July 2002 on Combating Trafficking in Human Beings', OJ EU L 203/1, 1 August 2002. See also Ryan, B., 'The United Kingdom', in Higgins, I., and Hailbronner, K., eds, *Migration and Asylum Law and Policy in the European Union* (Cambridge: Cambridge University Press, 2004), p. 438.

41   See *Report from the Commission to the Council and the European Parliament Based on Article 10 of the Council Framework Decision of 19 July 2002 on Combating Trafficking in Human Beings*, COM (2006) 187 final, 2 May 2006, p. 3.

42   See s. 4(1) of Asylum and Immigration (Treatment of Claimants, etc.) Act 2004, ch. 19.

43   See Art. 4 of the *Convention for the Protection of Human Rights and Fundamental Freedoms* (ECHR), Rome, 4 November 1950, as amended by Protocol no. 11. See also s. 4(4)(a) of f Asylum and Immigration (Treatment of Claimants, etc.) Act 2004, op. cit. note 42.

44   See s. 4(4)(b) of Asylum and Immigration (Treatment of Claimants, etc.) Act 2004.

45   See ibid., s. 4(4)(c)(i).

46   See ibid., s.4(4)(c)(ii).

47   See ibid., s. 4(4)(c)(iii).

48   See ibid., s. 4(4)(d)(i)(ii).

49   See ibid., s. 4(5)(a).

50   See ibid., s. 4(5)(b).

(d) a person uses or attempts to use him for any purpose within sub-paragraph
(i), (ii) or (iii) of paragraph (c), having chosen him for that purpose on the
grounds that—

(i) he is mentally or physically ill or disabled, he is young or he has a family
relationship with a person, and

(ii) a person without the illness, disability, youth or family relationship would be
likely to refuse to be used for that purpose.[51]

These new provisions have been inserted to ensure that the offence of trafficking
includes all those cases where the role of the victim is completely passive or when
a person is used as a tool for the benefit of other people.[52]

In conclusion, it is important to mention that the UK has ratified the Council of
Europe Convention on Trafficking in Human Beings[53] and the UNTOC Trafficking
Protocol.[54] Furthermore, after 2002, the UK introduced ad hoc legislation covering
not only traffic in prostitution, but also other forms of human trafficking that
have been defined by Framework Decision 2002/629/JHA, where the Council
required Member States to penalise them.[55] The fact that the UK has responded to
the requirements of the European Framework Decision on Trafficking in Human
Beings should also be emphasised.[56] Despite these advancements, the UK has
failed to participate in the Directive on the Protection of Human Trafficking and
People Smuggling Victims. This should be viewed negatively, because it is crucial
that the EU has a common approach to the protection of victims in order to identify
the criminal organisations involved.

Italian Law

A new Italian law on trafficking in human beings was introduced in 2003.[57] Prior
to this new legislation, Act 79/1958[58] punished trafficking in prostitutes and the
recruitment in Italy and abroad of persons for the purpose of sexual exploitation.[59]
Moreover, the Italian Court of Last Resort (Corte di Cassazione) stated that the

---

51   See s. 54 of Borders, Citizenship and Immigration Act 2009, ch. 11.

52   See s. 54 of *Explanatory Note of Borders, Citizenship and Immigration Act 2009*,
ch. 11.

53   See Council of Europe Convention on Trafficking, op. cit. note 19.

54   See UNTOC Trafficking Protocol, op. cit. note 18.

55   See Art. 1(1) of 'Council Framework Decision 2002/946/JHA of 28 November 2002
on the Strengthening of the Penal Framework to Prevent the Facilitation of Unauthorised
Entry, Transit and Residence, OJ EU L 328/1, 5 December 2002.

56   See 'Council Framework Decision 2002/629/JHA of 19 July 2002 on Combating
Trafficking in Human Beings', OJ EU L 203, 1 August 2002.

57   See Act 228/2003, 'Misure contro la tratta di persone', GU 195, 23 August 2003.

58   See Act 75/1958, 'Abolizione della regolamentazione della prostituzione e lotta
contro lo sfruttamento della prostituzione altrui', GU 55, 4 March 1958.

59   See ibid., Art. 3(7).

crime of trafficking in prostitutes in Article 3(7) of Act 75/1958 could have been punished in conjunction with the crime of *associazione per delinquere* (association between three or more persons with the intent to commit crimes).[60] Article 3(7) could not punish criminal organisations involved in trafficking in prostitution, but only individual acts committed for the purpose of trafficking in prostitution.[61] Article 416 of the Italian Penal Code punishes any form of criminal association.[62] Therefore, it could have been applied in conjunction with Article 3(7) of Act 75/1958.

Other provisions against trafficking in human beings dealt with the sexual exploitation of children, and were adopted in 1998.[63] Act 269/1998 is based on the UN Convention on the Rights of the Child,[64] which was ratified by Italy in 1991.[65] Act 269/1998 introduced for the first time into Italian law the concept of sexual exploitation of children, and established a special police unit to fight against this crime in co-operation with Europol and the police forces of other European countries.[66] Act 269/1998 did not include trafficking in children, but only their exploitation for the purpose of prostitution or for the purposes of producing, commercialising or possessing child pornography.[67]

In 1998, Legislative Decree 286/1998 introduced the concept of smuggling of migrants with the purpose of prostitution, exploitation of any person, and the exploitation of children for any purpose.[68] In 2002, Act 189/2002 inserted a new provision in Legislative Decree 286/1998[69] which punishes those smugglers of migrants who commit this crime with the intent of recruiting persons for the purpose of sexual exploitation, or children for any form of exploitation, with imprisonment for up to 15 years.[70] Act 189/2002 added the concept of sexual

---

60   See Art. 416 of 'Codice Penale. R.D.N. 1398, 19/10/1930', GU 251, 26 October 1930. See also Cass. Pen. Sez. 1 sent. 21, 7 January 2003, rv. 223024.

61   Ibid.

62   See Art. 416 of 'Codice Penale. R.D.N. 1398, 19/10/1930', op. cit. note 60.

63   See Act 269/1998, 'Norme contro lo sfruttamento della prostituzione, della pornografia, del turismo sessuale in danno di minori, quali nuove forme di riduzione in schiavitù', GU 185, 10 August 1998, which introduced Arts 600*bis*, 600*ter*, 600*quater*, 600*quinquies*, 600*sexies* and 600*septies* to 'Codice Penale. R.D.N. 1398, 19/10/1930', op. cit. note 60.

64   See *Convention on the Rights of the Child*, adopted by General Assembly Resolution 44/25 of 20 November 1989.

65   See Art. 1(1) of Act 269/1998, op. cit. note 8.

66   See ibid., Art. 16(5 and 6).

67   See Arts 600*bis*, 600*ter*, 600*quater* of 'Codice Penale. R.D.N. 1398, 19/10/1930', op. cit. note 60, as modified by Act 269/1998, op. cit. note 63.

68   See Art. 12(3) of Legislative Decree 286/1998, op. cit. note 8.

69   See Art. 11(1)(c) of Act 189/2002, op. cit. note 8, which introduced para. 3*bis* to Art. 12 of Legislative Decree 286/1998, op. cit. note 8.

70   Ibid.

exploitation to that of prostitution. The penalties for these crimes were increased by the new Act 94/2009.

Until 2003, Italian law on trafficking in human beings concentrated only on trafficking in prostitutes and on sexual exploitation. The major modification to Italian legislation on trafficking in persons was made by the introduction of Act 228/2003,[71] which modified previous provisions of the Italian Penal Code.[72] The previous Articles 600, 601 and 602 focused on the crimes of slavery and commercialisation of slaves. Article 600 stated that anyone who reduces a person to slavery shall be punished with imprisonment for 5–15 years.[73] Article 601 stated that the trafficking or commercialisation of slaves was punishable with imprisonment for 5–20 years.[74] Article 602 punished the purchase, cession, selling and possession of slaves with imprisonment for 3–12 years.[75] Act 228/2003 gave a more in-depth definition of the concept of reduction to slavery, specifying that it consists of any form of subjection suffered by an individual and committed by a person for the purpose of forced labour, forced sexual acts, begging or other acts of exploitation.[76] The reduction to slavery might be committed by threat, violence, deception, abuse of power or abuse of a position of physical or psychical inferiority or of a situation of necessity or by the promise of economic advantage or other profit for those persons who exercise authority over persons willing to be reduced to slavery.[77] In all these cases, the new Article 600 establishes punishment with imprisonment of 8–20 years.[78] The penalty was increased by one-third to a half if the crime of reduction to slavery is committed against a minor under 18 years old or for the purpose of prostitution or removal of organs.[79] The Italian Corte di Cassazione pointed that the new Article 600 defines the crime of reduction to slavery introduced by the Slavery Convention ratified in Italy in 1928.[80]

Article 601 defines the crime of trafficking in human beings as consisting of transportation of persons from one State to another with the intent of exploiting

---

71   See Act 228/2003, op. cit. note 57.

72   See Arts 600, 601, 602 and 416 of 'Codice Penale. R.D.N. 1398, 19/10/1930', op. cit. note 60, as modified by Arts 1,2,3,4 of Act 228/2003, op. cit. note 57.

73   See Art. 600 of 'Codice Penale. R.D.N. 1398, 19/10/1930', op. cit. note 60.

74   See ibid., Art. 601.

75   See ibid., Art. 602.

76   See ibid., Art. 600(1) as modified by Art. 1(1) of Act 228/2003, op. cit. note 57.

77   See Art. 600(2) of 'Codice Penale. R.D.N. 1398, 19/10/1930', op. cit. note 60, as modified by Art. 1(2) of Act 228/2003, op. cit. note 57.

78   See Art. 600(1) of 'Codice Penale. R.D.N. 1398, 19/10/1930', op. cit. note 60, as modified by Art. 1(1) of Act 228/2003, op. cit. note 57.

79   See Art. 600(3) of 'Codice Penale. R.D.N. 1398, 19/10/1930', op. cit. note 60, as modified by Art. 1(3) of Act 228/2003, op. cit. note 57.

80   See *Geneva Slavery Convention of 25/9/1926*, United Nations Treaty Series 212. See also the Act of Ratification, R.d. 26 April 1928, no, 1723. See also Cass. Pen. Sez. 6, sent. 81, 4 January 2005, rv. 230777.

these persons.[81] Under Italian law, the crime of human trafficking is committed by deception, force, threat, abuse of authority or abuse of the inferiority of the person subject to human trafficking.[82] Article 600 establishes imprisonment of 8–20 years for those who commit this crime.[83] Moreover, the penalty increases if minors under 18 years old are trafficked, or if persons are trafficked for the purposes of prostitution or removal of organs.[84] These provisions also punish with imprisonment of up to 20 years those who commercialise slaves.[85] The term of imprisonment for those who commercialise slaves will increase if the victim is a minor under 18 years old or if persons are commercialised for the purposes of prostitution or removal of organs.[86] The sexual exploitation of minors under 18 years old is also punished severely by Act 38/2006.[87] Act 228/2003 punishes criminal organisations that commit trafficking in human beings who force individuals into slavery and commercialise them.[88]

The Italian law on human trafficking meets the requirement of Framework Decision 2002/629/JHA,[89] although only Italy communicated to the Commission the measures taken to implement this framework decision in May 2005.[90] Italian law on human trafficking is also similar to the Council of Europe Convention on Action against Trafficking in Human Beings that Italy signed on 8 June 2005, although it has yet to ratify it.[91] Italian law also took into consideration the UNTOC Trafficking Protocol, because it has ratified it.[92]

In conclusion, British and Italian laws on human trafficking are very strict because they consider trafficking in human beings a form of slavery.

The next sections analyse British and Italian laws on irregular migration, and show that both legal systems are strict because they establish the penalty of expulsion for irregular migration.

---

81   See Art. 601(1) of 'Codice Penale. R.D.N. 1398, 19/10/1930', op. cit. note 60, as modified by Art. 2(1) of Act 228/2003, op. cit. note 57.

82   Ibid.

83   Ibid.

84   See Art. 601(2) of 'Codice Penale. R.D.N. 1398, 19/10/1930', op. cit. note 60, as modified by Art. 2(2) of Act 228/2003, op. cit. note 57.

85   See Art. 602(1) of 'Codice Penale. R.D.N. 1398, 19/10/1930', op. cit. note 60, as modified by Art. 3(1) of Act 228/2003, op. cit. note 57.

86   See Art. 602(2) of 'Codice Penale. R.D.N. 1398, 19/10/1930', op. cit. note 60, as modified by Art. 3(2) of Act 228/2003, op. cit. note 57.

87   See Act 38/2006 'Disposizioni in materia di lotta contro lo sfruttamento sessuale dei bambini e la pedopornografia anche a mezzo Internet', GU 38, 15 February 2006.

88   See Art. 416(3) of 'Codice Penale. R.D.N. 1398, 19/10/1930', op. cit. note 60, as modified by Art. 4 of Act 228/2003, op. cit. note 57.

89   See Art. 1 of Framework Decision 2002/629/JHA, op. cit. note 56.

90   See COM (2006) 187 final, op. cit. note 41.

91   See Council of Europe Convention on Trafficking, op. cit. note 53.

92   See UNTOC Trafficking Protocol, op. cit. note 54.

British and Italian Laws on Irregular Migration

British Law

The Immigration Act 1971 established that it is a criminal offence to over-stay in the UK or not to observe 'a condition of the leave'.[93] The Act also states that it is a criminal offence to obtain by deception or other means, or to attempt to obtain, the right of entering and remaining in the UK, or to take action in order to avoid or postpone an enforcement action against themselves.[94] The Act states that if a person continues to stay in the UK after a deportation order has been issued, they commit a criminal offence.[95] Moreover, in all these cases, according to the Act, irregular migrants may be arrested by a police or immigration officer without warrant.[96] The Immigration Act 1971 also establishes an expulsion procedure and the right of immigration officers to detain persons liable to examination or removal.[97]

British law states that irregular migrants can be detained until their removal, and it does not establish a time limit for detention.[98] The Asylum and Immigration Act 2006 states that a person who has been required to submit to further examination of their identity can be detained for a period not exceeding 12 hours,[99] but a person who does not have the right to stay in the UK, despite the modifications of the Asylum and Immigration Act 2006, can be detained for an indefinite period. The European Court of Human Rights (Strasbourg Court) has stated that detention of non-UK nationals can be allowed in the process of their deportation, with respect to the ECHR (the Human Rights Act 1998 in the UK).[100] Therefore, British law fulfils the requirements of the ECHR and the Strasbourg Court by establishing that irregular migrants can be detained if the Home Secretary wishes to remove them from British territory.[101] British law does not need to indicate a time limit for detention as long as the deportation process is in progress.[102] Irregular migrants

---

93   See s. 24(1(b)(ii)) of Immigration Act 1971 inserted by Immigration and Asylum Act 1999.

94   See ibid., s. 24.A((1)(a)).

95   See s. 24(1) of Immigration Act 1971, substituted by British Nationality Act 1981.

96   See ibid., s. 28(a)(1).

97   See ibid., s. 16(1).

98   See s. 362 (1) of Immigration Rules (HC 395), laid before Parliament on 23 May 1994 under s. 3(2) of the Immigration Act 1971.

99   See s. 16 (1)(b) of Schedule 2 of Immigration Act 1971 as substituted by s. 42(3) of Asylum and Immigration Act 2006.

100   See, in particular, Art. 5(1)(f) of Human Rights Act 1998, ch. 42. See also *A.* v. *Secretary of State for the Home Department* [2005] 2 WLR 87, paras 8 and 9, which quote the European Court of Human Rights case *Chahal* v. *United Kingdom* (1996) 23 EHRR 413.

101   See *R* v. *Governor of Durham Prison, ex p Hardial Singh* [1984] 1 WLR 704. See also *Privy Council in Tan Te Lam* v. *Superintendent of Tai A Chau Detention Centre* [1997] AC 97.

102   See *A.* v. *Secretary of State for the Home Department* [2005] 2 WLR 87, para. 8.

can be expelled and detained for an indefinite period because they do not enjoy the right of abode in the territory of their arrival,[103] and for this reason they are in a position 'in which a national could never find himself'.[104]

According to British law, a person who is expelled does not have the right to be heard by a judicial authority and to defend him or herself against the expulsion procedure.[105] Indeed, the expulsion is decided by an immigration officer, and the expelled person can only appeal against a deportation order that has already been decided.[106]

Finally, it must be highlighted that the Immigration Act 1971 allows the detention without charge of irregular migrants, as there is no provision in the Act which states that irregular migrants are detained because they have committed the crime of irregular entry or stay. The Act states that an irregular migrant can be detained 'where a person has failed to comply with or has contravened a condition or has remained without authority',[107] and not because they have been charged with the crime of irregular entry. The only provisions that refer to Sections 24 and 24 A, provisions that criminalise irregular migration, are those that establish the arrest of illegal entrants with or without warrant[108] and those on the right to search them with or without warrant.[109] There is no provision that states that irregular migrants are detained because they have committed the crime of illegal entry. A logical argument can be made that the British only criminalised irregular migration in order to justify their detention. Detention without charge should be prohibited because it does not take into consideration whether the persons detained are victims of human trafficking and people smuggling, or their potential victims or criminals. Criminals and victims are all detained together in the UK, including 'families with children ... and other vulnerable people'.[110] Whether the detained persons are human traffickers or victims of people smugglers, they should be legally protected – in other words, they should have the right to reside in EU territory. Differentiation between victims and their smugglers or exploiters is important to protect victims, and it could prevent their re-victimisation. If irregular migrants are returned to their countries of origin, they may risk re-victimisation by their exploiters or smugglers. Restrictive laws do not prevent re-victimisation. In Italy, for example, strict immigration laws allowed the expulsion of irregular migrants without checking whether they were victims of human traffickers. This negligence facilitates the re-victimisation of people previously smuggled and

---

103   See *Moustaquim* v. *Belgium* (1991) 13 EHRR 802, para. 13.

104   See *A.* v. *Secretary of State for the Home Department*, op. cit. note 102, para. 56.

105   See ss. 8 *et seq.* of the Immigration Act 1971, Schedule 2.

106   Ibid. See also ss. 63 *et seq.* of Immigration and Asylum Act 1999.

107   See s. 364(1) of Immigration Rules, op. cit. note 98.

108   See ss. 28A and 28AA of Immigration Act 1971.

109   See ibid., ss. 28B and 28C.

110   See *Amnesty International Report 2006: The State of the World's Human Rights*, p. 270.

trafficked, because smugglers and traffickers are left without control, and are free to recruit victims again.

The 'Operational Enforcement Manual' states that detention should only be used as a last resort, and it must be kept under continuous review.[111] Nevertheless, the British Joint Committee on Human Rights (Joint Committee) reported that in recent years there has been an increase in detention of irregular migrants (asylum seekers).[112] There are ten Immigration Removal Centres with a total capacity of 2,545 places, whereas ten years ago there were only 200 places.[113] The fact that the Nationality, Immigration and Asylum Act 2002 has changed the name of Detention Centres to Removal Centres confirms the increase in detention of asylum seekers.[114] The Home Office explained that the use of detention might be necessary if the identity of a person and the grounds of their claim are in the process of being decided, if there are well-founded concerns that a person will not respect the conditions of temporary admission or release, if the removal has to be made effective, and if it seems that the asylum claim may be decided quickly under the fast-track process.[115] The Home Office pointed out that the decision to detain is taken on a case-by-case basis.[116] However, the Joint Committee reported that detention of irregular migrants as applied in the UK breaches Article 5(1)(f) ECHR. The Joint Committee reported:

> that current practice in relation to the detention of asylum seekers not only fails to reflect the Home Office's own policy guidance but also breaches the right to liberty because it is arbitrary.[117]

The Joint Committee also reported that detention often becomes unlawful when an asylum seeker is detained for the purpose of being removed, but is held up due to difficulties in obtaining travel documents, which can cause the process to drag on for months.[118] There are methods that can reduce detention in removal centres,[119] called 'fast-track processes'. The 'fast-track' method is used in three detention centres, Harmondsworth, Yarl's Wood and Oakington, with great success. These processes permit a rapid decision on asylum claims, within less than a month

---

111   Ch. 38 of the Home Office's Operational Enforcement Manual, <http://www.ind. homeoffice.gov.uk/documents/oemsectiona/>, accessed 13 April 2007.

112   See House of Lords and House of Commons Joint Committee on Human Rights, *The Treatment of Asylum Seekers*, Session 2006–2007, 10th Report, HL 81 and HC 60-I, *Volume I: Report and Report and Formal Minutes*, p. 69.

113   Ibid.

114   Ibid. See also s. 66 of the Nationality, Immigration and Asylum Act 2002, ch. 41.

115   See House of Lords and House of Commons Joint Committee on Human Rights, *The Treatment of Asylum Seekers*, op. cit. note 112, p. 70.

116   Ibid.

117   Ibid.

118   See ibid., p. 71.

119   See ibid., p. 72.

including any appeal. Harmondsworth and Yarl's Wood sometimes operate a 'super-fast track', which may last no more than nine days. Nevertheless, the Joint Committee reported that some non-governmental organisations are concerned that similar short processes may cause unfair decision-making, and that it is unlikely that an asylum seeker will reveal in such a short time what happened in her or his country of origin. In addition, there have been reports that it is unlikely that victims of rape or sexual violence will disclose information on these offences in such a short process. It must be pointed out that at Yarl's Wood specifically, statistics show that between May 2005 and September 2006, 26 percent of women did not have legal representation, and only 2 percent of asylum appeals succeeded.[120] A lack of legal representation for those processed in the fast track has been reported by Southampton and Winchester Visitors Group, by the Association of Visitors to Immigration Detainees (AVID), the London Detainee Support Group (LDSG) and by the Immigration Law Practitioners' Association (ILPA).[121] The ILPA has also expressed concern about the length of detention in cases of fast-track processes.[122] The Joint Council for the Welfare of Immigrants (JCWI) has stated that 'any policy extending fast track detention beyond seven days must render detention arbitrary and unlawful'.[123]

Vulnerable people are also detained without taking into consideration their situation.[124] The Immigration Minister has argued that vulnerable adults should only be detained in exceptional circumstances.[125] Vulnerable people include pregnant women, unaccompanied children, the elderly, people suffering from medical conditions or who are mentally ill, people where there is independent evidence that they have suffered torture, and people with serious disabilities.[126] However, Bail for Immigration Detainees (BID) reported that:

> it is a common occurrence for people with severe mental health problems to be detained, for evidence of their mental health to be ignored, for their problems to remain untreated whilst they are detained and for their detention to continue despite contravening stated Home Office policy.[127]

Furthermore, the LDSG pointed out that: 'torture victims were not routinely released, even where healthcare staff within the detention centre reported evidence of torture to the Immigration Service'.[128] The Home Office also has a policy that

---

120   See ibid., pp. 72 and 73.
121   See ibid., p. 73.
122   Ibid.
123   Ibid.
124   See ibid., p. 75.
125   See ibid., p. 74.
126   Ibid.
127   Ibid.
128   Ibid.

asylum seekers who are children should not be detained.[129] Nevertheless, the number of detained families has increased over the last years. There have been estimates that in 2005, 1,860 children were detained under immigration powers, and the vast majority of them (85 percent) were asylum detainees. BID expressed absolute opposition to detention of children, and stated that:

> Being detained is a humiliating and degrading experience ... The use of handcuffs and officers wearing body armour criminalise families and increase the distress and confusion of children. ... [T]he current process of detention and removal does not currently consider the welfare of the child, and that children and their needs are invisible throughout the process ...[130]

The Joint Committee reported many dramatic stories about the detention of children and their families.[131] A Jamaican lady had been in the UK since 2000, and had been detained with her two children aged 8 and 10. She had been detained three times, and her daughter suffered from an ear infection and sometimes wanted to commit suicide.[132] In other instances, two children were separated from their breastfeeding mothers.[133]

There have also been reports that asylum seekers with families are usually arrested early in the morning without having the opportunity to contact legal representatives.[134] High Court judges have considered this type of arrest illegal. However, there is evidence that this practice still continues.

The ILPA also reported that the Immigration Service in many cases failed to give written reasons for detention.[135] Furthermore, Her Majesty's Inspectorate of Probation expressed concerns about the process of reviewing detention. It stated: 'we find that monthly (non-judicial) reviews are repetitive, do not reflect changed circumstances, including the longevity of detention, and in some cases are missing altogether'.[136] The right to apply for bail, allowed to anyone in immigration detention apart from those who are detained pending examination, is also often denied.[137] Many detainees have problems in exercising their rights because of language difficulties, lack of legal representation, or mental health issues. The majority of bail hearings are unsuccessful.

---

129   See ibid., p. 76.
130   See ibid., p. 77.
131   See ibid., p. 78.
132   See ibid., pp. 78 and 79.
133   See ibid., p. 93.
134   See ibid., p. 91.
135   See ibid., p. 83.
136   Ibid.
137   See ibid., p. 84.

The Joint Committee also expressed concern about the quality of healthcare provided to asylum seekers in detention centres.[138] The Royal College of Psychiatrists reported that:

> There were no regular visits to the centre by qualified mental health staff, no equivalent to community mental healthcare, no daycare and no outpatient care. The Society expressed concern about the lack of specialised provision for torture victims and the absence of protocols for the identification, assessment and treatment of substance misusers.[139]

Some detainees are not able to keep their HIV status private while in detention.[140] Violation of human rights has also been reported in detention centres.[141] The Joint Committee has highlighted that: 'asylum seekers have been subjected to excessive use of force whilst being taken into detention or during an attempt to remove them from the UK'.[142] Detention without charge of irregular migrants should also be prohibited, because it again is another violation of human rights.

In conclusion, it seems that detention without charge is not applied only in exceptional cases in the UK. Serious negligence has been reported by non-intergovernmental organisations and by the Joint Committee. This is the reason why these centres should be reformed so that the rights of more vulnerable people, which includes the victims of human trafficking, can be taken into account fully. Furthermore, victims of human trafficking, and victims of torture or other degrading treatment should be differentiated from other irregular migrants. They should obtain permanent visas that would allow law enforcement authorities to gain their trust in reporting their victimisers. For this purpose, they should be assisted by humanitarian organisations.

Italian Law

Act 94/2009 modified parts of Legislative Decree 286/1998 by adding new provisions on the criminalisation of irregular entry. Article 1 of Act 94/2009 has added Article 10*bis* to Legislative Decree 286/1998, which imposes a fine of up to

---

138   See ibid., p. 89.

139   See ibid., p. 88.

140   Ibid.

141   'Detention centre enquiry ordered: Allegations of racism and bullying at Oakington Immigration Centre are to be investigated by the prisons and probation ombudsman', BBC News, 3 March 2005, <http://news.bbc.co.uk/go/pr/fr/-/1/hi/uk_politics/4315467>, accessed 20 June 2005. See Shaw, Stephen, *Investigation into Allegations of Racism, Abuse and Violence at Yarl's Wood Removal Centre: A Report by the Prison and Probation Ombudsman for England and Wales*' (2004), <http://www.ppo.gov.uk/docs/special-yarls-wood-abuse-03.pdf>. See also *Amnesty International Report 2006*, op. cit. note 110.

142   House of Lords and House of Commons Joint Committee on Human Rights *The Treatment of Asylum Seekers*, op. cit. note 112, p. 95.

€10,000 on foreigners who irregularly enter or stay in Italian territory. This new provision is nonsensical, especially when we consider that those who are smuggled by sea cannot possibly afford to pay such fines because of their conditions of extreme poverty.

In the past, Italian law has been subject to Constitutional Court judicial review, as some parts of it were unconsitutional. Before the reform of 2009, Italian law required expulsion, not criminal penalties, for all irregular migrants. Criminal sanctions would only be applied if they did not leave Italian territory within five days after a period of detention that did not exceed 60 days.[143] Legislative Decree 286/1998[144] dealt with irregular migration, and it did not impose imprisonment on irregular migrants, but their expulsion.[145] Legislative Decree 286/1998 stated that a foreigner (other than European citizens) who entered Italian territory without applying for a residence permit or by avoiding checks established by Legislative Decree 286/1998 would be expelled. Legislative Decree 286/1998 also included the procedure to follow after an expulsion order. It stated that the expulsion order was to be carried out by the head of police administration (*questore*) without specifying a time limit. The provision also stated that the police authority (*prefetto*), had to take into account the social, working and family life of the foreigner before carrying out the expulsion order if the foreigner did not have valid identity documents. Expulsion was, rightly, not automatic.

Modifications to Legislative Decree 286/1998 were introduced by Act 189/2002 and Act 106/2002. These new Acts did not modify the administrative nature of irregular migration, they only facilitated measures for expulsion and made Legislative Decree 286/1998 more restrictive. The new Acts did not guarantee irregular migrants rights to appeal expulsion decisions. Therefore, it was evident that Italian law attempted to render irregular migration a crime without charge, because expulsion was imposed automatically on irregular migrants, whose personal freedom was heavily restricted, being accompanied to the frontier without consultation with a lawyer. This is why, in the short period since Act 189/2002 came into force, there has been an increase in cases before the Italian Constitutional Court.[146] This chapter examines one judgment of the Italian Constitutional Court in

---

143 See Art. 14*(5bis)* of Legislative Decree 286/1998, op. cit. note 8, as modified by Art. 13(1)(b) of Act 189/2002, op. cit. note 8.

144 A more in-depth study on Italian law written by the author of this book can be found in 'Assisting Illegal Immigration and Trafficking in Human Beings in Italian Law: Illegal Immigration between Administrative Infringement and Criminal Offence', in Guild, E., and Minderhoud, P., eds, *Immigration and Criminal Law in the European Union: The Legal Measures and Social Consequences of Criminal Law in Member States on Trafficking and Smuggling in Human Beings* (Leiden: Martinus Nijhoff, 2006) pp. 141–68.

145 See Art. 13 of Legislative Decree 286/1998, op. cit. note 8, Supplemento ordinario no. 139 as modified by Act 189/2002, op. cit. note 8, and Art. 2(1) of Act 106/2002, GU 133, 8 June 2002.

146 See 'Judgment of Constitutional Court no. 223, 8–15 July 2004', GU 28, 21 July 2004. See also 'Judgment of the Italian Constitutional Court no. 5, 13 January 2004', GU,

particular, because it thwarted the attempt to make irregular migration a crime. This Constitutional Court's judgment declared unconstitutional that part of Legislative Decree 286/1998, as modified by Act 106/2002.[147] The Italian Constitutional Court found it troubling that under Act 106/2002, an irregular migrant could be deported coercively before a tribunal could decide on the legality of a procedure which limited their personal freedom. Even though such a tribunal might ultimately reject the deportation procedure, it would have been too late due to the short period (48 hours) within which a deportation procedure had to be carried out. Such a finding by a tribunal would have no positive effect on the irregular migrant, as he or she would have already been deported from Italian territory without the opportunity to defend him or herself. Specifically, Act 106/2002 was in conflict with the principle of the Italian Constitution which establishes the ineffectiveness of a procedure that has not been executed within 48 hours by the tribunal. The Constitutional Court added that the right to a defence, a personal freedom, was also violated because modifications introduced by Act 106/2002 did not allow a foreign person to be heard by a judicial authority with the assistance of a lawyer. Following the judgment of the Constitutional Court, in September 2004 the government approved the new Legislative Decree 241/2004.[148] According to this Legislative Decree, the head of the police administration must inform the justice of the peace (*giudice di pace*) within 48 hours of the adoption of the expulsion order.[149] This measure will be suspended until the decision of the justice of the peace, who shall hear the foreigner subject to the deportation order with the assistance of a lawyer. Consequently, the tribunal no longer has any jurisdiction to oversee the case, and compared to the previous Act 106/2002, Legislative Decree 241/2004 does not require that an expulsion order be immediately effective.[150] Indeed, the new provision states that the justice of the peace cannot take any decision without the presence of a lawyer.[151]

Four years after the intervention of the Constitutional Court and the consequent law's amendment, in 2008 the government decided to adopt a new draft law which

21 January 2004; 'Ordinance no. 226, 8–15 July 2004', GU 28 21 July 2004.

147   See 'Judgment of the Italian Constitutional Court no. 222', 8–15 July 2004, GU 28, 21 July 2004.

148   See Art. 1 of Legislative Decree no. 241/2004, GU 216, 14 September 2004. See also 'Decree of Conversion in Law no. 271/2004', GU 267, 14 November 2004.

149   Ibid. The post of justice of the peace, established in Italy by Act 468/1999, has jurisdiction over minor crimes punishable by imprisonment up to four months, and contraventions. Thus, competence over irregular migration should have been transferred to the administrative judge unless the legislator had changed the administrative nature of irregular migration. Nevertheless, the legislator did not do this when irregular migration was still considered an administrative infringement according to Art. 13 of Legislative Decree 286/1998, and not modified in that part by Act 189/2002. After Act 94/2009 enters into force, the justice of the peace will have jurisdiction over the crime of irregular migration.

150   See Art. 13(5*bis*) of Legislative Decree 286/1998, op. cit. note 8. See also Art. 1(1) Legislative Decree 241/2004, op. cit. note 148.

151   See ibid., Art. 1(1).

criminalised irregular migration.[152] Indeed, a new provision of the draft law stated that a foreigner who enters Italian territory in violation of Legislative Decree 286/1998 shall be punished with imprisonment for six months to four years.[153] This provision has been criticised because it punishes the subjective status of a person, and not the conduct of the individual.[154] The Italian Association for Legal Studies on Immigration (ASGI) suggests that the best way to prevent irregular migration is by facilitating the entry of migrants for work. It must be emphasised that EU Member States need employees from outside the EU because there is shortage of working population in the EU.[155] Another issue raised by the ASGI is the fact that Italy does not have sufficient prisons to detain all the arrested irregular migrants, therefore this new provision would have been applied only to a minority of them. The majority of irregular migrants will not be able to afford lawyers, and it will be the responsibility of the Italian State to pay the potentially high costs of legal aid.[156] This especially applies to people smuggled by sea. How can they afford a lawyer if they are extremely poor? Act 94/2009 does not resolve this problem, because it criminalises irregular migration by the introduction of a pecuniary penalty. The new law criminalises a conduct, irregular migration, which does not include a *mens rea* component – the intention to commit a criminal offence. This is because irregular migrants smuggled by sea who leave their countries of origin certainly do not do so with the intention of committing a crime, but because they would otherwise die from poverty. Therefore, either the provision of Act 94/2009 which considers irregular migration a crime is a case of strict liability, or this Act punishes people smuggled by sea simply because they are poor. In other words, the *mens rea* of this crime would be the fact that people smuggled by sea leave their countries of origin because they are poor, and by doing so, they show their intention to commit a crime. A strong argument can be made that this new provision should be considered unconstitutional because, according to Article 27 of the Italian Constitution, criminal law is based on the principle of *nullum crimen sine culpa* ('no crime without culpability'). An argument that this provision is simply the State imposing strict liability on a particular crime, which is allowed by the Italian Constitution, would ultimately not prevail. This is due to the fact that the Italian Penal Code only allows strict liability in limited circumstances, for which a restrictive list is provided.

---

152   See Disegno di Legge no. 733 presented by the Italian Prime Minister before the Senato della Repubblica, 3 June 2008, <http://www.senato.it/service/PDF/PDFServer/BGT/00302495.pdf>.

153   My translation of ibid., Art. 9.

154   See material provided by Associazione Studi Giuridici sull'Immigrazione (ASGI), 'Osservazioni sulle Norme in Materia di Stranieri contenute nei Provvedimenti del "Pacchetto Sicurezza" approvati dal Consiglio dei Ministri nella riunione del 21/5/2008', <http://www.astrid-online.it/Immigrazio/Studi--ric/ASGI_pacchetto-sicurezza.pdf>, p. 13.

155   See Chapter 4 of this book.

156   See 'Osservazioni sulle Norme in Materia di Stranieri contenute nei Provvedimenti del "Pacchetto Sicurezza" approvati dal Consiglio dei Ministri nella riunione del 21/5/2008', op. cit. note 154, p. 14.

The more logical conclusion as to why the government has adopted this new law is that it has demagogic aims, intending to attract votes at the expense of addressing the problem of irregular migration in the most effective and serious way. An effective fight against irregular migration would require the adoption of a law on economic legal migration, which is absent in Act 94/2009. It is self-evident that most (if not all) the new provisions of the Act are principally addressed to repressive measures on irregular migration, which has widespread support among the Italian public. Paragraph 28 of Article 1 of Act 94/2009 has reduced funding for economic legal migration, while a new fund to return irregular migrants has been established by Article 14*bis* that Act 94/2009 has added to Legislative Decree 286/1998.

The demagogic approach adopted by the government has gained the support of the Italian people by misleading them. The ease with which the government deceives the Italian public, convincing them that the smuggling of migrants is a bigger problem than it actually is, is due to widespread ignorance in the Italian population. Most of them are not well informed about the fact that irregular migration caused by smuggling of migrants is not the main problem, as most irregular migrants do not enter Italian territory by this means, but by over-staying, as was shown in Chapter 4. Conversely, during the Parliamentary discussions of the draft law on irregular migration, the Italian media largely drew a correlation between stopping smuggling of migrants by sea and stopping irregular migration altogether.

The result of this misleading information was that most Italians, especially those living in northern Italy, where the phenomenon of irregular migration is more evident, supported the new law. Interviews held in Milan with people with intermediate education[157] showed that they were more likely to support this new law, thinking that it would solve the problem of irregular migration. The government reached their demagogic aim by misleading Italian people, as criminalising irregular migration is almost impossible. In fact, how can it be possible to 'catch' all the irregular migrants and criminalise them? Criminalising irregular migrants smuggled by sea will not help law enforcement authorities to gain the trust of these people, with the risk that they will always be reluctant to report their smugglers. There is also the risk that this new law would discourage victims of people trafficking from reporting their victimisers, as they will fear being criminalised. As stated above, this law is also nonsensical because it requires people who are usually extremely poor to pay fines they cannot possibly afford. The Opposition to the government did not seriously fight against the entry into force of this new law because irregular migration is a burning issue in Italy, and must be approached with great sensitivity. Any resistance to the government measure could be widely seen as an endorsement of irregular migrants. There was not even opposition against the provision of Act 94/2009 which, by introducing Article 9(2*bis*) to Legislative Decree 286/1998, prolonged the detention of irregular migrants in so-called Centres of Identification and Expulsion (CIE) from 60 days to 180 days. The provisions of Act 94/2009 on the criminalisation of irregular migration are now under examination by the Constitutional Court after that

---

157   Interviews held in Milan on 10–15 June 2009 and 20–27 August 2009.

the Tribunal of Pesaro and the Public Prosecutor of Turin requested a preliminary ruling.[158] They argue that the aim of the new provisions of Act 94/2009 is to expel the irregular migrants – something already provided for by provisions of Legislative Decree 286/1998. Therefore, there was no reason to criminalise irregular migration. They also argued that punishing irregular entry with a large financial penalty was excessive, considering the fact that, as emphasised above, most irregular migrants are poor and will never be able to afford payment.

Unfortunately, on 5 July 2010, for practical more than reasons founded on the Constitution, the Italian Constitutional Court has established that the new crime of irregular migration is not unconstitutional but it responds to the need of the Italian State to control migration flows. In this matter, the legislator has wide discretion, including the power to impose criminal sanctions to irregular migrants.[159]

In conclusion, the Italian government decided to criminalise irregular migration. This initiative might be counter-productive for many irregular migrants because many of them are victims of smugglers and traffickers and will be reluctant to co-operate with law enforcement authorities and report these criminals. As a result, irregular migrants risk remaining vulnerable to exploitation by criminal organisations.

The next sections examine how the UK and Italy deal with victims of the human trafficking and people smuggling by sea.

Reducing Victimisation

British Law and Human Trafficking Victims

British law did not provide for the protection of victims of human trafficking until the ratification of the Council of Europe Convention on Trafficking in Human Beings. This is a very welcome change, because Europol and the British Joint Committee on Human Rights have estimated that the UK is one of the main European countries of destination for victims of human trafficking for the purpose of sexual exploitation.[160] Since the convention was only ratified in April 2009, it is too premature to evaluate the application of this new law. Therefore, this section

---

158 See *Ordinanza del Tribunale di Pesaro – Sezione Penale, RNR 2823/09*, RG TRIB 829/09, 31 August 2009. See also *Questione di legittimità costituzionale dell'art. 10 bis D.L.vo n. 286/98 come introdotto dall'art. 1 co. 16 Legge 15 luglio 2009, n. 94 in relazione agli artt. 2, 3 co. 1 e 25 co. 2 Cost*, Public Prosecution Office of Turin, 15 September 2009.

159 See judgement of the Italian Constitutional Court no. 250, 15/7/2010 not yet published in the *Italian Official Journal*.

160 *Trafficking in Human Beings for Sexual Exploitation in the EU: A Europol Perspective*, <http://www.europol.eu.int/publications/SeriousCrimeOverviews/2005/THB_factsheet.pdf>, accessed 10 November 2005. See also House of Lords and House of Commons Joint Committee on Human Rights, *Human Trafficking*, Session 2005–2006, 26th Report, HL 245-I and HC 1127-I, *Volume I: Report and Report and Formal Minutes*, p. 28.

concentrates on the measures adopted to date by British law on the protection of victims of trafficking.

UK police forces have mainly focused on trafficking in human beings for sexual exploitation.[161] All the UK police forces are taking part in a variety of projects called Operation Pentameter, Operation Maxim and Operation Paladin Child.[162] Operation Pentameter is a funded multi-agency unit which involves 55 police forces in England, Scotland, Wales, Ireland, the Channel Islands, the UK Immigration Service, the National Criminal Intelligence Service, the Crown Prosecution Service and many non-governmental organisations.[163] The aim of this multi-agency unit is to prevent human trafficking for the purpose of sexual exploitation by arresting and prosecuting the perpetrators and by caring for the victims.[164] Operation Maxim is an anti-trafficking initiative led by the Metropolitan Police, and was established after the death of 58 Chinese people in a lorry in Dover.[165] Operation Maxim liaises with the Immigration Service and Passport Service to co-ordinate the work of the Human Smuggling Unit and the Metropolitan Polices Clubs and Vice Unit (CO14).[166] Operation Paladin Child was an initiative taken by the Metropolitan Police in partnership with the Immigration Service and the Children's charity the National Society for the Prevention of Cruelty to Children which was organised during August–November 2003.[167] The aim of Operation Paladin Child was to investigate cases of the abuse and exploitation of children.[168]

However, in the UK, the victims of human trafficking have been neglected compared to other persons such as asylum seekers. It was found that in the UK, the International Organization for Migration supports the return and reintegration of asylum seekers in their countries of origin,[169] while human trafficking victims' and people smuggling victims are not part of this programme.[170] Victims of people smugglers and human traffickers can only be provided with a ticket to return to their countries of origin after completing an application form where they sign

---

161   Interview with police officer Karen Kinger at Scotland Yard on 16 June 2006.

162   See House of Lords and House of Commons Joint Committee on Human Rights, *Human Trafficking*, op. cit. note 159, pp. 43 and 44.

163   <http://www.norfolk.police.uk/article.cfm?artID=7513&catID=549&bctrail=0, accessed 19 June 2006.

164   Ibid.

165   See House of Lords and House of Commons Joint Committee on Human Rights, *Human Trafficking*, op. cit. note 159, p. 43.

166   See ibid., pp. 43 and 44.

167   See ibid., p. 44.

168   Ibid.

169   Reintegration is fully supported by the author of this book if humanitarian organisations provide assistance to irregular migrants that means they do not return to their countries of origin in the state of poverty that led them to leave it in the first place.

170   See International Organization for Migration, *Voluntary Assisted Return and Reintegration Programme: VARRP. Reintegration Self-evaluation Results*, June 2004, p. 2.

a 'Declaration of Voluntary Return'.[171] No programme of integration has been established for those who risk being re-victimised when they return to their countries of origin. This is because they return to countries where they live in poor conditions without any assistance or support to start a business that could change their situation of poverty. Returning to a position of poverty will make victims of human trafficking easy targets for criminal organisations ready to traffic them again.[172] If human trafficking victims applied for asylum in the UK, they could participate in a programme of reintegration in their countries of origin which consists of obtaining financial support from the IOM for starting a business.[173] However, victims of people smuggling and human trafficking, many of whom live in conditions of slavery,[174] may not know British asylum law, or may be reluctant to approach public authorities or humanitarian organisations because they fear retaliation from the criminal organisations that have smuggled and exploited them.[175]

Finally, British legislation has been absolutely inadequate because there are no provisions that expressly protect victims of human trafficking and people smuggling.[176] The UK is not a party to the EC Directive on the Protection of Victims of Smuggling and Trafficking in Persons.[177] Moreover, the legislation against criminal organisations, although it has established a form of protection for persons who want to testify against criminal organisations, does not address the issue of human trafficking and people smuggling.[178] The reason for this is because this legislation states that those who can be offered protection must be resident in the UK and be witnesses in criminal proceedings against members of criminal organisations.[179] Victims of people smuggling and human trafficking are not mentioned in this legislation, and if they are irregular migrants, they cannot be protected because they are not legally resident in the UK. The Serious Organised Crime and Police Act (SOCA) 2005 is discriminatory because it grants protection to

---

171 See documents gathered from the IOM on 16 June 2006 at 21 Westminster Palace Gardens, Artillery Row, London SW1P 1RR.

172 See House of Lords and House of Commons Joint Committee on Human Rights, *Human Trafficking*, op. cit. note 159, p. 47.

173 See *Voluntary Assisted Return and Reintegration Programme*, op. cit. note 169, p. 5.

174 See Benzi, O., *Prostitute. Vi Passeranno Davanti Nel Regno Dei Cieli* (Milan: Arnoldo Mondatori Editore, 2001).

175 See later in this chapter, where it is shown that this fear is real, as on some occasions criminal organisations, for example, have killed family members of people who reported their exploiters.

176 See s. 145 of Nationality and Immigration Asylum Act 2002.

177 See 'Council Directive 2004/81/EC of 29 April 2004 on the Residence Permit Issued to Third-country Nationals Who are Victims of Trafficking in Human Beings or Who Have Been the Subject of an Action to Facilitate Illegal Immigration, Who Cooperate with the Competent Authorities', OJ EU L 261/19, 6 August 2004.

178 See ss. 82 *et seq.* of Serious Organised Crime and Police Act 2005.

179 See ibid., s. 82(1)(b) and Schedule 5.

victims of organised crimes only if they reside legally in British territory. Why are other victims neglected? It seems that the SOCA considers the fight against human trafficking as a priority, along with the fight against drug trafficking.[180] Nevertheless, if it does not provide assistance for victims of human trafficking and people smuggling, it is unlikely that it will reduce the incidence of these two crimes. Although there is no specific legislation covering victims of these two crimes, temporary residence permits may be granted to victims of human trafficking on a discretionary basis. The granting of these permits is based on whether they decide to support the law enforcement authorities in their investigations of the organisations behind these crimes.[181]

The UK has signed and ratified the UNTOC Convention and Protocols on Smuggling and Trafficking of Persons and the Council of Europe Convention on Trafficking, which requires the granting of a form of protection for victims of human trafficking.

In conclusion, the UK did not have ad hoc legislation on victims of smuggling and trafficking. While legislation on smuggling of migrants by sea is not necessary in the UK as they do not have to face this crime directly, it was to adopt specific legislation on human trafficking after the ratification of the Council of Europe Convention on Trafficking. The urgency arose because in the past, shelter for victims could only be provided on a discretionary basis to 25 victims of human trafficking for sexual exploitation.

The Poppy Project and its Inadequacy in Protecting Victims of Human Trafficking

The British Home Office funds the Poppy Project,[182] which provides a shelter for trafficked women who are not minors.[183] Children cannot be admitted to the Poppy Project.[184] In 2004, a centre was opened in Sussex to provide protection to children

180   See House of Lords and House of Commons Joint Committee on Human Rights, *Human Trafficking*, op. cit. note 159, p. 42.

181   See Obokata, T., 'Smuggling of Human Beings from a Human Rights Perspective: Obligations of Non-State and State Actors under International Human Rights Law', On *International Journal of Refugee Law* 7:2 (2005), p. 410.

182   <http://www.poppyproject.org> and <http://www.poppy.ik.com>; both websites were accessed on 16 February 2006. Please note that these URLs no longer relate to the Poppy Project, which can now be found online at <http://www.eaves4women.co.uk/POPPY_Project/POPPY_Project.php>.

183   Reply by e-mail received from the responsible for the Poppy Project, on 28 June 2006. Minors are often victims of human trafficking, and there is evidence that in Italy the 35 percent of trafficked women in the sexual market are girls aged under 18; 'Associazione Papa Giovanni XXIII and Prostitution in Italy and the Law', paper received on 19 April 2006 during interviews held in Rimini, p. 6.

184   See House of Lords and House of Commons Joint Committee on Human Rights, *Human Trafficking*, op. cit. note 159, p. 54.

aged 16–17.[185] However, this was closed after a few weeks, partly because there were not enough referrals.[186] Since 2004, no other projects have been organised in order to accommodate children who are victims of human trafficking.[187] The Poppy Project reported that children do not receive enough support, and it seems that children in the UK are put through the immigration and asylum process without recognition of their special needs to be protected from human traffickers.[188]

The Poppy Project can only accommodate up to 25 women victims of trafficking for sexual exploitation.[189] Trafficked women must meet specific criteria, which include having been brought to the UK, having worked as prostitutes in the last 30 days in the UK, having been forcibly exploited, having come forward to the authorities, and having shown the will to co-operate with the authorities.[190] Nevertheless, these criteria can be evaluated with much discretion,[191] and 15 of the 99 women accepted for the project in 2003–2006 did not meet all the criteria.[192] However, many women were not admitted because there was not enough space to accommodate them.[193]

The project is divided into two stages: one available for a period not exceeding four weeks, and another stage available for a period of 6–12 weeks.[194] In the first stage, the victim is given short-term accommodation, a health assessment, access to legal services, interpretation and translation services, information, and possibly support and liaison with police and immigration officials.[195] In the second stage, victims are required to co-operate with law enforcement authorities, and on the basis of this co-operation, they can obtain further support.[196] There are three facts concerning the Poppy project that must be pointed out. Firstly, the protection of victims of human trafficking for sexual exploitation may only be granted to victims who decide to co-operate with law enforcement authorities. This condition does not respect the requirements of Framework Decision 2002/629/JHA, which expressly specifies that the protection of human trafficking victims 'shall not be dependent on the report or accusation made by a person'[197] when the crime has been committed wholly in the territory of one EU Member State.[198] The Poppy

---

185 Ibid.
186 Ibid.
187 Ibid.
188 See ibid., p. 55.
189 <http://www.poppy.ik.com>, accessed 16 February 2006.
190 Ibid.
191 See House of Lords and House of Commons Joint Committee on Human Rights, *Human Trafficking*, op. cit. note 159, p. 52.
192 Ibid.
193 Ibid.
194 Ibid.
195 Ibid.
196 Ibid.
197 See Art. 7(1) of Council Framework Decision 2002/629/JHA, op. cit. note 56.
198 See ibid., Arts 6(1)(a) and 7(1).

Project can apply discretion to the criterion on the decision to co-operate with law enforcement authorities. However, this criterion should be completely abolished, because in many cases victims in the UK do not want to accuse their exploiters because they fear retaliation.[199] Secondly, the UK does not grant any form of legal protection to victims of human trafficking for purposes other than sexual exploitation. The Human Trafficking Centre established in October 2006 may change this situation, but it is still too early to evaluate this. Thirdly, the Poppy Project is the only non-governmental organisation that provides a shelter for some victims of human trafficking for sexual exploitation.[200] Another similar project should be organised in Glasgow, but at the moment the Poppy Project in London is unique in the UK. Moreover, other NGOs and voluntary organisations that offer assistance to human traffickers' victims do not receive enough funding, and for this reason they are unable to provide assistance in many cases.[201]

The people responsible for the Poppy Project were approached by the author, but only agreed to have an e-mail exchange, and it must be said that they did not demonstrate a willingness to co-operate with the research project. They simply sent some materials as an e-mail attachment, and from the material they provided, it seems that victims are hosted by the Poppy Project for eight months to a year, and afterwards many of them are returned to their countries of origin. Indeed, in the UK, victims of human trafficking can be recognised as asylum seekers under the Geneva Convention or other forms of protection under the Human Rights Act 1998 or the ECHR.[202] In some cases, victims of human trafficking for sexual exploitation have obtained the status of refugees or other forms of humanitarian protection because their countries of origin did not have adequate laws against human trafficking for sexual exploitation,[203] but not simply because they were victims of human trafficking. In another case, there was evidence that the claimant had been sexually exploited and that her husband would have been violent to her on her return. However, she was not granted the status of refugee or other humanitarian protection because her country of origin had adequate laws that could protect her.[204] All victims of human trafficking and people smuggling by sea should be granted legal protection and integration into the hosting society unless the country of origin they return to can offer some form of basic support. Even

---

199 See Joint Committee on Human Rights, op. cit. note 159, p. 47.

200 See <http://www.eaves4women.co.uk/POPPY_Project/Student_FAQs.php#q5>.

201 See House of Lords and House of Commons Joint Committee on Human Rights, *Human Trafficking*, op. cit. note 159, p. 53.

202 See Richards, S., Steel, M., and Singer, D., *Hope Betrayed: An Analysis of Women Victims of Trafficking and their Claims for Asylum*, (London: Eaves-Poppy Project, 2006), p. 12.

203 Home Office Immigration and Nationality Directorate, *Gender Issues in the Asylum Claim: Asylum Policy Instruction*, March 2004, <http://www.ind.homeoffice. gov.uk/ind/en/home_laws_policy/policy_instructions/apis/gender_issues_in_the.html>, accessed 24 April 2006.

204 Ibid.

if the countries of origin of human trafficking victims punish human trafficking, the victims will never be adequately protected from being exploited again. These situations will not change because the poverty which is the underlying cause will remain unaddressed. In addition, the restrictive approach adopted by the UK and the consignment of all irregular migrants to detention camps without any distinction between human traffickers and their victims may have facilitated the commission of human trafficking, especially because it is difficult to identify victims in detention centres. The Joint Committee on Human Rights revealed that victims of human trafficking, for example, have been kept in detention centres with other irregular migrants where it was impossible to distinguish victims from human traffickers.[205] One of the victims of traffic in prostitution hosted in accommodation provided by the Poppy Project reported that she was contacted again by her traffickers while she was in a detention centre.[206] Loanna, a girl from Africa, was invited by an Englishman to go to the UK to do domestic work for him. When she arrived in the UK, she was forced to work as a prostitute, and when she refused, she was beaten and threatened with arrest if she did not accept his terms. After six months, the police searched the house where she was hosted, and transferred her to a detention camp. Instead of granting protection to Loanna, a victim of human traffickers, the police decided to incarcerate her. Loanna continued to receive unwelcome visits from her trafficker, who would threaten her not to tell anybody about them, otherwise her family and she would be killed after her return to Africa. When she reported him, the visits stopped, although she continued to receive threatening telephone calls from people she had never met. When the police decided to surrender her from the detention centre and when she received assistance from the Poppy Project, these threatening acts stopped. However, Loanna is afraid to go out alone, and fears receiving punishment from her traffickers. It could be argued that Loanna's story is just one case, but how many are there that have remained unreported? What about victims of other forms of human trafficking, such as forced labour, child prostitution and trafficking in organs? These people are completely neglected and abandoned in detention camps, where they may receive daily threats. However, no one knows them, and no one knows how many of them are in a state of vulnerability.

The UK opened another multi-agency unit to deal with any form of human trafficking, which was operational from 2 October 2006.[207] It is called the UK Human Trafficking Centre (UKHTC) and is based in Sheffield.[208] The public prosecutor who deals with victims of human trafficking in the UKHTC was

---

205   See House of Lords and House of Commons Joint Committee on Human Rights, *Human Trafficking*, op. cit. note 159, p. 49.

206   <http://www.poppyproject.org/loanna/htm>, accessed 18 February 2006.

207   See 'Sex Slavery under Police Scrutiny', BBC News, 30 September 2006, <http://news.bbc.co.uk/1/hi/england/south_yorkshire/5383386.stm>.

208   See *Human Trafficking*, op. cit. note 159, pp. 42 and 43. See also <http://www.ukhtc.org/index.htm>.

approached about contributing to this research.[209] The public prosecutor said that the UKHTC deals with all victims of human trafficking, and not only with victims of trafficking for sexual exploitation. However, it is very difficult to persuade victims to report their exploiters, as they do not trust law enforcement authorities. Another problem that law enforcement authorities have to face every day is the fact that there are no reliable data on the crime, only on the number of recovered victims and their countries of origin, which are mainly Afghanistan, Iraq, Iran, Eritrea and sub-Saharan Africa. The public prosecutor was then asked if adopting a victim-centred approach to by giving victims long-stay visas, such as working visas, could enable law enforcement organisations to gain their trust, eventually persuading them to co-operate with their investigations. The public prosecutor said that there are some governments, such as the British government, which fear that such an approach might encourage more people to emigrate irregularly and make false claims in order to obtain permanent or working visas. However, the public prosecutor also said that there is no evidence that this risk is real, because a victim-oriented approach such as the one suggested has never been adopted for victims of people smuggling by sea. It must be added that it seems very unlikely that victims of smuggling by sea or trafficking would make false claims, as they fear retaliation from the criminal organisations directed towards them or their families in their countries of origin. These points are explored further in the next sections, where the situation of smuggling of migrants by sea and people trafficking in Italy is examined. Italian law approaches trafficking in human beings in a more advanced way. If all police forces in Italy applied the Italian law to victims of human trafficking and people smuggling, these offences could be dramatically reduced. However, there are two factors that should be considered. First of all, it has been found out that most Italian police forces, like British police forces, focus on human trafficking for sexual exploitation. Secondly, Act 189/2002 has contributed to the automatic expulsion of irregular migrants without encouraging police forces to investigate whether the irregular migrants are victims of human traffickers or people smugglers. Consequently, the application of the law on protection of victims of human trafficking has been left to the 'good will' of police forces which are keen to defeat human trafficking. This situation has been reported in Rimini, where police forces were respectful of the law on human trafficking and overcame human trafficking for sexual exploitation by reintegrating victims in Italian territory.

Italian Law on Protection of Human Trafficking Victims

Italy has ratified UNTOC and the Smuggling and Trafficking Protocols, but not the Council of Europe Convention against Trafficking in Human Beings. The ratification of this convention is essential to develop international co-operation against smuggling of migrants and trafficking in human beings. However, it could

---

209   Interviews held in London on 16 July 2009.

be argued that Italian legislation is much more advanced than the UK legislation on protection of victims of human trafficking because it establishes a form of legal protection for these victims and for victims of people smuggling.[210] The British Joint Committee on Human Rights stated:

> we were highly impressed by the way in which the proactive victim-centred approach adopted in that country has allowed such high numbers of trafficking victims to be supported and ultimately integrated into Italian society.[211]

The most important difference between Italian law on human trafficking and people smuggling and British law is embodied in Article 18 of Legislative Decree 286/1998.[212] This Article is revolutionary because it permits the integration of all victims of human trafficking into Italian society.[213] Article 18(1) of Legislative Decree 286/1998, which was not modified by Act 189/2002, states:

> When, during police's operations or inquiries or proceedings, for a criminal offence of the article 3 of Law 20 February 1958, n. 75[214] or one of those described at the article 380 of Criminal Procedure Code,[215] or during aid interventions of social services of local bodies, situations of violence or serious exploitations of a foreigner are found, and concrete dangers emerge for his or her life, as effects of trying to escape from the influence of an association dedicated to one of the above mentioned crimes, or because of the declarations made during preliminary enquiries or during the proceeding, the chief of the local Police headquarter, also on Public Prosecutor's proposal, or with the favourable opinion of the same authority, releases a special permit of staying to give the opportunities to the foreigners to escape from the violence and from the influence of the criminal organisation and to participate in an assistance and social integration program.[216]

---

210   See Art. 18(1) of Legislative Decree 286/1998, op. cit. note 8.

211   See *Human Trafficking*, op. cit. note 159, p. 63.

212   See Art. 18(1) of Legislative Decree 286/1998, op. cit. note 8.

213   The author is very grateful to Giampiero Cofano, co-ordinator of the Italian anti-trafficking organisation Association Pope John XXIII, for procuring the official English-language version of Art. 18 of Legislative Decree 286/1998. This version can also be found in *Tutela delle vittime del traffico di esseri umani e lotta alla criminalità. L'Italia e gli scenari europei. Rapporto di ricerca* (On the Road Edizioni, 2002), pp. 327–30.

214   This Act refers to sexual exploitation of women.

215   Art. 380 of *Codice di Procedura Penale*, Decreto del Presidente della Repubblica no. 447, 22 September 1988, refers to crimes of serious entity such as reduction to slavery and terrorism.

216   See official English version, op. cit. note 212, of Art. 18(1) of Legislative Decree 286/1998, op. cit. note 8.

This Article not only permits the integration of victims of human trafficking by issuing residence permits when the victims decide to co-operate with law enforcement authorities in order to arrest their traffickers, it also permits the integration of these people whether or not they decide to co-operate. By the wording of Article 18 of Legislative Decree 286/1998, the extension of protection to people who have been smuggled could be achieved because this Article states that if a foreigner is in 'situations of violence … and concrete dangers emerge for his or her life',[217] he or she can be issued a special permit to stay in Italy. Certainly, smuggled migrants by sea may encounter all these situations when they travel from their countries of origin to the EU by very poor means.

By applying Article 18 of Legislative decree 286/1998, the victims of smuggling of migrants by sea may seek the support of the police and may be provided with assistance and shelter in order to escape the criminal organisations that smuggled them. In one interview held in Rimini in Italy with the Head of the Investigative Office of Polizia di Stato (the Italian Police), he said that this Article can definitely be applied to any foreigner who wants to escape from the influence of criminal organisations. In fact, this Article has been applied to foreigners who were affiliates of criminal organisations and who decided to co-operate with law enforcement authorities in order to prosecute the criminals.

The next sections explain how Article 18 of Legislative Decree 286/1998 has been applied for the protection of victims of human trafficking, and particularly victims of human trafficking for the purpose of sexual exploitation. Specifically, the next section explores how Italian police in Rimini were able to defeat human trafficking for sexual exploitation by applying Article 18 of Legislative Decree 286/1998.

The Application of Article 18 of Legislative Decree 286/1998 and the Rimini Method

According to Legislative Decree 286/1998, when irregular migrants are arrested, police forces should investigate whether these people are victims of human trafficking, and not automatically expel them.[218] Nevertheless, the legislation introduced by the Italian government in 2002 does not make any reference to Article 18 of Legislative Decree 286/1998, and it attempted to make the expulsion automatic.[219] After the intervention of the Constitutional Court, the judicial authority must ratify the expulsion procedure. However, provisions adopted after the Constitutional Court's judgment do not specify that the judicial authority has to check whether the irregular migrant is a victim or potential victim of human trafficking. In other words, many irregular migrants may have been deported

---

217   See Art. 18(1) of Legislative Decree 286/1998, op. cit. note 8.
218   See ibid., Arts 13 and 18.
219   See ibid., Art. 13 as modified by Art. 12 of Act 189/2002, op. cit. note 8.

without investigating whether they were victims of human trafficking.[220] The British Human Rights Committee reported that in few isolated cases, victims were deported after having been informed of their rights under Article 18 of Legislative Decree 286/1998.[221]

In Rimini, the police authorities took the decision not to issue an automatic expulsion order, and they investigated whether the irregular migrants were also victims of trafficking for the purpose of sexual exploitation. They provided assistance to victims by explaining to them the rights they were entitled to invoke under Article 18. By this means, known as the Rimini Method, police forces defeated this form of trafficking in Rimini. The Rimini Method consisted of establishing trust between the police and victims of human trafficking in order to persuade them to co-operate in the arrest and prosecution of their exploiters. In order to achieve this, the police in Rimini sought the support of the Association Pope John XXIII.

The head of the investigative police office in Rimini asserted that the work of the Polizia di Stato in Rimini, the fact that they did not automatically expel irregular migrants, and the fact that they applied Article 18 of Legislative Decree 286/1998 correctly has become a model for other investigative offices of the Polizia di Stato in Italy. This is why the work carried out by the Polizia di Stato in Rimini is known as the Rimini Method.[222] The head of the investigative police office said that before 1998, the police had a legal obligation to deport victims of trafficking in human beings committed for sexual exploitation to their countries of origin after their arrest. The police emphasised that after the introduction of Article 18 of Legislative Decree 286/1998, their approach changed drastically, because this Article states that if prostitutes are victims of sexual exploitation and agree to report their exploiters, they can obtain permanent visas. This Article was crucial in the fight against human trafficking. The police in Rimini stated that the expulsion of prostitutes who were irregular migrants was counter-productive because these women, after being expelled and deported, would return to Italy again as victims of human trafficking. The application of Article 18 made a difference as it gave the police the opportunity to ask victims whether they could offer testimony in order to arrest their exploiters. The process was not straightforward, because victims did not want to report their exploiters. Victims feared them and their intimidatory power, and as emphasised in Chapter 2, the more people who are victims of criminal organisations are not integrated into the hosting society, the more they are influenced by those who intimidate them. The head of the police office in Rimini said that initially, although women lived in conditions of slavery and used to be tortured in order to force them to become prostitutes, they were reluctant to co-

---

220   See 'Associazione Papa Giovanni XXIII and Prostitution in Italy and the Law', op. cit. note 182, p. 9.

221   Ibid.

222   Interview with the head of the investigative police office of Polizia di Stato in Rimini, held on 12 June 2006.

operate because they feared retaliation against their families in their countries of origin. The police in Rimini highlighted that the peril of retaliation is real because it has been reported that in many cases, criminal organisations have killed family members of victims who decided to co-operate with the police. The first initiative was to ensure the integration of victims into Italian society. In this way, victims would be protected from the intimidating power of criminal organisations and the risk of retaliation. The head of the police office said that the Polizia di Stato gained the trust of victims and their integration by granting them permanent visas. This policy, supported by Article 18, led many women to co-operate with the police, who subsequently arrested the criminals involved in human trafficking for sexual exploitation. This was facilitated because the granting of long-term visas helped victims to understand that they could trust the law enforcement authorities. The permanent visas also gave victims the opportunity to integrate into Italian society by obtaining stable jobs. In this way, victims escaped the influence of criminal organisations and supported the investigations. Through the Rimini Method, prostitution on the streets of Rimini has been all but eliminated. In 1998, there were 700–800 prostitutes on the streets, now there are around ten, while the phenomenon of human trafficking, including the sexual exploitation of women, has increased in other parts of Italy where Article 18 has only been applied on a case-by-case basis, and not as a matter of course.[223] The police claimed that their investigations were successful because they also had the support of a humanitarian organisation in Rimini which contributed to convincing victims to trust the police. The process of integration of victims that led them to report their exploiters by the granting of long-term visas was conducted by the Association Pope John XXIII (hereafter 'the Association').

The Rimini Method and the Legal Protection of Human Trafficking Victims Who Do Not Co-operate with Police Forces

The co-ordinator of the Association, which was founded by Father Oreste Benzi in the 1950s, has been interviewed about the importance of Article 18 of Legislative Decree 286/1998.[224] The Association is one of 90 that exist in Italy that provide shelter to victims of human trafficking. This Association is similar to the British Poppy Project, although is larger and provides shelter not only to victims of human trafficking for sexual exploitation, but also to other victims of human trafficking. The victims assisted by the Association are minors under 18 years old who have been exploited by human traffickers for the purpose of begging in order to repay the costs of their journey to Italy. The Association provides a shelter for up to 400 victims per project, which lasts from a year to 18 months. This Association has its headquarters in Rimini, and smaller offices in the 20 regions of Italy. The

---

223   <http://www.pariopportunita.gov.it/DefaultDesktop.aspx?doc=596>,   accessed 28 June 2009.

224   Interview held in Rimini, 19 April 2006.

Association also has other centres abroad, in Bangladesh, Bolivia, Brazil, Chile, Kenya, Russia, Tanzania and Zambia, and it is also opening a centre in France. The co-ordinator of the Association has worked with victims of human trafficking since the early 1990s, and its centre in Rimini has provided shelter for 5,500 victims. Victims usually come from Eastern Europe, Latin America, Africa and Asia. Article 18 of Legislative Decree 286/1998 applies to all human trafficking victims, and it establishes that visas can be issued regardless of whether the victims decide to co-operate with law enforcement authorities. In the initial stages, victims report their exploiters and a collaboration with law enforcement authorities begins, and continues until the arrest and prosecution of the exploiters. Victims of human trafficking are offered assistance by one of the 90 associations that provide shelter and a programme of social reintegration. The associations that operate in Italian territory, including the Association Pope John XXIII, may also request Italian authorities to issue visas to victims who leave situations of exploitation. Therefore, the issue of a visa is not dependent on the agreement or refusal of victims to co-operate with law enforcement authorities. The aim of the law is to ensure that by issuing the visas, victims are no longer exploited by criminal organisations. In this way, Article 18 of Legislative Decree 286/1998 is very important, as it provides major incentives for victims to report their exploiters, encouraging them to seek assistance from the associations that can provide them with shelter. An example will serve to illustrate how this works.

The Association is made up of volunteers who provide help on a 24-hour basis. They look for victims of human trafficking on the streets, because it is unlikely that victims will report their exploiters to the police for fear of retaliation. Usually, people from Nigeria, for example, are trafficked by the same people who smuggled them into the country. People from Eastern Europe are usually sold by their smugglers to their traffickers when they reach their countries of destination. This difference results in people from Nigeria being more reluctant to co-operate with law enforcement authorities, because their exploiters are familiar with their families and can hurt them in retaliation. The exact opposite is the case for victims from Eastern Europe, whose exploiters are not in a position to retaliate against their families as they were not the ones who smuggled them into the country. Article 18 of Legislative Decree 286/1998 takes into consideration all these different factors, and for this reason decides not make the issuing of visas dependent on the willingness of victims to co-operate with law enforcement authorities.

The Association reassures victims of human trafficking by telling them that they will be protected and be provided with a residence permit and a job or the ability to study, as Article 18 of Legislative Decree 286/1998 provides.[225] In this way, victims do not go back on the streets, and can integrate fully into Italian society. This is the main reason why trafficking in human beings for sexual exploitation on the streets was defeated in Rimini.

---

225   See Art. 18(5) of Legislative Decree 286/1998, op. cit. note 8.

Should the victims of smuggling of migrants by sea also be protected by Article 18 of Legislative Decree 286/1998? Based on the success of the Rimini Method, the answer should be yes, with these victims being put in a position to trust law enforcement authorities. The co-ordinator of the Association John XXIII pointed out that there is a strong link between irregular migration and trafficking in human beings, because the people who are smuggled by criminal organisations in their countries of origin are subsequently trafficked in their countries of destination. The co-ordinator also stated that over his 12 years' experience in dealing with victims of human trafficking, it seems that it is rare that irregular migrants reach Italian territory without the support of criminal organisations. These criminal organisations eventually sell them to human traffickers, until the price of their journey is repaid, which could take their whole lives. This creates a vicious circle for victims of human traffickers and people smugglers by sea. If the Italian authorities expel irregular migrants without checking to see whether they are victims of human trafficking or people smuggling by sea, when these people are returned to their countries of origin, they will be contacted again by their exploiters. They will then return to Italian territory as victims of human trafficking or people smuggling once more. It has been reported that since the Italian government implemented restrictive laws against irregular migration, many potential victims have been returned to their countries of origin before it could be established whether they have been trafficked. Those who reach Italian territory are lucky, because many of them die during their exhausting trips. These are the reasons why people smuggled by sea should be protected and integrated into Italy by granting them visas, and thus applying Article 18 of Legislative Decree 286/1998 to them.

Victims of human trafficking and people smuggling by sea should be persuaded not to return to their countries of origin. They should also not be returned, to prevent their re-victimisation and possible death. Indeed, the story of a 21-year-old Albanian girl called Lauretta Kikia is very well known by the Association Pope John XXIII.[226] This girl was a victim of human trafficking for sexual exploitation until the Association provided shelter for her and a programme of integration. Lauretta was learning Italian, and had started to work in Italy. Unfortunately, she decided to return to Albania, although volunteers from the Association tried to convince her to remain in Italy. Conditions were not suitable for a safe return, but she went out of a desire to see her family again. After her return to Albania, she was recruited for the purpose of sexual exploitation and returned to Italy, where she was found dead in Tuscany in 2005. There are other dramatic stories like this.[227]

Other provisions under Act 228/2003 could also support the prevention of human trafficking. These provisions consist of establishing a fund for the benefit of

---

226   See <http://www.fides.org/ita/news/2005/0501/14_5015.html>.
227   See Benzi, *Prostitute. Vi Passeranno Davanti Nel Regno Dei Cieli*, op. cit. note 173.

human trafficking victims,[228] along with accommodation and health assistance.[229] Italian legislation foresaw the adoption of important preventive measures against human trafficking.[230] These measures consist of international co-operation, information campaigns, and co-operation with the countries of origins of human trafficking victims.[231]

The Protection of Victims of Smuggling of Migrants by Sea

Can Article 18 be Applied to People Smuggled by Sea?

As stated above in the discussion of the Rimini Method, the application of Article 18 is not linked to whether a victim decides to co-operate with law enforcement authorities. Article 18's aim is to ensure that a foreigner who is in a vulnerable position through being a victim of exploitation or violence can escape from the violence and influence of criminal organisations through a programme of assistance and social integration.[232] Article 18 can be applied by police forces on the proposal of the public prosecutor. In general, the application of Article 18 is left to the discretion of law enforcement authorities. Therefore, Article 18 can be applied to victims of smuggling if law enforcement authorities consider this appropriate. This statement was confirmed by the police based in the detention centre of Caltanissetta in Sicily. They said that Article 18 has been applied to victims of people smuggling who wanted to testify against boat skippers, for example.[233] When the police were asked if victims of smuggling were keen to report criminal organisations, the reply was that victims of people smuggling would never take the initiative to contact police forces and tell them that they were victims because these people are afraid that they or their families who live in their countries of origin could be killed or face other forms of retribution from the criminal organisations. The more vulnerable and unprotected these victims feel, the more likely they will be targeted by the criminal organisations. The threat that victims of people smuggling face from these criminals is real, and is supported by the testimony of police officers in Rimini, who stated during interview that there have been cases where families of victims who reported their traffickers have been murdered. Victims of smuggling, particularly those smuggled by sea and those subjected to human trafficking, would only report criminal organisations if police

---

228   See Art. 12(1 and 2) of Act 228/2003, op. cit. note 57.
229   See ibid., Art. 13.
230   See ibid., Art. 14(1).
231   Ibid.
232   See Consiglio di Stato, Sez. VI, 10 October 2006, no. 6023. See also T.A.R. Sicilia Catania Sez. II., 28 May 2007, no. 892.
233   Telephone interview with police based at the detention centre at Caltanissetta, 3 November 2008.

forces gained their trust. Article 18 could help police to achieve this result, because the issuing of a residence permit is not linked to a victim's willingness to offer testimony. Another factor in gaining the trust of victims is a political willingness to defeat smuggling of migrants by sea. The representatives of the Association Pope John XXIII in Rimini said that their effectiveness in implementing Article 18 was improved when political authorities in Rimini decided to get fully involved in combating trafficking in human beings for the purpose of sexual exploitation. However, seems that the national government does not share the same desire to fight trafficking in human beings: as stated above, they appear to focus entirely on enacting repressive measures on irregular migrants instead of adopting more progressive measures that have proven more effective. Research has shown that liberal approaches such as the Rimini Method have been more successful in countering trafficking.

The Italian government has set up commissions with the responsibility of monitoring the usefulness of projects attempting to implement Article 18, in order to decide which should receive funding. These commissions were expressly established by Regulation 102/2007,[234] and they may agree to finance a project at Lampedusa, a small Italian island which is the entry point for most of the irregular migrants coming from Africa. This project should involve the application of Article 18 to victims of smuggling, who will be encouraged to co-operate with law enforcement authorities in order to arrest and prosecute their smugglers. If successful, Lampedusa might provide a model that other southern Mediterranean European countries could decide to follow. The impact of Article 18 would be further enhanced if police from third national countries co-operated with the national police in Italy in their fight against criminal organisations based in the countries are involved in the smuggling of migrants by sea. In order to achieve this result, Europol should have competence to co-ordinate investigations carried out between EU Member States and third countries, and Frontex should co-operate with Europol. There are already legal measures in place to reinforce these two agencies, but they should be made more democratic in order to be accountable.

The next sections will focus on findings of interviews carried out in Lampedusa and in the Italian city of Siracusa. Lampedusa is the focus for research into trafficking in human beings and people smuggled by sea due to the strategic position of the island, which lies between Africa and Italy. Lampedusa had become the main place of landing for most of the irregular migrants smuggled by sea. Siracusa was chosen because of the success of its public prosecutors in defeating smuggling of migrants by sea through the application of Article 18.

---

234   See 'Regolamento per il riordino della Commissione per l'attuazione dell'articolo 18 del testo unico sull'immigrazione, operante presso il Dipartimento per i diritti e le pari opportunitá, a norma dell'articolo 29 del D.L. 4 luglio 2006, no 223, convertito, con modificazioni, dalla L. 4 agosto 2006, no. 248', GU 167, 20 July 2007.

People Smuggled by Sea and Their Situation in the Italian Island of Lampedusa

The phenomenon of people smuggling by sea is quite widespread in southern Mediterranean European countries such as Italy and Malta, since their location between North Africa and Europe makes them the transit countries of choice for many irregular migrants coming from Africa. The research shows that criminal organisations take advantage of the strategic position of Italy, and desperate people who have no alternative but to leave their countries of origin to escape poverty.[235] Research was carried out in one of the largest detention centres for irregular migrants in Italy located in the island of Lampedusa, situated between Italy and Libya. Lampedusa's strategic position gives an opportunity to develop a clear picture of the phenomenon of people smuggling by sea, and information gathered there could support changes in policy and law in all the EU Member States.

The first research interviews were conducted at Lampedusa on 1 October 2008. The centre is usually full of irregular migrants, but on this particular day it was not overcrowded as there had been no arrivals for some days. Many of the people hosted by the centre suffered from malnutrition, appearing tremendously underweight. Many of them were from sub-Saharan Africa, and suffered from starvation in their countries of origin. The first interview was with a police officer from the Polizia di Stato responsible for the centre. The police officer stated that the work of the police in Lampedusa consisted of identifying the irregular migrants, checking whether they had previous criminal records in Italy, and whether they had already tried to enter Italian territory. The author then asked the police officer whether they investigated the criminal organisations behind the smuggling. Investigations are not carried out by the Italian police in Lampedusa as this is the responsibility of Frontex. Officers from Frontex took time to explain the duties involved in their work in Lampedusa. The officers' job consists of checking whether there are criminals among the arrivals in Lampedusa, and whether the people smuggled by sea want to report the criminal organisations that transported them. The officers from Frontex went to great lengths to demonstrate why their work was very difficult and that they had not been successful in their investigations because the people smuggled by sea did not report the smugglers because they feared them. This has impeded the effectiveness of investigations, as convincing those smuggled by sea to report the criminal organisations that support them and to trust Frontex officers was very difficult. The reason is not merely because the irregular migrants do not speak Italian, but also because it is difficult to understand their cultures, and consequently convince them to trust the police. In other words, Frontex officers in Lampedusa understood how important was to conduct adequate investigations with the co-operation of those smuggled by sea, but this can only be obtained by gaining their trust. Irregular migrants hosted in Lampedusa needed to

---

[235] The author interviewed Italian Police and Italian Finance and Frontier Police (Guardia di Finanza) officers in Lampedusa on 2 and 3 October 2008.

communicate with people who understood their culture in order to be convinced to report the criminal organisations. The trust of irregular migrants could be gained by adopting the Rimini Method for victims of people smuggled by sea, because thanks to that method, the police in Rimini had succeeded in gaining this trust.

The Italian Red Cross and the International Organization for Migration (IOM) in Lampedusa have confirmed that smuggled people are reluctant to report their smugglers because they fear retaliation. These organisations, together with the UNCHR and Save the Children, have representatives in Lampedusa because they participate to a project called Praesidium.[236] In 2006, the Italian Ministry of Home Affairs, the UNCHR, the IOM and the Italian Red Cross obtained funding to participate in a project called ARGO 2005, and subsequently, they established the Praesidium project in Lampedusa. In 2007, Praesidium was extended to other detention centres in Sicily, at Trapani, Caltanissetta and Siracusa. Praesidium has allowed humanitarian organisations access to detention centres in order to assist irregular migrants who have been detained.

The author initially spoke to representatives of the UNHCR, who emphasised that their task consists of informing all irregular migrants of the possibility of applying for refugee status,[237] with territorial commissions deciding on the merits of each case. This issue was not explored in depth, and no interviews were held with representatives of Save the Children. The aim of this research and the visit to Lampedusa was to investigate whether people smuggled by sea were being given equal protection to victims of human trafficking. Therefore, particular attention was devoted to the Red Cross and IOM. These humanitarian organisations have different duties. The Red Cross monitors the health conditions of irregular migrants who are going to be transferred to other detention centres or who are going to be returned to their countries of origin. IOM informants stated that their tasks were to inform economic irregular migrants of the risks of their irregular status and to identifying victims of human trafficking.[238] Both organisations maintained that it was very difficult to identify victims of human trafficking because they feared retaliation from their exploiters, and for this reason remained silent.[239] In particular, the Red Cross has established two female teams in Lampedusa, headed by a nurse and a cultural mediator. One of the teams operates only in Lampedusa, and focuses on women and children, while the other team travels along the Sicilian coast to the other detention centres.[240] A representative of the Red Cross stated that the majority of women who arrive in Lampedusa have suffered sexual abuse by

---

236   The *Praesidium* is fully described in a document e-mailed by the Italian Red Cross to the author, 3 September 2008.

237   Telephone interview held with the representative of UNHCR in Lampedusa, 26 September 2008.

238   Interview in Lampedusa with the IOM representatives, 1 October 2008.

239   Interviews with Red Cross and IOM representatives in Lampedusa, 2 October 2008.

240   Document e-mailed by the Italian Red Cross on 3 September 2008, op. cit. note 235.

different groups over long periods. Such abuse was prevalent in Libya, either in prisons or on the streets. Interviews conducted by Human Rights Watch (HRW) in May 2009 also confirmed that asylum seekers detained in Libya had suffered serious violations of their human rights.[241]

The Red Cross representative emphasised that women who have been victims of human trafficking or other sexual abuses do not report the perpetrators. The representative said that a real victim of human trafficking needs someone to explain to her that she has been a victim. Some governments in the EU, such as the British government, state that victims of human trafficking should not be automatically granted visas because many of them would exploit the law by making false claims. The Red Cross representative discounted this possibility, arguing that victims are too scared and too intimidated by criminal organisations to falsify claims. The Red Cross and the IOM highlighted that if a person claimed to be a victim without prompting, their representatives would be very suspicious, because true victims only reveal their status very reluctantly, and only if the Red Cross and IOM representatives have gained their trust. This resembles the situation in Rimini discussed above.

The situation of people smuggled by sea is further complicated by the fact that in Lampedusa there is no mechanism of protection that focuses on these people. Certainly, there is Frontex, but it does not obtain information from those who have been smuggled. When asked whether they co-operated with Frontex in order to encourage irregular migrants to report criminal organisations who transported them, the IOM and Red Cross said that there was no co-operation with Frontex as it is not part of their work in Lampedusa. In other words, they have not obtained government funding to carry out investigations into the smuggling of migrants by sea. Public prosecutors in Siracusa stated that in Lampedusa the priority was to identify and transfer the irregular migrants from the island to other detention centres in Italy because the island aims to attract tourists, and the obvious presence of a detention centre might deter them from making Lampedusa their holiday destination.[242] However, this is not a good reason to avoid investigating the criminal organisations which are behind smuggling of migrants by sea, because the crime is committed on a large scale by exploiting the poor conditions of desperate individuals.

In conclusion, the interviews carried out in Lampedusa show that the phenomenon of smuggling of migrants by sea is not being combated effectively. This is due to the fact that preventative measures consist of enacting a restrictive law aimed at detaining irregular migrants who, after their expulsion, will likely return to the EU in the same manner. They will risk their lives, during desperate trips on boats in poor conditions, motivated by the chance of escaping the extreme poverty of their countries of origin. In Lampedusa, the focus is on finding the best

---

241 See Zaccaro, S., 'Italy-Libya: Migrants Returned to Face Abuse', IPS, 21 September 2009, <http://ipsnews.net/news.asp?idnews=48530>.

242 Interview held with the Public Prosecution Office of Siracusa, 9 January 2009.

way to remove irregular migrants. There is no co-operation between Frontex and humanitarian organisations in order to support investigations that could reduce the incidence of smuggling by tackling the criminal organisations involved. In Lampedusa, they have not adopted a more liberal approach that would try to persuade victims to testify against criminal organisations. It is impossible to say whether an approach comparable to the Rimini Method would be as effective for people smuggling by sea, because the method has never been tried in Lampedusa. Meanwhile, any decline in the number of irregular migrants smuggled every year by sea from Africa has been achieved by adopting tough measures that violate international conventions, EU law and national law. An alternative approach could not only avoid these violations, but lead to further reductions in the number of people smuggled by sea. It must also be emphasised that an approach similar to the Rimini Method is feasible because there are clear data on people smuggled by sea every year from Africa to Italy. The phenomenon is not uncontrollable, and it could be addressed in better ways.

Statistical Data on Lampedusa

The Italian Ministry of Home Affairs was contacted in order to obtain statistical data on the number of people smuggled by sea from Africa to Lampedusa. The intention was to access objective statistics on the scale of the crime. It was discovered that Ministry of Home Affairs does have precise data on people smuggled by sea, which suggests that migration flows by sea are not uncontrollable. Moreover, the data gathered also confirm that a only a small percentage of the total irregular migration is committed by sea, as shown in Chapter 4.

The data[243] show that the number of irregular migrants who reach the Italian island of Lampedusa by sea did not decline, but increased in 2008. Between January and December 2008, 30,657 irregular migrants arrived at Lampedusa by sea.[244] This number represents a significant increase compared to the year before, when only 22,455 irregular migrants landed. It is also an increase over the totals for 2006 – 21,400 – and 2004 – 22,824. Conversely, in 2009, since the Italian government adopted a tough policy on irregular migration, the incidence of smuggling of migrants by sea decreased, falling by 55 percent in the first six months of 2009 compared to the same period in 2008.[245] It must pointed out, however, that the government reached this objective by sending people back to Libya, where people are suffering brutal treatment and unsanitary conditions:

---

243   Data e-mailed to the author by the Department of Immigration of the Ministry of Internal Affairs, 10 October 2008.

244   Data from the Italian Ministry of Internal Affairs received by e-mail on 10 October 2008 and 29 September 2009.

245   Data from the Italian Ministry of Internal Affairs received by e-mail on 10 October 2008 and 3 November 2009.

A 24-year old Eritrean woman who was held in the Libyan migrant detention centres of Al Fellah and Misrata said 'All of the women had problems from the police. The police came at night and chose ladies to violate.'[246]

Abuses committed in Libya have also been confirmed by the Italian Red Cross and Frontex in Lampedusa. Those interviewed have stated that many victims of trafficking and smuggling hosted in this detention centre do not want to report their exploiters and smugglers because they do not trust the police, fearing they may commit the same abuses as the police in Libya. By rejecting irregular migrants smuggled by sea, Italy is violating the United Nations Convention on the Law of the Sea, which obliges States Parties to rescue people at risk of losing their lives at sea. Italy is also violating other international requirements, as many of the irregular migrants on the boats are asylum seekers, and others are victims of human trafficking.[247] Another fact to take into account is that the restrictive policy adopted by the government may be only be successful in the short term because, as Europol has pointed out,[248] criminal organisations are able to adapt their routes to avoid detection. In the long term, people smuggling by sea may not be defeated if it is only addressed by repression of irregular migrants without adequate investigations into the criminal organisations behind this crime.

Data from the Ministry of Home Affairs also show that irregular migrants who travel to Italy by sea often come from sub-Saharan Africa. In 2008, the top nationalities of irregular migrants landed by sea to Lampedusa were people from Nigeria (4,417), Somalia (4,320), Eritrea (2,918), Tunisia (2,492), Ghana (1,729) and Egypt (1,291). Four out of these six nations belong to sub-Saharan Africa (Nigeria, Somalia, Eritrea, Ghana). In 2007, the top nationalities were Egypt (5,131), Eritrea (3,007), Morocco (2,341), Algeria (1,762), Tunisia (1,417) and Nigeria (913). In 2006, the top nationalities were Morocco (8,146), Egypt (4,200), Eritrea (2,859), Tunisia (2,288), Ghana (530) and Nigeria (491). In 2005, the top nationalities were Egypt (10,201), Morocco (3,624), Eritrea (1,974), Tunisia (1,596), Sudan (732) and Ethiopia (718). In 2008, the number of people coming from sub-Saharan Africa increased. The only positive note in these data is the fact that the phenomenon of smuggling of migrants by sea is not out of control. The Italian government is in a position to know how many irregular migrants reach Italy through Lampedusa, and their nationality. The other thing to notice is that the top nationalities are not always the same, and these data may mean that criminal organisations are always able to adapt their routes as the controls and checks on others increase. This might be the reason why the proportions of nationalities constantly change. Irregular migrants who travel by sea in poor conditions should

---

246   See Zaccaro, 'Italy-Libya', op. cit. note 240.

247   On this point, see 'Esposto alla Commissione europea, al Comitato ONU per i diritti umani, al Commissario europeo per i diritti umani presso il Consiglio d'Europa, May–June 2009', *Diritto, Immigrazione e Cittadinanza* 11:3 (2009), pp. 266–77.

248   See Chapter 4 of this book.

be considered victims of smuggling of migrants by sea. This is because people coming from sub-Saharan Africa have two alternatives: either to die because of starvation in their countries of origin, or to leave their countries in the hope of finding a better life elsewhere. Criminal organisations take advantage of their state of poverty by offering them travel to Europe, albeit in very poor conditions. There should be reluctance to consider these people criminals. The Red Cross and police forces in Lampedusa said that these people often travel with their families, including very young children, and despite the situation, they are very dignified when they land at Lampedusa. They follow instructions given by the police without complaint. The police officers interviewed said that the children are very sympathetic to one other. One police officer offered a biscuit to a very young child, and he shared it with all the other children who were on the boat, although he was very hungry. In some cases, children are unaccompanied because they have lost their mothers during the trip from Africa to Italy, and when they land they still look for their mothers, not yet realising that they have died. The Red Cross pointed out that in some cases, children have watched their mothers raped in the desert while travelling from their countries of origin to Lampedusa, and they suffer serious psychological trauma. It is safe to say that mothers would not accept their children suffering in this way unless they were truly desperate. The Red Cross also said that there are men who have left their families in their countries of origin in search of a better life for themselves and their children. These men suffer separation from their families and risk their lives in the attempt. Are these people less deserving of protection than the victims of human trafficking? Could they assist police forces in their investigations of the criminal organisations that exploit their state of poverty? The research suggests that in the long term, smuggling of migrants by sea could be defeated by enlisting the support of its victims. This requires long-term thinking, but would pay off in the end, as it would prevent people suffering abuse and would reduce the commission of these crimes in the first place. Such an approach would be more successful if it was backed up by a common EU policy on economic migration, along with a common policy to improve economic conditions in the countries of origin, as was emphasised in Chapter 4.

The Siracusan Approach

Public prosecutors who dealt with people smuggling by sea and had conducted successful investigations in Siracusa were interviewed in January 2009. The way they deal with smuggling of migrants by sea will be referred to as the *Siracusan* Approach. This approach was created by a team of four public prosecutors working for the Public Prosecutor Office of the Tribunal of Siracusa who conduct investigations on smuggling of migrants by sea. In 2007, they admitted that the number of people smuggled by sea who landed in Siracusa by boat increased from

1,172 in 2006 to 1,975 in 2007.[249] This increase was their prime motivation for exploring ways to reduce the incidence of this crime by changing their focus to concentrate on the irregular migrants themselves. The General Public Prosecutor of Siracusa explained that there are different degrees of exploitation. The most serious is the crime of trafficking in human beings reduced to slavery. However, there is another kind of exploitation which is typical of smuggling of migrants by sea, as smugglers also exploit their victims' poverty. These victims have little choice regarding whether to leave their countries of origin. Extreme poverty forces them to leave even if they might prefer to stay. The public prosecutors in Siracusa also highlighted that most of those smuggled by sea die during their trips because their boats sink in the Mediterranean.

Criminal organisations are always prepared to attempt to return them to Italy, no matter how tough the law on irregular migration is. Therefore, the team in Siracusa approached smuggling of migrants by sea by applying different legal provisions under Legislative Decree 286/1998 to offer protection to the irregular migrants. These provisions allow people smuggled by sea to testify against their smugglers in exchange for a residence permits. The public prosecutors in Siracusa usually apply three provisions: Article 5(6) of Legislative Decree 286/1998, which addresses asylum seekers and people in need of subsidiary protection, who can obtain refugee status; Article 18 of Legislative Decree 286/1998, which also addresses human trafficking victims and was examined above, and Article 11(*cbis*) of Legislative Decree 394/1999, which states that any irregular is willing to testify in an investigation related to smuggling of migrants by sea can obtain a residence permit of no longer than three months' duration. The public prosecutors in Siracusa said that their investigations are usually successful when they apply Article 18 of Legislative Decree 286/1998 because it allows them to issue long-term visas, an essential instrument in gaining the trust of victims as it allows them to integrate these people by giving them jobs, allowing the migrants to escape the intimidating power of criminal organisations and increasing their willingness to report them. Nevertheless, public prosecutors cannot decide on their own what provisions to apply. These decisions are taken by the head of the police administration (*questore*), who takes orders from the Ministry of Home Affairs, which in turn operates under direction of the government. In other words, public prosecutors must obtain permission from the *questore* (and ultimately, the government) in order to apply Article 18. Public prosecutors in Siracusa emphasised that the *questore* in Siracusa has never denied them a residence permit on the basis of Article 18, which is another reason why the Siracusan Approach has been so successful. The public prosecutors said that Article 18 facilitates investigations that take a long time and require the presence of the victim in Italian territory in order to permit the arrest and punishment of the criminals involved. The public prosecutors also

---

249　See 'Procura della Repubblica press il Tribunale di Siracusa. Gruppo Contrasto Immigrazione Clandestina', data on irregular migrants smuggled by sea, collected in 2006, 2007 and 2008, document supplie by the Public Prosecutors in Siracusa, 9 January 2009.

highlighted that one positive aspect of this Article is the fact that the issuing of permanent residence permits is not reliant on those smuggled choosing to assist the police. Therefore, this Article encourages smuggled migrants to trust the public prosecutors (which takes time) and co-operate with them. Thanks to Article 18, the team of public prosecutors in Siracusa uncovered a criminal organisation which on various occasions smuggled 1,975 people from Egypt to Italy. Subsequently, they arrested the boat operators involved in this activity, who used to transport people from many different countries, including Egypt, Somalia, Eritrea, Ethiopia and Oromia, Sudan, especially the region of Darfur, Nigeria, Niger, Togo, Gambia, Sierra Lion, Ghana and Tunisia.[250] The public prosecutors in Siracusa stated that they were able to arrest the boat skippers, who were eventually sentenced to jail terms thanks to the co-operation of the Egyptian authorities.[251] Finally, the public prosecutors emphasised that their approach would not be a push factor encouraging many people to leave their countries of origin because those who do so are limited by where they live (in between the frontiers of various African countries) and their numbers cannot increase. Usually, all those who have the opportunity to leave their countries of origin decide to do so. Unfortunately, most of them (90 percent) die during their trips in the desert or on the boats carrying them from Libya to Italy. One public prosecutor emphasised that of every ten boats that leave Libya, only two or three successfully reach Lampedusa.

In January 2009, the author also interviewed the police officers who support the public prosecutors' work. They said that Article 18 facilitates investigations into smuggling of migrants by sea because once irregular migrants have obtained long-term visas, they have the opportunity to look for work, being integrated into Italian society, and are thus motivated to report their smugglers. Conversely, temporary residence permits granted under Article 11(*cbis*) do not include work permits. As a result, irregular migrants cannot support themselves, so they are less motivated to report their smugglers. Finally, the police in Siracusa confirmed that the fact that Article 18 does not make the issuing of a residence permit conditional on the willingness of victims to co-operate with law enforcement authorities is the most significant aspect of this law, because it gives the authorities time to gain the trust of victims and obtain testimony essential to investigations. Public prosecutors and police in Siracusa were subsequently asked whether there was a danger that victims of people smuggling would make false claims. The answer was that this risk exists for all crimes, not only for smuggling of migrants, but nevertheless, it could be avoided by comparing the accusations made by different irregular migrants. If their testimony is borne out and there are no inconsistencies, the public prosecutors and police will assume they are truthful. The most serious problem to tackle remains that of convincing smuggled migrants to report their smugglers despite fear of retaliation. This is why investigations begin when irregular migrants are rescued and still held on navy boats. The police approach

---

250 Ibid., p. 6.
251 See Judgment of the Tribunal of Siracusa issued on 31 October 2008.

them and ask if they can speak English. Irregular migrants who do not wish to co-operate out of fear will pretend not to understand anything, while others will speak English. Subsequently, the police divide them from the rest of the group and work hard to gain their trust. In this task, the police and public prosecutors in Siracusa are supported by humanitarian organisations such as the IOM, whose members also try to gain the irregular migrants' trust. Co-operation between the law enforcement authorities and humanitarian organisations is essential in order to encourage victims to report their smugglers. This kind of co-operation is totally absent in Lampedusa, where the government's only concern is to remove irregular migrants from the island without conducting any investigations. In Siracusa, the law enforcement authorities are successful because the police, Frontex, humanitarian organisations and public prosecutors co-operate to obtain relevant information from the irregular migrants. The author was told that investigations based on the testimony of irregular migrants could be more successful if Article 18 was widened. The public prosecutors explained that Article 18 only allows the issuing of residence permits and work permits, which can become permanent, to irregular migrants at risk of being under the influence of criminal organisations once they are in Italian territory. However, although this principle can be applied to victims of trafficking, it cannot be applied to smuggled migrants because once they have reached Italian territory most of them are no longer under the influence of a criminal organisation. In this case, the law states that they should be entitled to a three-month residence permit, which, according to the public prosecutors in Siracusa, is not enough because it allows law enforcement authorities too little time to work with those who have been smuggled. Expelling irregular migrants is no solution to the problem, and the public prosecutors stated that they have often interpreted Article 18 widely in order to obtain permission to use it in order to avoid losing important evidence that could only come from the irregular migrants. The public prosecutors also added that, on the basis of their ten years' experience of dealing with this crime, protecting the victims, not returning them, is the only productive solution to the problem. The public prosecutors emphasised that their investigations can only facilitate the arrest of boat skippers, and not of the organisers of this crime, who may be based outside the EU Member States. For this purpose, these investigations should be conducted by Frontex and Europol, which should have competence to deal with the police of third countries carrying out investigations into criminal organisations based outside the EU. Extending of the scope of competence of Europol, effective use of Frontex and the application of Article 18 of Legislative Decree 286/1998 could contribute to defeating smuggling of migrants by sea. Obviously, the application of this law must be accompanied by policies on legal migration, otherwise the efforts will be unsuccessful, as on the basis of the evidence, poor people will always try to escape from their countries of origin if they have no opportunities for survival.

These issues should be addressed by the governments of EU Member States because the problem of smuggling of migrants by sea is not only an Italian problem, as it the Italian Red Cross in Lampedusa has reported that the majority of the irregular migrants who reach the island do not want to stay in Italy, but want to go on to Denmark, France, the Netherlands, Sweden and the UK. Therefore, a change in policies and laws should be agreed by all Member States at EU level, because the phenomenon involves all of them, albeit indirectly, and also because isolated Member States are unable to deal with it. This is because the fight against smuggling takes time. In fact, the Rimini Method took six years to be successfully implemented. Member States should abandon their demagogic approach, which may contribute to gaining votes, but also aggravates the problem of people smuggling by sea, as this section has shown. The EU should take Article 18 as model and consider applying the law on subsidiary protection to victims of smuggling by sea even if they are not from countries where there is war or political instability, because smuggling is a form of exploitation.

In conclusion, it has been demonstrated that smuggling of migrants by sea and trafficking in human beings can be defeated by focusing on the victims of these two crimes. The EU should take this into consideration and promote the adoption of laws focusing on the protection of victims. This would encourage victims to report their smugglers and traffickers. Moreover, the EU should reinforce Europol and Frontex in order to facilitate more in-depth investigations concerning the criminal organisations that commit smuggling and trafficking and are based outside the EU.

A New EU Court to Deal with Smuggling of Migrants by Sea?

The Lisbon Treaty will enhance the jurisdiction of the Court of Justice over EU police and judicial co-operation, although the limitations of the EU Treaty remain. This is because Member States will still have the option to decide whether to allow the Court of Justice to rule in the criminal area.[252] It is thought that an adequate way to combat smuggling of migrants by sea could be achieved by creating a new court or section of the Court of Justice with the task of allocating jurisdiction. Smuggling of migrants by sea should be dealt with in this way because in studies over the years, it has been noted that Malta, Italy and Libya have often refused to rescue irregular migrants at sea because they have claimed that their boats are not in their territorial waters, so they did not have any obligation to do so. Irregular migrants have been often left on old boats at sea for days until a decision about their destination has been agreed by Libya, Italy and Malta. The Lisbon Treaty has now entered into force, and it is thought that Member States should consider creating a new court or section of the Court of Justice to allocate jurisdiction in cases similar to those described. The new court, which was discussed in Chapter 3, should decide how to resolve conflicts of jurisdiction between EU Member States (between Malta and Italy, for example). If the conflict is between Italy and Libya, a third non-EU country, this conflict should be considered as involving the EU and the third country, and it should be resolved between the EU and

---

252   See Chapter 3 of this book.

Libya, and not between Italy or Malta and Libya. Frontex and Europol should deal with the external relations of the EU by improving contacts between law enforcement agencies of EU Member States and third countries such as Libya. This co-operation could reduce conflicts of jurisdiction. Chapter 3 highlighted that the Commission considered this idea, though it was also emphasised that there are other steps that should be taken before creating this court. One of these consists of enhancing mutual trust between EU Member States, which is crucial in the fight against smuggling and trafficking. This is why the next sections analyse possible conflicts of jurisdiction that may prevent Member States co-operating with each other in combating smuggling and trafficking. The Italian and UK criminal justice systems will be compared, and it will be demonstrated that the EU is acquiring the legal instruments to resolve conflicts of jurisdiction and lack of mutual trust arising from differences in national legal systems.

Possible Conflicts of Jurisdiction

Extraterritoriality of Smuggling of Migrants and Trafficking in Human Beings and Possible Conflicts of Jurisdiction between the UK and Italy

British immigration law punishes assisting irregular migration, smuggling of migrants and trafficking in human beings if committed within British territory, or outside British territory if committed by:

> a British citizen, … a British overseas territories citizen, … a British National (Overseas), … a British Overseas citizen, … a person who is a British subject under the British Nationality Act 1981 …, and … a British protected person within the meaning of that Act.[253]

Italian immigration law does not expressly establish extraterritorial jurisdiction for perpetrators of assisting irregular migration, smuggling of migrants and trafficking in human beings. The reason for this is that all Italian legislation focuses on specific issues, such as immigration. General rules such as extraterritoriality are established by the Italian Penal Code and the Italian Criminal Procedure Code. These general rules apply to all Italian legislation. Specifically, the Italian Penal Code states that when an Italian citizen commits a crime abroad, they will be punished in Italian territory and according to Italian law when the Italian citizen is returned to Italian territory.[254] These provisions also apply to Legislative Decree 286/1998, Act

---

253 See s. 25 (5), 146(2), of Immigration Act 1971, op. cit. note 1. See also s. 5 of Asylum and Immigration (Treatment of Claimants, etc.) Act 2004, op. cit. note 42.

254 See Art. 9 of 'Codice Penale. R.D.N. 1398, 19/10/1930', op. cit. note 60.

189/2002 and Act 228/2003, because Italian extraterritorial jurisdiction concerns all offences punishable with imprisonment of no less than three years.[255]

The Italian and British laws both respond to Framework Decision 2002/946/JHA, which states that Member States shall ensure the punishment of assisting irregular migration with or without the purpose of a financial gain, if the crimes have been committed 'in whole or in part within its territory; ... by one of its nationals, or ... for the benefit of a legal person established in the territory of that Member State'.[256] The British and Italian laws also comply with the requirements of Framework Decision 2002/629/JHA.[257]

Nevertheless, the British and Italian laws do not permit the extradition of their nationals when the crime of assisting irregular migration has been committed. Under British law, this may be clarified by reading the Immigration Act 1971, as substituted by the Nationality, Immigration and Asylum Act 2002, which, as emphasised above, states that British citizens or nationals shall be punished in the UK or elsewhere if they have committed the crime of assisting irregular migration in the UK or outside British territory.[258] The same principles can also be applied to perpetrators of assisting irregular migration and human traffickers in Italy. Indeed, the Italian Penal Code states that nationals cannot be extradited, although this principle cannot be applied where international conventions require extradition.[259] Certainly, Italy and the UK allow extradition, although they may create obstacles to surrendering a criminal if they do not trust each other's legal systems and in order to protect their nationals.

Italy and the UK both belong to the EU, and both have signed and ratified the European Arrest Warrant Framework Decision.[260] Thus, modifications have been introduced to traditional extradition procedures. Furthermore, the Commission proposal on how to resolve conflicts of jurisdiction examined above[261] may help these two Member States to overcome difficulties related to conflicts of jurisdiction.

---

255   See ibid., Art. 9(1).

256   See Art. 4(1) of the Framework Decision 2002/946/JHA, op. cit. note 55.

257   See Art. 6(1) of Council Framework Decision 2002/629/JHA, op. cit. note 56. This Article states that: 'Each Member State shall take the necessary measures to establish its jurisdiction over an offence referred to in Articles 1 and 2 where: (a) the offence is committed in whole or in part within its territory, or (b) the offender is one of its nationals, or (c) the offence is committed for the benefit of a legal person established in the territory of that Member State.'

258   Ibid.

259   See Art. 13(4) of 'Codice Penale. R.D.N. 1398, 19/10/1930', op. cit. note 60.

260   See the UK Extradition Act 2003. See also Act 69/2005, 'Disposizioni per conformare il diritto interno alla decisione quadro 2002/584/GAI del Consiglio, del 13 giugno 2002, relativa al mandato d'arresto europeo e alle procedure di consegna tra Stati membri', GU 98, 29 April 2005.

261   See Chapter 3 of this book.

The next section examines possible conflicts of jurisdiction between British and Italian judicial authorities in dealing with smuggling of migrants and trafficking in human beings.

Conflicts of Jurisdiction in Dealing with Smuggling of Migrants and Trafficking in Human Beings

Conflicts of jurisdiction may primarily be caused by Framework Decision 2002/946/JHA, which states that Member States have to establish their jurisdiction when the crime of smuggling of migrants is committed 'in whole or in part within its territory'.[262]

According to Italian law, a person who commits a crime in Italian territory shall be punished under Italian criminal law.[263] The Italian Penal Code distinguishes between conduct crimes and result crimes. Indeed, it states that conduct crimes – crimes that are punished even if they did not occur – will be punished under Italian jurisdiction even if only one part of the conduct has been committed in Italian territory.[264] The Italian Corte di Cassazione confirmed this because it asserted that it is sufficient that one part of the crime, even if small, has been committed in Italian territory in order for Italian jurisdiction to apply to a specific case.[265] Moreover, the Penal Code states that a crime is committed in Italy if the event occurred on Italian territory.[266] The Italian Corte di Cassazione has also asserted that a person shall be sentenced in Italy when the event caused by a conduct occurred in whole or in part in Italian territory.[267] UNTOC calls these two types of jurisdictions 'subjective and objective variants of territorial jurisdiction'.[268]

In the UK, there are also conduct crimes and event crimes.[269] Hirst pointed out that possession crimes are typical conduct crimes.[270] In cases of possession crimes, the English Court of Appeal asserted that there are two elements that need to be proven in order to establish English jurisdiction on a crime committed in different States.[271] One of these elements is constituted by the fact that the defendant has a possession; another element shall be the defendant's intention to commit a crime by using this possession.[272] On another occasion, the English Court of Appeal

---

262   See Art. 4(1(b)) of the Framework Decision 2002/946/JHA, op. cit. note 56.

263   See Art. 6 of 'Codice Penale. R.D.N. 1398, 19/10/1930', op. cit. note 60.

264   See ibid., Art. 6(2).

265   See Cass. Pen. Sez. 6 sent. 96, 8 January 2003 r.v. 223007.

266   Ibid.

267   See Cass. Pen. Sez. 2 sent. 7051, 16 July 1981 (ud. 13 March 1981) rv. 149797.

268   See Chapter 2 of this book.

269   See Hirst, M. *Jurisdiction and the Ambit of the Criminal Law* (Oxford: Oxford University Press, 2003), pp. 118 *et seq.*

270   See *R v. El-Hakkaoui* [1975] 1 WLR 396, quoted in Hirst, *Jurisdiction and the Ambit of the Criminal Law*, op. cit. note 268, p. 119.

271   Ibid.

272   Ibid.

pointed out that in result crimes, English jurisdiction will be established 'if any part of the proscribed result takes place in England'.[273] Thus, in the UK there are the same rules as in Italian law – rules expressly recognised by international law, and precisely by UNTOC.

Smuggling of migrants and trafficking in human beings are conduct crimes because it is irrelevant whether an event of illegal entry or trafficking in persons has effectively occurred.[274] Therefore, if a criminal group organises an illegal journey for irregular migrants from Senegal to Italy, for example, and the event consisting of the arrival of the irregular migrants from Senegal in Italy did not occur, smugglers of these irregular migrants will be punished in Italian territory solely for having organised the illegal trip. Moreover, Italian jurisdiction will also apply when the criminal group has just purchased a boat in Italian territory in order to organise the irregular migrants' trip. However, if illegal documents are subsequently prepared in England with the aim of transferring irregular migrants to the UK, the UK could also claim jurisdiction because British law establishes that assisting irregular migration is punished if committed on its territory.[275] It is clear that conflicts of jurisdiction may arise between the UK and Italy because in this example, the smugglers of migrants have committed the conduct crime both in Italy and the UK. Indeed, Italy may also claim jurisdiction because the boat has been purchased in its territory, for example, or because some of the documents had been prepared in Italy. Which country should have jurisdiction in this case? Moreover, what would the consequences be if, after their arrival in Italy, the migrants smuggled from Senegal were transferred to the UK to be subsequently exploited?

The Council of Europe Convention on Trafficking in Human Beings[276] states that States Parties shall establish jurisdiction over the offence of trafficking in human beings when it is committed in their territory:

> on board a ship flying the flag of that Party; ... on board an aircraft registered under the laws of that Party; ... by one of its nationals or by a stateless person who has his or her habitual residence in its territory ... against one of its nationals.[277]

---

273   See *Secretary of State for Trade* v. *Markus* [1976] AC 35, 61.

274   See, respectively, Arts 1(1a and b) of Directive 2002/90/EC, op. cit. note 10. See also: Art. 3 of UNTOC Trafficking Protocol, op. cit. note 18; Art. 4 of the Council of Europe Convention on Trafficking, op. cit. note 19; Art. 3 of the Smuggling Protocol, op. cit. note 16; s. 25 of Immigration Act 1971, op. cit. note 1; Art. 12 of Legislative Decree 286/1998, op. cit. note 8.

275   See s. 25 (4(a)) of Immigration Act 1971, op. cit. note 1.

276   See Art. 31 of the Council of Europe Convention on Trafficking, op. cit. note 19.

277   See ibid., Art. 31(1).

The establishment of jurisdiction may be difficult either because the same crime has been committed in more than on State Party or because trafficking in human beings may be linked to smuggling of migrants committed in one or more States Parties. The European Council Convention on Action against Trafficking in Human Beings encourages co-operation and agreements among States Parties in order to establish 'the most appropriate jurisdiction for prosecution'.[278] However, such agreements may be difficult when States' criminal judicial systems differ. One of the reasons for this is that some States permit trials *in absentia*. Another reason is that in some States, all crimes have a statute of limitations which specifies the period within which crimes must be prosecuted or criminal penalties imposed. Moreover, it may be difficult to establish the most appropriate jurisdiction because in the UK investigations are carried out by the police or other agencies,[279] whereas in Italy investigations are conducted by public prosecutors and decisions on whether or not to prosecute are taken by the judicial authorities.[280] It must be pointed out that although the Italian and British criminal justice systems are similar because both are based on the accusatorial system since the new Italian Penal Code abolished the inquisitorial system and introduced a new criminal accusatorial system in 1988,[281] they may present conflicts of jurisdiction that are difficult to overcome. Further problems would arise in the fight against smuggling of migrants and trafficking in human beings if judicial co-operation involved other EU Member States' criminal justice systems, such as the inquisitorial system of Germany.[282] In countries with an inquisitorial legal system, the trial is more important than the pre-trial phase, as in this latter phase the prosecution is automatic.[283]

This is why the Commission's proposal on how to resolve conflicts of jurisdiction between EU Member States should be implemented. Indeed, the Commission's proposal would help Italy and the UK, for example, to find agreement on which jurisdiction is better suited to resolving their conflicts.

What about the EAW and mutual legal assistance? Although EU Member States may not place much trust in each other's legal systems, in some cases this has been proven wrong. Indeed, in some cases Member States have accepted each other's judgments without any further measures being adopted. Problems may arise in cases of cross-border crimes or when the judicial authorities of one Member State do not understand the legal system of another.

---

278   Ibid.

279   See the Police and Criminal Evidence Act 1984 (PACE), Code of Practice C, para. 11.4.

280   See Arts 416 *et seq.* of *Codice di Procedura Penale*, op. cit. note 214.

281   See Conso, G., and Grevi, V., *Profili del Nuovo Codice di Procedura Penale* (Padova: CEDAM, 1993), pp. xv *et seq.*

282   See Sanders, A., and Young, R., *Criminal Justice*, 2nd edn (Oxford: Oxford University Press, 2005), p. 320.

283   Ibid.

The next sections deal with the EAW, mutual legal assistance, and the EEW between the UK and Italy. In particular, the next section examines how the EAW has improved or may improve judicial co-operation between these two countries and whether the EAW can render the fight against assisting irregular migration and smuggling of migrants more effective. Indeed, more robust co-operation in criminal matters may be a deterrent against smugglers of migrants, for example, because it would be more difficult for them to find safe havens. The next section deals with judicial co-operation between the UK and Italy by comparing their criminal proceedings.

As stated above, British and Italian criminal proceedings are similar. Therefore, in Italy as in the UK, the pre-trial phase is very important and prosecution does not automatically follow when a suspect has been arrested.[284] Moreover, in Italy the judicial authorities decide whether or not to prosecute a person,[285] whereas in the UK the Crown Prosecution Service takes this decision.[286] Thus, although there are similarities between the two criminal judicial systems, judicial co-operation between Italy and the UK may present difficulties as a result of the different authorities which decide whether to prosecute in Italy (the judicial authorities) and in the UK (the police), and because the British system is based on common law, and the Italian system on civil law. The next sections deal with these difficulties and suggest how to overcome them.

The European Arrest Warrant in the UK and Italy

The Implementation of the European Arrest Warrant in the Italian and British Legal Systems

The EAW aims to develop mutual recognition of decisions taken by judicial authorities in the Member States of the EU. In the past, other instruments have been adopted for this purpose: the European Convention on Extradition of 1957, and the 1995 and 1996 Conventions on Extradition. However, the 1995 and 1996 Conventions on Extradition have not been ratified by Italy.[287] Thus, although the EU tried to simplify extradition procedures in its Member States in order to facilitate mutual judicial co-operation, Member States have not shown much confidence in these instruments. This is confirmed by the position of Member States regarding

---

284   See Conso, and Grevi, *Profili del Nuovo Codice di Procedura Penale*, op. cit. note 280, pp. xviii and xix. See also Sanders, and Young, *Criminal Justice*, op. cit. note 281, pp. 319 *et seq.*

285   See Conso, and Grevi, *Profili del Nuovo Codice di Procedura Penale*, op. cit. note 280, pp. 369 *et seq.*

286   See ss. 1 *et seq.* of the Prosecution of Offences Act 1985, ch. 23.

287   See <http://www.consilium.eu.int/accords>.

the 1995 and 1996 Conventions on Extradition,[288] which have not been ratified by some new Member States, as well as Italy.[289]

However, the EAW has replaced these Conventions on Extradition, including the 1957 Extradition Convention.[290] Moreover, the EAW has been ratified by all EU Member States, including Italy and the UK.[291] The next section examines the British and Italian Acts that transposed the EAW into their domestic laws.

The British and Italian Acts on the European Arrest Warrant

In the UK, the EAW has been incorporated into the Extradition Act 2003.[292] In Italy, the EAW has been incorporated by Act 69/2005.[293] The Extradition Act 2003 is divided into two parts. The first part concerns extradition concerning States that have implemented the EAW, although as Alegre and Leaf have pointed out, the scope of the first part of the Extradition Act 2003 is not limited to States that have implemented the EAW.[294] In any case, the majority of the measures on extradition would not apply to States that have not implemented the EAW Framework Decision.[295] These specific measures will apply in cases of extradition requests from Member States that have implemented the EAW Framework Decision.[296] The Extradition Act 2003 does not require the application of double criminality as an essential criterion for issuing extradition to other EU Member States for certain forms of serious crimes.[297] Smuggling of migrants, indicated in the list in Schedule 2 as 'facilitation of unauthorized entry and residence',[298] and trafficking in human beings are considered serious crimes for which double criminality is not required between EU Member States.[299]

---

288   See Chapter 3 of this book.

289   Ibid.

290   See Recital 5 of 'Council Framework Decision 2002/584/JHA of 13 June 2002 on the European Arrest Warrant and the Surrender Procedure between Member States', OJ EU L 190/1, 18 July 2002.

291   See Council of the European Union Doc. 16352/03 of 22 December 2003; Council of European Union Doc. 8687/05 ADD 1, 20 May 2005. See <http://ue.eu.int/cms3_Applications/applications/PolJu/details.asp?lang=EN&cmsid=720&id=71> for the other Member States.

292   See Extradition Act 2003, ch. 41.

293   See Act no. 69/2005, op. cit. note 259.

294   See ss. 1–68 of Extradition Act 2003. See also Alegre, S., and Leaf, M., *European Arrest Warrant: A Solution Ahead of its Time* (JUSTICE, 2003), p. 78.

295   See ibid., pp. 78 and 79.

296   See ss. 69–141 of Extradition Act 2003. This book only analyses Part 2 of this Act.

297   See ibid., Art. 64(2. See also ibid., s. 215, Schedule 2.

298   See also ibid., s. 215, Schedule 2.

299   See also ibid., ss. 64(2) and 215, Schedule 2.

Italian law also states that double criminality is not necessary for crimes such as human trafficking and people smuggling.[300] Therefore, if Italy requires extradition of a suspect regarding one of the crimes for which the EAW Framework Decision does not require double criminality, the UK should surrender the person accused of that crime.[301] The same principle should be applied if the UK requires extradition for an offence for which the EAW Framework Decision excludes the requirement of double criminality. Indeed, Italian law on the EAW explicitly allows extradition in these cases.[302] Therefore, it should be quite straightforward to obtain or approve extradition when assisting irregular migration, smuggling of migrants and trafficking in human beings have been committed. However, problems and conflicts between Member States judicial authorities may arise in cases of convictions *in absentia*, in case of precautionary custody and in the specific case of Italian criminal procedure,[303] when the period within which a criminal offender must be prosecuted has expired or the period within which a sentence must be served has expired (*prescrizione*).[304]

Issues of trials *in absentia* and expiration periods for crimes and criminal penalties are strictly related to each other in Italy, because the expiration period for crimes and criminal penalties is not suspended when the defendant is absent. Convictions *in absentia* are not allowed under UK law, and their admissibility in order to facilitate the application of the EAW may be in breach of the principle of fair trials, explicitly foreseen by Article 6 ECHR.[305] The UK judicial authorities will not apply the EAW in case of trials *in absentia* if two conditions are met.[306] One of these conditions concerns a person who has been convicted *in absentia* 'and who did not deliberately absent himself or herself'.[307] Another condition which can prohibit extradition in case of conviction *in absentia* will apply when 'there is no guarantee of a retrial or a review amounting to a retrial'.[308] On the basis of these provisions, it can be highlighted that British law does not completely exclude the extradition of a person convicted *in absentia*. Therefore, a person who was deliberately absent from a trial abroad cannot rely on the fact that trials *in absentia* are forbidden in the UK to avoid extradition. According to British law, a person who was not intentionally absent from a trial abroad may have the right to a retrial

---

300   See Art. 8(c)(d)(o) of Act 69/2005, op. cit. note 259.

301   See ibid., s. 215.

302   See Art. 8 of Act 69/2005, op. cit. note. 259.

303   See Art. 420*quater* of *Codice di Procedura Penale*, op. cit. note 214.

304   See Arts 157 *et seq.* and 172 *et seq.* of 'Codice Penale. R.D.N. 1398, 19/10/1930', op. cit. note 60.

305   See Alegre and Leaf, *European Arrest Warrant*, op. cit. note 293, p. 83. See also Art. 6 ECHR, op. cit. note 43.

306   See s. 20(3) of Extradition Act 2003.

307   See the section entitled 'Bars to Surrender', letter (i) of Annex A of Council of European Union Doc. 16352/03, 22 December 2003. See also s. 20(3) of Extradition Act 2003.

308   See 'Bars to Surrender', letter (i) of Annex A of Council of European Union Doc. 16352/03, op. cit. note 306. See also s. 20(5) of Extradition Act 2003.

abroad. Nevertheless, in Italian criminal law, the expiration period (*prescrizione*) applies to all crimes and criminal convictions.[309] The Corte di Cassazione asserted that the *prescrizione* was introduced to guarantee that a trial was concluded within a reasonable period with respect to Article 6 ECHR.[310] However, the 'right to a fair trial'[311] is a basis on which extradition of a person convicted *in absentia* may be refused by British judicial authorities[312] if a foreign judicial authority will not be able to guarantee a retrial of a person who was not deliberately absent from a trial,[313] as indicated above. Italian law cannot ensure that a trial will be revisited, because the establishment of an expiration period for crimes and convictions could create obstacles to a retrial. Indeed, a retrial may not be possible if the *prescrizione* expires.[314] This is because the expiration period could elapse during the retrial, leading to its suspension, since even if the person is convicted, she or he will not go to prison.[315]

Another problem may be caused by restrictions under Italian law on how long a person may be kept in custody or detention during investigations if she or he has not yet been charged (*decorrenza dei termini*).[316] Precautionary custody in Italian law consists of detention without charge or after a decision subject to appeal has been issued. Precautionary custody may be applied in specific circumstances such as complex investigations or if there is a risk that the accused may abscond.[317] In case of homicide, for example, the period of precautionary custody cannot exceed one year.[318] When the conditions listed above are not met, the period of detention without charge cannot exceed 96 hours from time of arrest.[319] Therefore, difficult situations may arise. A murderer convicted *in absentia* in Italy can be extradited from the UK to Italy if the person was not deliberately absent from the trial and the UK has obtained from Italy a guarantee of a retrial. Subsequently, if the person is kept in precautionary custody in Italy and if the retrial exceeds the time limit on precautionary custody, the offender, although convicted in a retrial, may remain unpunished if the permitted duration of detention without charge (*decorrenza dei termini*) has been exceeded. This situation could easily happen because evidence may have been lost while the person was absent from Italy or because witnesses may not be in Italy, or may even have died. These differences can be overcome because, as Knowles pointed out, Section 20(5) of the Extradition Act 2003 uses

---

309   Ibid.
310   See Cass Pen. Sez. 1 sent. 4216, 24 May 1986 (ud. 21 April 1986) rv. 172803.
311   See Art. 6 ECHR, op. cit. note 43.
312   Ibid.
313   See s. 20(5) of Extradition Act 2003.
314   See Art. 172 of 'Codice Penale. R.D.N. 1398, 19/10/1930', op. cit. note 60.
315   Ibid.
316   Ibid. See also Art. 303 of *Codice di Procedura Penale*, op. cit. note 214.
317   See ibid., Art. 274.
318   See ibid., Art. 303(1(3)).
319   See ibid., Art. 390.

the words 'would be entitled to a retrial'.[320] Therefore, 'an undertaking by the requesting state that the defendant will be given a retrial may be sufficient, even if he is not guaranteed a retrial as a matter of law'.[321] However, in the UK, the mere acceptance of a simple undertaking may not be respectful of Article 6 ECHR in a practical case, so the British judicial authorities may refuse to extradite an offender already judged *in absentia* in Italy. Certainly, Framework Decision 2009/299, examined in Chapter 4, which applies the principle of mutual judicial recognition to decisions rendered *in absentia*, may change the situation. This is because Article 2 of the framework decision amends the EAW Framework Decision by adding Article 4a. This Article states that although the executing judicial authority may refuse to execute the EAW if the person did not appear at trial, this provision can be derogated if the person was summoned in person and informed that the decision might be handed down even if they did not appear for trial. Moreover, the judicial authority may execute the EAW if the person was informed of the trial and gave a mandate to a legal counsellor to defend him or her at the trial or if the person refused a retrial or did not contest a judgment given *in absentia*. The new framework decision could facilitate the recognition of decisions made *in absentia* and the issuing of an EAW. However, there are also other issues related to precautionary custody that need to be considered. In Italy, although precautionary custody may extend much beyond 96 hours during investigations, it must comply with strict time limits set out by the Penal Code either during the investigations or during the prosecution.[322] However, in the UK, although the period of detention without charge cannot exceed 96 hours,[323] there are no strict limits on precautionary custody. According to British law, a period of detention without charge cannot exceed 24 hours during the investigation,[324] but in cases of serious crimes, this can be extended up to 36 hours[325] or a maximum of 60 hours.[326] The police may request a magistrate to grant a longer period of detention without charge as long as this does not exceed 96 hours.[327] However, much discretion is allowed when investigations are concluded and the prosecution stage starts. Indeed, when the prosecution starts, British law does not establish precise time limits on detention in the case of precautionary custody, unlike Italian law.[328] In England and Wales, for example, judicial authorities have to respect specific time limits when a person is kept in custody if the Secretary of State has imposed these time limits by

---

320   See s. 25(5) of Extradition Act 2003. See also Knowles, B., *Blackstone's Guide to the Extradition Act 2003* (Oxford: Oxford University Press, 2004), p. 65.
321   See ibid., p. 65.
322   See Art. 303 of the *Codice di Procedura Penale*, op. cit. note 214.
323   See ss. 40–47 of PACE, op. cit. note 278, although in case of terrorism, the detention without charge of suspected terrorists can go beyond these limitations; see ss. 23, 24 and 25 of Terrorism Act 2006.
324   See s. 41(1) of PACE, op. cit. note 278.
325   See ibid., s. 42(1).
326   See ibid., ss. 42 and 43.
327   See ibid., s. 44(3).
328   Ibid.

regulations.[329] Nevertheless, the imposition of these terms is not obligatory as it is in Italy, where there are specific provisions under the Italian Penal Code.[330]

Possible solutions to conflicts between Italy and the UK in allowing extradition according to the EAW Framework Decision in case of trial *in absentia* could be resolved by developing mutual trust in both judicial systems and by applying the amendments of Framework Decision 2009/299. In other words, Italian judicial authorities could give UK judicial authorities assurances that a trial *in absentia* of an offender has been lawful because the Italian Criminal Code considers a trial *in absentia* a last resort.[331] Moreover, if the UK requested an EAW, Italy might trust that the period of precautionary custody would not be unreasonable. However, would British judicial authorities trust Italian judicial authorities, or vice versa? Certainly, in some cases judicial authorities of EU Member States might trust each other, and in these cases no further action would be required. Mutual trust is very important in order to achieve the best results in countering criminal organisations that commit smuggling of migrants and trafficking in human beings.

In conclusion, trials *in absentia* could make the application of the EAW between Italy and the UK difficult. This is because these two States have to respect different regulations in imposing detention without trial. Thus, a retrial, an important condition required by the UK in order to extradite an offender judged *in absentia*, could be limited by the restrictions on detention without trial that apply in Italy. Moreover, the fact that the Italian system establishes precise limits on precautionary custody may prevent Italian authorities extraditing an offender to the UK because it has no such precise limits. Nevertheless, it has also been shown that the new framework decision on trials *in absentia* could resolve these problems. However, other issues arising from differences between EU Member States may lead to difficulties in the application of the EAW and the principle of mutual judicial recognition.

The next sections show that in some cases, the House of Lords and the Corte di Cassazione have exhibited a good deal of trust in other EU Member States' legal systems. They analyse how the House of Lords has dealt with the EAW in trials *in absentia*, how the Corte di Cassazione has dealt with the EAW in cases of lack of time limits on precautionary custody, and how difficulties caused by lack of mutual trust can be overcome.

The House of Lords' Judgments on the European Arrest Warrant

The House of Lords is aware of the importance of the European Arrest Warrant.[332] Indeed, it has emphasised that the EAW was established to replace the previous

---

329   See s. 22 of Prosecution of Offences Act 1985 as amended.
330   See Judgment of the Italian Corte di Cassazione.
331   See Arts 420 *et seq.* of *Codice di Procedura Penale*, op. cit. note 214.
332   See Council Framework Decision 2002/584/JHA, op. cit. note 289.

extradition procedure[333] and should be applied uniformly in all EU Member States (*Dabas*).[334] Moreover, the House of Lords maintained that the EAW is based on the principle of mutual judicial recognition and that it was established to accelerate extradition, and for this purpose, the requested Member State 'should surrender the person to the requesting member state speedily and without investigating the merits of the proposed prosecution'.[335] Finally, the House of Lords is aware that EU Member States should surrender the person concerned on the assumption that other EU Member States' judicial authorities will guarantee a fair trial, because EU Member States share common values and recognise common rights.[336] Indeed, in *Dabas*,[337] the EAW was issued without difficulties. In this case, the appellant had committed solely on the Spanish territory the crime of complicity in Islamic terrorism in relation to the bombing attack of 11 March 2004.[338] Moreover, the House of Lords did not impede the application of the EAW because issues related to differences in EU Member States' criminal systems did not arise.

Problems may arise when crimes have a cross-border dimension or when EU Member States' judicial authorities are unfamiliar with other EU Member States' legal systems and thus do not trust each other. Indeed, in one case the British judicial authorities showed an absolute lack of trust towards other EU Member States and tried to find any excuse, even elaborating the Extradition Act 2003, to prevent the extradition of a person who had committed the crimes of assisting irregular migration and trafficking in human beings through Belgium.

On the basis of the EAW Framework Decision,[339] the King's Prosecutor in Brussels requested the extradition of a person who had facilitated the irregular entry and residence of Ecuadorian citizens in Europe through Brussels by falsifying documents and who had subsequently committed people trafficking.[340] In the UK, the EAW Framework Decision had been implemented and it was inserted in Part 1 of the Extradition Act 2003. This Act indicates that EU Member States are Category

---

333   See *European Convention on Extradition 1957*, ETS no. 24, 13 December 1957. See also: *Benelux Treaty on Extradition and Mutual Assistance in Criminal Matters*, 616 UNTS 120, 1962; 'Convention drawn up on the basis of Article K.3 of the Treaty on European Union, on Simplified Extradition Procedure between the Member States of the European Union', OJ EU C 78/2, 10 March 1995; 'Convention Drawn up on the Basis of Article K.3 of the Treaty on European Union, Relating to Extradition between the Member States of the European Union', OJ EU C 313/21, 23 October 1996.

334   See Opinions of the Lords of Appeal for Judgment in the Cause *Dabas (Appellant)* v. *High Court of Justice, Madrid (Respondent) (Criminal Appeal for Her Majesty's High Court of Justice)* [2007] UKHL 6, para. 42.

335   See ibid., para. 58.

336   See ibid., para. 4.

337   Ibid.

338   See ibid., para. 1.

339   See Framework Decision 2002/584/JHA, op. cit. note 289.

340   See *Office of the King's Prosecutor, Brussels* v. *Armas and Others* [2005] 3 WLR 1079.

1 territories.[341] Moreover, the Extradition Act 2003 abolishes the requirement of double criminality between the UK and EU Member States for certain offences.[342] The accused, Armas, was convicted and sentenced to five years' imprisonment *in absentia* for having committed the crimes of assisting irregular migration, forgery of documents and trafficking of persons.[343] These crimes constitute extraditable offences in EU Member States, even when the double criminality requirement is not satisfied.[344] In 2004, the deputy senior district judge in the UK discharged the defendant on the basis that the extradition could not been applied according to Section 65(2)[345] nor Section 65(3) of the Extradition Act 2003.[346] The reason why Section 65(2) could not apply was because some conduct was committed in the UK.[347] Instead, this section states that a person can only be extradited to another EU Member State if the crime has not been committed in any part of British territory.[348] Section 65(3) could not apply because if the legislator had had the intention to apply this subsection in a case where offences were committed partly in the UK and partly in another EU Member State, it would have established that the offender could have been extradited even if only a part of the conduct had been committed in an EU Member State.[349] Section 65(3) states that a person can be extradited to an EU Member State if he or she has committed the entire conduct in that Member State.[350] Certainly, Framework Decision 2002/584/JHA does not rule out the possibility of excluding extradition when a crime has been committed

---

341   See Arts 1–68 of Extradition Act 2003. See also [2005] 3 WLR, op. cit. note 339, para. 9. See also Alegre and Leaf, *European Arrest Warrant*, op. cit. note 293, p. 78.
342   See s. 64(2) Part 1 and s. 215, Schedule 2 of Extradition Act 2003. See also Alegre and Leaf, *European Arrest Warrant*, op. cit. note 293, pp. 78 and 79.
343   See [2005] 3 WLR, op. cit. note 339, paras 1 and 12.
344   See s. 215, Schedule 2 of Extradition Act 2003.
345   See [2005] 3 WLR, op. cit. note 339, para. 13. See also s. 65(2) of Extradition Act 2003, which states: '(2) The conduct constitutes an extradition offence in relation to the category 1 territory if these conditions are satisfied – (a) the conduct occurs in the category 1 territory and no part of it occurs in the United Kingdom; (b) a certificate issued by an appropriate authority of the category 1 territory shows that the conduct shows that the conduct falls within the European framework list; (c) the certificate shows that a sentence of imprisonment or another form of detention for a term of 12 months or a greater punishment has been imposed in the category 1 territory in respect of the conduct.'
346   See [2005] 3 WLR, op. cit. note 339, para. 13. See s. 65(3) of Extradition Act 2003, which states: '(3) The conduct also constitutes an extradition offence in relation to the category 1 territory if these conditions are satisfied – (a) the conduct occurs in the category 1 territory; (b) the conduct would constitute an offence under the law of the relevant part of the United Kingdom if it occurred in that part of the United Kingdom; (c) a sentence of imprisonment or another form of detention for a term of 4 months or a greater punishment has been imposed in the category 1 territory in respect of the conduct.'
347   See [2005] 3 WLR, op. cit. note 339, para. 13.
348   See s. 65(2)(a) of Extradition Act 2003.
349   Ibid.
350   See ibid., s. 65(3)(a).

partly or entirely on the territory of the executing State, although it states that this decision is only optional.[351] In any case, the fact that a British court adopted this restriction on crimes that are mostly transnational and committed on a large scale clearly demonstrates the diffidence of this State towards an instrument that had been created to accelerate the investigation of crimes and imposition of punishments on criminals and the lack of trust in other EU Member States' judicial systems.

The King's Prosecutor in Brussels was allowed by the divisional court to appeal against this decision, and in the appeal the judge confirmed the previous judgment and held that the offences charged against the appellant were part of the European framework list of the Extradition Act 2003, Schedule 2.[352] However, the offences had been partly committed in the UK, thus Section 65(2)(a) could not be applied.[353] Furthermore, Section 65(3)(a) could also not be applied, because the offence was not committed entirely in Belgian territory.[354] It could be argued after this judgment that national law implementing the EAW Framework Decision could apply this framework decision restrictively. However, the problem might be resolved if the UK prosecuted a person who has partly committed a crime in the UK. It must also be added that the House of Lords disagreed that extradition to another EU Member State should only be allowed when the crime has wholly occurred in the territory of that EU Member State. Indeed, the House of Lords was not completely convinced that Section 65(3) could not apply.[355] In other words, some of the Lords disagreed that the extradition should have been excluded because parts of the conduct had been committed in the UK.[356] They rejected the argument that Section 65(3) did not apply to offences committed partly in an EU Member State. On the contrary, they held that Section 65(3) would have excluded extradition only if the requirement of double criminality had not been fulfilled. They also pointed out that the Extradition Act 2003 incorporated the EAW Framework Decision,[357] that the EAW was designed to facilitate the extradition of offenders, and that EU Member States would be unlikely to decline extradition.[358] The House of Lords pointed out that the EAW is based on mutual recognition that can only be applied if there is mutual trust and confidence between EU Member States.[359] Moreover, the Lords also asserted that there is in the UK:

---

351   See Art. 4(7)(a) of Framework Decision 2002/584/JHA, op. cit. note 289.

352   See [2005] 3 WLR, op. cit. note 339, paras 14 and 15. See also s. 215, Schedule 2 of Extradition Act 2003.

353   See [2005] 3 WLR, op. cit. note 339, para. 15.

354   Ibid.

355   See ibid., para. 17.

356   Ibid.

357   See ibid., para. 20.

358   See ibid., para. 22.

359   See ibid., para. 23.

a lack of confidence in the ability of the criminal justice arrangements of other Member States to measure up to the standards of our own, and a corresponding lack of trust in the ability of the new system to protect those against whom it might be used. Now that the argument is over and the new system is in force it has to earn that trust by the way it is put into practice. The system has, of course, been designed to protect rights. Trust in its ability to provide that protection will be earned by a careful observance of the procedures that have been laid down.[360]

The House of Lords then added that EU Member States should extradite offenders between themselves with respect to the principle of mutual recognition expressly recognised by the EAW Framework Decision.[361] Therefore, it is the case that the framework decision allows EU Member States to refuse extradition if an offence has been committed in whole or in part in the executing Member State's territory.[362] Moreover, it is the case that on the basis of this framework decision, the UK adopted Section 65(3), which requires that the offender has to be in the territory of the requesting State when the crime for which he or she is accused is committed, and that the crime must have been committed in its entirety in the requesting State.[363] It is also the case that this latter criterion is difficult to apply when crimes such as human trafficking have been committed because these crimes have a transnational dimension.[364] Consequently, the House of Lords concluded that there are sufficient grounds to extradite an offender if the effects of the criminal conduct lead to harm within the requesting territory.[365] Thus, on the basis of this assertion, the House of Lords reached two conclusions. First, it pointed out that the extradition could not have been allowed under Section 65(2)(a) of the Extradition Act 2003 because the conduct partly occurred in the UK.[366] Second, it held that the extradition could have been allowed under Article 65(3) of the Extradition Act 2003 because the correct interpretation of this provision should not require that the conduct has only occurred outside the UK.[367] Therefore, at the end, they agreed that the extradition could have been allowed. However, although the House of Lords showed some willingness to extradite the offender, it dismissed the appeal because the Belgian extradition request did not satisfy the requirements

---

360   Ibid.
361   See ibid., para. 32. See also Art. 2(2) of Framework Decision 2002/584/JHA, op. cit. note 289.
362   See [2005] 3 WLR, op. cit. note 339, para. 32. See also Art. 4(7)(a) of Framework Decision 2002/584/JHA, op. cit. note 289.
363   See [2005] 3 WLR, op. cit. note 339, paras 33 and 34.
364   See ibid., para. 34.
365   See ibid., para. 40.
366   See ibid., para. 49.
367   Ibid.

of Section 2(5) of the Extradition Act 2003.[368] In other words, the Belgian request did not specify that the defendant convicted *in absentia* was unlawfully at large.[369] Moreover, because it was impossible for the House of Lords to inquire of the Belgian judicial authorities whether the person was or was not unlawfully at large, as this request would be contrary to the EAW, whose purpose is to expedite the extradition of offenders,[370] the House of Lords dismissed the appeal. The House of Lords could have given a more restrictive interpretation of the Extradition Act 2003 in order to allow the EAW on the basis of the principle of recognition, as the Corte di Cassazione did.

To summarise, the House of Lords recognised that although a crime can be committed partly on British territory, the offender can be extradited to an EU Member State if the negative effects of the crime are felt mainly in that EU Member State. However, the House of Lords dismissed the appeal because it showed a lack of trust towards the Belgian authorities which had applied the conviction *in absentia*. In other words, the House of Lords did not understand the trial *in absentia* because the Belgian judicial authorities did not explain whether Armas was unlawfully at large, so it decided to discharge the defendant. Lack of trust and lack of knowledge of Belgian criminal procedure caused the House of Lords to take this decision. It could be that judicial authorities of another Member State where trial *in absentia* is admissible would have given a different response. In this way, not only can the uniform interpretation of the EAW in the EU Member States be jeopardised, but also the effectiveness of judicial co-operation to combat cross-border crimes. For all these reasons, the amendments to the EAW framework decisions introduced by Framework Decision 2009/299 are considered highly adequate.

The next section examines two judgments of the Corte di Cassazione on the EAW.

The Corte di Cassazione's Judgments on the European Arrest Warrant

In a recent case (*Cusini*) the Corte di Cassazione did not extradite an Italian citizen called Rosanna Cusini to Belgium because the Belgian judicial authorities did not specify in their request the time limit of precautionary custody that, as emphasised above, Italian law holds must be expressly indicated because it cannot

---

368   See ibid., para. 42. See also s. 2(5) of Extradition Act 2003, which states: 'The statement is one that – (a) the person in respect of whom the Part 1 warrant is issued is alleged to be unlawfully at large after conviction of an offence specified in the warrant by a court in the category 1 territory, and (b) the Part 1 warrant is issued with a view to his arrest and extradition to the category 1 territory for the purpose of being sentenced for the offence or of serving a sentence of imprisonment or another form of detention imposed in respect of the offence.'

369   See [2005] 3 WLR, op. cit. note 339, para. 55.

370   See ibid., para. 57.

be discretionary.[371] Cusini was accused of swindling in Belgium, where she had already been arrested and released on caution.[372] Therefore, there was a pending procedure against Cusini. The Court of Appeal of Venice allowed the extradition of Cusini because the requirement of double criminality in Italy and in Belgium regarding swindling was respected.[373] Cusini appealed against the decision of the Court of Appeal of Venice before the Corte di Cassazione. First, Cusini pointed out that the EAW was not the original document, but a copy sent by fax.[374] However, the Corte di Cassazione found this submission unfounded because the EAW cannot be acquired in its original form as it is a document issued by a domestic authority of one EU Member State and forwarded to the other EU Member States.[375] Therefore, it is impossible for one EU Member State to receive the original document.[376]

Second, Cusini highlighted that the crime was committed in part in Italy, and not in Belgium, because she returned to Italy at the end of 2002, while the crime had been committed between 2002 and 2004,[377] whereas, according to Act 69/2005, the EAW cannot be granted if a part of one crime has been committed in Italy.[378] However, the Corte di Cassazione held on this point that the allegations against Cusini only concerned criminal offences committed in Belgian territory, and not in Italian territory. Thirdly, Cusini emphasised that the Belgian authorities' allegations were too generic and did not indicate the evidence against her.[379] In other words, the request did not precisely indicate the reasons why the EAW was requested.[380] However, the Corte di Cassazione held that by the wording of the request, the allegation was clear enough because all the charges against the offender were clearly indicated, although the reasons for the request were not expressly stated. It is true that indication of the precise reasons for the arrest warrant is essential under Italian law, but a similar request cannot be imposed on other EU Member States if it is easy to understand the reasons why the EAW has been requested by referral to request and charges.

Finally, Cusini highlighted the failure of the Belgian judicial authorities' request to indicate the maximum time limit for precautionary custody expressly indicated by Article 18(e) of Act 69/2005 as an obstacle to the issue of the EAW.[381] On this point, the Corte di Cassazione observed that EC law is part of the domestic law, and that the domestic law of EU Member States should be interpreted in conformity

---

371   See Cass. Pen, sez. 6, sent. 16542, 15 May 2006 (ud. 8 May 2006).
372   See ibid., para. 3.
373   See ibid., para. 4.
374   See ibid., para. 6.
375   Ibid.
376   Ibid.
377   See ibid., para. 7.
378   Ibid. See also Art. 18(p) of Act 69/2005, op. cit. note 259.
379   See para. 8 of Cass. Pen. sez. 6, sent. 16542, op. cit. note 370.
380   Ibid.
381   See para. 9 of Cass. Pen. sez. 6, sent. 16542, op. cit. note 370. See also Art. 18(e) of Act 69/2005, op. cit. note 259.

with EC law.[382] The Corte di Cassazione emphasised that in Belgium and in England, no maximum time limit for precautionary custody is established.[383] This is because in these two EU Member States there are periodical judicial controls on precautionary custody, so it is not established that a person should be released if the maximum time limit for precautionary custody has elapsed.

The Strasbourg Court held that domestic laws do not violate Article 5(3) of the ECHR if they do not indicate the maximum time limit for precautionary custody.[384] On the contrary, the Strasbourg Court held that it is better not to indicate precise time limits for precautionary custody, but to evaluate the limits to apply on a case-by-case basis, unless fundamental rights are not respected in the requesting State. However, the Corte di Cassazione observed that a maximum time limit for precautionary custody should be applied with respect for Article 13(4) of the Italian Constitution, on which Act 69/2005 is based. Moreover, the Corte di Cassazione pointed out that EC law is part of domestic law, and therefore, as the Court of Justice held in *Pupino*, the national law should be interpreted in conformity with framework decisions. Nevertheless, the legal obligation to conform interpretation of national law to framework decisions ceases when it is in breach of national law.[385] Therefore, this limitation makes it impossible for the Court of Justice to deliver a preliminary ruling on this point. Furthermore, the Corte di Cassazione observed that it was not possible to raise the issue of the constitutionality of Article 18(e) of Act 69/2005 because this provision respects Article 13(4) of the Italian Constitution and because a similar request would prolong the detention of Cusini. Consequently, the Corte di Cassazione annulled the previous decision of the Court of Appeal and ordered the immediate release of Cusini.[386]

Negri has argued that this decision risks making it impossible to apply the EAW and enable the free circulation of judgments of EU Member States courts in the criminal area.[387] Moreover, the judgment of the Corte di Cassazione could make it preferable to apply the traditional extradition procedures, because the latter established the extradition of an Italian citizen without the need for the Corte di Cassazione to intervene. For this reason, the EAW that was established to overcome the formalities that made extradition very slow could prove a less adequate instrument than traditional extradition.

---

382   See para. 9.1 of Cass. Pen. sez. 6, sent. 16542, op. cit. note 370. The Corte di Cassazione quoted Case C-105/03 [2005] 2 CMLR 63 *Criminal proceedings against Maria Pupino*.

383   See para. 9.2 of Cass. Pen. sez. 6, sent. 16542, op. cit. note 370.

384   See Corte di Cassazione are *Stogmuller c. Autriche* v. *Austria* 10 November 1969 (1979–80) 1 EHRR 155; *Erdem c. Allemagne* v. *Germany* (2002) 35 EHRR 15 ECHR; *Tomasi* v. *France* (1993) 15 EHRR 1.

385   See para. 47 of Case C-105/03, op. cit. note 381.

386   See para. 10 of Cass. Pen. sez. 6, sent. 16542, op. cit. note 370.

387   See Negri, G., 'Arresto Europeo a Raggio Ridotto', *Il Sole 24 Ore*, 19 May 2006.

The author believes that the Corte di Cassazione made a similar judgment because it did not trust the Belgian judicial system. In any case, it must be admitted that the EAW Framework Decision allows EU Member States to apply their constitutional rules.[388] Consequently, through this ruling, the Corte di Cassazione applied a power allowed by the EAW Framework Decision.

Nevertheless, it must be mentioned that in a recent case the Corte di Cassazione reinterpreted Article 18(e) of Act 69/2005.[389] Indeed, the Corte di Cassazione explained that the aim of the EAW Framework Decision is to grant extradition on the basis of the principle of mutual trust between EU Member States.[390] For this reason, Article 18(e) of Act 69/2005 must be interpreted as requiring equivalent guarantees in case of precautionary custody, rather than a non-existent and unrealistic perfect homogeneity of EU Member States' legal systems.[391] Certainly, there are EU Member States that, like Italy, specify maximum terms for precautionary custody,[392] such as France, Greece, Malta, Poland, Portugal, the Czech Republic, Romania, Slovakia and Spain. Nevertheless, there are other EU Member States which provide continuous reviews at regular intervals, although they do not set out an explicit maximum term for precautionary custody.[393] These legal systems provide implicit maximum terms for precautionary custody, so they have to be considered respectful of Article 18(e) of Act 69/2005.[394] This seems to be the case with Belgium, Sweden and Finland, for instance.[395] From the wording of the court, the list seems not to be exhaustive. Therefore, the UK is also part of this list.

In conclusion, the Corte di Cassazione did not extradite an Italian citizen who committed swindling to Belgium because the Belgian system does not establish a maximum period for precautionary custody. Nevertheless, in a more recent judgment the Corte di Cassazione reviewed its position on the basis of the mutual trust on which the EAW Framework Decision is based. The House of Lords in one case also extradited a person on the basis of mutual trust. Therefore, some EU Member States apply the EAW Framework Decision extensively, although not always, because EU Member States do not know enough about each other's criminal systems and thus do not trust each other. Therefore, it is important to establish mutual trust between EU Member States to ensure the full compliance of all EU Member States with the EAW Framework Decision.

---

388 See para. 12 of Framework Decision 2002/584/JHA, op. cit. note 289.
389 See Cass. Pen, sez. unite, sent. 4614/2007, 5 February 2007.
390 See ibid., para. 9.
391 Ibid.
392 See ibid., para. 7 of the judgment.
393 See ibid., para. 8 of the judgment.
394 See ibid., paras 9 and 10 of the judgment.
395 See ibid., para. 9 of the judgment.

Other problems may prevent European integration in the criminal area. One of these concerns the *prescrizione* when the UK requests extradition of a person from Italy to the UK. The next section examines this specific possibility.

Other Problems Related to the European Arrest Warrant between Italy and the UK

Italian law has established precise time limits within which a criminal offender can be tried and punished.[396] However, a recent Act has changed Italian law in this respect,[397] and greater discretion is now given to judges in establishing these time limits.[398] Moreover, the duration of these limits has been reduced compared to the previous legislation.[399]

However, these time limits still exist. Furthermore, the EAW Framework Decision considers lapse of time a ground for refusal.[400] As a result, if the UK requests extradition of persons who have committed crimes which, according to Italian law, can no longer be prosecuted because the time limits have been exceeded, the UK request will be rejected. Indeed, Italian law does not permit application of the EAW when the crime or criminal penalty periods have expired[401] because in these cases a person can no longer be prosecuted.[402] However, the predetermined expiration period decided by the Italian judicial authorities may appear too short for British judicial authorities, so problems related to jurisdiction may arise between them. Moreover, if the Italian judicial authorities required the extradition of a person from the UK, the UK might refuse this request 'by reason of the passage of time if (and only if) it appears that it would be unjust or oppressive to extradite him'.[403] Indeed, Italy is a civil law country, and Italian judicial authorities have to respect

---

396   See Art. 157 of 'Codice Penale. R.D.N. 1398, 19/10/1930', op. cit. note 60.

397   Compare Art. 157 (1 and 2) of 'Codice Penale. R.D.N. 1398, 19/10/1930', op. cit. note 60, with Art. 6 of Act 251/2005, 'Modifiche al codice penale e alla legge 26 luglio 1975, n. 354, in material di attenuanti generiche, di recidiva, di giudizio di comparazione delle circostanze di reato per I recidivi, di usura e di prescrizione', GU 285, 7 December 2005, which modified Art. 157(1 and 2) of 'Codice Penale. R.D.N. 1398, 19/10/1930', op. cit. note 60.

398   See Art. 157(1) of 'Codice Penale. R.D.N. 1398, 19/10/1930', op. cit. note 60, as modified by Act 251/2005, op. cit. note 396, with Art. 157(1 and 2) of 'Codice Penale. R.D.N. 1398, 19/10/1930', op. cit. note 60, previous modification.

399   See Art. 157(1) of 'Codice Penale. R.D.N. 1398, 19/10/1930', op. cit. note 60, as modified by Act 251/2005, op. cit. note 396 with Art. 157(3,4 and 5) of 'Codice Penale. R.D.N. 1398, 19/10/1930', op. cit. note 60, previous modification.

400   See para. 12 and Art. 4(4) of Framework Decision 2002/584/JHA, op. cit. note 289.

401   See Art. 18(1(n)) of Act 69/2005, op. cit. note 396.

402   See Art. 157 of 'Codice Penale. R.D.N. 1398, 19/10/1930', op. cit. note 60, as modified by Act 251/2005, op. cit. note 396.

403   See s. 82 of Extradition Act 2003.

the rule of *nullum crimen nulla poena sine lege*.[404] The UK also has to respect this rule explicitly recognised by the ECHR.[405] However, the UK being a common law country, this rule has been respected when criminal offences have been defined with sufficient certainty.[406] Therefore, sufficient certainty concerning expiration periods in the UK consists of according discretion to judicial authorities in the determination of those times for crimes and criminal penalties in the UK.[407] These impediments to the EAW should be overcome by amending the EAW Framework Decision. In this way, time limits could be applied more narrowly by EU Member States in order to facilitate the surrender of the persons concerned.

Mutual Legal Assistance between the UK and Italy

The Mutual Legal Assistance Convention[408] entered into force in the UK on 22 December 2005.[409] Italy has not yet ratified this convention.[410] Moreover, Italy has not implemented the Protocol on Mutual Legal Assistance.[411] In any case, mutual legal assistance between Italy and the UK should be based on the UK's Crime (International Co-operation) Act 2003 and on Articles 723 *et seq.* of the Italian Penal Procedure Code. Mutual legal assistance (*rogatoria* in Italian criminal proceedings) may be useful in order to enable the arrest of smugglers of migrants and traffickers in human beings. It may also prevent conflicts of jurisdiction between different Member States, and in the specific case analysed here, between Italy and the UK. Indeed, mutual legal assistance, as specified above, consists of requesting assistance from another State in order to obtain evidence abroad against a person alleged to have committed a crime in the requesting State. The Crime (International Co-operation) Act 2003 provides for situations where British

---

404   See Art. 25(2) of 'Costituzione della Repubblica Italiana', GU 298, 27 December 1947, Edizione Straordinaria. See also Art. 7 ECHR, op. cit. note 43; Mantovani, F., *Diritto Penale* (Padova: CEDAM, 1992), pp. 39 *et seq.*

405   See Art. 7 ECHR, op. cit. note 43.

406   See Ashworth, A., and Redmayne, M. (2005), *The Criminal Law Process* 3rd edn (Oxford: Oxford University Press, 2005), p. 34.

407   Ibid.

408   See 'Convention of 29 May 2000 Established by the Council in Accordance with Article 34 of the Treaty on European Union, on Mutual Assistance in Criminal Matters between the Member States of the European Union', OJ EU C 197/1, 12 July 2000. See also 'Protocol, Established by the Council in Accordance with Article 34 of the Treaty on European Union, to the Convention on Mutual Assistance in Criminal Matters between the Member States of the European Union', OJ EU C 326/1, 21 November 2001.

409   See <http://www.consilium.eu.int/accords>.

410   Ibid.

411   Ibid. See also 'Council Act of 16 October 2001, Establishing, in Accordance with Article 34 of the Treaty on European Union, the Protocol to the Convention on Mutual Legal Assistance in Criminal Matters between the Member States of the European Union (2001/C 326/01)', OJ EU C 326/1, 21 November 2001.

authorities need to obtain evidence and the when British authorities are requested to send evidence abroad.[412] The Act states that judicial authorities may apply for assistance in obtaining evidence when it appears:

> that an offence has been committed or that there are reasonable grounds for suspecting that an offence has been committed, and ... that proceedings in respect of the offence have been instituted or that the offence is being investigated.[413]

The Act also states that evidence may be sent by a territorial authority to a requesting State 'in connection with ... criminal proceedings or a criminal investigation being carried on outside the United Kingdom ...'.[414] The Italian Penal Procedure Code foresees mutual legal assistance requested from a foreign judicial authority and assistance requested from Italian judicial authorities to foreign judicial authorities.[415] In both cases, the Italian Minister of Justice decides whether to send the evidence requested or to apply for evidence being sent to the Italian judicial authorities.[416] Indeed, the UK Crime (International Co-operation) Act 2003 imposes conditions that must be met in order for a foreign judicial authority to obtain evidence from British judicial authorities.[417] One of these is that according to the law of the requesting country, an offence 'has been committed or ... there are reasonable grounds for suspecting that such an offence has been committed ...'.[418] Another condition to be met is that proceedings must 'have been instituted in that country or ... an investigation into the offence is being carried on there'.[419]

The Italian Minister of Justice can in certain circumstances deny requests by other States for evidence to be sent from Italy.[420] Moreover, the decision to agree or refuse to send or obtain evidence is decided by the Minister of Justice, and not by the judicial authorities. Ample discretion is left to the Minister of Justice, who, for example, may decide to refuse a request of assistance in obtaining evidence if the request might discriminate against a person for reasons related to gender, race, religious belief, nationality, language, political opinions and so on.[421] British law does not have a similar provision, so the first obstacle to mutual legal assistance

---

412 See ss. 7 *et seq.* and 13 *et seq.* of Crime (International Co-operation) Act 2003.

413 See ibid., s. 7(1(a and b)).

414 See ibid., s. 14(1(a)). This section also highlights that mutual legal assistance can be provided in connection with administrative proceedings and investigations. However, this book will not analyse this possibility because its aim is to focus on the two crimes of smuggling of migrants and trafficking in human beings.

415 See Arts 723(1) 727(1) of *Codice di Procedura Penale*, op. cit. note 214.

416 See ibid., Arts 723(1) and 727(1).

417 See s. 14 (2(a and b)) of Crime (International Co-operation) Act 2003.

418 See ibid., s. 14 (2(a)).

419 See ibid., s. 14 (2(b)).

420 See Art. 723(1) of *Codice di Procedura Penale*, op. cit. note 214.

421 Ibid.

may result from the different means by which mutual legal assistance is executed. Moreover, there are differences in the way evidence is gathered and admitted to the trial stage.

Because of all the problems mentioned in this section, mutual legal assistance in case of the commission of smuggling of migrants and human trafficking can be difficult to achieve. If the UK and Italy, for example, accepted that jurisdiction over smuggling of migrants should be given to the British judicial authorities, although only one part of the crime has been committed in the UK, the British judicial authorities could require the Italian authorities to send evidence against suspects to the UK. However, would evidence sent by Italian judicial authorities to the UK be admitted by the British judicial authorities? According to English law on criminal evidence, for example, the court may refuse to admit evidence:

> if it appears to the court that, having regard to all the circumstances, ... the admission of the evidence would have such an adverse affect on the fairness of the proceedings that the court ought not to admit it.[422]

It can be predicted that advocates would be keen to exclude evidence coming from abroad and not gathered by the British police or other British agencies if this evidence incriminated the defendant, since they could complain that evidence from abroad does not respect domestic law. This problem may be resolved through increased police co-operation between Member States. However, police co-operation may not always be sufficient to resolve these problems. Indeed, if the crime of smuggling of migrants has been initially committed in Italy and thereafter in the UK, co-operation between the British and Italian police could not have been considered necessary when the crime was initially committed without involving British territory if, for example, criminals only had connections with criminal organisations based in Senegal, and not in the UK. Police co-operation would only have been requested if UK territory or British nationals had been involved in the commission of this offence. Moreover, there is the question of admissibility of hearsay evidence under the Italian and British criminal systems. According to British law, hearsay is 'a statement not made in oral evidence in the proceedings ... admissible as evidence of any matter stated'.[423] In Italy, hearsay consists of information given by persons who do not want to reveal their identity to the police.[424] The Italian Penal Procedure Code states that the judicial authorities cannot request the police to reveal the names of persons who inform them of the commission of a criminal offence,[425] but their information cannot be admitted as evidence at trial.[426] In the UK, hearsay evidence can be admissible in certain

---

422 See s. 78(1) of PACE, op. cit. note 278.
423 See s. 114(1) of Criminal Justice Act 2003.
424 See Cass. Pen. 28 July 2003 no. 31739, rv. 226201.
425 See Art. 203(1) of *Codice di procedura penale*, op. cit. note 214.
426 Ibid.

cases.[427] An example may serve to clarify the issue. The UK and Italy agree to confer jurisdiction to Italian judicial authorities on smuggling of migrants in order to prevent conflicts of jurisdiction on this crime. Subsequently, the UK transfers the evidence gathered from the British police to the Italian judicial authorities. In this case, there could be a risk that the Italian judicial authorities consider this evidence inadmissible because it contravenes the rules on hearsay. When implemented by Member States, the EEW may resolve these problems as it permits the exchange of evidence between EU Member States on the basis of the issuing State's law, which in this example would be the UK. Italy should simply accept this evidence. The Mutual Legal Assistance Convention, which establishes the exchange of evidence on the basis of the requesting State's law, may not be applied between Italy and the UK because Italy has not implemented this convention. Moreover, it is desirable that the law of the issuing State be applied, because the issuing State should decide to transfer evidence on the basis of its domestic law. However, the EEW also requires a high level of mutual trust, because the requesting state should be able to apply the evidence based on the issuing State's law on the basis of mutual trust that could be constructed if common rules on defendants and suspects are approved in the EU. Consequently, it is desirable that the proposals of the Commission be implemented and that the fundamental rights of defendants and suspects are protected in the same way throughout EU Member States. This is the first goal that should be achieved.

Conclusions

This chapter highlighted a variety of issues. The UK and Italy have adopted restrictive laws on irregular migration. Their laws are so tough that it is difficult to distinguish victims of human trafficking and people smuggling from their smugglers and exploiters. Both legal systems criminalise irregular migration, and this is very disconcerting because it seems that Italian law punishes people smuggled by sea just because they are poor.

Italy has a very advanced law on the protection of human trafficking, and this law has been successful in investigations of trafficking in human beings (through the Rimini Method) and smuggling of migrants by sea (through the Siracusan Approach). Police forces were successful because they were supported by the victims, who agreed to testify against their smugglers and traffickers. It is difficult to gain the trust of these victims because they have often been victims of abuse, and they also fear retaliation from the criminal organisations. This is why it is important to provide them with a shelter where they can be reassured and eventually come to trust the law enforcement authorities and decide to testify against criminal organisations involved in the commission of these two crimes. This approach is feasible because the smuggling of migrants by sea is

---

427   See s. 114(1) of Criminal Justice Act 2003.

not uncontrollable. Indeed, this chapter has shown that the Italian government knows exactly how many people are smuggled by sea through the small island of Lampedusa.

However, this chapter has also shown that Italian law creates obstacles to the protection of victims, as it relies too heavily on repressive measures against irregular migrants without considering the fact that some of them are victims of smuggling of people by sea and human trafficking. By adopting this policy, the Italian government has ignored international conventions and EU law which obligate Member States to rescue people in danger and provide a shelter to asylum seekers and victims of human trafficking.

The UK has progressed in the fight against trafficking in human beings because it has ratified the European Council Convention on Trafficking. Nevertheless, this Member State also gives priority to legal measures against irregular migration. EU Member States should fight against smuggling and trafficking by enhancing EU police and judicial co-operation. This can only be done by enhancing mutual trust between their judicial systems.

This chapter cited four important cases before the House of Lords and the Corte di Cassazione where it has been shown that mutual trust may sometimes exist between EU Member States' judicial authorities, but that this is not always the case. This is why the author applauds the entry into force of the Lisbon Treaty, which will strengthen police and judicial co-operation through the intervention of the European Parliament by adopting legal measures in these fields. The Lisbon Treaty will also facilitate the establishment of a common policy on migration through more significant interventions by the European Parliament in decision-making procedures on immigration. In this way, it is hoped that in the future, a more adequate law based on the Rimini Method and the Siracusan Approach will be adopted at EU level to combat smuggling of migrants by sea and the trafficking of people.

Chapter 6
Conclusion

Findings of this Book

This book has shown that trafficking in human beings and smuggling of migrants by sea could be countered by a process of integrating the victims of these two crimes. The process of integration should consist of granting long-term visas to victims of these two crimes, to encourage them to trust law enforcement authorities and to testify against their smugglers and traffickers. In this way, trafficking in human beings and smuggling of migrants by sea have been successfully fought against in Rimini (the Rimini Method) and Siracusa (the Siracusan Approach). The Rimini Method has shown that trafficking in human beings for the purpose of sexual exploitation, for example, has been defeated by issuing permanent visas to victims of human trafficking and a programme of integration into Italian society. This integration programme was necessary in order to ensure that victims of human trafficking escaped from the intimidating power of the criminal organisations that victimised them. This is the reason why Article 18 of Legislative Decree 286/1998 does not make the issuing of long-term visas conditional on the victims deciding to co-operate with law enforcement authorities. The same thoughts can be applied to the smuggling of migrants by sea, although in this specific case there is no law that considers the people smuggled by sea as victims. There is Directive 2004/81 on the protection of victims of human trafficking, which was analysed in Chapter 4. However, this directive is ambiguous because it leaves Member States the choice to extend the law on protection of victims of human trafficking to victims of people smuggling. There should be no free choice in the case of smuggling of migrants by sea. This book has demonstrated that they are victims because these people are forced to leave their countries of origins due to their extreme state of poverty. This is the reason they should be considered victims of human trafficking. Chapter 5 of this book explained that there are different degrees of victimisation. Subjection to slavery is one form of victimisation. Trafficking of persons is different from the smuggling of migrants, because people who are the victims of people smuggling are not forced to leave their countries of origin by other people, but by circumstances which do not depend on them. However, these circumstances put these people in a state of vulnerability, thus exposing them to being exploited by criminal organisations which smuggle them by taking advantage of their state of poverty. One must take into consideration the fact that people smuggled by sea often become victims of trafficking, because they must repay the price of their journey. This is the reason why this book has tried to demonstrate that people smuggled by sea need to be protected by the issuing of long-term visas. In order to demonstrate this, it was necessary to travel to Sicily, to the island of Lampedusa and the city of Siracusa. At these locations, research showed that people smuggled by sea are usually from Sub-Saharan Africa, most of them dying during their trip in the desert or on boats from Libya to Italy. Research also showed that the smuggling of migrants by sea is not uncontrollable, as was once wrongly thought. While there are no reliable data on trafficking, there are sufficient data on the smuggling of migrants by sea, specifically data on people smuggling by sea that originates in North Africa and into Sicily. This is why it is believed that this crime should be dealt with following the Siracusan Approach. The Siracusan Approach, which is similar to the Rimini Method, sees public prosecutors, in co-operation with the head of police administration (*questore*) and the IOM, being able to grant long-term visas to people smuggled by sea. These people eventually decided to identify their smugglers to the law enforcement authorities because, by granting them long-term visas, those authorities helped the victims of smuggling to escape the intimidation of organised crime. Unfortunately, the Rimini Method and the Siracusan Approach are not widely applied because the government prefers to expel irregular migrants rather than seeking their help in fighting against the criminal organisations involved in the commission of these two crimes. It is important to point out that the granting of a long-term visa is up to the *questore*, who must answer to the government, and therefore must to follow its directives.

In addition, the UK and Italy, two EU Member States, have not only criminalised irregular migration, but have also created detention centres to house irregular migrants prior to deportation, overlooking the requirement of Article 5(1)(f) ECHR. In these detention centres, irregular migrants are detained without charge, and it has been alleged that their human rights are frequently violated.

British law on human trafficking has been lacking until the ratification of the Council of Europe Convention on Trafficking in Human Beings. This is due to British law's failure to address the crime of human trafficking more broadly. The defect in the approach taken by British law is that it only addresses human trafficking for sexual exploitation, providing shelter to only a limited number of victims. Other categories have been completely neglected. However, progress was made in 2006, when the UK Human Trafficking Centre (UKHTC) was opened in Sheffield, and in 2009, which saw the UK enforcing the Council of Europe Convention against Trafficking.

Italian law is unreasonable because it criminalises irregular migration by applying a pecuniary penalty to people who enter the Italian territory irregularly. By doing this, Italian law does not take into account that those who are smuggled by sea will not be able to afford to pay this penalty. Moreover, it seems that the criminalisation of irregular migrants is either a case of strict liability, which the Italian Constitution only admits for an exclusive list of crimes, or the criminalisation of poverty, as explained in Chapter 5.

Now that the UK has ratified the Council of Europe Convention against Trafficking, it should have a more open approach on the issue. Moreover, the UK should co-operate with other EU Member States in order to contribute to enhancing EU police and judicial co-operation so that an EU criminal judicial area can be constructed. The UK should opt in to all measures on migration to reduce human trafficking and people smuggling. Hopefully, now that the Lisbon Treaty has entered into force, the people of the EU will push their governments to participate in a common policy on immigration. Such a policy would reduce irregular migration, as explained in Chapter 4.

Smuggling of migrants and trafficking in human beings would definitely be defeated if poverty in countries not belonging to the EU was defeated. Smuggling and trafficking are not new crimes. Italians have been victims of these crimes for years. Unfortunately, Italians seem to have forgotten about this. Historically, many Italians were the victims of human trafficking.[1] It is estimated that 80,000 Italian children were the victims of human traffickers in the nineteenth century.[2] Carminello Ada, for example, was an Italian child of five years old who was sold in Italy by his parents to an Italian human trafficker.[3] Subsequently, he went to London by foot to work as a busker, where, according to his Italian 'owner', he did not earn enough.[4] For this reason, his 'owner' tied Carminello's hands and feet, hung him on a wall, and murdered him by biting and beating his body.[5] How many Carminellos will be trafficked from Africa, Eastern Europe or other parts of the world and murdered in the EU today? There are no data on this issue, and while many children may be murdered, the UK does not participate to EU migration measures, because it is worried about losing its sovereignty on migration. Moreover, Italian legislators, by criminalising irregular migration, have forgotten where Italians come from. Italian legislators have forgotten the way Italian migrants were stereotyped abroad. 'Chianti',[6] 'dagoes',[7] 'macaroni'[8] and 'wops'[9] have been the most widespread nicknames for Italian migrants. Italian legislators should have applied a more sensitive law on irregular migration that should have

---

1   See Stella, G.A., *L'Orda. Quando gli albanesi eravamo noi* (Milan: Edizione Rizzoli, 2002), pp. 91–114.

2   See Stella, G.A., and Franzina, E., 'Brutta gente. Il razzismo anti-italiano', in *'L'emigrazione Italiana e gli Stati Uniti. Verso L'America* (Roma: Donzelli Editore, 2005), p. 223.

3   See Stella, *L'Orda*, op. cit. note 1, p. 114.

4   Ibid.

5   Ibid.

6   From the name of the famous wine from Tuscany that for Americans represented all Italian red wines, called 'dago red'; see Stella, *L'Orda*, op. cit. note 1, p. 285.

7   This nickname was widespread in Anglo-Saxon countries and used to stereotype all Latin people, especially Italians. Some say that it stems from 'finally, they go'. Others say that it is derived from 'until the day goes' (in the sense of a day labourer). There are others who think that it stems from Diego, a common Spanish and Mexican name. However, the most likely origin seems to be from 'dagger', because Italians were stereotyped as people who would readily stab others; see Stella, *L'Orda*, *op. cit.* note 1, p. 286.

8   'Pasta eaters'; see ibid., p. 287.

9   'Without passport' or 'without papers'; see ibid., p. 288.

taken into account the main cause of migration: poverty. The reason for doing so is to recognise that in the past, Italians have been discriminated against and criminalised because they emigrated for reasons of poverty.[10] Now the trafficking of Italian persons does not exist any more. The reason for this is because economic conditions in Italy have dramatically improved since the nineteenth century. Therefore, on one hand poverty should be addressed in order to prevent human trafficking and people smuggling, and on the other hand EU police and judicial co-operation should be strengthened. In order to achieve this latter objective, laws aimed at resolving conflicts of jurisdiction should be strengthened at the EU level. The Lisbon Treaty should be welcomed, because it overcomes the concerns of the EU Treaty which did not allow the European Parliament to co-legislate in decision making concerning the areas of freedom, security and justice. There is hope that the ratification of the Lisbon Treaty will facilitate the democratic process in the criminal area and in immigration issues. The Lisbon Treaty will achieve EU integration in the areas of freedom, security and justice.

It could be that one day, the citizens of the EU may consider it ideal to establish a European criminal court, which at the moment is considered by the Commission to be *extrema ratio* ('a last resort'). The establishment of a new criminal court may require Member States to accept limits on their sovereignty. Now that the Lisbon Treaty has entered into force and common rules on suspects and defendants in the EU will be created, Member States may enhance mutual trust in each other's legal systems. This may prove necessary in order to create a new criminal court to deal with conflicts of jurisdiction concerning cross-border crimes, as outlined in Chapter 5. However, if Member States do not trust each other's legal systems, they may be reluctant to comply with the requirements of the EAW Framework Decision, for instance. They may not want to set aside their constitutions in order to apply the EAW Framework Decision. Setting aside national constitutions may be necessary in order to implement third pillar measures that could really support a concrete fight against criminal organisations, such as those that commit smuggling of migrants and trafficking in human beings. However, setting aside national constitutions would mean recognising the EU's supremacy in the criminal area. How can this be achieved if there are no common rules on suspects and defendants? Consequently, one hopes that the Lisbon Treaty will establish these rules. It must be emphasised that at the moment, the application of measures such as the EAW Framework Decision is left to national courts of last resort. Therefore, one hopes that national courts interpret their constitutions broadly, as the Corte di Cassazione did, in order to comply fully with the EAW Framework Decision and other third pillar measures. Now that the Lisbon Treaty has entered into force, it is expected to clarify the relationship between the criminal area and national sovereignty. This will be achieved by including the participation of the European Parliament and national parliaments in decision making procedures involving freedom, security and justice.

---

10   See Stella, *L'Orda*, op. cit. note 1.

Bibliography

Unless indicated otherwise, all URLs cited in the text and this Bibliography were accessible at time of writing (May 2010).

International Sources

Geneva Slavery Convention of 25/9/1926, UN Treaty Series 212.

Convention on the Prevention and Punishment of the Crime of Genocide of 1948, UN Treaty Series 78:277.

Convention for the Protection of Human Rights and Fundamental Freedoms, Rome, 4 November 1950.

Convention Relating to the Status of Refugees Adopted on 28 July 1951 by the United Nations Conference of Plenipotentiaries on the Status of Refugees and Stateless Persons, convened under *General Assembly Resolution 429 (V) of 14 December 1950*, entered into force 22 April 1954, in accordance with Article 43.

United Nations Convention on the Law of the Sea (UNCLOS), Montego Bay, 10 December 1982.

Convention on the Rights of the Child, adopted by General Assembly Resolution 44/25 of 20 November 1989.

Protocol to Prevent, Suppress and Punish Trafficking in Persons, Especially Women and Children, Supplementing the United Nations Convention against Transnational Organized Crime, A/RES/55/25, Doc. A/55/383, 8 January 2001, <http://www.unodc.org/pdf/crime/a_res_55/res5525e.pdf>.

Protocol against the Smuggling of Migrants by Land, Sea and Air, Supplementing the United Nations Convention against Transnational Organized Crime, A/RES/55/25, 8 January 2001, <http://www.unodc.org/pdf/crime/a_res_55/res5525e.pdf>.

United Nations Convention against Transnational Organized Crime, A/RES/55/25, Doc. A/55/383, 8 January 2001, <http://www.unodc.org//pdf/crime/a_res_55/res5525e.pdf>.

Legislative Guide for the Implementation of the Protocol against the Smuggling of Migrants by Land, Sea and Air, Supplementing the United Nations Convention against Transnational Organized Crime, United Nations Centre for International Crime Prevention, 2003.

Legislative Guide for the Implementation of the Protocol to Prevent, Suppress and Punish Trafficking in Persons, Especially Women and Children, Supplementing the United Nations Convention against Transnational Organized Crime,

Global Alliance Against Traffic in Women, 2004, <http://www.unodc.org/pdf/crime/legislative_guides/03%20Legislative%20guide_Trafficking%20in%20Persons%20Protocol.pdf>.

Legislative Guide for the Implementation of the United Nations Convention against Transnational Organized Crime and the Protocol Thereto, United Nations Office on Drugs and Crime, 2004.

Draft Council of Europe Convention on Action against Trafficking in Human Beings, Opinion no. 253 (2005) of the Parliamentary Assembly, <http://assembly.coe.int/Documents/AdoptedText/ta05/EOPI253.htm>.

Council of Europe Convention on Action against Trafficking in Human Beings, CM (2005) 32 Addendum 1 final, 3 May 2005, <http://conventions.coe.int/Treaty/EN/Treaties/Html/197.htm>.

Report of the United Nations International Law Commission, 57th Session, A/60/10, 2005.

The State of Food Insecurity in the World 2005, Food and Agriculture Organization of the United Nations, 2005, <ftp://ftp.fao.org/docrep/fao/008/a0200e/a0200e.pdf>.

World Migration: Cost and Benefits of International Migration, Geneva: International Organization for Migration, 2005.

The State of Food Insecurity in the World 2006, Food and Agriculture Organization of the United Nations, 2006, <http://download.repubblica.it/pdf/FAOSOFI2006.pdf>.

European Sources

Treaties and Conventions

European Convention on Extradition 1957, ETS no. 24, 13 December 1957.

Benelux Treaty on Extradition and Mutual Assistance in Criminal Matters, 616 UNTS 120, 1962.

'Convention Drawn Up on the Basis of Article K.3 of the Treaty on European Union, on Simplified Extradition Procedure between the Member States of the European Union', OJ EU C 78/2, 10 March 1995.

'Convention Based on Article K.3 of the Treaty on European Union, on the Establishment of a European Police Office (Europol Convention)', OJ EU C 316, 27 November 1995.

'Convention Drawn Up on the Basis of Article K.3 of the Treaty on European Union, Relating to Extradition between the Member States of the European Union', OJ EU C 313/12, 23 October 1996.

'Convention on Simplified Extradition Procedure between the Member States of the European Union: Explanatory Report', OJ EU C 375/4, 12 December 1996.

'Convention Relating to Extradition between the Member States of the European Union: Explanatory Report (Text Approved by the Council on 26 May 1997)', OJ EU C 191/13, 23 June 1997.

'Convention of 29 May 2000 Established by the Council in Accordance with Article 34 of the Treaty on European Union, on Mutual Assistance in Criminal Matters between the Member States of the European Union', OJ EU C 197/1, 12 July 2000.

Charter of Fundamental Rights of the European Union, 2000/C 364/01, 18 December 2000.

'Explanatory Report on the Convention of 29 May 2000 on Mutual Assistance in Criminal Matters between the Member States of the European Union', OJ EU C 379/7, 29 December 2000.

'Programme of Measures to implement the Principle of Mutual Judicial Recognition of Decisions in Criminal Matters, 2001/C 12/02', OJ EU C 12/10, 15 January 2001.

'Final Report on the First Evaluation Exercise: Mutual Legal Assistance in Criminal Matters', OJ EU C 216/14, 1 August 2001.

'Council Act of 16 October 2001, Establishing, in Accordance with Article 34 of the Treaty on European Union, the Protocol to the Convention on Mutual Assistance in Criminal Matters between the Member States of the European Union', OJ EU C 326/1, 21 November 2001.

'Protocol Amending the Convention on the Establishment of a European Police Office (Europol Convention) and the Protocol on the Privileges and Immunities of Europol, the Members of its Organs, the Deputy Directors and the Employees of Europol', OJ EU C 312/1, 16 December 2002.

'Consolidated Version of the Treaty Establishing the European Community', OJ EU C 325/33, 24 December 2002.

'Consolidated Version of the Treaty on European Union', OJ EU C 325/1, 24 December 2002.

'Brussels Declaration on Preventing and Combating Trafficking in Human Beings, Council Conclusions of 8 May 2003, 2003/C 137/01', OJ EU C 137/1, 12 June 2003.

'Treaty Establishing the Constitution for Europe 2004', OJ EU C 310/1, 16 December 2004.

Consolidated Version of the Treaty Establishing the European Community, C 321 E/1, 29 December 2006.

'Consolidated Version of the Treaty on European Union and the Treaty on the Functioning of the European Union', OJ EU 2010/C 83/01, 30 March 2010.

European Union Council Documents

'Council Joint Action of 29 November 1996 Establishing an Incentive and Exchange Programme for Persons Responsible for Combating Trade in Human

Beings and the Sexual Exploitation of Children', OJ EU L 322/7, 12 December 1996.

'Council Joint Action of 27 February 1997 Adopted by the Council Concerning Action to Combat Trafficking in Human Beings and Sexual Exploitation of Children', OJ EU L 63/2, 4 March 1997.

'Joint Action of 29 June 1998, 98/428/JHA of 29 June 1998 Adopted by the Council on the Basis of Article K.3 of the Treaty on European Union, on the Creation of a European Judicial Network', OJ EU L 191/4, 7 July 1998.

'Council Act 1999/C 26/03 of 3 November 1998 Laying Down Rules Concerning the Receipt of Information by Europol from Third Parties', OJ EU C 26/17, 30 January 1999.

'Council Act of 12 March 1999 Adopting the Rules Governing the Transmission of Personal Data by Europol to Third States and Third Bodies', OJ EU C 88/1, 30 March 1999.

'The Schengen Acquis: Council Decision 1999/435/EC of 20 May 1999', OJ EU C 176, 10 July 1999.

'Presidency Conclusions of the Tampere European Council', SN 200/99, 15 and 16 October 1999.

'Decision 293/2000/EC of the European Parliament and the Council of 24 January 2000 Adopting a Programme of Community Action (the Daphne Programme) (2000 to 2003) on Preventive Measures to Fight Violence against Children, Young Persons and Women', OJ EU L 34/1, 9 February 2000.

'Council Decision 2000/C 106/01 of 27 March 2000 Authorising the Director of Europol to Enter into Negotiations on Agreements with Third States and Non-EU-related Bodies', OJ EU C 106/1, 13 April 2000.

'Council Decision of 29 May 2000 to Combat Child Pornography on the Internet', OJ EU L 138/1, 9 June 2000.

'Council Recommendation 2000/C 289/13 of 28 September 2000 to Member States in Respect of Requests Made by Europol to Initiate Criminal Investigations in Specific Cases', OJ EU C289/8, 12 October 2000.

'Council Decision 2001/87/EC of 8 December 2000 on the Signing, on Behalf of the European Community of the United Nations Convention against Transnational Organised Crime and its Protocols on Combating Trafficking in Persons, Especially Women and Children, and the Smuggling of Migrants by Land, Air and Sea', OJ EC L 30/44, 1 February 2001.

'Council Directive 2001/40/EC of 28 May 2001 on the Mutual Recognition of Decisions on the Expulsion of Third Country Nationals', OJ EU L 149/34, 2 June 2001.

Laeken European Council of 14 and 15 December 2001.

'Council Decision 2002/187/JHA of 28 February 2002 Setting up Eurojust with a View to Reinforcing the Fight against Serious Crime', OJ EU L 63/1, 6 March 2002.

'Council Framework Decision 2002/584/JHA of 13 June 2002 on the European Arrest Warrant and the Surrender Procedures between Member States', OJ EU L 190/1, 18 July 2002.

'Council Framework Decision 2002/629/JHA of 19 July 2002 on Combating Trafficking in Human Beings', OJ EU L 203/1, 1 August 2002.

'Council Directive 2002/90/EC of 28 November 2002 Defining the Facilitation of Unauthorised Entry, Transit and Residence', OJ EU L 328/17, 5 December 2002.

'Council Framework Decision 2002/946/JHA of 28 November 2002 on the Strengthening of the Penal Framework to Prevent the Facilitation of Unauthorised Entry, Transit and Residence of 28 November 2002', OJ EU L 328/1, 5 December 2002.

'Council Directive 2003/86/EC of 22 September 2003 on the Right of Family Reunification', OJ EC L 251/12, 3 October 2003.

'Council Resolution 2003/C 260/03 of 20 October 2003 on Initiatives to Combat Trafficking in Human Beings, in Particular Women', OJ EU C 260/4, 29 October 2003.

'Council Directive 2003/110/EC of 25 November 2003 on Assistance in Cases of Transit for the Purpose of Removal by Air', OJ EU L 321/26, 6 December 2003.

'Council Framework Decision 2004/68/JHA of 22 December 2003 on Combating the Sexual Exploitation of Children and Child Pornography', OJ EU L 13/44, 20 January 2004.

'Council Directive 2003/109/EC of 25 November 2003 Concerning the Status of Third-country Nationals Who are Long-term Resident', OJ EC 2004 L 16/44, 23 January 2004.

'Council Regulation (EC) No. 377/2004 of 19 February 2004 on the Creation of an Immigration Liaison Officers Network', OJ EU L 64/1, 2 March 2004.

'Regulation (EC) No. 491/2004 of the European Parliament and of the Council of 10 March 2004 Establishing a Programme for Financial and Technical Assistance to Third Countries in the Areas of Migration and Asylum (AENEAS)', OJ EU L 80/1, 13 March 2004.

'Decision 803/2004/EC of the European Parliament and the Council of 21 April 2004 Adopting a Programme of Community Action (2004 to 2008) to Prevent and Combat Violence against Children, Young Persons and Women and to Protect Victims and Groups at Risk (the Daphne II Programme)', OJ EU L 143/1, 30 April 2004.

'Council Decision 2004/512/EC of 8 June 2004 Establishing the Visa Information System (VIS)', OJ EU L 213/5, 15 June 2004.

Eurojust: Co-operation Agreement with the Kingdom of Norway, Council Doc. 11641/04, 23 July 2004.

'Council Decision 2004/573/EC of 29 April 2004 on the Organisation of Joint Flights for Removal from the Territory of Two or More Member States, of

Third-country Nationals Who are Subjects of Individual Removal Orders', OJ EU L 261/28, 6 August 2004.

'Council Directive 2004/81/EC of 29 April 2004 on the Residence Permit Issued to Third-country Nationals Who are Victims of Trafficking in Human Beings or Who Have Been the Subject of an Action to Facilitate Illegal Immigration, Who Cooperate with the Competent Authorities', OJ EU L 261/19, 6 August 2004.

'Council Directive 2004/82/EC of 29 April 2004 on the Obligation of Carriers to Communicate Passenger Data', OJ EU L 261/24, 6 August 2004.

Draft Multiannual Programme: The Hague Programme – Strengthening Freedom, Security and Justice in the European Union, Doc. 13993/04 JAI 408, 27 October 2004.

'Council Regulation (EC) No. 2007/2004 of 26 October 2004 Establishing a European Agency for the Management of Operational Cooperation at the External Borders of the Member States of the European Union', OJ EU L 349/1, 25 November 2004.

'Council Decision 2004/927/EC of 22 December 2004 Providing for Certain Areas Covered by Title IV of Part Three of the Treaty Establishing the European Community to be Governed by the Procedure Laid Down in Article 251 of that Treaty', OJ EU L 396/45, 31 December 2004.

Council and Commission Action Plan Implementing the Hague Programme on Strengthening Freedom, Security and Justice in the European Union, Adopted by the JHA Council of 2 and 3 June 2005, Doc. 9778/2/05 REV 2, 10 June 2005.

Proposal for a Directive of the European Parliament and of the Council on Common Standards and Procedures in Member States for Returning Illegally Staying Third-country Nationals, COM (391) 2005, 1 September 2005.

'Commission Decision 2005/687/EC of 29 September 2005 on the Format for the Report on the Activities of Immigration Liaison Officers Networks and on the Situation in the Host Country in Matters Relating to Illegal Immigration', OJ EU L 264/8, 8 October 2005.

'Regulation (EC) No. 562/2006 of the European Parliament and of the Council of 15 March 2006 Establishing a Community Code on the Rules Governing the Movement of Persons Across Borders (Schengen Borders Code)', OJ EU L 105/1, 13 April 2006.

'Council Regulation (EC) No. 168/2007 of 15 February 2007 Establishing a European Union Agency for Fundamental Rights', OJ EU L 53/1, 22 February 2007.

EU Council Document: Proposal for a Council Framework Decision on Certain Procedural Rights in Criminal Proceedings Throughout the European Union, Doc. 8182/07, 2 April 2007.

'Decision 779/2007/EC of the European Parliament and the Council of 20/6/2007 Establishing for the Period 2007–2013 a Specific Programme to Prevent and Combat Violence against Children, Young People and Women and to Protect

Victims and Groups at Risk (Daphne III Programme) as Part of the General Programme "Fundamental Rights and Justice"', OJ EU L 173/19, 3 July 2007.

'Regulation (EC) No. 863/2007 of the European Parliament and of the Council of 11 July 2007 Establishing a Mechanism for the Creation of Rapid Border Intervention Teams and Amending Council Regulation (EC) No. 2007/2004 as Regards that Mechanism and Regulating the Tasks and Powers of Guest Officers', OJ EU L 199/30, 31 July 2007.

'Regulation (EC) No. 296/2008 of the European Parliament and of the Council of 11 March 2008 Amending Regulation No. 562/2006', OJ EU L 97/60, 9 April 2008.

'Council Framework Decision 2008/909/JHA of 27 November 2008 on the Application of the Principle of Mutual Recognition to Judgments in Criminal Matters Imposing Custodial Sentences or Measures Involving Deprivation of Liberty for the Purpose of their Enforcement in the European Union', OJ EU L 327/27, 5 December 2008.

'Directive 2008/115/EC of the European Parliament and of the Council of 16 December 2008 on Common Standards and Procedures in Member States for Returning Illegally Staying Third-country Nationals', OJ EU L 348/98, 24 December 2008.

'Council Decision 2008/976/JHA of 16 December 2008 on the European Judicial Network', OJ EU L 348/130, 24 December 2008.

'Council Framework Decision 2008/978/JHA of 18 December 2008 on the European Evidence Warrant for the Purpose of Obtaining Objects, Documents and Data for Use in Proceedings in Criminal Matters', OJ EU L 350/72, 30 December 2008.

'Council Framework Decision 2009/299/JHA of 26 February 2009 Amending Framework Decisions 2002/584/JHA, 2005/214/JHA, 2006/783/JHA, 2008/909/JHA and 2008/947/JHA, Thereby Enhancing the Procedural Rights of Persons and Fostering the Application of the Principle of Mutual Recognition to Decisions Rendered in the Absence of the Person Concerned at the Trial', OJ EU L 81/24, 27 March 2009.

'Council Decision 2009/371/JHA of 6 April 2009 Establishing the European Police Office (Europol)', OJ EU L 121/37, 15 May 2009.

European Commission Documents

Communication from the Commission to the Council and the European Parliament on a Community Immigration Policy, COM (2000) 757 final, 22 November 2000.

Communication from the Commission to the Council and the European Parliament on an Open Method of Coordination for the Community Immigration Policy, COM (2001) 387, 11 July 2001.

Proposal for a Council Directive on the Conditions of Entry and Residence of Third-country Nationals for the Purpose of Paid Employment and Self-employed Economic Activities, COM (2001) 386, 11 July 2001.

Communication from the Commission to the Council and the European Parliament on a Common Policy on Illegal Immigration, COM (2001) 672 final, 15 November 2001.

Green Paper on Criminal-law Protection of the Financial Interests of the Community and the Establishment of a European Prosecutor, COM (2001) 715 final, 11 December 2001.

Proposal for a Council Directive on the Short-term Residence Permit Issued to Victims of Action to Facilitate Illegal Immigration or Trafficking in Human Beings Who Cooperate with the Competent Authorities, COM (2002) 71 final, 11 February 2002.

Green Paper on a Community Return Policy on Illegal Residents, COM (2001) 672 final, 10 April 2002.

Communication from the Commission to the Council and the European Parliament: Towards Integrated Management of the External Borders of the Member States of the European Union, COM (2002) 233 final, 7 May 2002.

'Proposal for a Comprehensive Plan to Combat Illegal Immigration and Trafficking in Human Beings in the European Union', OJ EU C142/23, 14 June 2002.

Communication from the Commission to the Council and the European Parliament: Integrating Immigration Issues in the European Union's Relations with Third Countries, COM (2002) 703, 3 December 2002.

Communication from the Commission to the Council and the European Parliament. Wider Europe-Neighbourhood: A New Framework for Relations with our Eastern and Southern Neighbours, COM (2003) 104, 11 March 2003.

Communication from the Commission to the Council, the European Parliament, the European Economic and Social Committee and the Committee of the Regions on Immigration, Integration and Employment, COM (2003) 336, 3 June 2003.

Communication from the Commission to the European Parliament and the Council in View of the European Council of Thessaloniki on the Development of a Common Policy on Illegal Immigration, Smuggling and Trafficking in Human Beings, External Borders and the Return of Illegal Residents, COM (2003) 323 final, 3 June 2003.

Proposal for a Council Decision on the Conclusion, on Behalf of the European Community, of the United Nations Convention against Transnational Organized Crime, 2003/0195 (CNS) COM (2003) 512 final, 28 August 2003.

Proposal for a Council Framework Decision on the European Evidence Warrant for Obtaining Objects, Documents and Data for Use in Proceedings in Criminal Matters, COM (2003) 688, 14 November 2003.

Proposal for a Council Framework Decision on Certain Procedural Rights in Criminal Proceedings throughout the European Union, COM (2004) 328, 28 April 2004.

Communication from the Commission. European Neighbourhood Policy: Strategy Paper, COM (2004) 373 final, 12 May 2004.

Communication from the Commission to the Council and the European Parliament. Area of Freedom, Security and Justice: Assessment of the Tampere Programme and Future Orientations, COM (2004) 401, 2 June 2004.

Communication from the Commission to the Council, the European Parliament, the European Economic and Social Committee and the Committee of the Regions: First Annual Report on Migration and Integration, COM (2004) 508, 16 July 2004.

Green Paper on Mutual Recognition of Non-custodial Pre-trial Supervision Measures, COM (2004) 562, 17 August 2004.

Proposal for a Regulation of the European Parliament and of the Council Laying Down General Provisions Establishing a European Neighbourhood and Partnership Instrument, COM (2004) 628 final, 29 September 2004.

Commission Staff Working Paper: Annual Report on the Development of a Common Policy on Illegal Immigration, Smuggling and Trafficking of Human Beings, External Borders, and the Return of Illegal Residents, SEC (1349) 2004, 25 October 2004.

Green Paper on an EU Approach to Managing Economic Migration, COM (2004) 811, 11 January 2005.

Communication from the Commission to the Council and the European Parliament: Communication on the Mutual Recognition of Judicial Decisions in Criminal Matters and the Strengthening of Mutual Trust between Member States, COM (2005) 195, 19 May 2005.

Council and Commission Action Plan Implementing the Hague Programme on Strengthening Freedom, Security and Justice in the European Union, Adopted by the JHA Council of 2 and 3 June 2005, Doc. 9778/2/05 REV 2, 10 June 2005.

Communication from the Commission to the Council on the Monitoring and Evaluation Mechanism of the Third Countries in the Field of the Fight against Illegal Immigration, COM (2005) 352, 28 July 2005.

Proposal for a Directive of the European Parliament and of the Council on Common Standards and Procedures in Member States for Returning Illegally Staying Third-country Nationals, COM (391) 2005, 1 September 2005.

Proposal for a Council Framework Decision on the Protection of Personal Data Processed in the Framework Police and Judicial Cooperation in Criminal Matters, COM (2005) final, 4 October 2005.

'Commission Decision of 29 September 2005 on the Format for the Report on the Activities of Immigration Liaison Officers Networks and on the Situation in the Host Country in Matters Relating to Illegal Immigration', OJ EU L 264/8, 8 October 2005.

Fighting Trafficking in Human Beings: An Integrated Approach and Proposals for an Action Plan, COM (2005) 514 final, 18 October 2005.

Communication from the Commission to the European Parliament and the Council on the Implications of the Court's Judgment of 13 September 2005 (Case C-176/03 Commission *v.* Council*)*, COM (2005) 583 final/2, 24 November 2005.

Communication from the Commission to the European Parliament and the Council on the Implications of the Court's Judgment of 13 September 2005, COM (2005) 583 final/2, 24 November 2005.

Communication from the Commission: Policy Plan on Legal Migration, COM (2005) 669, 21 December 2005.

Green Paper On Conflicts of Jurisdiction and the Principle of Ne Bis in Idem in Criminal Proceedings, COM (2005) 696, 23 December 2005.

Commission Staff Working Document: Annex to the Green Paper on Conflicts of Jurisdiction and the Principle of Ne Bis in Idem in Criminal Proceedings, SEC (2005) 1767, 23 December 2005.

European Neighbourhood and Partnership Instrument (ENPI): Regional Strategy Paper (2007–2013) and Regional Indicative Programme (2007–2010) for the Euro-Mediterranean Partnership, EUROMED.

'Speech by Benita Ferrero-Waldner, European Commissioner for External Relations and European Neighbourhood Policy on "Combating Trafficking in Human Beings": The EU's Response', 17 March 2006, <http://www.osce.org/item/18396.html>.

'Withdrawal of Commission Proposals Following Screening for their General Relevance, their Impact on Competitiveness and Other Aspects', OJ EU C 64/3, 17 March 2006.

Green Paper on the Presumption of Innocence, COM (2006) 174, 26 April 2006.

Report from the Commission to the Council and the European Parliament Based on Article 10 of the Council Framework Decision of 19 July 2002 on Combating Trafficking in Human Beings, COM (2006) 187 final, 2 May 2006.

Proposal for a Council Framework Decision on the European Evidence Warrant (EEW) for Obtaining Objects, Documents and Data for Use in Proceedings in Criminal Matters, Council Doc. 11235/06, 10 July 2006.

Proposal for a Regulation of the European Parliament and of the Council Establishing a Mechanism for the Creation of Rapid Border Intervention Teams and Amending Council Regulation (EC) No. 2007/2004 as Regards the Mechanism, COM (2006) 401, 19 July 2006.

Proposal for a Council Framework Decision on the European Supervision Order in Pre-trial Procedures between Member States of the European Union, COM (2006) 468, 29 August 2006.

Proposal for a Council Decision Establishing the European Police Office (EUROPOL), COM (2006), 817, 20 December 2006.

Opinion of the Joint Supervisory Body of Europol (Opinion 07/07) with Respect to the Proposal for a Council Decision Establishing the European Police Office (Europol), 5 March 2007.

Communication from the Commission to the Council and the European Parliament on the Role of Eurojust and the European Judicial Network in the Fight against Organized Crime and Terrorism in the European Union, COM (2007) 644, 23 October 2007.

Communication from the Commission to the European Parliament, the Council, the European Economic and Social Committee and the Committee of Regions: Towards a Common Immigration Policy, COM (2007) 780, 5 December 2007.

European Parliament Report with a Proposal for a European Parliament Recommendation to the Council on Development of an EU Criminal Justice Area (2009/2012 (INI)), A6-0262/-2009, 8 April 2009.

Other EU Sources

'Information Concerning the Date of Entry into Force of the Treaty of Amsterdam, 1999/C 120/13', OJ EU C 120/24, 1 May 1999.

Europol Annual Report 2004, <http://www.aretusa.net/download/centro%20documentazione/02documenti/4-orga/internazionali/D-04-INT-17en.pdf>.

Eurojust Annual Report 2004, <http://www.eurojust.europa.eu/press_releases/annual_reports/2004/Annual_Report_2004_EN.pdf>.

'Act of the Joint Supervisory Body of Eurojust of 2 March 2004 Laying Down its Rules of Procedure', OJ EU C 86/1, 6 April 2004.

Eurojust Annual Report 2005, <http://www.libertysecurity.org/article1509.html>.

'Trafficking in Human Beings for Sexual Exploitation in the EU: A Europol Perspective', <http://www.europol.eu.int/publications/SeriousCrimeOverviews/2005/THB_factsheet.pdf>, accessed 12 December 2005.

Barcelona Declaration Adopted at the Euro-Mediterranean Conference of 27– 28/11 1995, <http://ec.europa.eu/comm/external_relations/euromed/bd.htm>, accessed 21 June 2006.

The Policy: What is the European Neighbourhood Policy?, <http://ec.europa.eu/comm/world/enp/policy_en.htm>.

Europol Annual Report 2006, <http://www.europol.europa.eu/publications/Annual_Reports/EuropolAnnualReport2006.pdf>.

Europol Annual Report 2007, <http://www.europol.europa.eu/publications/Annual_Reports/Annual%20Report%202007.pdf>.

Europol Annual Report 2008, <http://www.europol.europa.eu/publications/Annual_Reports/Annual%20Report%202008.pdf>.

'Strategic Agreement between the European Agency for the Management of Operational Cooperation at the External Borders of the Member States of the European Union', <http://www.europol.europa.eu/legal/agreements/Agreements/Strategic%20cooperation%20agreement%20Frontex.pdf>.

'The Treaty of Lisbon and the Court of Justice of the European Union', Court of
   Justice of the European Communities, Press Release No. 104/09, 30 November
   2009, <http://europa.eu/rapid/pressReleasesAction.do?reference=CJE/09/
   104&format=HTML&aged=0&language=EN&guiLanguage=en>.

The Court of Strasbourg's Jurisprudence

Colozza v. *Italy* (1985) 13 EHRR 516.
Salabiaku v. *France* (1988) 13 EHRR 379.
Soering v. *United Kingdom* (1989) 11 EHRR 439.
Barberà, Messegué and Jabardo v. *Spain* (1989) 11 EHRR 360.
Moustaquim v. *Belgium* (1991) 13 EHRR 802.
Tomasi v. *France* (1992) 15 EHRR 1.
Kemmache v. *France*, judgment of 24 November 1994, Series A no. 296-C.
Chahal v. *United Kingdom* (1996) 23 EHRR 413.
Murray v. *UK* (1996) 22 EHRR 29.
H.L.R. v. *France* (1997) ECHR 23.
Berrehab v. *The Netherlands* (1998) EHRR 138.
Witold Litwa v. *Poland*, no. 26629/95, ECHR 2000-III.
Einhorn v. *France*, Application no. 71555/01, 16 October 2001 (unreported).
Krombach v. *France* (2001) ECHR 88.
Medenica v. *Switzerland* (2001) ECHR 395.
Conka v. *Belgium* 51564/99 (2002) ECHR 14.
Slivenko v. *Latvia* (2003) ECHR 2002-II.
Smirnova v. *Russia* (2003) 8.
Saadi v. *United Kingdom*, Application no. 13229/03.
Somogyi v. *Italy* (2004) ECHR 203.
Siliadin v. *France* (2005), European Court of Human Rights, Ser. A no.
   73316/05.
Stoichkov v. *Bulgaria* (2005) ECHR 186.
Sejdovic v. *Italy* [GC], ECHR (2006).

The Court of Justice of the European Communities' Jurisprudence

Case 26/62 *Van Gend & Loos* [1963] ECR 1.
Case 35/76 *Simmenthal* v. *Italian Minister for Finance* [1976] ECR 1871.
Case 50/76 *Amsterdam Bulb* [1977] ECR 137.
Case C 106/77 *Simmenthal* [1978] ECR 629.
Case 203/80 *Casati* [1981] ECR 2595.
Case 231/83 *Cullet* [1985] ECR 305.
Case 294/83 *Parti écologiste 'Les Verts'* v. *European Parliament* [1986] ECR
   1339.

Case C-80/86 *Kolpinghuis Nijmegen* [1987] ECR 3969.

Case 68/88 *Commission* v. *Greece* [1989] ECR 2965.

Case C-299/86 *Drexl* [1988] ECR 1213.

Case C-2/88 *Zwartveld and Others* [1990] ECR I-3365.

Case C-70/88 *European Parliament* v. *Council of the European Communities (Chernobyl)* [1990] ECR I-2041.

Joined Cases C-6/90 and C-9/90 *Andrea Francovich and Others, Danila Bonifaci and Others* v. *Italian Republic ECR* [1991] I-5357.

Case 1/91 *Draft Treaty on a European Economic Area* [1991] ECR I-6079.

Case C-300/89 *Commission of the European Communities* v. *Council of the European Communities* [1991] ECR I-2867.

Joined Cases C-13/91 and C-113/91 *Debus* [1992] ECR I-3617.

Joined Cases C-358/93 and C-416/93 *Bordessa and Others* [1995] ECR I-361.

Case C-265/95 *Commission* v. *France* [1997] ECR I-6959.

Case C-175/97 *Commission* v. *France* [1998] ECR I-963.

Joined Cases C-10/97 to C-22/97 *IN. CO. GE'90 and Others* [1998] ECR I-6307.

Case C-226/97 *Lemmens* [1998] ECR I-3711.

Case C-109/01 *Secretary of State for Home Department* v. *Hacene Akrich* [2003] ECR I-09607.

Case C-186/98 *Nunes and de Matos* [1999] ECR I-4883.

Case C-201/02 *Wells* [2004] ECR I-723.

Joined Cases C-187 and 385/01 *Gozutoc and Brugge* [2003] ECR I-1345.

Case T-338/02 *Segi and Others* [2004] ECR II-1647.

Case C-105/03 *Criminal proceedings against Maria Pupino* [2005] 2 CMLR 63.

Case C-160/03 *Spain* v. *Eurojust* [2005] ECR I-2077.

Case C-176/03 *Commission* v. *Council* [2005] ECR I-7879.

Case C-469/03 *Miraglia* [2005] ECR I-2009.

Joined Cases C-465/02 and 466/02 *Germany and Denmark* v. *Commission* [2005] ECR I-0000.

Case C-436/04 *Van Esbroeck* [2006] ECR I-2333.

Case 467/04 *Gasparini* [2006] ECR I-0000.

Case C-150/05 *Van Straaten* [2006] ECR I-0000.

Case C-540/03 *Parliament* v. *Council* [2006] ECR I-5769.

Case T-228/02 *OMPI* v. *Council* [2006] ECR II-4665.

Cases C-354/04 P *Gestoras Pro Amnistía and Others* v. *Council* [2007] ECR I-1579.

Case C-355/04 P *Segi and Others* v. *Council* [2007] ECR I-1657.

Case C-303/05 *Advocaten voor de Wereld VZW* v. *Leden van de Ministerraad* [2007] ECR I-3633.

Case C-288/05 *Kretzinger* [2007] ECR I-6441.

Case C-367/05 *Kraaijenbrink* [2007] ECR I-6619.

Case C-357/09 PPU *Kadzoev*, judgment of 30 November 2009, not yet reported.

British Primary Sources

Sexual Offences Act 1956.
Immigration Act 1971.
Police and Criminal Evidence Act 1984.
Prosecution of Offences Act 1985.
Nationality Immigration and Asylum Act 2002.
Immigration Rules (HC 395).
Extradition Act 2003.
Crime (International Co-operation) Act 2003.
Criminal Justice Act 2003.
Sexual Offences Act 2003.
Asylum and Immigration (Treatment of Claimants, etc.) Act 2004.
Serious Organised Crime and Police Act 2005.
Terrorism Act 2006.
Asylum and Immigration Act 2006.
Borders, Citizenship and Immigration Act 2009, ch. 11.
Explanatory Note of Borders, Citizenship and Immigration Act 2009, ch. 11.
House of Lords Select Committee on the European Union, *Europol's Role in Fighting Crime*, Session 2002–2003, 5th Report, HL 43, 28 January 2003.
House of Lords Select Committee on the European Union, *The Future Role of the European Court of Justice*, Session 2003–2004, 6th Report, HL 47, Minutes of Evidence.
House of Lords Select Committee on the European Union, *Judicial Cooperation in the EU: The Role of Eurojust*, 23rd Report, HL 138, 21 July 2004.
International Organization for Migration (IOM), *Voluntary Assisted Return and Reintegration Programme: VARRP. Reintegration Self-evaluation Results*, June 2004.
The Criminal Law Competence of the EC: Follow-up Report, Session 2006–2007, 11th Report, HL 63, Minutes of Evidence.
House of Lords and House of Commons Joint Committee on Human Rights, *Human Trafficking*, Session 2005–2006, 26th Report, HL 245-I and HC 1127-I, 13 October 2006.
House of Lords and House of Commons Joint Committee on Human Rights, *The Treatment of Asylum Seekers*, Session 2006–2007, 10th Report, HL 81 and HC 60-I, *Volume I: Report and Report and Formal Minutes*.
House of Lords Select Committee on the European Union, *Europol: Coordinating the Fight against Serious and Organized Crime*, Session 2007–2008, 12 November 2008.

British Jurisprudence

R v. *El-Hakkaoui* [1975] 1 WLR.

Secretary of State for Trade v. *Markus* [1976] AC 35.

Kakis v. *Government of Cyprus* [1978] 1 WLR 779, 782.

R v. *Governor of Pentonville Prison ex p Tarling* [1979] 1 WLR 1417.

R v. *Governor of Durham Prison ex p Hardial Singh* [1984] 1 WLR 704.

Privy Council in Tan Te Lam v. *Superintendent of Tai A Chau Detention Centre* [1997] AC 97.

Re Davies [1998] COD 30.

Shah and Islam [1999] INLR 144.

Secretary of State for the Home Department v. *Lyudmila Dzygun (Immigration Appeal Tribunal)*, Appeal no. CC-50627-99 (00TH00728), 13 April 2000.

A. v. *Secretary of State for the Home Department* [2005] 2 WLR 87.

Office of the King's Prosecutor, Brussels v. *Armas and Others* [2005] 3 WLR 1079.

Opinions of the Lords of Appeal for Judgement in the Cause Dabas (Appellant) v. *High Court of Justice, Madrid (Respondent) (Criminal Appeal for Her Majesty's High Court of Justice)* [2007] UKHL 6.

Italian Primary Sources

'Codice Penale. R.D.N. 1398, 19/10/1930', *Gazzetta Ufficiale* no. 251, 26 October 1930.

'Costituzione della Repubblica Italiana', *Gazzetta Ufficiale* no. 298, 27 December 1947, Edizione Straordinaria.

Act 75/1958, 'Abolizione della regolamentazione della prostituzione e lotta contro lo sfruttamento della prostituzione altrui', *Gazzetta Ufficiale* no. 55, 4 March 1958.

Codice di Procedura Penale, Decreto del Presidente della Repubblica no. 447, 22 September 1988.

Act of 6 March 1998, 'Disciplina dell'immigrazione e norme sulla condizione dello straniero', *Gazzetta Ufficiale* no. 59, 12 March 1998 no. 40. Law 30 December 1986, no. 943, 'Norme in materia di collocamento e di trattamento dei lavoratori extracomunitari immigrati e contro le immigrazioni clandestine', *Gazzetta Ufficiale* no. 8, 12 January 1987.

Legislative Decree 25 July 1998, no. 286, 'Testo unico delle disposizioni concernenti la disciplina dell'immigrazione e norme sulla condizione dello straniero', *Gazzetta Ufficiale* no. 191, 18 August 1998, Suppl. Ord. no. 139.

Act of 7 June 2002, no. 106, 'Conversione in legge, con modificazioni, del decreto-legge 4 aprile 2002, no. 51, concernente disposizioni urgenti recanti misure di contrasto all'immigrazione clandestine e garanzie per soggetti colpiti da provvedimenti di accompagnamento alla frontiera', *Gazzetta Ufficiale* no. 133, 8 June 2002, <http://www.parlamento.it/parlam/leggi/02106l.htm>.

Act of 30 July 2002, no. 189, 'Modifica alla normativa in materia di immigrazione e di asilo', *Gazzetta Ufficiale* no. 199, 26 August 2002, Supplemento ordinario, <http://www.parlamento.it/parlam/leggi/021891.htm>.

Act 228/2003, 'Misure contro la tratta di persone', *Gazzetta Ufficiale* no. 195, 23 August 2003.

Law Decree of 14 September 2004, no 241, 'Disposizioni urgenti in materia di immigrazione', *Gazzetta Ufficiale* no. 216.

'Decree of Conversion in Law no. 271/2004', *Gazzetta Ufficiale* no. 267, 14 November 2004.

Act no. 69, 'Disposizioni per conformare il diritto interno alla decisione quadro 2002/584/GAI del Consiglio, del 13 giugno 2002, relative al mandato d'arresto europeo e alle procedure di consegna tra gli Stati membri', *Gazzetta Ufficiale* no. 98, 29 April 2005.

Rapporto Annuale 2005 sullo 'stato della sicurezza in Italia', 14 August 2005, <http://www.interno.it//assets/files/&/20058141464>, accessed 23 March 2007.

Legge 15 July 2009, no. 94, 'Disposizioni in material di sicurezza pubblica', *Gazzetta Ufficiale* no. 170, 25 July 2009, Supplemento ordinario no. 128.

Italian Jurisprudence

Cass. Sez. III *Gius. Pen.* 1962, II 81, m. 68.

Cass. Pen. Sez. 2 sent. 7051, 16 July 1981 rv. 149797.

Cass Pen. Sez. 1 sent 4216, 24 May 1986 rv. 172803.

Cass. Pen. Sez. 6 sent. 7455, 26 June 1992, rv. 190897.

Cass. Pen. Sez 6 sent. 10721, 12 October 1998 rv. 211741.

Tribunale di Roma, 15 February 2001, <http://eugius.supereva.it/sentenza_anticopyright.htm>, accessed 16 June 2005.

Cass. Pen. Sez. 1 sent. 21, 7 January 2003, rv. 223024.

Cass. Pen. Sez. 6 sent. 96, 8 January 2003 rv. 223007.

Cass. Pen. 28 July 2003 no. 31739, rv. 226201.

Judgment of the Italian Constitutional Court no. 5, GU, 13 January 2004.

Judgment of the Italian Constitutional Court no. 222, 'Sentenza 8–15 luglio 2004', GU no. 28, 21 July 2004.

Cass. Pen. Sez. 6, sent. 81, 4 January 2005, rv. 230777.

Cass. Sez. III sent. 3368/2005, 16 April 2005.

Cass. Pen, Sez. 6, sent. 16542, 15 May 2006 (ud. 8 May 2006).

Cass. Pen, Sez. unite, sent. 4614/2007, 5 February 2007.

Request of Declaration of Inconstitutionality Requested by the Tribunale di Pesaro – Sezione Penale, RNR 2823/09, RG TRIB 829/09, 31 August 2009.

Questione di legittimità costituzionale dell'art. 10 bis D.L.vo n. 286/98 come introdotto dall'art. 1 co. 16 Legge 15 luglio 2009, no. 94 in relazione agli artt.

2, 3 co. 1 e 25 co. 2 Cost, Public Prosecution Office of Turin, 15 September 2009.

Secondary Sources

Books

Alegre, S., and Leaf, M., *European Arrest Warrant: A Solution Ahead of its Time*, London: JUSTICE, 2003.

Ashworth, A., and Redmayne, M., *The Criminal Law Process*, 3rd edn, Oxford: Oxford University Press, 2005.

Bade, K.J., *Legal and Illegal Immigration into Europe: Experiences and Challenges*, Ortelius-lezing, 2003.

Benzi, O., *Prostitute. Vi Passeranno Davanti Nel Regno Dei Cieli*, Milan: Arnoldo Mondatori Editore, 2001.

Blake, N., and Husain, R., *Immigration, Asylum and Human Rights*, Oxford: Oxford University Press, 2003.

Conso, G., and Grevi, V., *Profili del Nuovo Codice di Procedura Penale*, Padova: CEDAM, 1993.

Delmas-Marty, M., and Vervaele, J.A.E., *The Implementation of the Corpus Juris in the Member States*, Mortsel: Intersentia, 2000.

Di Nicola, A., 'Trafficking in Human Beings and Smuggling of Migrants', in Reichel, P., ed., *Handbook of Transnational Crime and Justice*, London: Sage Publications, 2005, pp. 181–203.

Falcone, G., *Cose di Cosa Nostra*, RCS Rizzoli Libri, 1991.

Fijnaut, C., 'Police Co-operation and the Area of Freedom, Security and Justice', in Walker, N., ed., *Europe's Area of Freedom, Security and Justice*, Oxford: Oxford University Press, 2004, pp. 241–82,.

Hailbronner, K., 'Asylum Law in the context of a European Migration Policy', in Walker, N., ed., *Europe's Area of Freedom, Security and Justice*, Oxford: Oxford University Press, 2004, pp. 41–88.

Hirst, M., *Jurisdiction and the Ambit of the Criminal Law*, Oxford: Oxford University Press, 2003.

Joutsen, M., 'International Instruments on Cooperation in Responding to Transnational Crime', in Reichel, P., ed., *Handbook of Transnational Crime and Justice*, London: Sage Publications, 2004.

Knowles, B., *Blackstone's Guide to the Extradition Act 2003*, Oxford: Oxford University Press, 2004.

Lonbay, J., 'Free Movement of Persons in the European Union: The Legal Framework', in Arnull, A., ed., *Accountability and Legitimacy in the European Union*, Oxford: Oxford University Press, 2002, pp. 437–52.

Mantovani, F., *Diritto Penale*, Padova: CEDAM, 1992.

Pastore, E., 'Visas, Borders, Immigration: Formation, Structure, and Current Evolution of the EU Entry Control System', in Walker, N., ed., *Europe's Area of Freedom, Security and Justice*, Oxford: Oxford University Press, 2004, pp. 89–142.

Peers, S., 'Family Reunion and Community Law', in Walker, N., ed., *Europe's Area of Freedom, Security and Justice*, Oxford: Oxford University Press, 2004, pp. 143–97.

Peers, S., *EU Justice and Home Affairs*, Harlow: Pearson Education, 2000.

Peers, S., 'Statewatch Analysis: Transferring the Third Pillar', *Statewatch*, May 2006, <http://www.statewatch.org/news/2006/may/analysis-3rd-pill-transfer-may-2006.pdf>.

Peers, S., *EU Justice and Home Affairs Law*, Oxford: Oxford University Press, 2006.

Peers, S., 'Statewatch Analysis: EU Reform Treaty Analysis 1: JHA Provisions', *Statewatch*, 2 August 2007, <http://www.statewatch.org/news/2007/aug/eu-reform-treaty-jha-analysis-1.pdf>.

Peers, S., 'Statewatch Analysis: The EU's JHA Agenda for 2009', *Statewatch*, 2009, <http://www.statewatch.org/analyses/eu-sw-analysis-2009-jha-agenda.pdf>.

Richards, S., Steel, M., and Singer, D., *Hope Betrayed: An Analysis of Women Victims of Trafficking and their Claims for Asylum*, London: Eaves-Poppy Project, 2006.

Ryan, B., 'The United Kingdom', in Higgins, I., and Hailbronner K., eds, *Migration and Asylum Law and Policy in the European Union*, Cambridge: Cambridge University Press, 2004, pp. 431–54.

Sanders, A., and Young, R., *Criminal Justice*, 2nd edn, Oxford: Oxford University Press, 2005.

Stella, G.A., *L'Orda. Quando gli albanesi eravamo noi*, Milan: Edizione Rizzoli, 2002.

Stella, G.A., and Franzina, E., 'Brutta gente. Il razzismo anti-italiano', in *'L'emigrazione Italiana e gli Stati Uniti. Verso L'America*, Roma: Donzelli Editore, 2005, pp. 213–41.

Stille, A., *Excellent Cadavers: The Mafia and the Death of the First Italian Republic*, New York: Vintage, 2006.

Van Den Wyngaert, C., 'Eurojust and the European Public Prosecutor in the *Corpus Juris* Model: Water and Fire?', in Walker, N., ed., *Europe's Area of Freedom, Security and Justice*, Oxford: Oxford University Press, 2004, pp. 201–39.

Varese, F., *The Russian Mafia: Private Protection in a New Market Economy*, Oxford: Oxford University Press, 2001.

Legal Journal Articles

Albrecht, H.J., 'Fortress Europe? – Controlling Illegal Immigration' *European Journal of Crime, Criminal Law and Criminal Justice* 10:1 (2002): 1–22.

Alegre, S., and Leaf, M., 'Mutual Recognition in European Judicial Cooperation: A Step Too Far Too Soon? Case Study – the European Arrest Warrant', *European Law Journal* 10:2 (2004): 200–217.

Arnull, A., 'From Bit Part to Starring Role? The Court of Justice and Europe's Constitutional Treaty', *Yearbook of European Law* 24 (2005): 1–25.

Bagaric, M., and Morss, J., 'State Sovereignty and Migration Control: The Ultimate Act of Discrimination?', *Journal of Migration and Refugee Issues* 1 (2005) 1: 1–26.

Bhabha, J., and Zard, M., 'Smuggled or Trafficked', *Forced Migration Review* 25 (May 2006): 6–8.

Bhabha, J., and Zard, M., 'Human Smuggling and Trafficking: The Good, the Bad and the Ugly', <http://www.fmreview.org/pdf/bhabha&zard.pdf>, accessed 6 May 2007.

Brinkmann, G., 'The Immigration and Asylum Agenda' *European Law Journal* 10:2 (2004): 190–91.

Cholewinski, R., 'The Need for Effective Individual Legal Protection in Immigration Matters', *European Journal of Migration and Law* 7:3 (2005): pp. 237–62.

Corstens, G.J.M., 'Criminal Law in the First Pillar?', *European Journal of Crime, Criminal Law and Criminal Justice* 11:1 (2003): 131–44.

Deen-Racsmany, Z., and Blekxtoon, R., 'The Decline of the Nationality Exception in European Extradition?', *European Journal of Crime, Criminal Law and Criminal Justice* 13:3 (2005): 5–36 and 317–63.

Douglass-Scott, S., 'The Rule of Law in the European Union: Putting the Security into the "Area of Freedom, Security and Justice"', *European Law Review* 29:2 (2004): 219–42.

Emiliou, N., 'Subsidiary: An Effective Barrier Against "the Enterprises of Ambition?"', *European Law Review* 17 (1992): 383–407.

'Esposto alla Commissione europea, al Comitato ONU per i diritti umani, al Commissario europeo per i diritti umani presso il Consiglio d'Europa, May–June 2009', *Diritto, Immigrazione e Cittadinanza* 11:3 (2009): 266–77.

Harding, C., 'The Offence of Belonging: Capturing Participation in Organised Crime', *Criminal Law Review* (2005): 690–700.

Jimeno-Bulnes, M., 'European Judicial Cooperation in Criminal Matters', *European Law Journal* 9:5 (2003): 614–30.

Lenaerts, K., and Corthaut, T., 'Of Birds and Hedges: The Role of Primacy in Invoking Norms of EU law', *European Law Review* 31:3 (2006): 287–315.

Obokata, T., 'Smuggling of Human Beings from a Human Rights Perspective: Obligations of Non-State and State Actors under International Human Rights Law', *International Journal of Refugee Law* 7:2 (2005): 394–415.

Obokata, T., 'Trafficking of Human Beings as a Crime against Humanity: Some Implications for the International Legal System', *International and Comparative Law Quarterly* 54:2 (2005): 445–57.

Pacurar, A., 'Smuggling, Detention and Expulsion of Irregular Migrants A Study on International Legal Norms, Standards and Practices', *European Journal of Migration and Law* 5 (2003): 259–83.

Papagianni, G., 'Free Movements of Persons in the Light of the New Title IV TEC: From Inter-governmentalism towards a Community Policy', *Yearbook of European Union* 21 (2001–2002): 107–62.

Peers, S., 'Implementing Equality? The Directive on Long Term Resident Third Country Nationals', *European Law Review* 29:4 (2004): 442.

Peers, S., 'Mutual recognition and Criminal Law in the European Union: Has the Council Got it Wrong?', *Common Market Law Review* (2004): 5–36.

Peers, S., 'Readmission Agreements and EC External Migration Law', *Statewatch* 17, <http://www.statewatch.org/news/2003/may/readmission.pdf>, accessed 14 June 2005.

Peers, S., 'Rights of Criminal Suspects and EU Law', *Statewatch*, <http://www.statewatch.org/news/2007/apr/Statewatch-analysis-crim-proced.pdf>.

Peers, S., 'Salvation Outside the Church: Judicial Protection in the Third Pillar after the *Pupino* and *Segi* Judgements', *Common Market Law Review* 44 (2007): 883–929.

Peers, S., 'Statewatch Briefing: Vetoes, Opts-out and EU Immigration and Asylum Law', *Statewatch*, revised version, 23 December 2004, <http://www.statewatch.org/news/2004/dec/eu-immg-opt-outs3.pdf>, accessed 4 May 2005.

Peers, S., 'The Future of the EU Judicial System and EC Immigration and Asylum Law', *European Journal of Migration and Law* 7:3 (2005): 263–74.

Peers, S., 'Transferring the Third Pillar', Statewatch, <http://www.statewatch.org/news/2006/may/analysis-3rd-pill-transfer-may-2006.pdf>, accessed 15 May 2006.

Plachta, M., 'European Arrest Warrant: Revolution in Extradition?', *European Journal of Crime, Criminal Law and Criminal Justice* 11:2 (2003): 178–94.

Rogers, N., 'Immigration and the European Convention on Human Rights: Are New Principles Emerging?', *European Human Rights Law Review* 8:1 (2003): 53–64.

Smartt, U., 'Human Trafficking: Simply a European Problem?', *European Journal of Crime, Criminal Law and Criminal Justice* 11:2 (2003): 164–77.

Vassallo Paleologo, F., 'Obblighi di protezione e controlli delle frontiere marittime', *Diritto Immigrazione e Cittadinanza* 9:3 (2007).

Waismer, M., 'The "Battle of the Pillars": Does the European Community Have the Power to Approximate National Criminal Laws?', *European Law Review* 29:5 (2004): 613–35.

Weyembergh, A., 'Approximation of Criminal Laws, the Constitutional Treaty and the Hague Programme', *Common Market Law Review* 42:6 (2005): 1,592.

Other Articles

Adepoju, A., 'Review on Research and Data on Human Trafficking in Sub-Saharan Africa', in Laczko, F., and Gozdziak, E., eds, *Data and Research on Human Trafficking: A Global Survey*, Geneva: International Organization for Migration, 2005, pp. 76–98.

'Barcone disperso al largo di Linosa "Ho visto buttare al largo sei corpi"', *La Repubblica*, 4 August 2005, <http://www.repubblica.it/2005/e/sezioni/cronaca/sbarchinuovi/lampe168/lampe168.html>.

'Circeo, Ghira è morto 11 anni fa scoperta la tomba a Melilla', *La Repubblica*, 29 October 2005, <http://www.repubblica.it/2005/j/sezioni/cronaca/ghiracirceo/andreaghira/andreaghira.html>.

'Clandestini poveri da assolvere se non vanno via', *Melting Pot Europa*, 18 September 2006, <http://www.meltingpot.org/articolo8545.html>.

'Clandestini, sei dispersi in mare circa 400 sbarcati nelle ultime ventiquattro ore', *La Repubblica*, 24 September 2005, <http://www.repubblica.it/2005/i/sezioni/cronaca/sbarchi3/libialampe/libialampe.html>.

'Crime and punishment', *The Economist*, 24–30 June 2006: 14.

'Detention centre enquiry ordered: Allegations of racism and bullying at Oakington Immigration Centre are to be investigated by the prisons and probation ombudsman', BBC News, 3 March 2005, <http://news.bbc.co.uk/go/pr/fr/-/1/hi/uk_politics/4315467>, accessed 20 June 2005.

'Fortress Europe – L'osservatorio sulle vittime dell'immigrazione clandestina', *Melting Pot Europa*, 6 February 2007, <http://www.meltingpot.org/articolo9778.html>.

'Gela, la tragedia dei clandestini 11 corpi sulla spiaggia', *La Repubblica*, 11 September 2005, <http://www.repubblica.it/2005/i/sezioni/cronaca/sbarchi3/sbarchi3/sbarchi3.html>.

'Lampedusa, immigrato muore legato al barcone della speranza', *La Repubblica*, 16 August 2005, <http://www.repubblica.it/2005/h/sezioni/cronaca/prualampedusa/prualampedusa/prualampedusa.html>.

'Mafia suspects held in "Godfather" town', BBC News, 5 June 2002, <http://news.bbc.co.uk/1/hi/world/europe/2027306.stm>.

'Migrants land in Mauritania', News24, 12 February 2007, <http://www.news24.com/News24/Africa/News/0,2-11-1447_2068220,00.html>.

'Mueren 28 immigrantes frentes a las costas de Mauritania cuando se dirigìan en caiucos a Canarias', *El Mundo*, 13 August 2006, <http://www.elmundo.es/elmundo/2006/08/12/espana/1155400365.html>.

Negri, G., 'Arresto Europeo a Raggio Ridotto', *Il Sole 24 Ore*, 19 May 2006.

Pecoraro, A., 'Lampedusa, la strage dimenticata dei migranti', *Il Manifesto*, 24 February 2007.

Price, T., and Twomey, J., 'Beauty in hiding as sex slave monster is jailed', *Daily Express*, 17 September 2005.

'Profile: Bernardo Provenzano'. BBC News, 11 April 2006, <http://news.bbc. co.uk/1/hi/world/europe/4899512.stm>.

'Sex slave rings man cleared', UK Newsquest Regional Press, 23 September 2005.

Shaw, Stephen, *Investigation into Allegations of Racism, Abuse and Violence at Yarl's Wood Removal Centre: A Report by the Prison and Probation Ombudsman for England and Wales*, 2004, <http://www.ppo.gov.uk/docs/ special-yarls-wood-abuse-03.pdf>.

Spano', L., '"Mi hanno venduta per 600 euro". Anche un poliziotto agli arresti', *La Repubblica Palermo*, 14 October 2005, <http://www.ilpassaporto.kataweb. it/dettaglio.jsp?id=40442&c=1>, accessed 20 December 2005.

'Tunisia si capovolge barca', *La Repubblica*, 4 October 2004, <http://www. repubblica.it/2003/j/sezioni/cronaca/sbarchi2/tuni/tuni.html>.

Zaccaro, S., 'Italy-Libya: Migrants Returned to Face Abuse', IPS, 21 September 2009, <http://ipsnews.net/news.asp?idnews=48530>.

Conference Papers

Cholewinski, R., 'The Criminalisation of Migration', draft paper presented to the ILPA, British Institute for International and Comparative Law and JUSTICE Conference on 'How Much Freedom, Security and Justice? Developments in EU Asylum and Immigration Law', 13–14 May 2005.

De Burca, Grainne, 'The ECJ's Tobacco Advertising Judgement', Centre for European Legal Studies, Occasional Paper no. 5, University of Cambridge, 9 December 2000.

Interviews and Other Sources

'Procura della Repubblica press il Tribunale di Siracusa. Gruppo Contrasto Immigrazione Clandestina', data on irregular migrants smuggled by sea, collected in 2006, 2007 and 2008. Interview with the co-ordinator of the anti-trafficking organisation Association John XXIII in Rimini, Italy on 19 April 2006.

Interviews by e-mail with those responsible for the Poppy Project in London on 24 April 2006 and 28 June 2006.

Interview with the Head of the Investigative Office of Polizia di Stato in Rimini, 12 June 2006; telephone interview on 21 June 2006.

Informal interviews in London at the International Organization for Migration and at Heathrow Airport on 16 June 2006.

Interview with police officers at Scotland Yard (London) on 16 June 2006.

Interview at the detention centre in Lampedusa (Italy) with Frontex and other police forces on 1–3 October 2008.

Interviews with the Red Cross and International Organization for Migration in Lampedusa on 2 October 2008.

Data e-mailed to the author of this book by the Department of Immigration of the Ministry of Internal Affairs on 10 October 2008.

Data from the Italian Ministry of Internal Affairs received by e-mail on 10 October 2008 and 29 September 2009.

Judgment of the Tribunal of Siracusa issued on 31 October 2008.

Interviews with public prosecutors in Siracusa on 8 January 2009.

Document handed in by the Public Prosecutors in Siracusa on 9 January 2009.

Report of 'Procura della Repubblica Press Oil Tribunale di Siracusa-Gruppo Interforze Contrasto Immigrazione Clandestina 2007', document received by the Public Prosecutors on 9 January 2009.

Interviews held in Milan on 10–15 June 2009 and 20–27 August 2009.

Interviews with the public prosecutor of the UKHTC, London, July 2009.

Index